PRAISE FOR *VIRI DIGNITATEM*

"The fruit of wide reading and years of research, David Delaney's *Viri Dignitatem: Personhood, Masculinity, and Fatherhood in the Thought of John Paul II* offers an overview of the great Polish Pope's somewhat scattered and fragmentary thought on 'the masculine genius' and the vocation of fatherhood. Delaney systematizes John Paul II's ideas and presents them in the context of his philosophical and theological method and his vision of the embodied human person as male and female. He carefully examines the internal coherence of this anthropology as well as objections and criticisms that have been leveled against it over the years. Delaney reads widely, writes clearly, and thinks deeply about the issues he treats. The result is a book that is both substantive yet accessible to a wide audience. This volume will be welcomed by students and scholars as an important contribution to John Paul II studies. Highly recommended."

John S. Grabowski
The Catholic University of America

———————•———————

"*Viri Dignitatem: Personhood, Masculinity, and Fatherhood in the Thought of John Paul II* fills a void in the scholarship on Pope St. John Paul II. In this book, Dr. Delaney takes a deep dive into John Paul's thought to present the sainted pope's insights into the meaning of masculinity and fatherhood. While many are aware that John Paul II articulated an explicit theology of femininity and motherhood, Dr. Delaney successfully shows that understanding John Paul's more implicit theology of masculinity and fatherhood is essential to understanding other areas of his thought, especially his insights into the human person. In the course of this exquisitely researched book, through the thought of John Paul II, Dr. Delaney presents a theology of human personhood, sexual difference, masculinity, and fatherhood. In an era of relativism and subjectivism that treats these realities as fungible, *Viri Dignitatem*, by mining the thought of John Paul II, moors the reader in reality."

Perry J. Cahall
Pontifical College Josephinum

"With the publication *of Viri Dignitatem*, David H. Delaney has made an enormous contribution to what, until now, has been considered a lacuna in the work of Pope St. John Paul II. Dr. Delaney's extensive analysis illuminates a critically important dimension of the late Holy Father's project: that it reflects a profound understanding not only of womanhood but of masculinity as well. This volume is a rich and well-considered treatment of the foundational elements of John Paul's anthropological framework, his account of sexual difference, and the way in which both inform the philosopher-pope's theology of masculinity and fatherhood. *Viri Dignitatem* will be a valuable resource for those of us intent on arriving at a coherent and comprehensive account of man and woman, their identities, and their mission in the world."

Deborah Savage
Franciscan University of Steubenville

———————•———————

"This crucial work fills an important lacuna in the anthropological thought of John Paul II on personhood and sexual difference. At a time when the very notion of masculinity is under assault ('toxic masculinity') and when sexual difference stands at the precipice of losing all meaning (the roles of male and female have become interchangeable and unmoored from any firm biological reality), Delaney provides us with a return to sanity through the lens of John Paul II. But more than a simple return to sanity, this work offers a plumbing of the depths on an aspect of John Paul II's anthropology that has garnered too little attention over the years. Most appreciated is Delaney's contribution on fatherhood. There is perhaps no notion in greater need of recovery and supportive reflection than fatherhood. To that end, this work proves invaluable. A must-read."

Paul Gondreau
Providence College

RENEWAL WITHIN TRADITION

SERIES EDITOR: MATTHEW LEVERING

Matthew Levering is the James N. and Mary D. Perry Jr. Chair of Theology at Mundelein Seminary. Levering is the author or editor of over thirty books. He serves as coeditor of the journals *Nova et Vetera* and the *International Journal of Systematic Theology*.

ABOUT THE SERIES

Catholic theology reflects upon the content of divine revelation as interpreted and handed down in the Church, but today Catholic theologians often find the scriptural and dogmatic past to be alien territory. The Renewal within Tradition Series undertakes to reform and reinvigorate contemporary theology from within the tradition, with St. Thomas Aquinas as a central exemplar. As part of its purpose, the series reunites the streams of Catholic theology that, prior to the Council, separated into neo-scholastic and *nouvelle theologie* modes. The biblical, historical-critical, patristic, liturgical, and ecumenical emphases of the Ressourcement movement need the dogmatic, philosophical, scientific, and traditioned enquiries of Thomism, and vice versa. Renewal within Tradition challenges the regnant forms of theological liberalism that, by dissolving the cognitive content of the gospel, impede believers from knowing the love of Christ.

PUBLISHED OR FORTHCOMING

Reading the Sermons of Thomas Aquinas: A Beginner's Guide
Randall B. Smith

The Culture of the Incarnation: Essays in Catholic Theology
Tracey Rowland

Self-Gift: Humanae Vitae *and the Thought of John Paul II*
Janet E. Smith

On Love and Virtue: Theological Essays
Michael S. Sherwin, O.P.

Aquinas on Beatific Charity and the Problem of Love
Christopher J. Malloy

The One Church of Christ: Understanding Vatican II
Stephen A. Hipp

*O Lord, I Seek Your Countenance: Explorations
and Discoveries in Pope Benedict XVI's Theology*
Emery de Gaál

*One of the Trinity Has Suffered:
Balthasar's Theology of Divine Suffering in Dialogue*
Joshua R. Brotherton

The Bible and Catholic Ressourcement: *Essays on Scripture and Theology*
William M. Wright IV

*Conforming to Right Reason: On the Ends of the Moral Virtues
and the Roles of Prudence and Synderesis*
Ryan J. Brady

Vessel of Honor: The Virgin Birth and the Ecclesiology of Vatican II
Brian A. Graebe

*The Love of God Poured Out: Grace and the Gifts of
the Holy Spirit in St. Thomas Aquinas*
John M. Meinert

A Living Sacrifice: Liturgy and Eschatology in Joseph Ratzinger
Roland Millare

The Primacy of God: The Virtue of Religion in Catholic Theology
R. Jared Staudt

*The Trinitarian Wisdom of God: Louis Bouyer's
Theology of the God-World Relationship*
Keith Lemna

*The Order and Division of Divine Truth:
St. Thomas Aquinas as Scholastic Master of the Sacred Page*
John F. Boyle

Christ, the Logos of Creation: An Essay in Analogical Metaphysics
John R. Betz

A Bride Adorned: Mary–Church Perichoresis in Modern Catholic Theology
John L. Nepil

*Religious Liberty and the Hermeneutic of Continuity:
Conservation and Development of Doctrine at Vatican II*
R. Michael Dunnigan

Viri Dignitatem

VIRI DIGNITATEM

·

Personhood, Masculinity, and Fatherhood in the Thought of John Paul II

DAVID H. DELANEY

EMMAUS
ACADEMIC
Steubenville, Ohio
www.emmausacademic.com

EMMAUS
ACADEMIC

Steubenville, Ohio

www.emmausacademic.com
A Division of The St. Paul Center for Biblical Theology
Editor-in-Chief: Scott Hahn
1468 Parkview Circle
Steubenville, Ohio 43952

Library of Congress Cataloging-in-Publication Data applied for
ISBNs 978-1-64585-357-2 hardcover | 978-1-64585-358-9 paperback |
978-1-64585-359-6 ebook

Cover design and layout by Emma Nagle and Allison Merrick

Cover image: *Deploration of Abel* by Philippe de Champaigne, 1656

In memory of my father,
Hal Delaney (1932–1998)

Table of Contents

Introduction

Viri Dignitatem investigates St. John Paul II's account of the meaning of human personhood, masculinity and sex difference, and fatherhood. This book had its origins in plans to investigate the topic of the male-only Catholic priesthood. The approach was to employ insights on the meaning of sex difference from John Paul II's now well-known theology of the body in order to understand better the anthropological foundation for the Church's teaching on the male priesthood. The focus changed when it was discovered that greater study was required into John Paul's understanding of the meaning of sex difference as it applies to men and fatherhood. From there it was a short step to recognizing the necessity for a deeper investigation into this great thinker's theology of masculinity and fatherhood.

Regardless of what they think about it, all who write about such things acknowledge that John Paul II had much to say about women and motherhood. The contrary is the case with respect to men and fatherhood. Supporters and critics alike agree that in comparison to his treatment of femininity, John Paul II almost seemed to ignore men and fatherhood. As we will see, his view of the dignity of both women and men is complementarily lofty. Since he was never able to write a major document on the dignity and vocation of men to complement his 1988 apostolic letter on women and motherhood entitled *Mulieris dignitatem* (On the Dignity and Vocation of Women), it seems appropriate then to entitle a work drawing from the breadth of his writings in order to fill this gap *Viri Dignitatem*.

John Paul the Great was a profound theologian and philosopher whose life's work contributed to a renewal in Catholic theology in the loosely organized *Communio* school. His particular philosophical and theological concerns provide great insights into the human person. His thought as it relates to masculinity and fatherhood is an essential aspect of his anthropological project. However, his oblique treatment of men and fatherhood together with his innovative philosophical approach tend to obscure the topic for most readers. This effort intends to be a contribution toward a remedy to this situation.

Moreover, a fresh look at the theological meaning of masculinity and fatherhood seems a timely one for a variety of reasons, which we will look at more closely as we go along. Amidst the great crisis of fatherhood in the West that has been noted by so many in the late twentieth century, from Church leaders and those involved in marriage and family apostolates to sociologists and social commentators, fatherhood has attracted increased interest. While he did not directly address the topic in a major work, John Paul II's commitment to the complementarity of sex difference suggests that there has to be at least an incipient theology of masculinity and fatherhood in his writings. Having already invested considerable effort in coming to understand the late Pope's anthropology and his theology of sex difference, I recognized that this criticism was only partly justified. In fact, my initial study convinced me that John Paul did indeed have an implicit theology of men and fatherhood within his writings.

THE PROJECT

Karol Wojtyła studied the human person as a moral agent in his book entitled *Person and Act* in the original Polish, who fulfills himself by acting with knowledge and freedom to choose the authentic good. This work is a key to understanding his philosophical anthropology. His later theology of the body catecheses builds upon his philosophical anthropology to show that the human person who acts is always either male or female. These catecheses contribute to a theological anthropology, which fleshes out his philosophical anthropology. His theological anthropology penetrates personhood more deeply, showing that sex difference fundamentally determines personhood and characterizes the manner of acting which leads to fulfillment.

Wojtyła's anthropology is decidedly theological, beginning with the revelation that man is created in the image of the Trinitarian God and most clearly understands himself in light of the Incarnate Son. The revelation that man, as male and female, is also an image of God is *sine qua non* for understanding the implications of masculinity and fatherhood in his thought. For embodied personhood, one's sex difference more profoundly conditions the manner in which he experiences, acts, chooses the authentic good, and so fulfills himself as a human person than any other single aspect of his personhood. Sex difference is essential to the meaning of the human person.

The foundation for Karol Wojtyła's theology of fatherhood begins in Wojtyła's early philosophical work in ethics. His exploration led him to the study of human personhood disclosed in experience and action. While teaching at the Catholic University of Lublin, later as auxiliary bishop and finally as archbishop of Kraków, he continued his interest in human personhood. During this pre-papal period, his writings show a sustained concern for the human person as an individual, as well as for the person in relation to others. He finds that the person in action reveals himself as an individual who simultaneously is defined in a certain way through his relationships with others.

These two elements, individuality and relationality, underlie Wojtyła's later thought on sexual differentiation in the human person and form the basis of his theology of fatherhood. At the same time, his pastoral work with a group of young families precipitated his reflections on fatherhood, resulting in what would become the last of his plays, entitled *Radiation of Fatherhood*, along with a short essay entitled "Reflections on Fatherhood" which summarized the play's main ideas.[1] While Wojtyła's philosophical works are essential for understanding his view of the human person, this play is his first work exploring human fatherhood and is essential to understanding his thinking on men and fatherhood.

John Paul II began a catechetical exposition of a central aspect of his Christian anthropology during his Wednesday General Audience catecheses, which lasted from September 1979 to November 1984, now generally referred to as his theology of the body. These catecheses are particularly significant for John Paul's thinking on fatherhood. In them, he examines the human person as sexually differentiated in terms of the two elements mentioned above: (a) the person as an individuated subject and (b) the person as created to be in relationships with others. John Paul employs phenomenology in this examination. He finds himself justified in using phenomenology because of the manner in which one's actions reveal the person. Further, he finds that sexual difference, in part, constitutes the "being" of the person. His phenomenological analysis helps to show that a person's "being" is also, in some ways, constituted by his relations to others, which then indicates that sexual differentiation also must shape the person's interpersonal relations.

---

[1] See Karol Wojtyła, *Radiation of Fatherhood*, in *The Collected Plays and Writings on Theater: Karol Wojtyła*, trans. Bolesław Taborski (Berkeley: University of California Press, 1987); "Reflections on Fatherhood," *Znak* (May 1964), reprinted in *Collected Plays and Writings*, 365–68.

These findings have direct relevance for his theology of fatherhood. This aspect of John Paul's anthropology also provides the basis for his theology of women and motherhood outlined in his apostolic letter *Mulieris dignitatem*. This theology of women and motherhood is prominent in other writings as well, such as the encyclical *Redemptoris mater,* the apostolic exhortation *Familiaris consortio* (*FC*), his 1994 letter to families written for the year of the family, and his 1995 letter to women for the Fourth World Conference on Women in Beijing. He also shows special concern for women and women's issues in his encyclicals *Laborem exercens, Sollicitudo rei socialis,* and *Evangelium vitae*, and in his apostolic exhortations *Christifideles laici* and *Vita consecrata.*

However, as previously mentioned, John Paul II seemingly did not devote the same level of attention to the topic of masculinity or human fatherhood. While he addresses human fatherhood directly in one paragraph of *FC* and obliquely throughout his apostolic exhortation *Redemptoris custos*, these do not approach the volume of direct treatment that he gives to women and motherhood. Nor can one point to an explicitly worked-out theology of human fatherhood. However, this dearth of dedicated works concerning human fatherhood is not the case for divine fatherhood. For example, he explores the fatherhood of God in his second encyclical, *Dives in misericordia*, and he subsequently dedicated a series of Wednesday General Audience catecheses to the same topic.

John Paul often cites Ephesians 3:15 to affirm that all human fatherhood, as well as motherhood, has its source in God. As such, in his writings some attributes of God's fatherhood provide an analogous theology of human fatherhood. Additionally, a close reading of his papal writings reveals that he often presents many aspects of his theology of women in reference to men. Just as one must understand the female in relation to the male, one must understand fatherhood in relation to motherhood. Thus, one can recover significant components of a theology of human fatherhood from his writings, to include both natural and spiritual fatherhood.

In John Paul's thought, spiritual fatherhood describes aspects of the fatherly vocations of both natural fathers and priests. However, in this work I will primarily focus on natural human fatherhood. For John Paul II, natural fatherhood is more than simply biological fatherhood. Rather, it includes all aspects of the common, everyday experience of being a man and a father, encompassing both biological and adoptive fathers. This experience is both in contrast to, as well as in cooperation with, women and mothers.

I would like to suggest that properly understanding John Paul II's theology of fatherhood is fundamental for adequately appropriating a large part of his papal thought. Because there has been no systematization of John Paul II's theology of fatherhood, there is a significant possibility that readers may not adequately understand those of his writings which presuppose his anthropology. This could play a part in some of the criticisms of his anthropology, especially those which bear on sexual differentiation.

While there is an extensive body of work which assesses the late Holy Father's view of personhood, few have published on the manner in which he views sex difference and its relation to the human person. Many have written on his view of women and motherhood, albeit mostly from a critical, feminist perspective. However, it appears that no one has yet attempted to extract and systematize his theology of fatherhood which he disperses throughout his writings.

If I am correct in claiming that a proper appreciation of John Paul's theology of fatherhood is requisite for a robust understanding of his thought, and especially of those aspects which bear on sexual difference, then it seems to me that a systematic exposition and evaluation of his theology of fatherhood would be of particular value. It would provide a more complete understanding of the late pope's anthropology in terms of sex differentiation and the "completion" of his theology of women and motherhood with a theology of men and fatherhood. Together these would provide a more thorough understanding of his thought which bears on anthropology and sex, to include clarifying the manner in which John Paul views sex difference as associated with human personhood.[2]

THIS BOOK'S ORGANIZATION

This book is organized into four parts. Part 1 investigates John Paul's anthropology and explicates his concept of person. As we will find, masculinity constitutes one complementary mode of human personhood, and fatherhood (properly understood) can be understood as the fulfillment of the masculine *telos*. These points dictate our project in this first part, which will look at the person, especially in terms of personal fulfillment, and the metaphysical description which underlies his account of personhood.

---

[2] For the sake of concision, throughout this book I will occasionally use the term "the author" or "our author" to refer to John Paul II. In addition, John Paul II has noted that his style of writing includes a regular use of italics in order to draw emphasis to a point he wishes to make. All italics in his quotes are original, as is the case with other quotes. In the rare case I use italics for emphasis, I will make it clear in a footnote.

Part 2 will expand the study of personhood to its complementary aspects with the aim of providing an account of masculinity. It will take our metaphysical description of personhood and compare it to his account of sex difference to arrive at a metaphysical description of sex difference that coheres with both accounts of sex difference and personhood. It will then lay the foundation for the fulfillment of the person in relation to his sex. While part 2 is aimed at understanding masculinity, its complementary character means it cannot be adequately understood except in relation to femininity, so the better portion of it applies to both sexes.

With John Paul's theological anthropology of the sexually differentiated human person worked out, part 3 proceeds to identify a systematized theology of masculinity and human fatherhood. We will see that fatherhood is the calling to fulfill the potency of masculinity. Since masculinity has meaning only in the face of femininity, fulfillment of the paternal vocation will necessarily have reference to motherhood.

Part 4 will evaluate our account of John Paul II's theology of masculinity and fatherhood in terms of its self-consistency and adequacy by considering criticisms brought against it by other authors and by looking at what I have found to be possible issues.

Part One

HUMAN PERSONHOOD

CHAPTER 1

The Human Person

As we proceed, we will find that personhood, masculinity, and fatherhood are not three different topics within Karol Wojtyła's anthropology. Rather, they are all interrelated and inseparable aspects of what it means to be human. Human personhood does not exist in the concrete, other than as masculine and feminine persons. While there is certainly much more in common than is different between male and female persons, the entire manner in which each experiences and possesses himself and experiences the world is in some way colored by his masculinity or femininity. Therefore, we must begin our project by first addressing what is common to both persons before we can explore what is distinct in their sex differences, how it is unique to the masculine person, and what it means for fatherhood. However, before we can start, it is essential we briefly address a fundamental question determining how we are to interpret Karol Wojtyła work.

THOMIST OR PHENOMENOLOGIST?

Anyone investigating Karol Wojtyła's thought must first engage the debate concerning his use of Thomism and phenomenology because the former provides a self-consistent metaphysical system for articulating an anthropology that is completely lacking in the latter. One cannot correctly understand Wojtyła's anthropology without an adequate understanding of the manner in which he uses Thomism and phenomenology. Deciding the debate is a necessary first step because the debate not only directly affects his view of the human person but also affects one's ability to properly interpret those texts which presuppose his anthropology.

A significant number of commentators believe that our author's writings give clear evidence that he is a Schelerian phenomenologist.[1] For

---

[1] Karol Wojtyła studied Max Scheler's phenomenological project for his "habilitation"

THE HUMAN PERSON

example, Ronald Lawler seems to find a methodological priority to Wojtyła's phenomenology based on a quote from *The Acting Person*: "Only after this careful phenomenological study would one proceed to the metaphysical analysis of man."[2] However, Robert Harvanek goes much further when he addresses the "controversy about Karol Wojtyła's philosophical allegiance. Is he a Lublin Thomist (Andrew Woznicki) or a Schelerian phenomenologist (Anna Tymieniecka)?"[3]

Harvanek sides with Tymieniecka, concluding: "John Paul II should not be interpreted from the perspective of neo-thomism or neo-scholasticism. He is not working in ontology or metaphysics, nor in Aristotelian epistemology and methodology. Rather, he should be interpreted from the point of view of Munich phenomenology and Scheler."[4] Finally, Stephen Dinan says that although Aristotle's and Aquinas's influences are present, Kant's and Scheler's phenomenology dictate his thinking.[5] If this substantive phenomenological priority is accurate, then we must spend considerable effort in understanding Scheler before beginning our project.

As it turns out, an adequate familiarity with Wojtyła's writings shows that those who would advocate for a phenomenological priority, much less exclusivity, are seriously mistaken. Rather, it is obvious he consistently maintains a fundamental adherence to Thomism and Thomist metaphysics throughout his life.[6] However, Karol Wojtyła is also a phenomenologist.

---

dissertation, with the idea of determining if it had anything to offer Christian ethics. For helpful summaries of Scheler's influence on Wojtyla, see Kenneth L. Schmitz, *At the Center of the Human Drama* (Washington DC: The Catholic University of America Press, 1993), 30–57; and Rocco Buttiglione, *Karol Wojtyła: The Thought of the Man Who Became John Paul II*, trans. Paolo Guietti and Francesca Murphy (Grand Rapids, MI; Cambridge, UK: William B. Eerdmans Publishing Co., 1997), 54–82.

2 Ronald Lawler, *The Christian Personalism of Pope John Paul II* (Chicago: Franciscan Herald Press, 1982), 19–20.

3 Robert F. Harvanek, S.J., "The Philosophical Foundations of the Thought of John Paul II," in *The Thought of Pope John Paul II: A Collection of Essays and Studies*, ed. John M. McDermott (Rome: Editrice Pontificia Università Gregoriana, 2000), 1.

4 Harvanek, "Philosophical Foundations," 19.

5 See Stephen Dinan, "The Phenomenological Anthropology of Karol Wojtyła," *New Scholasticism* 55 (1981): 318.

6 The twentieth century brought with it much debate about the correct interpretation of St. Thomas, as well as debate about which of the different schools of Thomism most influenced Karol Wojtyła. These various Thomisms include a traditional form of strict interpretation which more or less refuses to go beyond or correct anything that the Angelic Doctor explicitly wrote. The leading figure in this form of Thomism in the early twentieth century was Wojtyła's director for his first dissertation on Thomism and St. John of the Cross, Réginald Garrigou-Lagrange. In addition, there are those

Thomist metaphysics forms his philosophical foundation, but he integrates Scheler's phenomenological method, appropriately purified of what he calls Cartesian errors.[7] Space limits me from providing a detailed examination of Wojtyła writings to demonstrate this fact, but a brief summary will suffice.

For example, let us look at St. Thomas's philosophical ethics. One of Thomas's central themes is the *actus humanus*. His use of the Latin term suggests its Thomist provenance. The underlying Thomist articulation of the concept is integral to Wojtyła's ethics because it uniquely shows that "all the faculties of the human soul work to perfect the human being, so they all contribute to the development of the person."[8] In a series of six

---

who follow Joseph Maréchal's transcendental Thomism, Jacques Maritain's existential Thomism, Étienne Gilson's existential-historical Thomism, Joseph de Finance's "act" Thomism, Cornelio Fabro's participatory Thomism, and the Thomism developed at the Catholic University of Lublin (see Schmitz, *Center of the Human Drama*, 34). Schmitz indicates that Wojtyła's self-formation in philosophy made him conversant in all of these forms of Thomism. Stefan Swieżawski, who was the one who invited Wojtyła to take the Ethics Chair at Lublin, indicated that Wojtyła was integral to the Lublin school's attempt "to 'discover' the true St. Thomas" whose realist metaphysics was the foundation of their project "to continue the . . . development of European metaphysics and philosophy extending from medieval to contemporary times" (Stefan Swieżawski, "Karol Wojtyła at the Catholic University of Lublin," in *Person and Community: Selected Essays*, vol. 4, trans. Theresa Sandok, O.S.M. [New York: Peter Lang, 1993], xiii). Rocco Buttiglione says that Swieżawski was particularly influenced by the existential Thomism of Maritain and Gilson (see Buttiglione, *Thought of the Man*, 38). Buttiglione indicates that during Wojtyła's time at Lublin, the philosophy department became a place of vibrant interchange among the traditional form of Thomism, an existential Thomism open to phenomenology, and a Polish version of transcendental Thomism oriented toward "a fundamentally personalistic philosophy" (Buttiglione, *Thought of the Man*, 38). By the time of John Paul II's *magnum opus, Person and Act*, Buttiglione finds Wojtyła is grounded in Garrigou-Lagrange's version of traditionalist Thomist Realism, which is amplified by Lublin's version of existential Thomism, most similar to Gilson's existential-historical Thomism (see Buttiglione, *Thought of the Man*, 355ff.). This was a Thomism that opened itself up to the insights obtained through Wojtyła's own phenomenological project.

[7] These errors can be generalized under a single error in which human consciousness is divorced from the metaphysically concrete human person. Wojtyła is critical that this divorce reduces the person to being a center of a stream of conscious thought and experience with no substantiality. See, e.g., Karol Wojtyła, "In Search of the Basis of Perfectionism in Ethics," in *Person and Community*, 55, originally published in Polish as "*W poszukiwaniu podstaw perfekcjoryzmu w etyce*," *Roczniki Filozoficzne* 5, no. 4 (1955–57): 303–17. Wojtyła consistently uses the adjectives "Cartesian" and "post-Cartesian" for errant philosophical systems which reject metaphysics and posit a dualism between body and spirit. I will follow his convention in this book.

[8] Karol Wojtyła, "Thomistic Personalism," in *Person and Community*, 169.

articles on various matters of philosophical ethics, published very early (between 1955 and 1959),[9] he invariably uses Aristotle and St. Thomas as the solution to errors he finds in the ethical theories of Immanuel Kant and Max Scheler.[10] In these works, Wojtyła explains that Kant and Scheler surely have contributions to make in the field of ethics but he relies on Thomist metaphysics to avoid their Cartesian errors.

Wojtyła is explicit that one must begin with Thomism when he states that "phenomenology can indirectly assist us in overcoming certain errors in view of the will that arise from an improper relation to the empirical facts, but it cannot serve as a tool for the sort of interpretation of ethical experience upon which ethics as a normative science is based."[11] Rather, he takes "the view of the human act developed by Thomas Aquinas [as] an adequate interpretation of ethical experience."[12] He faults both Kant's and Scheler's systems of ethics because they eliminate the capacity for personal perfection by separating human consciousness from the concreteness of human being (esse). Perfection is possible only where there is a metaphysically concrete person in which the fruit of virtuous activity can perdure.[13]

Wojtyła says that metaphysics is the necessary grounding for this objectivity. He finds that Thomist philosophical and theological insights provide "a whole series of additional constitutive elements" which prove fruitful for an insightful study of personalism.[14] He rejects all post-Cartesian philosophical meditations on personhood which result in a split between the somatic and psychic aspects of the human being and in a "hypostatization of consciousness . . . [where] consciousness becomes an independent subject of activity, and indirectly of existence, occurring somehow alongside the body."[15] In order to ground the person in "being," Wojtyła consistently returns to Aristotelian-Thomist metaphysics.

Thomism continues to underlie St. John Paul II's theological method and content throughout his papal magisterium. There is perhaps no better place to see this than his encyclical *Fides et ratio*. He is emphatic about the

---

[9] The first four were published in the journal *Roczniki Filozoficzne*, the fifth in *Roczniki Teologiczno-Kanoniczne*, and the sixth in *Znak*.

[10] See Wojtyła, *Person and Community*, 3–99.

[11] Karol Wojtyła, "The Will in the Analysis of the Ethical Act," in *Person and Community*, 20–21.

[12] Wojtyła, "Ethical Act," 20.

[13] See Wojtyła, "Basis of Perfectionism," 55.

[14] Wojtyła, "Thomistic Personalism," 165.

[15] Wojtyła, "Thomistic Personalism," 169. Wojtyła is concerned about the destructive influence of post-Cartesian philosophers and their "hypostatization of consciousness," which reduces the person to a stream of consciousness.

indispensable place of metaphysics in authentic Catholic theology, high-lighting anthropology as an example in which it cannot be dispensed.[16] He reminds that the magisterium promotes Thomas as a model and guide for theological studies.[17] Catholic theologians need to embrace Thomas's methodology, such as the relationship between faith and reason and its practical implications for the role of philosophy in doing theology. Thomist metaphysics is enduring because it has its foundation in the act of being, and this reveals and explains the intimate relationship between God and creation, which itself confirms the relationship between faith and metaphysical reasoning.[18]

John Paul II is a committed Thomist. As such, he does not merely appropriate the content of St. Thomas's thought, he also follows Thomas's method. This permits him to integrate into his own method and content, truth wherever he finds it. Accordingly, one should not be surprised to see that he has integrated the valid insights of contemporary phi-losophy into his Thomism and Thomist metaphysics, while carefully screening out modern philosophical errors. Many scholars adequately familiar with his work find this to be true, especially in terms of his Thomist-phenomenological project.[19]

---

[16] See John Paul II, Encyclical Letter on the Relationship between Faith and Reason *Fides et ratio* (September 14, 1998), AAS 91 (1999), 5–88; (Boston: Pauline Books & Media, 1998), §83. Here he states:

> We cannot stop short at experience alone; even if experience does reveal the human being's interiority and spirituality, speculative thinking must penetrate to the spiritual core and the ground from which it rises. Therefore, a philosophy which shuns metaphysics would be radically unsuited to the task of mediation in the understanding of revelation. . . . Metaphysics thus plays an essential role of mediation in theological research. A theology without a metaphysical horizon could not move beyond an analysis of religious experience nor would it allow the *intellectus fidei* to give a coherent account of the universal and transcendent value of revealed truth. If I insist so strongly on the metaphysical element, it is because I am convinced that it is the path to be taken in order to move beyond the crisis pervading large sectors of philosophy at the moment, and thus to correct certain mistaken modes of behavior now widespread in our society.

[17] See *Fides et ratio*, 78.
[18] See *Fides et ratio*, 97.
[19] Scholars who agree this is the case include Douglas Flippen, who finds John Paul successfully integrated the observations of phenomenology vis-à-vis human conscious-ness with a Thomist metaphysical anthropology ("Was John Paul II a Thomist or a Phenomenologist?" *Faith and Reason* [Spring 2006]: 65–106). Philippe Jobert finds a complementarity between John Paul II's and St. Thomas Aquinas's metaphysical approach to anthropology, with the latter asking, "What is man," and the former asking, "Who is

The likely reason the debate began is to be found in the history behind the initial English translation of Karol Wojtyła's magnum opus, *Osoba i Czyn*

---

man," and studying the concrete totality of the human person to answer the question ("Complémentarité de l'anthropologie de Saint Thomas d'Aquin et de l'anthropologie de Jean Paul II," in *Antropologia Tomista. Atti del IX Congresso tomistico internazionale* [Città del Vaticano: Libreria Editrice Vaticana, 1990], 432–37). Jerzy W. Gałkowski, a friend and former colleague of Wojtyła's at the Catholic University of Lublin (KUL), has no doubt that his friend's thought is based upon Thomism and that his project from the beginning of his time at KUL was to synthesize Thomism and phenomenology; to miss this is to lose the proper sense of his work (Gałkowski, "The Place of Thomism in the Anthropology of K. Wojtyła," *Angelicum* 65 [1998]: 181). Lawrence B. Porter says that John Paul II's approach is "a highly original synthesis which cannot be character-ized as either simply Thomistic or simply Schelerian . . . [but a] remarkable synthesis of Thomist and phenomenological thought" ("Gender in Theology: The Example of John Paul II's *Mulieris dignitatem*," *Gregorianum* 77, no. 1 [1996]: 103). Antoine Nachef says John Paul II's approach is an innovation that could be characterized as an extension of Thomism in which he fleshes out Thomist metaphysical concepts with experiential insights (see Antoine E. Nachef, *The Mystery of the Trinity in the Theological Thought of Pope John Paul II* [New York: Peter Lang Publishing, 1999], 49). Buttiglione says that Wojtyła's philosophical program provides confirmation of the Thomist ontology of the human person with an amended form of Scheler's phenomenology and its anal-ysis of personal experience (see *Thought of the Man*, 82). John J. Conley says that his phenomenological method is a major factor in forming his methodology, while his phi-losophy of action derives more from scholasticism than from phenomenology which he thinks is the main difficulty many have in reading the Saint's work ("The Philosophical Foundations of the Thought of John Paul II: A Response," in *The Thought of Pope John Paul II: A Collection of Essays and Studies*, ed. John M. McDermott [Rome: Editrice Pontificia Università Gregoriana, 2000], 23, 28). Gerald McCool finds that although Scheler's phenomenology of values influenced Wojtyła by heightening his sensitivity to the importance of self-awareness, his metaphysics and his theology remained con-sistently Thomist ("The Theology of John Paul II," in *The Thought of Pope John Paul II*, 31). Kenneth Schmitz performs a detailed analysis of Karol Wojtyła's philosophical anthropology and comes to the same conclusion, that the author's project is an origi-nal, but critical, adaptation of Husserl's phenomenology as a method for studying the dynamisms of human consciousness into Thomist metaphysics (*Center of the Human Drama*, 126–30). Thomas Petri confirms John Paul II's dependence upon Thomist anthropology in his theology of the body and that the combination of Thomism with phenomenology was his project in *Person and Act* and throughout his work, although Petri states it is beyond the scope of his study to assess whether John Paul II's project was successful or whether such a project can be successful (Thomas Petri, O.P,. *Aquinas and the Theology of the Body: The Thomistic Foundations of John Paul II's Anthropology* [Washington, DC: The Catholic University of America Press, 2016], 125). George H. Williams says that "Beneath the ice on which Wojtyła, like a figure skater, displays his phenomenological configurations, lie the deep waters of Thomism, recently freshened

(*Person and Act*). In English it is given the title *The Acting Person*.[20] It is a book in which Wojtyła uses phenomenology to investigate the human person and his fulfillment, in and through action. Many have noted the deficiency of this English translation.[21] The most common criticism one finds is the decision by the editor, Anna-Teresa Tymieniecka, to delete a large percentage of Wojtyła's references to Thomist metaphysics and to render technically precise Latin phrases in contextually appropriate (according to her estimation) phenomenological terminology.[22] It seemed to be her purpose, for unknown reasons, to recreate Wojtyła as a pure Schelerian phenomenologist. Tymieniecka died in 2014 and in 2021

---

by a neopatristic anthropology, that like Aristotelian anthropology, can presuppose that what is said about the Christian man can, for Christian reasons, be said about man in general" (George Huntston Williams, *The Mind of John Paul II: Origins of His Thoughts and Action* [New York: The Seabury Press, 1981], 188–89).

[20] Karol Wojtyła, *The Acting Person*, trans. Andrezej Potocki, ed. A. Tymieniecka, Analecta Husserliana: The Yearbook of Phenomenological Research, vol. 10 (Dordrecht: Reidel Publishing Co., 1979). In this work, I will use the title *Person and Act* when referring to the book and its general content. I will use *The Acting Person* only when referring explicitly to the first English translation and when quoting from it.

[21] See Schmitz, *Center of the Human Drama*, 59–60, in which he provides a discussion of several other critics of the English translation; George Weigel, *Witness to Hope* (New York: Harper Collins Publishers, Inc., 1999), notes 174–75; and Buttiglione, *Thought of the Man*, 113n1. Buttiglione says the translation is "unreliable, or at least shadowed by doubts." In fact, George H. Williams sees such a great discontinuity between the original and the English translation that he treats the two as completely separate works in his book *Mind of John Paul II*, 186–218.

[22] Tymieniecka was a Polish-born American phenomenologist who was the founder and editor of *Analecta Husserliana*, and who studied phenomenology under one of Husserl's principal students, Roman Ingarden. Tymieniecka's editorial decision greatly distorts the work for the readers of the English version, and cloaks the Thomist presuppositions operative throughout the entire text. Even for someone unfamiliar with the Polish language, the failure to find in the English translation the numerous Latin phrases and references to St. Thomas and Aristotle in the Polish text will make this deficiency readily apparent. Though many have identified the need for a corrected English translation, apparently Dr. Tymienicka would not allow one to be published even though a corrected version has been prepared (see Weigel, *Witness to Hope*, 175–76n). In fact, her control apparently extended to the Polish publication rights. Williams notes that "in a review of *The Acting Person* in the London Times Literary Supplement, 4 April 1980, a distinguished Polish philosopher had intimated that there would appear a new Polish edition of the original *Osoba I Czyn* and in reply, ibid., 15 August 1980, Dr. Tymieniecka, said that no other but hers in Polish retroversion would be possible by reason of contracts and copyrights and she disclosed a letter with date from His Holiness in which, presumably in Polish, he referred warmly to the common enterprise in English as 'my, thy, and our work'" (Williams, *Mind of John Paul II*, 376–77n1).

The Catholic University of America Press published *Person and Act and Related Essays* as the first volume of the English language critical edition of Karol Wojtyła's works.[23] This edition corrects the problematic editorial bias of the first English translation. It might be hoped that this corrected translation will help bring to an end the confusion about the late Holy Father's philosophical project.

John Paul II's integration of phenomenology and Thomist phenomenology is motivated first by the need for a concrete, self-consistent, and anthropologically adequate metaphysical system for understanding the human person, which he sees as uniquely provided for in Thomist metaphysics. Second, he recognizes that in order to address many contemporary questions adequately, there is an urgent need for a philosophical method of analysis that can distinguish the universal human experience within the dynamisms of human consciousness from those experiences that are particular to the individual person.

For the latter goal, John Paul II adopts methods and valid insights about the human person discovered by modern philosophical innovations, namely phenomenology, while correcting modern, false metaphysical presuppositions. For these reasons, the author's anthropological writings associated with this integration provide important insights about his method of study and his understanding of the human person. Clearly then, a thorough study of his anthropology calls for an examination of these philosophical texts as a precursor. We can then turn to those writings that reveal the features of human personhood which John Paul finds in divine revelation in order to flesh out his theological anthropology.[24] This is a first and necessary step toward understanding the masculine person and his fulfillment in fatherhood.

THOMIST PHENOMENOLOGY AND THE HUMAN PERSON

In terms of anthropology, I would say that St. Thomas Aquinas, Aristotle, Max Scheler, and Immanuel Kant are some of the most significant

---

[23] Karol Wojtyła, *Person and Act and Related Essays* (Washington, DC: The Catholic University of America Press, 2021). I received this second, critical edition too late in the publishing process to update my references and quotes, so all references in this book will be to the first English edition, *The Acting Person*.

[24] My purpose here is not to provide a complete account of St. John Paul II's understanding of the human person, but to emphasize his phenomenological project and especially his metaphysical presuppositions. For a more robust treatment of John Paul's manifold view of the human person, see J. Brian Bransfield, *The Human Person: According to John Paul II* (Boston: Pauline Books & Media, 2010).

influences on Karol Wojtyła.[25] Amongst the various influences, he grounds his understanding of "person" in St. Thomas's categories. Even more, he finds that Thomist philosophical and theological insights provide "a whole series of additional constitutive elements" that prove fruitful for an insightful study of personalism.[26]

Wojtyła admits that the scholastic tradition did not develop the particular experiences of consciousness found in modern philosophy.[27] However, he expresses concern that many modern thinkers have tried to understand the person as a personal subject by focusing exclusively on consciousness, even reducing the subject to his consciousness, though they have discovered valid insights. For Wojtyła, Kant and Scheler are of particular interest, but he objects to what he calls their post-Cartesian dualism. This dualism results in a rejection of the scholastic understanding of the human person as a metaphysically concrete *suppositum*.[28]

These post-Cartesian intellectuals replace *suppositum* with a concept of the human person that is nothing more than the center of a stream of consciousness. Nevertheless, Wojtyła is certain that philosophers can authentically advance the understanding of the human person by using valid aspects of modern insights, especially using new tools of an appropriately adapted phenomenology. However, he is adamant that the person must remain grounded in "being," and Thomist metaphysics is ideally, if not uniquely, suited for maintaining this realism.

---

[25] This is not to suggest that there have not been numerous other influences. In addition to the previously mentioned figures representing the various schools of Thomism (see p. 10n6), Schmitz identifies other figures such as Aristotle, St. Thomas, Immanuel Kant, Max Scheler, St. Augustine, Maurice Blondel, Gabriel Marcel, Emmanuel Mounier, Paul Ricoeur, Emmanuel Levinas, and Martin Buber (*Center of the Human Drama*, 34–36). However, it is beyond the scope of this work to provide a more detailed analysis of his philosophical and theological influences. It seems reasonable for this study to focus on Aristotle, St. Thomas, Kant, and Scheler since the author explicitly addresses these thinkers in most of his philosophical writings, and as Schmitz says, "Wojtyła's thought defines itself most directly . . . in confrontation with the practical philosophy of Immanuel Kant and even more with Kant's phenomenological critic, Max Scheler" (*Center of the Human Drama*, 36).

[26] Wojtyła, "Thomistic Personalism," 165.

[27] See Karol Wojtyła, "The Person: Subject and Community," in *Person and Community*, 225–26, originally published in Polish as "Osoba: Podmiot i wspólnota," *Roczniki Filozoficzne* 24, no. 2 (1976): 5–39.

[28] *Suppositum* is a scholastic term employed by St. Thomas Aquinas to distinguish among various ways of being. A *suppositum* is a real being, which exists, has perfect unity, is that in which inheres various accidents of the particular being, and makes whole the particular entity. An intelligent *suppositum* is called a person.

Writing in the Polish journal *Znak* in 1961, then Auxiliary Bishop Karol Wojtyła of Kraków provides an outline of those aspects of Thomism which are essential to his program of personalism.[29] Wojtyła says that

---

[29] John Paul II explains how his interest in personalism originated in a response to questions put forth by the Italian media and published in book form. In what is a rather long quotation, he summarizes his entire anthropological project:

> I must say that my concern for "the acting person" did not arise from the disputes with Marxism or, at least, not as a direct response to those disputes. I had long been interested in *man as person*. Perhaps my interest was due to the fact that I had never had a particular predilection for the natural sciences. I was always more fascinated by man. While studying in the Faculty of Literature, man interested me inasmuch as he was a creator of language and a subject of literature; then, when I discovered my priestly vocation, man became the *central theme of my pastoral work*. By this point the war had ended and the controversies with Marxism were in full swing. In those years, my greatest involvement was with young people who asked me questions, not so much about the existence of God, but rather about *how to live*, how to face and resolve problems of love and marriage, not to mention problems related to work. The memory of those young people from the period following the German occupation has always remained with me. In a certain sense, with their doubts and with their questions, they showed me the way. From our meetings, from my sharing in the problems of their lives, a book was born, the contents of which is summarized in the title *Love and Responsibility*. My book on the acting person came later, but it was also born of the same source. In some ways it was inevitable that I would arrive at this theme from the moment I began to deal with questions concerning human existence—questions asked by people not only in our time but in every time. . . . So the development of my studies centered on man—on the human person—can ultimately be explained by my *pastoral concern*. And it is precisely from a pastoral point of view that, in *Love and Responsibility*, I formulated the concept of a personalistic principle. This principle is an attempt to translate the commandment of love into the language of philosophical ethics. *The person is a being for whom the only suitable dimension is love.* We are just to a person if we love him. This is as true for God as it is for man. Love for a person excludes the possibility of treating him as an object of pleasure. This is a principle of Kantian ethics . . . but [Kant] did not fully interpret the commandment of love. . . . *The true personalistic interpretation of the commandment of love is found in the words of the Council*: "When the Lord Jesus prays to the Father so that "they may be one" (John 17:22), He places before us new horizons impervious to human reason and implies a similarity between the union of divine persons and the union of the children of God in truth and charity. This similarity shows how man, who is the only creature on earth that God wanted for his own sake, can fully discover himself only by the sincere gift of himself" (*Gaudium et spes* 24). Here we truly have an adequate interpretation of the commandment of love. Above all, *the principle that a person has value by the simple fact that he is a person* finds very clear expression: man, it is said, "is the only creature on earth that God has wanted for his own sake." At the same time the Council emphasizes

St. Thomas was not only acquainted with the concept of personhood but that he clearly defined it.[30] This is not to say that he was as familiar with the "problem of personalism."[31] However, Thomas's clear description of the person provides a solid point of departure for personalism.[32] For Wojtyła, personalism is not so much a theory of the person as it is "practical and ethical."[33] His personalist approach begins by way of Immanuel Kant's moral imperative, which indicates one must always treat a person as an end and never as an object.

This moral imperative had an early, positive impact on Wojtyła, even while he judges Kant's anthropology to be ultimately unsatisfactory. He finds that Kant does not properly understand either the person or the Gospel commandment to love, but rather sees his moral imperative as an externally imposed duty.[34] Wojtyła transforms Kant's imperative into his own personalistic norm, which he articulates in *Love and Responsibility*, by locating the meaning of man in his having been created with the freedom to choose the good—ultimately he must have the freedom to love. For

---

that the most important thing about love is the sincere gift of self. In this sense *the person is realized through love*. Therefore, these two aspects—the affirmation of the person and the sincere gift of self—not only do not exclude each other, they mutually confirm and complete each other. *Man affirms himself most completely by giving of himself.* This is the fulfillment of the commandment of love.

(John Paul II, *Crossing the Threshold of Hope,* ed. Vittorio Messori, trans. Jenny McPhee and Martha McPhee [New York, NY: Alfred A. Knopf, Inc., 1994], 199–202).

[30] See Wojtyła, "Thomistic Personalism," 165.

[31] Wojtyła, "Thomistic Personalism," 165.

[32] Wojtyła, "Thomistic Personalism," 165.

[33] Wojtyła, "Thomistic Personalism," 165.

[34] Wojtyła explains his thinking behind his belief that the Kantian imperative needs to be reformulated:

It becomes clear that if the commandment to love, and love that is the object of this commandment, are to possess meaning, then we must base them on a different principle from the principle of utilitarianism, on another axiology, and on another fundamental norm. In the given case it will be the personalistic principle and norm. As a principle formulated negatively, this norm states that the person is a kind of good that is incompatible with using, which may not be treated as an object of use and, in this sense, as a means to an end. Hand in hand with this goes the positive formulation of the personalistic norm: the person is a kind of good to which only love constitutes the proper and fully-mature relation. And this positive content of the personalistic norm is precisely what the commandment to love brings out.

(Karol Wojtyła, *Love and Responsibility*, trans. Grzegorz Ignatik [Boston: Pauline Books & Media, 2013], 25).

Wojtyła, Kant's duty imperative that one must always act in such a way that the person is an end and not merely an instrument must be reformulated to allow for the fact that the person who is the object of his own activity also has his own personal ends.[35]

God reveals to a person his particular goals, and it is necessary that the person himself understand and freely choose whether or not to accept and strive for them. Every person's ultimate fulfillment is found in ongoing acceptance for himself of Christ's gift of salvation, but all have their unique paths to this. Only with the freedom to choose can man truly fulfill himself. This reformulation of the principle lies at the foundation of the right to every human freedom. So while accepting Kant's imperative, Wojtyła finds Kant's duty-based anthropology to be fatally inadequate because it does not account for the essential role of freedom.

Kant's influence on Wojtyła to consider the human person in terms of an "end" leads him to see it to be entirely consonant with his anthropology based in Thomist metaphysics.[36] Reconsidering his anthropological project from this personalist perspective allows Wojtyła to begin his development of a Christian personalism that would come to dominate his philosophical and theological thought. However, Thomas's *analogia entis* is a primary influence on Wojtyła's understanding of the human person, something he finds wanting in Kant.[37] He begins with the divine archetype of human personhood. For St. Thomas, personhood is the highest perfection in the world of creatures, so it must be realized to an unmatched degree of perfection in God.

Wojtyła employs Thomas's general theological approach in which he uses the tools of analogy, supereminence, and remotion in his reflection upon divine revelation about God in order to gain insights into his creation and vice versa.[38] Wojtyła applies this methodology in his analysis of the human person. In particular, Wojtyła accepts St. Thomas's view that there is an analogy between the human person and every other person (divine and angelic), and so he is able to employ the Boëthian definition in his anthropology.[39]

Throughout the rest of his writings on the matter, Wojtyła will insist

---

[35] See Wojtyła, *Love and Responsibility*, 9–11.

[36] See Wojtyła, "Thomistic Personalism," 165–69.

[37] See Wojtyła, "Thomistic Personalism," 166.

[38] For a discussion of these concepts, see Thomas Aquinas, *Summa contra gentiles* I, 14, 29, 30.

[39] "*Persona est rationalis naturae individua substantia*" (The person is an individual substance of a rational nature) (Wojtyła, "Thomistic Personalism," 167).

that the substantiality of the human person must be preserved. However, divine and angelic persons are pure spirit, and so there are also vast differences between human persons and angelic persons, and of course the differences are even greater for divine persons. This Thomist methodology leads Wojtyła to specific features of the human person that he finds essential for any adequate anthropology.

St. Thomas adopts Aristotle's hylomorphic theory to describe the nature of the human person as a *compositum* of body (matter) and soul (form).[40] It is of fundamental importance for Wojtyła that the soul is the substantial form of the human being.[41] However, he highlights the attributes which are proper to the human person, making the person unique among all other created hylomorphs. Among these are the fact that the soul is a spiritual substance and the principle of the unique life and activity of the human person. He identifies intellect and free will as the most significant faculties of the soul because they manifest and actualize the soul's spiritual constitution.[42] These faculties are also significant in that they are the primary means by which a person brings about his individual moral and psychological character.

Wojtyła identifies in Thomism the fundamental attributes of human consciousness to which he eventually applied his modified Schelerian method in *Person and Act*. He of course adds that "as the substantial form of the body, the soul also has, in addition to spiritual faculties, faculties that are intrinsically dependent on matter."[43] These faculties are primarily associated with the senses which involve cognition and those faculties that St. Thomas refers to as "appetitive."[44] Because these faculties all belong to

---

[40] For St. Thomas, the human substantial form (i.e., the soul) perdures beyond the death of the body (see *Summa Theologiae* Ia, q. 75, a. 6 [hereinafter *ST*]). It is debated whether Aristotle held to the continued existence of the rational soul after death. All quotations from the *Summa* herein are taken from St. Thomas Aquinas, *Summa Theologica* (Allen, TX: Christian Classics, repr. 1981).

[41] See *ST* Ia, q. 76, a. 4.

[42] See Wojtyła, "Thomistic Personalism," 168.

[43] Wojtyła, "Thomistic Personalism," 168.

[44] St. Thomas distinguishes between the rational powers, animal powers, and vegetative powers in the human person. All of the rational powers are proper to man, which include the intellect and will. The animal powers are based on the senses. However, while man shares most of his animal powers with other animals, he does not share all of them. Among these, Thomas distinguishes between those which deal with sense knowledge and those which are appetites. The cognitive senses include the five senses, imagination, memory, judgment, and common sense. The sensitive appetite is further comprised of the concupiscible and irascible powers. The concupiscible powers are those which provide the inclination to seek that which is suitable according to the senses such as love, desire,

the concrete human person, they all have a role to play in forming and perfecting the human person in both his moral and psychological aspects. This integral view of the human person is a hallmark of Thomism and is foundational to the thought of Karol Wojtyła.

This integral anthropology is especially apparent in the manner in which he integrates all the faculties of the person into personal formation and perfection. Wojtyła explicitly attributes the split between the somatic and psychic aspects of the human being to the ill fruits of post-Cartesian philosophies of personhood. This split results in the unacceptable assumption that the person is reduced to his faculty of consciousness, and that this person-consciousness' existence is in some manner independent of the body.[45] This dis-integrated approach is pathologically reductive in Wojtyła's view. It is wanting because it cannot integrate the body with the spiritual soul, and it completely lacks the understanding of the latter as the body's substantial form and the principle of the human person's entire life and activity.[46]

The consequences of this hypostatization of consciousness include a one-sided emphasis on freedom as complete independence from all constraint and making lived experience and consciousness into absolutes. The person loses his concreteness and becomes nothing more than an artifact of lived experiences, reducing man's essence to consciousness and self-consciousness.[47] Rather, along with St. Thomas, Wojtyła considers consciousness and self-consciousness to be "derivative" of the person's rational nature. In other words, they subsist accidentally in the person and so they cannot replace him.[48]

Consciousness arises from the human person's rational nature and allows the person to act in freedom through the will. His free will permits the person to be master over his own actions. However, to be able to act in complete freedom the person must first fully possess himself. In other words, he must be master over his own person, which means that he is master over his own will.[49] For St. Thomas, the human person is always a

---

joy, hate, aversion, and sorrow. The irascible powers are those powers in the senses which incline one to avoid that which is a hindrance to what is suitable or that will inflict harm, and include hope, courage, fear, despair, and anger (see *ST* Ia, qq. 77–89).

[45] See Wojtyła, "Thomistic Personalism," 169.

[46] See Wojtyła, "Thomistic Personalism," 169.

[47] See Wojtyła, "Thomistic Personalism," 170.

[48] See Wojtyła, "Thomistic Personalism," 170.

[49] Wojtyła uses the term "self-possession" to describe the person who is master over his will,

concrete being (*suppositum*) who actualizes his potency through thinking and free will.

Thomas's understanding of the relationship between existence and action arises out of this connection. Wojtyła finds this relationship expressed well in the scholastic axiom *operari sequitur esse*.[50] However, he discovers limitations in Thomist metaphysics. He says that it is thoroughly objective in its approach and lacks adequate tools for studying the human person's lived experiences that would enable it to analyze consciousness and self-consciousness in terms of unique expressions of the human person as a subject.[51] Wojtyła resolves this limitation in Thomism's ability to study and generalize the interior dynamisms of the person by augmenting it with phenomenology.

Eight years after the preceding article was written, Cardinal Wojtyła published his major work, *Osoba i czyn*, in which he applies his modification of Scheler's phenomenological method to his investigation of the human person as revealed in the human act (*actus humanus*).[52] Wojtyła begins this work by justifying his integration of Thomist metaphysics with the phenomenological method based upon the premise that *operari sequitur esse* means the person is revealed through his acting. This dictum allows phenomenology to draw universal insights from an analysis of the empirical data of lived experience because "being" (i.e., existence) is the act from which the person draws all subsequent action.[53]

This philosophy of existence itself justifies the ontological unity of the person and his acts. So the *actus humanus* reveals the *suppositum humanum*. The phenomenological tool Wojtyła uses to analyze the interiority of the human person, who is characterized by the concept of consciousness and especially self-consciousness, is Edmund Husserl's *epoché*,[54] though Wojtyła has a modified understanding of *epoché*.

---

and "self-determination" to describe when the self-possessed person makes use of this self-mastery in exercising his will.

[50] Act follows being or "to act" follows "to be." St. Thomas preferred the infinitive because it is a verb form which, especially in the case of *esse*, indicates "being" is always in "act."

[51] See Wojtyła, "Thomistic Personalism," 170–71.

[52] Again, the first controversial English translation of Wojtyła's book *Osoba i Czyn* (*Person and Act*) is entitled *The Acting Person*.

[53] Wojtyła says: "In its basic conception, the whole of *Person and Act* is grounded on the premise that *operari sequitur esse*: the act of personal existence has its direct consequences in the activity of the person. And so action, in turn, is the basis for disclosing and understanding the person" (Wojtyła, "Subject and Community," 260n6).

[54] Husserl was a German-Czech philosopher (1859–1938) and mathematician who is regarded as the founder of phenomenology. Therefore, Husserl in some sense was the

Epoché is a term borrowed from Greek skepticism to refer to the "phenomenological reduction," or the suspending of "intentionalities" and neutralizing of "doxic modalities."[55] When one applies this approach to the study of consciousness, it assists in the investigation of intentional acts directed toward phenomena (or extra-subjective, objective contents) and so it allows the abstraction of consciousness such that one can treat it as a subject. However, Wojtyła cautions that one must apply this method with the caveat that one may use it *only* for analysis; the analytical method does not infer the underlying reality.[56]

Wojtyła continually emphasizes that one can perform this "subjectification" of consciousness only for the sake of analysis. A phenomenologist must not mistake this *epoché* for a philosophy of reality or of the human being.[57] He says that this mode of analysis of consciousness can be fruitful so long as it is understood to be simply a method of analysis.[58] Scheler's failure to realize that *epoché* is simply methodological and does not reflect reality is Wojtyła's fundamental critique of Scheler.[59] His criticism of Scheler, therefore, is not so much with his use of the method itself but rather with Scheler's metaphysical presuppositions and faulty conclusions derived from valid insights.

Scheler's contention that the human person is not a substance but just a conscious unity of lived experiences is Wojtyła's primary criticism of

---

ultimate influence on Scheler's phenomenology. However, Scheler never actually studied under Husserl and was in fact critical of some of his methodologies. He independently developed his own "Munich school" of phenomenology. Wojtyła also studied Husserl and Dietrich von Hildebrand so his phenomenology is not appropriated solely through Scheler. Nevertheless, there is general agreement that Scheler is the dominant influence on his phenomenology. See Nachef, *Mystery of the Trinity*, 15–18; Williams, *Mind of John Paul II*, 115–40; Schmitz, *Center of the Human Drama*, 30–57; Buttiglione, *Thought of the Man*, 54–82.

55 See Robert Sokolowski explains that this "phenomenological reduction" is a "bracketing" or the suspension of our beliefs (i.e., neutralizing "doxic modalities") where we bracket the world, putting it into virtual parentheses to consider it precisely as we are conscious of it (i.e., the phenomenological "intentionalities"). *Introduction to Phenomenology* (Cambridge: Cambridge University Press, 2000), 49.

56 Ontologizing the method results in reductionist thinking; it is a great error of modern thought to presuppose that because one can study things in parts, methodologically abstracting some aspect from the whole, that the whole is little more than an accumulation of parts.

57 This, I believe, is Wojtyła's essential modification of Husserl's *epoché*.

58 See Wojtyła, "Subject and Community," 226.

59 See, for example, "The Problem of the Separation of Experience from the Act in Ethics," and "Basis of Perfectionism," 51–55, in *Person and Community*.

Scheler's project and all post-Cartesian anthropology.[60] However, the phenomenological method purged of this faulty post-Cartesian presupposition has the capacity to analyze the interior aspects of the person effectively. This is accomplished when the insights derived from the phenomenological method are located within a system grounded in the metaphysical realism of the person as a concrete, subsistent entity. Wojtyła's project leads to the recognition "that human beings are subjects—and even subjects completely *in actu*, so to speak—only when they experience themselves as subjects."[61]

In fact, Wojtyła believes that it is only by taking into consideration consciousness and how it functions that one can understand and analyze the relation between the human self and the metaphysical human *suppositum*.[62] Consciousness plays a mediating role within the person, helping him to constitute the self within the entire framework of his existence and actions. It is for this reason that an analysis of consciousness leads to the realization that it is the person who acts and who is the agent of the action. It is through action then, that we come to recognize the significance of the relational aspects of the human person.

To summarize, Wojtyła's study of human personhood, from his early philosophical writings up through *Person and Act*, identifies several key ideas for this topic: 1) He is adamant about the metaphysical "concreteness" of the person (i.e., the *suppositum*) that is provided for in Thomist anthropology. 2) He adopts the hylomorphic theory in which the human person is the unity of body (matter) and soul (substantial form). 3) He also finds that Thomist metaphysics provides the point of departure for a phenomenological analysis of the interiority of a person (i.e., his consciousness) in its dictum that "act follows existence." Thus, a study of consciousness can reveal universal features of personhood. 4) Finally, he recognizes that an acting agent implies relationality.[63] The revelation of the person through his actions, the metaphysically concrete person, and the person as relational all stand out as important features of the person. However, Wojtyła bases his certainty in this philosophical anthropology upon divine revelation. He finds these same features, which he has uncovered through reason, also revealed in Scripture and Tradition.

---

[60] See Schmitz, *Center of the Human Drama*, 44.
[61] Wojtyła, "Subject and Community," 227.
[62] See "Subject and Community," 227.
[63] In this book, I will use the terms "relationality" and "relational" to indicate metaphysical relations which give rise to relationships between and among people.

THE HUMAN PERSON AND REVELATION

John Paul II's first series of Wednesday audience catecheses, unof-
ficially entitled a theology of the body,[64] provide his most in-depth
look at the human person in light of divine revelation.[65] His exegetical approach[66] here includes in part, modern biblical criticism,[67] human

---

[64] The Wednesday catecheses ran from September 5, 1979, to November 28, 1984. John
Paul II, *Man and Woman He Created Them: A Theology of the Body*, trans. Michael
Waldstein (Boston: Pauline Books and Media, 2006).

[65] Many Scripture scholars criticize John Paul II's use of Scripture because to them he seems to
ignore modern findings. Terrence Prendergast is one such scholar who is representative of
this portion of the biblical studies academy (see "'A Vision of Wholeness': A Reflection on
the Use of Scripture in a Cross-Section of Papal Writings" in *The Thought of Pope John Paul
II: A Collection of Essays and Studies*, ed. John M. McDermott [Rome: Editrice Pontificia
Università Gregoriana, 2000], 69–91). He locates the criticism of John Paul II's use of
Scripture in his seeming to ignore the "findings" of modern critical scholarship. Prendergast
admits that he shares this criticism. For example, he points out John Paul's "easy movement
between one or other Gospel" (80–81). A modern graduate student in biblical studies is
taught that he must first perform a thorough source critical evaluation of the texts he wishes
to exegete before he can consider using texts from two different Gospels. Prendergast exemplifies what has been a widespread presupposition in Catholic biblical scholarship in the last
several decades. Namely, this is the view that any approach other than historical/literary/
source criticism is not academically sound. However, this view seems to be waning with the
return of the desire to find the religious meaning of the text. The past dean and vice rector
of the *Biblicum*, James Swetnam, S.J., says: "Father Prendergast's choice of assured norms
for judging the pope's use or non-use of modern biblical scholarship is a reminder that only
until fairly recently 'literary criticism' in the world of biblical studies involved above all the-
orizing about sources. Only in the past twenty years has there been a major shift in emphasis
to trying to discover above all what a biblical text means as it stands" (James Swetnam, S.J.,
"'A Vision of Wholeness': A Response," in *The Thought of Pope John Paul II*, 93). One of
Prendergast's concerns is the dearth of references to current academic theories in John Paul
II's more authoritative writings. Assuming, as he suggests, that Prendergast's position is the
common one among papal critics, it would seem that the underlying reason for much of the
criticism has been an uncritical appropriation of the presuppositions and findings of critical
scholarship, a realization to which many scholars are now coming. Swetnam argues that
"unqualified negativity about John Paul's use of Scripture is not warranted; not infrequently
it is insightful and inspiring. But when Father Prendergast's findings are viewed from the
perspective of the pope's statements to the Pontifical Commission, the pope emerges as a
wistful biblist. If he seems to be wistful, perhaps his wistfulness is caused by his vague suspicion that despite his willingness to learn from contemporary biblical scholarship he is
still to some extent on the outside of the Bible looking in. And this can only be because,
to a certain extent, contemporary biblical scholarship is in the same position" (Swetnam,
"Response," 96–97).

[66] For discussion of Catholic methods and tools of biblical interpretation see The Pontifical
Biblical Commission (PBC), *The Interpretation of the Bible in the Church*, trans. Libreria
Editrice Vaticana (Boston: Pauline Books & Media, 1993).

[67] See, for example, his references to source/form criticism (i.e., the documentary

sciences,[68] phenomenological hermeneutics,[69] the theological tradition
of the Church,[70] and canonical criticism.[71] In these catechetical meditations, John Paul begins with the Matthean text on the indissolubility of
marriage which takes him immediately back to "the beginning."[72] John
Paul uses the methods and tools catalogued above to find the human
person revealed to himself in the two creation narratives of Genesis.

In his discussion of Genesis 2:20, John Paul shows that man discovers
himself as different from the animals through the fact that among them,
the man finds no suitable helpmate. Therefore, the man sees himself as
alone in all of creation. John Paul believes this solitude to be a fundamental problem for the human person which, in a sense, precedes the fact of
sex difference.[73] He clarifies that he means prior not in a chronological
sense but existentially. By its very nature, solitude in the body is shared by
everyone prior to revelation of the diversity of complementary sex difference. This fundamental problem of being alone in the presence of creation,
which he calls "original solitude," brings to the first man the experience of
self-knowledge. John Paul II observes that because man discovers himself
to be different from the animals, he understands himself to be unique.

---

hypothesis) in John Paul II, *Man and Woman*, 134, 137–43, 146–54, 157, 169–76; and
textual/literary criticism in reference to philological development: *'āḏām, tardēmāʰ,
ḥălôm*, in *Man and Woman*, 156–61, 158–61nn12–16, and *yāḏaʿ* ("to know") in *Man
and Woman*, 206, and especially 206n31.

[68] See, for example, his recourse to cultural anthropology in *Man and Woman*, 138, and
especially 138n4, with reference to myth and philosophical systems in the study of the
development of *eros* in Platonic philosophy.

[69] See, for example, his treatment of shame in *Man and Woman*, 171–73. For better or
worse, I have introduced the term "phenomenological hermeneutics." However, phenomenology falls under the officially recognized categories of philosophical hermeneutics,
sociological methods, cultural anthropology, and psychological and psychoanalytical
considerations. See PBC, *Interpretation of the Bible*, 59–65, 76.

[70] See, for example, John Paul II's recourse to Patristic authors and Church Councils in his
treatment of preternatural gifts and concupiscence in *Man and Woman*, 239–49; see also
282n44 and ff.; see also footnote 51.

[71] See, for example, his integrated view of marriage in Genesis, Matthew, and Mark in *Man
and Woman*, 131–33, as an example of his use of canonical criticism.

[72] John Paul justifies this movement from Matthew to Genesis based on the following
verses: "And Pharisees came up to him and tested him by asking, 'Is it lawful to divorce
one's wife for any cause?' He answered, 'Have you not read that he who made them *from
the beginning* [emphasis mine] made them male and female'" (Matt 19:3–4).

[73] See John Paul II, *Man and Woman*, 147–48. The date in parentheses refers to the date the
address was given. This date is important for correlating the many versions and translations of his Wednesday audience catecheses.

This self-knowledge helps to form his subjectivity and reveals himself to be a person.[74]

The author also finds that divine revelation shows how man manifests self-determination in the choice that God gives him regarding the tree of the knowledge of good and evil.[75] John Paul II's analysis of the first two chapters of Genesis reveals the features of self-consciousness and self-determination as fundamental features of human personhood. In addition to these features, he also finds that these texts show the person is relational. Even in the context of original solitude John Paul II sees the relational aspect of man's personhood manifested.

Genesis shows this relationality in man's relationship to God in two ways. The first creation narrative shows that God created man in His image. The second narrative reveals him as one who is in a covenant relationship with God. The man is the subject of this covenant; he is a person who has as his Partner, the Absolute. In this partnership, man is given the freedom to choose between good and evil, between life and death. The partnership between man and his Creator further reveals to the man his creaturely dependence upon his Partner which demands his complete submission (see Gen 2:16–17). The man is alone among all other creatures, but he is partner with the Absolute in a one-of-a-kind, unrepeatable relationship.[76]

The man's relationship with God manifests his constitution as a human person. This relationship requires that the man exercise his gifts of self-determination and free will in accordance with the truth of who and what he is.[77] As a human person, man must participate in perfecting his own constitution by his choices and actions for the good. Revelation reveals man's relationality, and it shows the person to be a body-soul composite.

In his analysis of the Genesis creation narrative, John Paul II is quick to ensure that his readers do not mistake human personhood to be something of a post-Cartesian construct. He points out that it is not

---

[74] See *Man and Woman*, 146ff.

[75] He says that man's choice to eat or not eat of the tree "adds the aspect of choice and self-determination (that is, of free will) to the outline of man described above. In this way, man's image as a person endowed with his own subjectivity appears before us as finished in its first sketch. The concept of original solitude includes both self-consciousness and self-determination" (*Man and Woman*, 151).

[76] *Man and Woman*, 151.

[77] I.e., this is the truth of man's fulfillment through his partnership with God through his dependence on and submission to his Creator.

consciousness alone that reveals human personhood. In other words, the experiences of self-awareness and self-determination reveal the person, but man also discovers himself to be a person through his corporeality. More specifically, he discovers himself to be a person through his ability to be the source of self-determined action which is only possible because of his bodily makeup. All of this is revealed through John Paul's phenomenological analysis of the inspired text. He also uncovers an original description of human consciousness beginning in the second chapter of Genesis in which the man discovers his bodiliness along with its meaning.

The man's discovery is not based on a metaphysical analysis but in the concrete experience of himself as a subject. John Paul II says that "man is a subject not only by his self-consciousness and by self-determination, but also based on his own body. The structure of this body is such that it permits him to be the author of genuinely human activity. In this activity, the body expresses the person."[78] He will affirm this last phrase again and again: "The body expresses the person," and it is especially the activity of the body which expresses the person. The body and its activity reveal both the inherent and the intentional meaning of the entire person. The biblical text confirms the profound unity of body and soul. Scripture reveals more about this unity in the dual, complementary modes of humanity, the person as male and female.

Through the process of naming the animals and finding none to be a suitable partner, the man discovers that his difference from the other animals is discovered through the body's essential meaning.[79] Yet its meaning is not discovered through the body alone, nor even primarily through the body. The Genesis text reveals that it is more the "invisible" that determines man than what can be seen.[80] Furthermore, and this is essential for understanding fatherhood, it is in the differences between the male and female bodies that one cognitively understands the meaning of the body, and that one therefore can discern the human person. John Paul calls this the "spousal meaning of the body."

The body's spousal meaning indicates that because man is made male and female, in the image of God, it is directly due to sex difference that the first man can see himself as a gift to the first woman. The *communio personarum* (the communion of persons) of the Trinity further confirms this

---

[78] John Paul II, *Man and Woman*, 154. The body expressing the person is a critically important finding in Scripture which also corresponds with his hylomorphic anthropology.

[79] See *Man and Woman*, 155–56.

[80] See *Man and Woman*, 155–56.

fact. The ineffable Trinitarian communion is the archetype for the union that the structure of the body, as male and female, makes possible. The spousal configuration of the body indicates that the person is created for life-giving love. The body is the foundation and manifestation of marriage, what John Paul II calls the "primordial sacrament."

Marriage is primordial in that it exists from the very beginning of man's existence, before written history. It is a sacrament in that it is a visible sign constituted within man revealing something that at the same time is invisible. This sign is in the body, which makes man's complementary masculinity and femininity visible, and this complementary sex difference reveals his structure as a relational being made for fruitful love. Only the body has the capacity to make the invisible, visible. The material aspect of human nature reveals the immaterial, that is, the spiritual and even the divine. God created the body in order to manifest in the visible order, the "mystery hidden from eternity in God."[81] This corresponds exactly with John Paul's hylomorphic metaphysics.

The body and soul are an ontological unity, and because of this, the visible body reveals the invisible soul. Thus, divine revelation confirms the hylomorphic unity discovered through philosophical inquiry. They both point to the integral nature of body and soul, the importance and purpose of the body in the visible world, and perhaps also to the logical implication, therefore, that the body has more than a profane purpose. The body reveals a) man's transcendence over the animals and b) man's participation in the *communio personarum* of the Trinity, while at the same time it c) expresses the person in his sexual structure as an interpersonal, fruitful gift, and, d) through its action, it expresses the self.[82]

These important features of our author's anthropology emphasize the oneness of a composite human nature, the essential aspects of the human person and his fulfillment, the person's complementary structure, and the implications of feminine and masculine complementarity for personal fulfillment. His writings detailing the threats to the person also serve to highlight the features of the person he thinks are most significant.

---

[81] *Man and Woman*, 203.
[82] See *Man and Woman*, 241–42.

THREATS TO THE HUMAN PERSON

John Paul II believes the human person is threatened today.[83] Cartesian thinking, which has disassociated the soul from the body, underlies this threat, and manifests itself in many contemporary philosophical errors and their consequent ethical problems. Many of today's problems arise from this misunderstanding of the human person, which at its root is a matter of reductionism.[84] The consequences of reductionism are particularly destructive to the human person's relationships with other persons, especially in the family. In his Letter to Families, John Paul II identifies modern rationalism as one consequence of Cartesianism. Like ancient Manichaeism, modern rationalism also presupposes a radical split between the body and soul, resulting in a diminishment of the body to mere matter; matter that per se has no ethical value but is free to be manipulated and dominated according to the caprice of prevailing values (e.g., efficiency, utility, productivity, pleasure, etc.).[85] Such a reduction gives way to the separation between morality and the body.

Man loses a sense of who he is and the person, marriage, the family, and society all suffer for it. While the philosophical underpinnings of Manichaeism and modern rationalism are different, the results are the same. For this reason, John Paul calls modern rationalism a new form of Manichaeism in which soul and body are opposed to one another as polar

---

[83] See John Paul II, Apostolic Exhortation on the Role of the Christian Family in the Modern World *Familiaris consortio* (November 22, 1981), AAS 74 (1982), 114–37, §4. The peril has significantly increased since he wrote this more than forty years ago.

[84] Adolfo Barrachina says that John Paul's addressing of this problem is the primary focus of *Redemptor hominis*. The encyclical addresses the threatened human person by proposing the truth about his unparalleled dignity. Barrachina states that man's dignity comes from the fact that the Son of God assumed flesh and joined Himself with all of humanity. Through the Incarnation, together with His life, death, and Resurrection, Christ has definitively illuminated the most profound aspects of man's existence. See Adolfo Barrachina Carbonell, "La Trilogía Trinitaria de Juan Pablo II: Claves para su Lectura e Interpretación," *Anales Valentinos* 26 (2000): 201–30.

[85] However, Cartesian neo-Manichaeism's beliefs about the soul differ from ancient Manichaeism, as would be expected. Ancient Manichaeism's philosophical system was Neoplatonic, while neo-Manichaeism arises from Cartesian rationalism, which today doubts the soul. Elsewhere John Paul II locates the reductive motivation of modern rationalism in a faulty application of methods of scientific investigation to anthropology: "We are, in fact, the children of an age in which, due to the development of various disciplines, this integral vision of man can easily be rejected and replaced by many partial conceptions that dwell on one or another aspect of the *compositum humanum* but do not reach man's *integrum* or leave it outside their field of vision" (John Paul II, *Man and Woman*, 220).

opposites.[86] It loses sight of the fact that the spiritual soul is the source of life for the body, and so man is no longer understood to be a person and subject of his actions. John Paul sees the ramifications of this errant thinking in cultural ills such as a view of human sexuality not as something to be held in ineffable awe as when Adam first beheld Eve (see Gen 2:23), but as an area suited for manipulation and exploitation.

This modern rationalism has an inherent proclivity to reductionism because it relies solely on exhaustive cognitive comprehension. As such, it cannot tolerate mystery, and so rationalists cannot think of God as the infinite Christian God. If they acknowledge him at all, it is in the form of a "vague deism."[87] If there can be no mystery in God, then the mystery of the human person must all the more be reduced to that which scientific inquiry can circumscribe. John Paul rejects this reductive premise, affirming the mystery of the human person through one of his fundamental anthropological tenets: "*Christ reveals man to himself.*"[88] This precept makes the Incarnation pivotal for understanding his account of human personhood.

John Paul heads off any charge of Manichaeism against the Church's teaching concerning concupiscence, explaining that a desire that manifests itself as a lust of the flesh does not negate the body as a constituent aspect of human nature.[89] Rather, it affirms the significance of the body for determining man's being and his identity as a freely acting subject. As such, the body shares in the dignity of the human person. This is true because the body, as the object of desire, is recognized as a good.

John Paul argues that Christianity cannot be reconciled with any school of thought that considers the body to be evil. The Incarnation and Resurrection both attest to its inherent goodness. It is concupiscence which gives each person the proclivity to pervert the good urges that are integral to being a human person.[90] Manichaeism results in thinking which is at odds with Christianity. It negates the value of the human body and of sex and likewise distorts the value of the human person, who is either male or female, a union of body and soul.

Rather, the authentic Christian ethos is found in Jesus's words from

---

[86] See John Paul II, Letter to Families *Gratissimam sane* (February 2, 1994), AAS 86 (1994), 868–925 (New Hope, KY: Urbi Et Orbi Communications, 1994), §19 (hereinafter, Letter to Families).
[87] Letter to Families.
[88] *Gaudium et spes*, §22.
[89] See *Man and Woman*, 307–308.
[90] See *Man and Woman*, 307–308.

his Sermon on the Mount which requires the transformation of the person in order to purify this desire.[91] A purified conscience is able to realize and express the value of the body and sex difference as constituent aspects of the person that enable the communion of persons which lies at the root of God's plan for the human person. The post-Cartesian disassociation of the body from the soul, arising from the rejection of hylomorphism has given rise to modes of thinking that devalue the person and sex. A correct understanding of the person is paramount for a harmonious society.

John Paul considers a true anthropology to be the one key for solving many of the world's social ills. To accept the dignity and value of each person, we must understand authentic human personhood. Writing on the hundredth anniversary of Pope Leo XIII's *Rerum novarum*, John Paul II states that all of the Church's social doctrine as espoused by Leo presupposes an authentic anthropology in which the human person is recognized as having a unique and irreplaceable value.[92] Man is the only creature on earth that God created for his own sake. Man's dignity arises first from the fact that he is created in the image of God. Faulty views of the person have resulted in social distortions such as totalitarian governmental structures which are hostile to the human person. An example with which John Paul was all too familiar was socialism as it was manifested in Eastern Europe.

Marxist socialism reduced the person to simply one element in a larger social organism, thereby subordinating the person to the needs of the larger body. It failed to recognize the integrality of self-determination and free will for the person, further reducing the person solely to his socially beneficial relationships.[93] Neither does John Paul exempt democratic institutions from his warnings. He admonishes that "[a]uthentic democracy is possible only in a State ruled by law, and on the basis of a correct conception of the human person."[94] He is concerned that the various offspring of Cartesian dualism, in all sectors of society, have annihilated the authentic meaning of the human person.

The remedy for this is a correct understanding of the human person including: a) his inherent dignity derived from his creation in the image of God; b) his proper relation to society in which he loses none of his authentic self-determination and free will; c) his unity of body and soul in which neither can be denigrated without denigrating the person; and d)

---

[91] See *Man and Woman*, 307–308.
[92] See John Paul II, Encyclical Letter on the Hundredth Anniversary of Rerum Novarum *Centesimus annus* (May 1, 1991), AAS 83 (1991), 793–867, §11.
[93] See *Centesimus annus*, §13.
[94] *Centesimus annus*, §46.

his mystery which is revealed in the Incarnation. In addition to these four truths about the human person, John Paul II also emphasizes the uniqueness of the human person.

UNIQUE, UNREPEATABLE, INCOMMUNICABLE

Wojtyła explains that the term "person" first of all indicates the uniqueness and unrepeatability of the human person. The person is one who is very much more than simply one sample from a larger population. Rather, "[he] has in himself something more, some particular fullness and perfection of being. To emphasize this fullness and perfection the word 'person' must necessarily be used."[95] Manifesting man's individual distinctiveness begins with the person's rational ability. There is no other creature in the observable cosmos which has demonstrated the ability to reason.

The fact that reason makes man different from the rest of the cosmos, even among the highest of other animals, is highlighted by Boëthius's definition of a person as an individual substance of a rational nature (*individua substantia rationalis naturae*).[96] However, Boëthius's definition by itself is insufficient. Other dimensions of human personhood also are needed to reveal his uniqueness, to show that each person is incommunicable. Chief among these are the power of self-determination and its enabling faculty of free will. Wojtyła states that "*no one else can want for me. No one can substitute his act of will for mine.*"[97]

Antoine Nachef shows that in Wojtyła's view, it is through the agency of self-determination that we come to understand ourselves as acting subjects who exist and act individually among other acting subjects.[98] A person actualizes his unique individuality through self-determination exercised in freedom. A further requirement becomes apparent here, and that is for self-determination to be possible I must first fully possess myself.[99] So self-possession is also an integral attribute of the human person which makes him incommunicable. Incommunicability, especially due to self-possession and self-determination, has an ontological and an ethical implication.[100] Let us now turn to these implications .

---

[95] Wojtyła, *Love and Responsibility*, 4.

[96] See Wojtyła, *Love and Responsibility*.

[97] Wojtyła, *Love and Responsibility*, 24.

[98] See Nachef, *Mystery of the Trinity*, 24.

[99] See Wojtyła, *The Acting Person*, 107–108.

[100] I.e., ontologically each person has temporal continuity, it is always that person who chooses to act. The ethical implications arise because ultimately only the person can

Wojtyła recognizes that his view of the person will cause difficulties for some. This is especially true for those influenced by the reductive presuppositions too often associated with practitioners of the natural sciences. Wojtyła accepts the insights of science but rejects any methodological reductionism covertly extended into metaphysical extrapolations. The body is more than simply an organism. It is integral to human nature and to the person, and only because of this can it be the medium through which the person expresses himself.[101] The body's seamless integration in the person and his personal incommunicability mean that the body itself also has an ethical meaning. John Paul argues that almost all moral issues implicating the body are moral because the body is the inseparable, visible expression of the soul and of the freely acting person who, when he acts freely in the world, has a moral responsibility for these bodily acts, whether acting by himself or in his relationships with others.[102]

The ethical problem that John Paul II focuses on in his *Man and Woman* catecheses is the proper meaning and use of human sexuality. To explain the meaning of sex, he makes use of his earlier findings in these catecheses which show that the person's structure as a body-soul unity is a reflection of, and a participation in, the *communio personarum* of the Trinity. The naked human body reveals this image most intimately through its masculinity and femininity. The complete giving of one person to the other, in reciprocal fashion, is part of the "language of the body."[103] To act in truth means to obey this language, this spousal system, and so from this Trinitarian anthropology he finds the rationale for the Catholic teaching on sexuality.[104]

The texts which focus on uniqueness, unrepeatability, and incommunicability, emphasize the person's rational ability, free will, and self-determination, and show that these attributes have implications for human ethical behavior. Presupposing this, John Paul II repeatedly invokes three phrases from *Gaudium et spes* to articulate the value and purpose of the human person, which I propose form the fundamental hermeneutical

---

choose for himself because only he can exercise his free will. Because he has reason, an intellect, and free will, all of his free acts comprise moral decisions which accrue to him.

[101] See Wojtyła, *Love and Responsibility*, 186–87.

[102] See *Man and Woman*, 364–65.

[103] *Man and Woman*, 367–69. John Paul uses the term "language" in terms of the body in the sense of the body acting as a visible witness, or "prophet," of the truth which God has written into the human person. John Paul II infers this total gift of one spouse to another by analogy of the marital *communio personarum* with the Trinitarian *communio personarum*.

[104] See *Man and Woman*, 367–69.

principles for the understanding of his anthropology. The first is directly from Genesis revealing that man is made in the image of God.[105] The second is that Christ reveals man to himself.[106] The third is that man can only authentically fulfill himself through a sincere gift of self.[107]

CREATED IN THE IMAGE AND LIKENESS OF GOD

Fernando Moreno says this first hermeneutic principle is the truth about man which John Paul II proclaimed to the world from the beginning of his pontificate.[108] The source of man's personal dignity is the fact that God makes man in his own image. It also provides an interpretive key revealing the human person's metaphysically concrete constitution alongside other features of personhood, such as his personal dignity and relationality.

John Paul deduces that relationality constitutes human personhood from man's being made in the image of a Trinity of persons. It is for this reason that he believes "man made in the image of the Trinity" is perhaps the deepest theological truth about man.[109] He says that "[image and likeness mean] not only rationality and freedom as constitutive properties of human personhood, but also, from the very beginning, the capacity of

---

[105] "For sacred Scripture teaches that man was created 'to the image of God,' as able to know and love his creator." *Gaudium et spes*, §12; *Vatican Council II: The Conciliar and Post Conciliar Documents*, 1988 rev. ed., ed. Austin Flannery, O.P. (Northport, NY: Costello Publishing Company, 1987), 913.

[106] "In reality it is only in the mystery of the Word made flesh that the mystery of man truly becomes clear. For Adam, the first man, was a type of him who was to come, Christ the Lord, the new Adam, in the very mystery of the revelation of the Father and of his love, *fully reveals man to himself* and brings to light his most high calling" (emphasis mine). *Gaudium et spes*, §22; Flannery, *Vatican Council II*, 922. Thomas McGovern says that this second idea has become the theme of John Paul II's pontificate. See Thomas McGovern, "The Christian Anthropology of John Paul II," *Josephinum Journal of Theology* 8, no. 1 (2001): 138.

[107] "It follows then, that if man is the only creature on earth that God has wanted for its own sake, man can fully discover his true self only in a sincere giving of himself." *Gaudium et spes*, §24; Flannery, *Vatican Council II*, 925.

[108] See Fernando Moreno, "La verdad sobre el hombre en el Magisterio de Juan Pablo II," *Scripta Theologica* 20, nos. 2–3 (1988): 684.

[109] John Paul says: "[The Trinitarian concept of the 'image of God'] constitutes perhaps the deepest theological aspect of everything one can say about man. In the mystery of creation—the basis of the original and constitutive 'solitude' of his being—man has been endowed with a deep unity between what is, humanly and through the body, male in him and what is, equally humanly and through the body, female in him. . . . In this way, we find ourselves within the very bone marrow of the anthropological reality that has the name body" (*Man and Woman*, 164).

having a personal relationship with God, as 'I' and 'you,' and therefore the capacity of having a covenant, which will take place in God's salvific communication with man."[110] So the implications of man's having been made in the image of God include his dignity, rationality, and free will, and a special type of relationality. Man's constitution as a person gives him the capacity for personal communion with God. Man's capacity for God infers a vocation.

Each person's vocation starts with the call to a relationship of personal intimacy with God. One must unite himself to God through obedience to his will in order to hear his call and to receive the grace needed to respond to it. Therefore, because man's constitution demands that he faithfully follow his vocation if he is to find authentic actualization, union with God is the only path to authentic personal fulfillment. The Blessed Virgin is the icon of the perfect realization of this vocation to personal fulfillment through union with God.[111] Among corporeal creatures, only "man is *capax Dei*: capable of knowing God and of receiving the gift he makes of himself. Created in the image and likeness of God (see [Genesis] 1:26), man is able to live in a personal relationship with him and to respond with loving obedience to the covenant relationship his Creator offers him."[112]

Looking at vocation and personal fulfillment from another angle, one can view this relationship between each person and God in terms of "act." John Paul indicates that the *actus humanus* is integral to personal fulfillment in his discussion of "image" and work. Man's vocation to work comes directly from his being made in the image of God, to be a co-creator with him.[113] Thus to be fully actualized as a human person one must use his rational faculties and his self-determination to work out his actualization (i.e., holiness) in the particular vocation he is given.[114] It is only because man is made in the image of God that he can have a vocation that shares

---

[110] John Paul II, Encyclical Letter on the Holy Spirit in the Life of the Church and the World *Dominum et vivificantem* (May 18, 1986), *AAS* 78 (1986), 809–900, §34.

[111] See John Paul II, Apostolic Letter on the Dignity and Vocation of Women *Mulieris dignitatem* (August 15, 1988), AAS 80 (1988), 1653–1729, §5.

[112] John Paul II, *A Catechesis on Salvation History*, vol. 6, *The Trinity's Embrace: God's Saving Plan* (Boston: Pauline Books and Media, 2002), 105.

[113] John Paul II understands work as a "vocation" in a broad sense of the term vocation. In his holistic thought, God calls man to perfect himself in every aspect of his life. Man must freely respond to God's call in everything, including his particular "vocation" of work. John Paul II refers to the idea of work as a vocation twice in his Encyclical Letter on Human Work *Laborem exercens* (September 14, 1981), AAS 73 (1981), 577–647, §§11, 26.

[114] See *Laborem exercens*, §6.

in the work of the Creator.[115] The person-actualizing effect of the *actus humanus* is a recurring theme in John Paul II's thought, having ontological ramifications for the human person.

John Paul analyzes human work from its subjective perspective. He finds that work is always an *actus personae*, an act of the person in which imbues himself in his entirety—body and soul.[116] The whole person participates whether the work is manual or intellectual. He draws the parallel between work as an enterprise that engages the whole person and the soteriological promise of the gospel message which is directed to the salvation of the whole person, and so concerns itself with human work. The gospel calls the person to an interior effort in which the spiritual person is infused with and inspired by the theological virtues of faith, hope, and love. Through this grace, God condescends to elevate man's human works so as to make him a coworker in his plan of salvation, giving man's works the dignity of redemptive effect.

We have seen several anthropological features resulting from man's having been created in the image of God. Man has a) inherent dignity, b) reason, c) free will, d) self-determination, e) status as a relational being with God and other created persons, and f) the ability to perfect himself through his free actions by cooperating with grace in his vocation. Man's capacity for fulfillment is a calling to which he must obediently respond if he is to achieve it. *Gaudium et spes* is a primary text for the author in terms of understanding the human person and his vocation to perfect himself. It also provides the next important principle for understanding the author's anthropology.

CHRIST REVEALS MAN TO HIMSELF

Gaudium et spes §22 is the origin of the second hermeneutical principle: Christ reveals man to himself. J. Honoré argues that John Paul II finds in Christ alone both the expression of the truth of the human person and the meaning of man's existence and destiny. Failing to understand him, we remain a mystery to ourselves.[117] This principle constitutes the essential foundation of John Paul's theological anthropology.[118] His anthropology presupposes the Chalcedonian teaching that Jesus is both fully God and

---

[115] See *Laborem exercens*, §25.

[116] See *Laborem exercens*, §24. This idea articulates the main argument of *Person and Act*.

[117] See J. Honoré, "Christ the Redeemer, Core of John Paul II's Teaching," in *John Paul II: A Panorama of His Teachings* (New York: New City Press, 1989), 21.

[118] See Nachef, *Mystery of the Trinity*, 109.

fully man. More specifically, Jesus Christ is one divine person fully possessing the divine nature who joins to himself a fully human nature, without mixture, confusion, separation, or division of the two natures.[119]

John Paul II cites Pope Damasus to make clear that the Son of God had to become fully human, while losing nothing of his divinity, for the salvation of humanity to be possible.[120] This is important for salvation first, but it is also important for anthropology, that is, for understanding who we are. With this Christology as his point of departure, John Paul identifies and corrects several modern theological errors.

He asserts that the christological teachings of the ecumenical councils authoritatively proclaim "the truth about the human and divine natures, their duality and union in the person of the Word, the properties and faculties of human nature and their perfect harmony and subordination to the dominion of the divine 'I.'"[121] Jesus Christ is the example *par excellence* for each person who must submit and conform his will to God's. But Christ's having done so also makes it possible for those united with him to do the same. While the council fathers used terms and language of the time, they did not choose them haphazardly.

Conciliar formulations have an ability to transcend culture and time. They are not limited to a particular philosophical system or theological school. Therefore, it is illegitimate for men of today to impose Cartesian philosophical presuppositions on these texts. Theologians who reject the ability of dogmatic formulations to transcend theological and philosophical systems artificially introduce problems which impact this second hermeneutical principle.

John Paul identifies one such problem in anthropology, which arises when theologians reject a foundational distinction in traditional Christology. The Trinitarian distinction between person and nature is also essential for a coherent account of the Incarnation.[122] Those who fall prey to a new form of scholasticism, in which they uncritically appropriate new notions and terminologies from various scientific and philosophical schools while failing to discern the meaning these new expressions provide in terms of a common, universal understanding, often return to condemned formulations about the Incarnation. This happens to those

---

[119] See John Paul II, *A Catechesis on the Creed*, vol. 2, *Jesus, Son and Savior* (Boston: Pauline Books and Media, 1996), 320–30.

[120] See John Paul II, *Jesus, Son and Savior*, 324.

[121] John Paul II, *Jesus, Son and Savior*, 336–37.

[122] See John Paul II, *Jesus, Son and Savior*, 337. We will see this also has relevance to human personhood.

who uncritically adopt structuralist, relativist, existentialist, and subjectivist presuppositions in the philosophy of language and in hermeneutical systems common to modern philosophical schools of thought.

Proponents of such thought reject the ancient concepts and terminology as having been influenced by outdated thinking that is unable to convey to modernity the mystery of the living Christ. This crisis of language also relativizes and claims as obsolete the content of Nicene and Chalcedonian dogmas themselves, supposing they have nothing intelligible to convey to modern ears. This has resulted in a return to the condemned Nestorian position that claims there to be a human person in Christ. John Paul warns that such decadence results in theological claims that contradict revealed truth.[123]

The abandonment of the distinction between person and nature has led to much confusion, in part because of the loss of precision these concepts provide. It also leaves the practitioner open to a reductive understanding of human personhood. The mistake they make in giving Jesus human personhood, permitted by abandonment of the person-nature distinction, also follows from the Cartesian premise about the person held by some phenomenologists. In the case of the Incarnation, Jesus's personhood is simply a collection of experiences of consciousness, or it is simply his awareness of the divine within him.[124] John Paul warns that this post-Cartesian decadence cannot provide an adequate understanding of the Incarnation, of authentic human personhood, or a compelling articulation of human experience.

For the human person, personhood is experienced as a substantial unity of all aspects of one's bodily and spiritual makeup. For Jesus Christ, this principle of unity is the source of all created substance, the Second Person of the Trinity. The human experience of personhood is of one who possesses this nature; a person is one who possesses this particular body and soul. Jesus Christ experiences this possession of his humanity in a human manner. Nevertheless, it is the divine person who possesses his human nature. The distinction between nature and person allows us to describe reasonably divine revelation's assertion that Jesus is both fully man and fully God. He can indeed have a complete human nature without being a human person. In fact, for our salvation and for authentically understanding ourselves, this must be so. The Incarnation then also

---

[123] See John Paul II, *Jesus, Son and Savior*, 337.
[124] See John Paul II, *Jesus, Son and Savior*, 337–38.

strongly implies that human personhood must be analogical to divine personhood in terms of categories of being.[125]

The Incarnation also is the exemplar by which we come to understand both ourselves and our calling. Jesus Christ, the Second Adam, restores man's likeness to God, a likeness that was forfeited by the first Adam who left his children distorted by sin. Indeed, not only is the likeness restored in Christ but also the fact that God the Son assumed human nature reveals man's ineffable dignity. John Paul says that in a sense, Jesus unites each man to himself through his Incarnation.[126]

Man sees the heights of his dignity through the Incarnation which unites each person individually to the Incarnate Word. This is the good news; it is profound and amazing that man could possibly have such dignity. This good news "is also called Christianity."[127] Man sees in Christ his own "supreme calling" to holiness and to docility to God's will.[128] Man further sees in the Cross and Resurrection not only his calling to suffer with Jesus but also his calling to a return to his original destiny for happiness.[129] Christ is our model for how we are to live on earth in imitation of God; and if we are faithful, he is also the model for how we will live out our eternity.

Jesus Christ is also the one who enables this vocation to be lived. Only in Christ's redemption and our participation in the divine nature is it possible for man to realize his imitation of God.[130] Jesus demonstrated this after the Resurrection when he showed himself in his spiritualized body manifesting the pure soul's glory, first to the women and then to his disciples.[131] The Resurrection then shows not only the promise of our future glory but also the anthropological truth about the unity of body and soul and the permanent value of the body. John Paul says that "the truth about the resurrection had a *key meaning for the formation of theological anthropology as a whole*, which could simply be considered an '*anthropology of the resurrection*.'"[132] He once again relies on the Angelic Doctor for the

---

[125] We will take this up in chapter 4.

[126] See John Paul II, Encyclical Letter at the Beginning of His Papacy *Redemptor hominis* (March 4, 1979), *AAS* 71 (1979), 257–324, §8.

[127] *Redemptor hominis*, §10.

[128] John Paul II, *Jesus, Son and Savior*, 304.

[129] See John Paul II, *Jesus, Son and Savior*, 348.

[130] See John Paul II, *Jesus, Son and Savior*, 408.

[131] See John Paul II, *Jesus, Son and Savior*, 503.

[132] *Man and Woman*, 390.

metaphysics to explain the importance of the Resurrection of the body for anthropology.

He notes that St. Thomas Aquinas, through his meditations on the resurrection of the body, came to center his anthropology, and particularly the relation of the soul to the body, more on Aristotle than on Plato. St. Thomas's Christian modification of Aristotle's hylomorphic theory describes well the final and everlasting state of the person as a unity of body and soul, and attests to the compositeness of the human person. John Paul says that Plato, by contrast, saw the union of body to soul as a temporary situation. But it was not Aristotle's theory that gave rise to Thomas's theology. Rather, Thomas discovered in Aristotle a philosophical system which corresponds to divine revelation.

This system begins not with metaphysics but with the Resurrection, whereby Christ reveals the truth of human nature and so the truth of the human person. Namely, that man is an integral union of body and soul, a unity that was forfeited with the fall but restored by Christ. John Paul finds that the truth of this second hermeneutical principle is more important today than ever. He suggests that while modernity has progressed in its knowledge of such things as human psychology and the material world in general, man is still a great unknown to himself.[133] This ignorance extends to marriage and family life. Therefore, the world needs the gospel, not only for soteriological ends, but also for societal good.

For John Paul, the most profound fount of knowledge about the body is the Incarnate Word who reveals man to himself.[134] The Incarnation reveals the mystery and dignity of the person, including his body, and it hints at his metaphysical constitution. The Resurrection shows the truth of the seamless integration of the body-soul unity and man's vocation. This second hermeneutical principle therefore indicates the importance of the interpersonal and societal relations for the person, and this relational aspect of man is brought to the fore in the final principle.

MAN FULFILLS HIMSELF ONLY THROUGH A SINCERE GIFT OF SELF

This third hermeneutical principle is possibly one of the most often quoted by John Paul II. The fact that man can fulfill himself only through a sincere gift of self in some ways is the summary of his understanding of the meaning of the human person and his fulfillment. One necessary aspect of

---

[133] See Letter to Families, §19.
[134] See Letter to Families, §19.

the character of authentic self-giving and fulfillment will be shown to be given by the person's masculinity or femininity. The essence of fulfillment will be seen to be ordered by what it means to be a father (and mother). This principle is also infused with almost all of the most important theological, metaphysical, and ethical aspects of John Paul II's anthropology, especially from the perspective of his account of personhood.

Understanding the depths of this simple statement, along with its practical implications, will require us to delve into the Trinitarian and christological underpinnings of his anthropology. We will have to explore what he means by the human person and develop his philosophical account of personhood and personal fulfillment from metaphysical and experiential perspectives using both his Thomist anthropology and his phenomenological analyses.

We will also have to investigate John Paul's understanding of masculinity and fatherhood in relation to personhood, and their implications for personal fulfillment before we are ready to begin extracting his theology of fatherhood from his writings and extrapolating its practical implications in areas in which he is not explicit. Perhaps most insightful will be the metaphysical account of personhood and sex difference which will arise from his writings.

This metaphysical account will provide the key for understanding the coherence of his anthropology, for extracting implicit features of masculinity and fatherhood, and for determining the practical implications which we have mentioned. It will also help us to understand the manner in which one's choices change the person for good or evil by accruing to him the moral value of his choices and subsequent actions.

The account will aid us in resolving the perennial metaphysical problem of sex difference vis-à-vis human nature. That is, how can it be so important to the person if it is only accidental? In so doing, it will allow us to show why the relationship between sex difference and human personhood immutably defines an essential aspect of who one is as a human person. It will also reveal the significance of masculinity (and femininity) for personal fulfillment.

This principle serves a two-fold purpose for our project. Not only does it prove to be a key for understanding John Paul II's account of personhood, masculinity, and fatherhood, but it also provides something of the roadmap for this project. In tracing the analogy of being from the Trinity to the human person, a task required by the context of this principle given in *Gaudium et spes* §24, I found that the effort seemed to lay out for me the steps needing to be taken in order to articulate the account we will see in this work.

John Paul II's pastoral experience and academic work together served to focus his attention on the problem of the meaning of life and what it means to be human in terms of personal fulfillment. This together with his earlier work in the theater leads to our final concept.

THE *DRAMATIS PERSONAE*

The concept of the *dramatis personae* is an important category for understanding Karol Wojtyła's anthropology.[135] Owing perhaps to his early theatrical interest, Wojtyła adopts a dramatic approach in his theological anthropology, explaining that one can envision the person in terms of a personal drama. He uses the etymological origins of "drama" to suggest that the personal "act" in its relation to love sets the stage for the drama of interpersonal relations.[136] This statement summarizes in some respects, his view of the human person whose meaning and fulfillment is found in relation to the manner in which he chooses and acts with respect to others. His awareness of this meaning seems to be implicit already in the plays he wrote, beginning with his undergraduate work at Jagiellonian University in Kraków in the early 1940s.

Schmitz shows that even in these early years, Wojtyła was drawn to the study of the relationship between word and action.[137] He takes for his study of the phenomenon experiences from Polish history as well as lessons from significant events in salvation history. The youthful, future pope seemed to be fascinated with the written and spoken word in all of its variety of forms. He began his studies at the outbreak of World War II, where he experienced the horror of the Nazi occupation of his homeland. In an attempt to keep alive Polish culture in peaceful rebellion against Nazi attempts to annihilate it, he and his classmates began a clandestine spoken theater troupe which would be called the Rhapsodic Theater Company. It is here that we see how his precocious inquiry into word and action led to

---

[135] I acknowledge that this term does not occur with much frequency in the author's writings. I have found two occurrences: one in *Love and Responsibility*, 96, and another occurrence in *Man and Woman*, 143. However, the concept of life as a drama is quite prevalent in his writings as pope. For example, see *Redemptor hominis*, §§15-16; *Dives in misericordia*, §5; *Fides et ratio*, §45; *Reconciliatio et paenitentia*, §7; and implicitly throughout *Christifideles laici*, but explicitly in §44.

[136] Wojtyła, *Love and Responsibility*, 96–97.

[137] See Schmitz, *Center of the Human Drama*, 2.

his discovery of the relationship between truth and action, and so its role in forming the human person begins to take shape.

Schmitz summarizes themes in six of the plays written by Wojtyła between wartime Poland and the early 1960s, themes that reveal the fundamental elements that shaped his mature philosophy of the human person and human action.[138] Many themes come to the fore in his plays, such as hope and trust in the midst of suffering in his second play, *Job: A Drama from the Old Testament.*

Wojtyła explores the social responsibility of the artist with respect to his art in *Our God's Brother,* a play he began while he was still in formation for the priesthood. However, underlying themes of these dramas seem increasingly to revolve around the manner in which truth determines the meaning of the human person and his fulfillment, his freedom to choose to pursue the truth and his fulfillment, and the negative consequences for himself and his freedom if he chooses against truth. Ultimately, the relationship between truth and actions done intentionally and in freedom will be shown to be the foundation of love.

Love as a personal "act" is key for understanding and living out all interpersonal relations and in all their variety. His pastoral work as a university chaplain, which began in 1949, deepened his focus on the problem of love in the fallen world as he formed his *Rodzinka* (little family) of students with whom he began to spend considerable time, understanding their particular questions, concerns, and challenges. This pastoral experience is reflected in the themes and content of his plays *The Jeweler's Shop* and *Radiation of Fatherhood*, and it resulted in his book *Love and Responsibility*. The personally constituting phenomenon of an intentional choice made in freedom so defines his understanding of love and personal fulfillment, it will form his pastoral style.

Wojtyła's pastoral encounters with the growing group of students who would become his *Środowisko* always took the form of dialogue.[139] He would discuss with a student the problem at hand, its difficulties, and the possible consequences of decisions. They would contextualize the issue in terms of the meaning of the human person and his fulfillment. However,

---

[138] See *Center of the Human Drama*, 2–29, for a very helpful summary of each of Wojtyła's plays.

[139] This Polish term means "environment" or "milieu." It was the name that a group of university students gave to themselves with whom Wojtyła would regularly meet when he was the parochial vicar and university chaplain at the Collegiate Church of St. Florian in Kraków. The *Środowisko* attracted up to two hundred students from the Jagiellonian University and other nearby institutions of higher learning. See Weigel, *Witness to Hope*, 94ff.

he would never tell the young person what he must do. To do so might deprive him of the opportunity to transform himself. Therefore, at the end of the conversation, Wojtyła would leave him with the challenge still "you have to decide."[140]

It seems for Wojtyła, the concept of the *dramatis personae* indicates the intimate connection among one's personal "act" done in his interpersonal relationality with another, the act executed with intentionality and done in freedom (Thomas's *actus humanus*), and the self-determining (with more or less freedom) and self-constituting (as good or evil) effects of these acts. Detailing the metaphysical foundations of this concept along with practical implications for the many decisions in the drama of a man and father will constitute another aspect of this project.

JOHN PAUL AND THE HUMAN PERSON AT A GLANCE

In this chapter, we have seen an overview of John Paul II's understanding of the human person. Several significant aspects of the human person have stood out and merit closer examination. John Paul II emphasizes the critical importance of the metaphysical concreteness of the person (i.e., the *suppositum*). He makes the case for this in his philosophical analysis, in his exploration of divine revelation, in his texts on threats to the human person, and throughout his other direct and indirect writings on the human person.

John Paul II adopts hylomorphism as the best system to metaphysically describe the person. He also finds in his philosophical assessment that the person is, at his core, a relational being. His explications of divine revelation and his magisterial teaching show that man's relational constitution is due to his creation in the image of the Trinity of persons, a *communio personarum*, which points to the essence of complementarity for personhood. Man's relationality to God and to others is an essential attribute of human personhood because it is through this relationality that he perfects himself as a person. We already see suggestions of the metaphysical category of human personhood.

The ontological actualization of one's personhood is possible because he has an intellect and free will, which give him the capacity for self-possession and self-determination, and because of these, his choosing and acting have ethical implications. Thus, he can perfect himself by choosing the good or distort himself by choosing evil. Because he has this

---

[140] Weigel, *Witness to Hope*, 105.

choice, it follows that his calling to perfection is a vocation to which he must respond. The *dramatis personae* suggests that love as a personal act is that act which unites the person as metaphysically concrete to the person as relational and the person who reveals himself through act. It points to his fulfillment in relation to others through truth and love, and considering the sexual complementarity of personhood, points to the vocation of fatherhood.

In summary, the preceding top-level analysis indicates that a) the person revealed through act, b) the person as metaphysically concrete, and c) the person as relational who relates through acts of love leading to fulfillment are the three main features of personhood which require a more thorough investigation. The next three chapters will look at each of these in turn.

CHAPTER 2

Person and Act

Karol Wojtyła's insight that the person is revealed in "act," as intimated earlier, is fundamental to his view of the integral person as a unity of body, soul, and "act." Wojtyła undertakes his project to integrate phenomenological insights of universal dynamic properties of the human person with the Thomist philosophy of being in *Person and Act*. In this chapter, I will look at the salient aspects of Wojtyła's anthropology from this work for my study. I will not attempt a summary of the work, for which competent references already exist.[1] Rather, I intend to explore the manner in which "act," in this context I mean particularly the *actus humanus* or "man acts," causes relationality to become quasi-substantial.[2]

---

[1] For example, see Kenneth L. Schmitz, *At the Center of the Human Drama: The Philosophical Anthropology of Karol Wojtyla/Pope John Paul II* (Washington, DC: The Catholic University of America Press, 1993), 58–89; George Huntston Williams, *The Mind of John Paul II: Origins of His Thoughts and Action* (New York: The Seabury Press, 1981), 186–218; Rocco Buttiglione, *Karol Wojtyła: The Thought of the Man Who Became John Paul* II, trans. Paolo Guietti and Francesca Murphy (Grand Rapids, MI: William B. Eerdmans Publishing Co., 1997), 117–76; Ignacy Dec, "Person als Subjekt. Zum Personbegriff bei Karol Wojtyła," *Theologie und Glaube* 76 (1986): 294–307; Luigi Rulla, *Anthropology of the Christian Vocation*, vol. 1, *Interdisciplinary Bases* (Rome: Gregorian University Press, 1986), 102–12; and Stephen Dinan, "The Phenomenological Anthropology of Karol Wojtyła," *New Scholasticism* 55 (1981): 317–30.

[2] The language here may be somewhat tenuous, but it is intended to acknowledge the general view which considers there to be a great gulf between the view of the human person as a relation and as substance. For a discussion of this issue, see John Grabowski, "Person: Substance and Relation," *Communio* 22 (1995): 139–63. Mark Henninger describes the debate over the ontological status of relations, which began with St. Thomas Aquinas's adoption of Aristotle's categories, and attempts to reconcile questions that they raised. Mark G. Henninger, S.J., *Relations: Medieval Theories, 1250–1325* (Oxford: Clarendon Press, 1989). For our purposes, it is not necessary to engage the debate over the ontological status of relations. It is sufficient to show that Wojtyła can legitimately hold the

CONSCIOUSNESS AND EFFICACY

The first section of *Person and Act* addresses consciousness and efficacy.[3] Consciousness is foundational for the acting person because only a conscious actor can be responsible for his actions. Efficacy describes the means by which the conscious actor effects his responsible choices. These factors are precursors to the capacity for man acts to achieve quasi-substantiality. Wojtyła begins his study in this section by looking at the way in which Thomist metaphysics understands the human act. That is, he begins with the *suppositum*, the subject of all predications, together with the concepts of potency and act. For the human person, potencies proper to human nature preexist in the soul.

They await actualization by an act originating in the soul, which is the source of all acts. This metaphysics is the starting point for Wojtyła's *Person and Act*[4] and within this metaphysics, potency and act are his chief analytical tools.[5] But these metaphysical categories cannot completely account for all that is properly human in an act. Therefore, Wojtyła applies

---

Thomist view of "person" and "relation" together with the view of human relations as "quasi-substantial. In other words, certain relations (of the type constituting persons) are not accidents in themselves even if their effects can be described in terms of accidental forms. They have their own existence, their own essence, but neither are they substance. They seem to be their own category of being, someplace in between substance and accidents. This much is certain: this is the case for divine persons. Nevertheless, Henninger's study shows that even without quasi-substantiality, it is possible to see relations as changing the person ontologically. For St. Thomas there are two types of relations: real and logical. Real relations are manifested as accidental forms, which inhere in a substance and receive their existence from the substance of the subject in which they inhere (Thomas Aquinas, *De ente et essentia*, ch. 6). Henninger finds that in St. Thomas's comments on *The Metaphysics*, that "action and passion or active and passive potencies are the only causes of real relations" (Henninger, *Relations*, 18). Therefore, a person's action will cause the generation of an accidental form within his own substantial form (i.e., in his soul). Thus, in Thomism, the mechanism exists for relations of the real type to ontologically change the person.

[3] Wojtyła explains his concept of efficacy in phenomenological terms: "The starting point in our argument will be the experiential difference that is discernible in the totality of man's dynamism between man's acting and what happens in man. An examination of the facts discloses that it is the moment of efficacy that determines this fundamental difference. In this case the moment of efficacy is to be understood as the having of the experience of 'being an actor'" (Karol Wojtyła, *The Acting Person*, trans. Andrezej Potocki, ed. A. Tymieniecka, Analecta Husserliana: The Yearbook of Phenomenological Research, vol 10 [Dordrecht, Holland: Reidel Publishing Co., 1979], 66).

[4] See Buttiglione, *Thought of the Man*, 129.

[5] See Jerzy W. Gałkowski, "The Place of Thomism in the Anthropology of K. Wojtyła," *Angelicum* 65 (1998): 189.

his phenomenological method to explore further the human particulars of human act, especially the dynamisms of consciousness. As we have said, consciousness is not the whole of the human person but rather it is *"an intrinsic and constitutive aspect of the dynamic structure, that is, of the acting person."*[6] Consciousness is not a reality that is separate and cut off from the body. Rather, it is the content of experience that comes about by the subject's acting and being.[7] Consciousness has a function in man's understanding of himself as the cause of his acts.

Through consciousness, man has the experience of efficacy. That is, he experiences himself as the source of his actions.[8] Efficacy then distinguishes between what merely happens passively in man and the *actus humanus*. This line of thinking explains why Wojtyła sees the person as manifested in act. In fact, because of this there are some theologians who misconstrue Wojtyła's point of departure with the *actus humanus* to suggest that he thinks that existence begins in act, or as Nachef puts it, that Wojtyła's thought is mistakenly taken to infer "I act, therefore I am."[9]

However, this mistakes Wojtyła's method with the content of his thought, or perhaps as suggested earlier, it mistakes his method for that of a rigid Schelerian phenomenologist. This contradicts Karol Wojtyła's view. It is rather the case that Wojtyła believes when one experiences his own subjectivity, in the context of his being self-possessed and self-determined, he reveals to himself virtually everything contained within himself as a metaphysically concrete human subject.[10] Wojtyła often employs the scholastic phrase *operari sequitur esse* as we have already seen. In other words, he recognizes that metaphysically, existence must precede action but epistemologically it is action that manifests to the human person, the fullness of his existence. One must appreciate Wojtyła's Thomism to avoid this error.

Following a more detailed analysis, Wojtyła finds that efficacy is

---

[6] Wojtyła, *The Acting Person*, 31.

[7] See Wojtyła, *The Acting Person*, 33.

[8] See Wojtyła, *The Acting Person*, 66.

[9] Antoine E. Nachef, *The Mystery of the Trinity in the Theological Thought of Pope John Paul II* (New York: Peter Lang Publishing, 1999), 25. For examples of theologians who mistake Wojtyła on this point, see Robert F. Harvanek, S.J., "The Philosophical Foundations of the Thought of John Paul II," in *The Thought of Pope John Paul II: A Collection of Essays and Studies*, ed. John M. McDermott (Rome: Editrice Pontificia Università Gregoriana, 2000), 12; Avery Dulles, "The Prophetic Humanism of John Paul II," *America* 169 (1993): 7; *The Encyclicals of John Paul II*, ed. J. Michael Miller (Indiana: Our Sunday Visitor Publishing Division, Our Sunday Visitor, Inc., 1996), 28, cited in Nachef, *Mystery of the Trinity*, 25n66.

[10] See Nachef, *Mystery of the Trinity*, 25–26.

possible due to two foundational attributes of consciousness, the reflective (or mirroring) and the reflexive functions.[11] The latter is the one which has the function of shaping the subject through his experience as the self-determining author of the act. It appears to Wojtyła that man's reflexive experience "is the ground on which the dynamic relation, or rather interrelation, between the person and the action is actualized."[12] The reflexive function is significant, then, because it is here that the acting subject experiences himself as the actor who is himself responsible for his own actions.

The discovery of the reflexive function of consciousness is not possible solely with metaphysical analysis. Schmitz shows that while metaphysics captures being and action as belonging properly to the subject, it is the reflexive function of consciousness that reveals interiorly the reality of the entire person in the experience of his living out his actions.[13] However, this is not to say that Wojtyła's findings are not compatible with metaphysical analysis. Rather, Wojtyła considers the above phenomenological insights to correlate well with Thomist metaphysics. Wojtyła states:

> Considering the experiential cohesion of the whole human [*operari*][14] with his [*esse*],[15] we are led to accept . . . [the Thomistic basis for this cohesion].[16] [I]t is human nature that constitutes the appropriate basis for the cohesion of the subject-man—whatever

---

[11] Schmitz believes that "the mention of 'mirroring' puts one immediately in mind of the medieval Latin sense of *speculum, speculari*, and *speculatio*—terms that stand for the properly theoretical activity of the mind" (Schmitz, *Center of the Human Drama*, 71–72). This leads him to suggest that "mirroring" and "enlightening" are echoes of traditional Aristotelian-Thomist metaphysics, but especially that of "Augustinianism and medieval *Lichtmetaphysik*" (Schmitz, *Center of the Human Drama*, 72).

[12] Wojtyła, *The Acting Person*, 57. Reflexive experience is the experience of oneself as the subject of the action.

[13] See Schmitz, *Center of the Human Drama*, 75.

[14] The English translation, *The Acting Person*, uses "functioning" but the original Polish uses the Latin *operari*, which makes it clear that Wojtyła is thinking in terms of Thomist metaphysics. My thanks go to Fr. Jaroslaw Gamrot for his help with the Polish and for providing all of the corrected English translations of the Polish throughout this book.

[15] The English translation uses "existence," but the original Polish uses the Latin *esse*. The Latin indicates that Wojtyła has in mind the substantial nature of the human person.

[16] The translator leaves the following out of the English translation: "nie widać żadnej trudności w zaakceptowaniu tomistycznej podstawy tej spójności." This translates as "the Thomistic basis for this cohesion." In addition, the sentence ends with "cohesion." The next sentence begins "It is human nature" instead of the current English "We are led to accept that it is human nature." The sense of the original Polish has Wojtyła emphasizing

kind of inner dynamism it has—with any of its dynamizations. Of course, nature as the basis of this dynamic cohesion really inheres in the subject, while the subject itself having personal existence is a person. . . . The integration of human nature, of humanness,[17] in and by the person has as its consequence the integration of all the dynamism proper to man in the human person.[18]

The integration of dynamic subjective experience into the person belongs to human nature, but Wojtyła is quick to point out that unlike Platonism, in which the universal is that which is most real, "nature" exists only in the instantiated individual. This integration of the person and his experience is significant enough for Wojtyła to dedicate the third part of *Person and Act* to this subject. To prepare the way to discuss this integration, Wojtyła draws out the implications of consciousness and efficacy. He finds that the subject's consciousness of the experience of efficacy leads him to the experience of transcendence.

TRANSCENDENCE OF THE PERSON IN THE ACT

Wojtyła devotes the second part of *Person and Act* to exploring the way the person can experience self-transcendence in action. By self-transcendence he means that the person goes beyond himself; he is not a self-enclosed ego. Dulles attributes Wojtyła's (and later John Paul II's) emphasis on transcendence to his experiences in working on *Gaudium et spes*. Wojtyła embraces the Council's paradoxical declaration that man can only find his fulfillment in giving himself away in love to others.[19] Wojtyła made this insight a centerpiece of his anthropology. Fallen man has the task of overcoming the temptation to egocentrism; he must transcend himself if he is to fulfill his potency as an "ex-centric" being.

One discovers transcendence in the experiences of obligation, responsibility, freedom, and moral truthfulness. As such, transcendence reveals that there is something beyond the corporeal world; in other words, it suggests a spiritual dimension. This in turn leads to the search for the spirit's

---

that there is no contradiction between Thomism and our phenomenological experience, an important idea that is lost in the English translation.

[17] The English translation adds "of humanness," which is not in the original Polish. This leaves a misimpression that Wojtyła may not mean "nature" in a metaphysical sense.

[18] Wojtyła, *The Acting Person*, 84.

[19] See Avery Dulles, "John Paul II and the Mystery of the Human Person," *America* 190, no. 3 (2004): 11.

source and subsequently to the relation between the spiritual and corporeal aspects of the person. Wojtyła traces the outlines of this analytical approach:

> This notion of "spirituality" may serve as the key to the understanding of the complexity of man. For we now see man as the person, and we see him first of all in his acting, in the action. He then appears in the field of our integral experience as somebody material, as corporeal, but at the same time we know the personal unity of this material somebody to be determined by the spirit, by his spiritual nature and spiritual life. Indeed, the very fact that the personal—as well as the ontic—unity of the corporeal man is ultimately [established][20] by man's [spirituality][21] allows us to see in him the ontic composite of soul and body, of the spiritual and the material elements.[22]

Experience indirectly suggests that the person is a body-soul unity, but Wojtyła leaves the proof for the existence of this composite unity to metaphysics. Nevertheless, this unity is the source of man's capacity for self-transcendence, which gives rise to the possibility of self-determination.

Self-determination which is enabled by self-possession and free will is fundamental to transcendence.[23] In fact, Wojtyła points out that when one "wills" he does not simply endeavor to accomplish some goal, he actually endeavors and simultaneously decides. For this reason, Wojtyła says that whenever anyone says "I will" with a full, sincere commitment, he exercises and experiences the self-possession and self-governance that is unique to the human person.[24] It is only due to self-determination that it is possible

---

[20] "Established" more fittingly translates the Polish *stanowi* than does "commanded," which is used in the English translation, as it better conveys the sense of the Polish term. The former term carries within it the metaphysical sense of the "form" which both establishes and continues to give shape to "matter."

[21] "Spirituality" better translates the Polish *duchowość* than does "spiritual factor," which is used in the English translation, because it more properly suggests that the spiritual realm is an integrated dimension of the person rather than a separate (i.e., Cartesian) "factor."

[22] Wojtyła, *The Acting Person*, 185.

[23] Transcendence, as implied earlier, means that in acting the person transcends himself as *suppositum* in the sense of traditional metaphysics, because his acts emerge from his free will and self-determination (see Schmitz, *Center of the Human Drama*, 81, and footnote 41). Free will and self-determination are distinct in Wojtyła's thought. Free will is a faculty by which the person exercises his capacity for self-determination.

[24] See Wojtyła, *The Acting Person*, 147.

for an action to penetrate to and inhere in the core of the person.[25] But at the same time, the author is careful to emphasize that one must not misunderstand free will and self-determination as radically autonomous liberty. They include

> ontological autonomy [and] . . . dependence on [my "I"].[26] It includes the indispensable and essential moment of [dependence upon][27] "truth," and it is this moment that ultimately [gives shape to][28] freedom.[29] For human freedom is not accomplished or exercised in bypassing truth but, on the contrary, by the person's realization and surrender to truth. The dependence on truth marks out the borderlines of the autonomy appropriate to the human person.[30]

---

[25] See Wojtyła, *The Acting Person*, 150.

[26] "My 'I'" is a more literal rendering of the Polish *własnego „ja."* While Wojtyła certainly uses the term "the ego" elsewhere, here he does not. Certainly this is to emphasize the person, the acting subject. However, it would also seem to help avoid the Kantian implications of the "transcendental ego" which carries with it the post-Cartesian sense of the person as simply the center of a stream of conscious experiences with no metaphysical substance.

[27] The English translation has "reference to" for the Polish *zależność*. However, the Polish means "dependence upon." The English translation does not capture the necessity Wojtyła indicates for exercising freedom in accord with the truth of the created order.

[28] The English translation has "determines" for the Polish *kształtuje*. However, "gives shape to" better suggests the positive sense in which acting in accord with the truth actualizes the manner in which the person experiences his freedom.

[29] Freedom in truth was a major concern for Wojtyła. Thomas McGovern explains that Archbishop Wojtyła made substantial contributions to the Second Vatican Council's document on religious freedom, *Dignitatis humanae*. McGovern recounts that

> at the third session of the Council, in September 1964, quoting St. John's text, "The truth shall set you free" (John 8:32), [Wojtyła] requested that the relationship between truth and freedom should be emphasized more strongly, even to the point of affirming that there can be no freedom without truth. How often would we hear him repeat the same thesis, especially in his encyclical *Veritatis Splendor*! In his intervention on October 22, 1965, at the final session of the Council, he requested that the text of *Dignitatis Humanae* should underline a basic theme of Christian Personalism—man's responsibility in relation to the truth. If freedom and responsibility are not situated in the context of truth, there is a danger of favoring religious indifferentism.

Thomas McGovern, "The Christian Anthropology of John Paul II," *Josephinum Journal of Theology* 8, no. 1 (2001): 136–37.

[30] Wojtyła, *The Acting Person*, 154.

The authentic formation of the person's transcendence occurs when one surrenders himself to truth, and fully, freely wills in conformity with this truth.[31] It is only in truth that the person is able to *fulfill* himself in action, which Wojtyła calls "the normative function" of conscience.[32] The conscience's normative function and the foundation of the entire structure of self-governance and self-possession is located in choosing to be truthful, motivated by the conscience.[33] Transcendence integrates truth, freedom and conscience into the ontological constitution of the person, which suggests personhood has an ontology not articulated in Aristotle's ten categories of being.

Wojtyła considers transcendence to be "the constitutive feature of the person" because of transcendence's relation to the value of moral truth.[34] The person realizes his transcendence through the pursuit of the truth and its value.[35] It is through this transcendence that the person fulfills himself. In fact, transcendence and personal fulfillment are nearly synonymous

---

[31] See Wojtyła, *The Acting Person*, 159.

[32] Wojtyła, *The Acting Person*, 161. "Fulfillment" is a key concept for Wojtyła. He defines it as a synonym for the person's self-determined act. He states that

> [t]he fact that every performance of an action means fulfillment makes "to fulfill" almost synonymous with "to perform." This is why fulfillment seems to be the best homologue of the term "act," indicating the fullness which corresponds to a definite possibility or potentiality. In our approach we are looking for what could be an adequate manner of expressing the person as the subject and the agent of an action and at the same time of expressing an action as the authentic act of a person. When we speak of "performing an action" we see the person as the subject and the agent while the action itself appears as a consequence of the efficacy of the agent. This consequence is external with regard to the person, but it is also internal to, or immanent in, the person. Moreover, it is both transitive and intransitive with regard to the person. In either case it is most strictly connected with the will, which we already saw in the preceding chapter to consist in both self-determination and intentionality. Self-determination is something more basic for the will, and it is to it that the fundamental significance of freedom is related.

(*The Acting Person*, 149–50).

[33] See Wojtyła, *The Acting Person*, 162.

[34] Wojtyła, *The Acting Person*, 166.

[35] Dulles shows that this grounding of freedom in truth remains fundamental in John Paul II's magisterium. Dulles says: "While glorifying in freedom, the pope insists that it is not an end in itself but a means of personally adhering to the true good, as perceived by a judgment of conscience. 'Authentic freedom,' he writes, 'is never freedom "from" the truth but always freedom "in" the truth' (VS, No. 64)" (Dulles, "Mystery of the Human Person," 11).

terms. But the mechanism through which the person achieves transcendence is by forming himself, through self-possession and self-governance, in accord with his obligations to truth. It is not simply "by the intentionality of volitions nor through self-determination but *through his sense of obligation as the peculiar modification of self-determination and intentionality*"[36] that he transcends and fulfills himself.[37]

INTEGRATION OF THE PERSON IN THE ACT

The confluence of Thomist metaphysics with the insights of phenomenology is fundamental to Wojtyła's entire project in which he studies "act" as it reveals the person. In particular, he finds that the attributes of human consciousness identifiable through the study of human action disclose the Thomist "form," or human soul.[38] Wojtyła admits that while the phenom-

---

[36] Wojtyła, *The Acting Person*, 169.

[37] Wojtyła explains why he has chosen the concept of transcendence for the union of the person with his self-determined act, which presumes the person is guided by the truth, as the way to self-fulfillment:

> It is in and through [man's] acting, in and through the action, that we see him in this highly specific structure. Thus the person and the action constitute together an intimately cohesive, dynamic reality, in which the action is the manifestation and the explanation of the person and the action. This parallelism of manifestation and explanation is characteristic for the phenomenological method. The concept of the "transcendence," . . . is well fitted to the method; it serves our attempts to interpret the inherent essence of the experience "man acts," to objectify that which allows the acting person to manifest himself and be visualized as the person. Since manifestation comes together with explanation, the concept of "transcendence" not only expresses the essence of the phenomenological insight in what concerns the person but also explains the person in his dynamic cohesion with the action.

> (*The Acting Person*, 180).

[38] But Wojtyła says this is not a direct experience of the soul:

> We have, in fact, submitted that man had no direct experience of his soul. Experience of the transcendence of the person in the action together with all the elements and aspects of this experience is in no way equivalent to a direct experience of the soul. Similarly, we have to assert that experience of integration (in connection with the transcendence of the person in the action) cannot be identified with the experience—the direct discovering and experiencing—of the soul-body relation. Both the reality itself of the soul and that of the soul's relation to the body are in this sense transphenomenal and extraexperiential. Nevertheless, the total and comprehensive experience of man shows the soul as real and as staying in relation to the body. They have been both discovered and

enological method is not directly responsible for revealing the person as a body-soul unity, the method nevertheless highlights the unity of the person. Phenomenology and metaphysics support each other. While the former suggests this compound unity of body and soul, the latter provides the convincing demonstration that this is the case.[39] This integration of phenomenology and metaphysics allows Wojtyła to incorporate the dynamics of interior personal experience with the universality of metaphysical personhood.

Wojtyła's integral understanding of the human person extends from the body-soul unity to man's free, self-determining actions. In fact, he declares that in the sum of man's experience, action is the point about which the whole body-soul composite integrates itself "into the specific person-action unity."[40] In Wojtyła's thinking, the unity of the person and his volitional action has priority over the unity of body and soul in the integral personal experience.[41] It is the reflexive experience of action

---

are continuously being discovered in the philosophical reflection resulting from human experience.

(*The Acting Person*, 256–57).

[39] Wojtyła says that the demonstration of this unity

belongs to metaphysics, in which throughout the ages thinkers have been unraveling the nature of man as a being consisting of soul and body, of spirit and flesh. . . . [T]here is no question but that the original conception of man as a person—though it is accessible to the original intuition within the frame of phenomenological insight—has to be completed and supplemented by the metaphysical analysis of the human being. Thus, while the experience of the personal unity of man shows us his complex nature, the attempt at a deepened understanding of this complexity allows us in turn [to understand the *compositum humanum*] as the one and ontically unique person.

(*The Acting Person*, 186). See also *The Acting Person*, 257, where Wojtyła reiterates the inability of phenomenology to understand the body-soul relation without the categories provided by Thomist metaphysics. However, grounded in these categories, "common sense experience" of the body and soul can help to discover their unity in the human person. The English translation uses "to interpret human nature" for the phrase *zrozumieć compositum humanum* in the original Polish. The phrase "to understand the *compositum humanum*" more precisely translates the Polish. The English translation obscures Wojtyła's sense of the objectivity, or the givenness, of the *compositum humanum*.

[40] Wojtyła, *The Acting Person*, 197.

[41] Wojtyła finds that "the person-action unity has precedence over the psychosomatic complexity. Such is the case especially with integration. This is clearly indicated by the fundamental significance of the integration as well as of disintegration of the acting person. The subordination of the subjective ego to the transcendent ego—that is to say, the synthesis of efficacy and subjectiveness—in itself implies the complexity as well as

which serves to integrate the person, body and soul, and gives him a type of identity with his action. This is a fundamental point for Wojtyła. One's experience of his own self-determined action and its resulting personal fulfillment manifest the integral unity of person and action.[42] This is not simply a psychological affectivity but rather a manifestation of a "deeply cohesive reality;"[43] in other words, it is a unity of the person, body-soul, in and through his act.

It is evident then, while acts have some transient, temporal and external aspects to them, for Wojtyła they also have a lasting effect in the person's interiority, on making him not "what" (i.e., substance) but "who" (i.e., relation) he is.[44] The enduring product of self-determined action resides in the personal structure of self-determination and in a very real way makes the action a concrete aspect of the person; the person's "engagement in

---

the unity of man as a psycho-physical entity" (*The Acting Person*, 196). The Polish again does not use "ego" but rather "*ja*," which more literally translates as "I." See footnote 26 of this chapter for a discussion of this. Also, note the distinction between Wojtyła's term "transcendent" and the Kantian "transcendental." This is a priority in experience, not an ontological priority. Thus, this statement does not undermine my previous agreement with Nachef that Wojtyła holds that "being" precedes "act."

[42] Wojtyła indicates that his anthropological project is "concerned with the person and the action not as two separate and self–sufficient entities but—and we have emphasized this from the start—as a single, deeply cohesive reality. [Inasmuch] as this cohesion has real existence, it must be reflected in comprehension or interpretation. If so, then undoubtedly the existential and essential cohesion of the person and the action is best and most adequately expressed by the fulfillment resulting from performance of an action" (*The Acting Person*, 149). The English translation inserts "insofar" which is not in the Polish. Since this English structure requires an introductory adverb, "inasmuch" better reflects the sense of the Polish. The English translation restructures the original Polish, which reads more like the following: "This cohesion takes place in reality; therefore, it (i.e., the cohesion) must take place in understanding/interpretation." Wojtyła uses the Polish *czyli* to indicate the necessary equivalence of "understanding" and "interpretation" in this situation, so there is no question about the reality of the cohesion. However, the English translation intimates otherwise. Wojtyła here is criticizing phenomenologists who would not recognize objective reality.

[43] Wojtyła, *The Acting Person*, 149.

[44] Wojtyła states that "in the inner dimension of the person, human action is at once both transitory and relatively lasting, inasmuch as its effects, which are to be viewed in relation to efficacy and self-determination, that is to say, to the person's engagement in freedom, last longer than the action itself. The engagement in freedom is objectified—because of its lasting repetitive effects and conformably to the structure of self-determination—in the person and not only in the action, which is the transitive effect" (*The Acting Person*, 151).

freedom is objectified."[45] He states this more succinctly: "Human actions once performed do not vanish without a trace: they leave their moral value, which constitutes an objective reality intrinsically cohesive with the person, and thus a reality also profoundly subjective."[46] The enduring reality is at once ontological and moral.

The fulfillment to which Wojtyła continually refers is an ontological reality in the person. Therefore, if one chooses moral evil, he fails to achieve self-fulfillment. It is only through the free choice of the moral good that authentic self-fulfillment can occur. While the author allows for fulfillment in every action from an ontological perspective, his Thomist mind prefers the term "non-fulfillment" in the realm of morality.[47] In addition, the ontological importance of the action for the person is driven much more by the "moral [goodness][48] of the action and [not as much][49] by the mere performance of the action itself."[50] The person thus most perfectly integrates himself in his action when the action itself is one which is positively good in the moral realm.

PARTICIPATION

Wojtyła devotes the last part of *Person and Act* to the subject of participation. He explains here that truth, act, and self-fulfillment all coalesce in a dynamic reality of interpersonal obligation. Conscience is not the inward turned "subjectiveness" of post-Cartesian thinking. Rather, the person's conscience, which provides a sense of duty to another, has an objective correlate in the moral order. It is for this reason that the moral order both

---

[45] Wojtyła, *The Acting Person*, 151.
[46] Wojtyła, *The Acting Person*, 151.
[47] I.e., there is no ontological existence of evil. The person, therefore, who chooses evil fails to fulfill himself.
[48] The English translation uses "virtuality" for the Polish *dobroć*, which more precisely means "goodness." It is not clear what the translator/editor intends by "virtuality," but the term obfuscates the clarity of "moral goodness."
[49] The English translation has "and not" for the Polish *nie tyle*, which means "not as much." A more precise rendering of this paragraph would be as follows: "The moral values are so established for the person, that true fulfillment of the person takes place not through the act alone but also through the moral goodness of the act." In other words, the English translation excludes the performance of the act in the true fulfillment of the person. Wojtyła does not exclude it at all. Rather, he places the greater weight on the act's moral goodness.
[50] Wojtyła, *The Acting Person*, 153.

applies and also has consequences well beyond the individual person.[51] Self-fulfillment depends in part upon the person's interpersonal relations with other persons, namely, his acting in accord with the obligations he has because he is a member of a community. Wojtyła asserts that one experiences the truth of interpersonal obligation in his conscience because it is an external moral norm. His conclusions about integration reveal the necessary structure for man's participation in society in order to fulfill himself.

Recall that the moral dimension has an ontological effect on personal self-fulfillment governed by the close interaction of person, free will, self-determination, truth, and action. Therefore, the person's free response to his community obligations, which must be guided by truth, also has an ontological effect on the person.[52] This free response in truth to intersubjective obligations toward the common good is what Wojtyła refers to as "participation." "The ability to share in the [human nature][53] itself of every man is the very core of all participation and the condition of the personalistic value of all acting and existing 'together with others.'"[54] He defines participation in relational terms.

Wojtyła says that man's ability to share in the humanity of every other human person is at the core of what it means to "act" and to "exist" with others.[55] Therefore, participation allows the person to join his action with the actions of others in which both he and they transcend and fulfill themselves together.[56] It is in part because of the submission of the self to the good of the community that this transcendence can take place. So Wojtyła admonishes that "in the acting and being together with others the system of reference of the neighbor and that of the membership of a community have to interpenetrate each other and become mutually complementary. Any separation between them is inadmissible and dangerous because

---

[51] See Wojtyła, *The Acting Person*, 163–64.

[52] This follows because community obligations are external moral norms which arise from the created order.

[53] The English translation uses "humanness" for the Polish *człowieczeństwie*, which more precisely means "human nature." "Human nature" better reflects the "givenness," or the objective reality, of the nature of the human being, given Wojtyła's Thomism.

[54] Wojtyła, *The Acting Person*, 295.

[55] Wojtyła uses the idea of sharing in the humanity of others to indicate the ontological reality of interpersonal relationality. He wants to distinguish a simple formal membership in a group from the dynamic aspects of participation which go deep into the person's interiority together with the universal dimensions of human nature. See *The Acting Person*, 295.

[56] See Wojtyła, *The Acting Person*, 271.

it leads to downright alienation."[57] While Wojtyła does not develop his thinking on participation in *Person and Act* as much as he will in later work, even at this point it is possible to see the significance of the ontological value of participation.[58] Participation, or fulfillment through joint, interpersonal action, will be a key concept for Karol Wojtyła's thought on human fatherhood.

PERSON AND ACT IN FATHERHOOD

Person and Act introduces the major philosophical keys for Wojtyła's understanding of the human person and lays a necessary foundation for this study of human fatherhood. The human person is an integrated union of body and soul. With all of the faculties of this psychosomatic unity, especially through acts arising from self-determining free will (*actus humanus*), man fulfills himself in transcendence if the acts are done in truth for the good of the other and the common good.[59] Participation indicates that a person achieves self-fulfillment in a community and not through isolated self-actualization. If fatherhood is the fulfillment of masculinity, which we have yet to demonstrate, we now see that we must understand more fully the truth of masculinity and of fatherhood if the masculine person is to fulfill himself through self-transcendence, integration, and participation.

Before we get there, there is more we need to look at in terms of the structure of the person. Implicit in the person's ability to reveal and perfect himself through the *actus humanus* are the concrete substantiality and the relationality of the person. There must be a concrete subsisting person in which the effects of these acts are to inhere. Additionally, for self-fulfillment through his action with and for others, there must be some substantiality to one's interpersonal relations. Thus, this analysis has confirmed the significance of the remaining two features of personhood, which I previously identified as requiring a more detailed analysis. In the next chapter, I will take up the first of these: the human person as metaphysically concrete.

---

[57] Wojtyła, *The Acting Person*, 297.

[58] See Karol Wojtyła, "The Person: Subject and Community," in *Person and Community: Selected Essays*, vol. 4, trans. Theresa Sandok, O.S.M. (New York: Peter Lang, 1993).

[59] I.e., they are morally good.

CHAPTER 3

Metaphysics and Human Personhood

Metaphysical concreteness is of particular concern for Karol Wojtyła because it provides the solution to the problem of post-Cartesian dualism in understanding the human person. His system of metaphysics is Thomist, and the aspect of Thomism he employs to guarantee a concrete human personhood is hylomorphism. In this chapter we will look at 1) Wojtyła's terminology, 2) the way he uses the hylomorphic theory, and 3) the implications of hylomorphism for his anthropology.

TERMINOLOGY

It perhaps is best to go back to Wojtyła's early work on Thomistic personalism to see how he uses the Thomist vocabulary when dealing with the term "person" in order to better clarify Wojtyła's meaning. He finds that St. Thomas uses the Latin *persona* quite abundantly for the Trinitarian persons but very sparingly in reference to the human person. However, Wojtyła asserts that Thomas's use of the term for the Trinitarian relations, nevertheless, also applies to humans because St. Thomas explicitly states that "whatever is a true perfection in the created world must be found in the highest degree in God, and so the person, too, which signifies the highest perfection in the world of creatures, must be realized in an incomparably more perfect degree in God."[1]

---

[1] Karol Wojtyła, "Thomistic Personalism," in *Person and Community: Selected Essays*, vol. 4, trans. Theresa Sandok, O.S.M. (New York: Peter Lang, 1993), 166. This is his restatement of St. Thomas's articulation of the supereminence of person as applied to God in his *Summa Theologiae*: "I answer that, Person signifies what is most perfect in all nature— that is, a subsistent individual of a rational nature. Hence, since everything that is perfect must be attributed to God, forasmuch as His essence contains every perfection, this name person is fittingly applied to God; not, however, as it is applied to creatures, but in a more

He points out that Thomas's use of Boëthius's philosophical definition of person as *persona est rationalis naturae individua substantia* is the foundation for St. Thomas's definition of the human person, who is an individual of a rational nature, which is not self-subsistent but rather that a rational nature subsists in a person.[2] The person, and not the rational nature, is the subject of two particularly important predications—being and action. Wojtyła notes that two significant properties of a rational nature, which only become "concretized" in the person, are reason and freedom, so that the person exists and acts based upon these fundamental properties of a rational nature. So it is that the essential predications of a human being—existence and act—inhere in the person. The person must act in conformity with all those properties of a rational nature, the most significant being reason and freedom.

There are several terms that Wojtyła uses which bear on his understanding of the human person, and I suggest a brief survey of these terms will shed more light on the way he understands the concreteness of the human person.[3] The first term, "human being," he defines as "an individual (*individua substantia*) of a rational nature."[4] We have already discussed the term "person" above, which to summarize is that in which the rational nature subsists. While these first two terms might seem identical, for Wojtyła they are not. Wojtyła uses the term "human being" as a definition of the human substance, whereas "person" is the subsistent subject of that being, the "subject of existence and action."[5]

The next term, *suppositum*, is the past perfect participle of the Latin verb *suppōnō* which means "to place under," and as a participle it was used by the scholastics as a term "for the subject of all predications."[6] The significance of this term for Wojtyła is that it rescues human experience from pure subjectivity, which was a negative consequence of the "philosophy of consciousness."[7] *Suppositum* as a metaphysical term maintains the objective nature of "being" and the objective aspect of human experience inherent in a Thomist

---

excellent way; as other names also, which, while giving them to creatures, we attribute to God; as we showed above when treating of the names of God." *ST* Ia, q. 29, a. 3, resp.

2   Wojtyła, "Thomistic Personalism," 167.

3   These terms include human being, person, *suppositum*, consciousness, and self.

4   Wojtyła, "Thomistic Personalism," 167.

5   Wojtyła, "Thomistic Personalism," 167. We will explore the category of being for this subsistent substance in the next chapter.

6   Bernard Lonergan, *Collected Works of Bernard Lonergan*, ed. Frederick Crowe and Robert Doran, vol. 2, *Verbum: Word and Idea in Aquinas* (Toronto, Canada: University of Toronto Press, 1997), 318.

7   Wojtyła, "The Person: Subject and Community," in *Person and Community*, 219.

philosophy. It is the equivalent of the Greek *hypostasis* and so it is the technical metaphysical term for person. While the term is metaphysical, at the same time for Wojtyła, it provides an entrance into human subjectivity.

This entrance comes about because *suppositum* incorporates into itself the whole of human experience. It can do so because knowledge, which is metaphysical at its root, integrates experience into the human person.[8] Furthermore, *suppositum* shows that this person is a real being, a real subject, who experiences and incorporates this experience through existence and action and who is characterized by free will. Wojtyła summarizes the meaning of the term, declaring that "*suppositum* is the fundamental expression of the whole experience of the human being."[9]

Fourthly, Wojtyła uses the term "consciousness." As we have seen, it is clear that consciousness is a fundamental aspect of the person, but it is not an independent subject.[10] The person, unlike the modern conception, is not merely a unity of experiences but is a concrete subsisting entity (still in need of a category of being at this point). And so consciousness is rather "something derivative, a kind of fruit of the rational nature that subsists in the person."[11] Consciousness does not carry within it either the faculty of the will or self-determination. So one could call consciousness a formal specification of man, but it is not the entirety of the person. This in no way undermines its importance.

Consciousness provides a significant, constitutive function for the person. It interiorizes everything that one comes to know. Consciousness, and especially self-consciousness, plays a key role in linking the *suppositum* to the last term we are looking at: "self." Wojtyła succinctly characterizes the role of consciousness in terms of self, saying: "The self is nothing other than the concrete *suppositum humanum*, which, when given to itself by consciousness (self-consciousness) in the lived experience of action, is identical with the self-possession and self-governance that comes to light as a result of the dynamics of the personal efficacy that is self-determination."[12]

---

[8] Knowledge for St. Thomas is a metaphysical exchange of forms in which he indicates that in a sense, the knower becomes the known; see *ST* I, q. 14, a. 1. For a helpful summary of Thomas's epistemology, see Étienne Gilson, *The Philosophy of St. Thomas Aquinas*, trans. Edward Bullough (New York: Barnes and Nobles Books, 1993), 231–83. For a specific discussion of the knower becoming the known, see especially 264–65.

[9] Wojtyła, "The Person: Subject and Community," 223.

[10] See "The Person: Subject and Community," 220–28; "Thomistic Personalism," 169–71; and "In Search of the Basis of Perfectionism in Ethics," 49–55, in *Person and Community*.

[11] Wojtyła, "Thomistic Personalism," 170.

[12] Wojtyła, "Subject and Community," 231.

Wojtyła begins with the metaphysically concrete constitution of the human person and then locates within him (the *suppositum*, self) the dynamisms of lived experience which the person requires to act and fulfill himself in the world. The self is the *suppositum*, but it implies faculties and functions which metaphysics includes, but that metaphysics as a method of analysis cannot penetrate. Metaphysics does not have the tools to investigate the entirety of the human experience, such as the interiorization of the human experience. Wojtyła's integration of the phenomenological method of analysis with Thomist metaphysics opens for him a clearer picture of the interior person, permitting him to incorporate more fruitfully the findings of contemporary sciences.

Our review of some of Wojtyła's terminology affirms that he throws away nothing of Thomist metaphysics for his anthropology. Rather, he identifies the areas of Thomism that he must supplement with phenomenology in order to penetrate the interiority of person and his dynamic experiences. The self reveals the interior dynamics of the *suppositum* and all of those functions needed for the acting person. Consciousness is a constituent interior aspect of the person but cannot be mistaken as a synonym for it.

THE CONCRETE PERSON AND THE HYLOMORPHIC THEORY

The concreteness of the person is essential to John Paul II's anthropology. This includes concreteness in both a metaphysical sense as well as in the sense of an instantiated individual.[13] But while these are cognitively distinct, ontologically the latter follows upon the former. For this study, the metaphysical aspect of the concreteness of the person is of particular concern. The unity of a substantial form and a material body, described by hylomorphism, provides the philosophical framework for John Paul II's assertion that the human person is metaphysically concrete.[14]

---

[13] I have in mind the distinction between a Platonic metaphysics, in which the nature of an object exists separately from its material instantiation (i.e., the form), and a Thomist metaphysics, where a nature only exists in the concrete instances (i.e., a specific form united with, or rather "in-forming," matter). John Paul II points to his Thomist preference in his first encyclical when he says, "We are not dealing with the 'abstract' man, but the real 'concrete,' historical man. We are dealing with each man . . . man in his unique unrepeatable human reality, which keeps intact the image and likeness of God himself" (John Paul II, Encyclical Letter at the Beginning of His Papacy *Redemptor hominis* [March 4, 1979], *AAS* 71 [1979], 257–324, §13).

[14] I should address a possible critique of this claim. Anselm Min states that John Paul II's

Let us now investigate more precisely how our author uses hylomor-phic theory for his description of the human person. Wojtyła says that one cannot understand the body apart from the soul because the meaning of both lies in the human person, who is a unity of body and soul.[15] To try to understand one in isolation from the other inevitably will lead to reduc-tionism. This unity is a reality which was "advanced in the traditional philosophy of Aristotle and Aquinas, which from the likeness of man to the other beings of the visible world discovers in him alongside of the *hylic* or material element also the element of *morphe* or form; hence the theory of hylomorphism and the analysis of the human being carried out within its frame."[16]

Hylomorphism is so integral to Wojtyła's anthropology that he finds it necessary to show the personal experience of hylomorphic unity can be verified through phenomenological analysis, and that its features can be demonstrated in Scripture. He shows that the unity described by hylo-morphic theory has been employed by the magisterium and theologians

criticism of Aristotelian Thomism is such that John Paul finds it "inadequate to serve as the unifying basis of the concrete totality of man." Anselm K. Min, "John Paul II's Anthropology of Concrete Totality," *American Catholic Philosophical Association Proceedings* 58 (1984): 120–29. However, it appears to me that Min is limiting meta-physics to the concept of nature. His argument that nature is only a potentiality that must be "concretized" in an individual being is true. However, it is reductionist to reduce metaphysics to the concept of nature, when in reality it is an entire philosophy of being. It is clear that John Paul II is committed to metaphysics as the ground for concreteness for the person (see John Paul II, Encyclical Letter on the Relationship between Faith and Reason *Fides et ratio* [September 14, 1998], AAS 91 [1999], 5–88; *Fides et ratio* [Boston: Pauline Books & Media, 1998], §§43–44, 46, 61, 76, 82–84, 97, 105). Min's criticism of metaphysics as unable to penetrate the dynamic, personal subjectivity of the acting person does correspond to Wojtyła's assessment of metaphysics in *Person and Act*, but his rhetorical severity concerning metaphysics as a whole certainly does not. In addition, Min's recognition that the concrete person is the totality of his being and acting is also a competent presentation of Wojtyła's position. What Min seems to miss, however, is that Wojtyła believes that Thomist metaphysics in fact encompasses the concrete totality of the human person. Wojtyła observes that the dynamic aspects of the person cannot be penetrated with the tools available to this philosophy of being. However, when grounded in metaphysics, phenomenology provides additional insights and enrichment to the Thomist approach, not a replacement for it. For Karol Wojtyła, metaphysics provides the necessary foundation for the concreteness of the person; it does not exclude the totality of the person, even if it cannot deeply penetrate its dynamic aspects.

15 See Karol Wojtyła, *The Acting Person*, trans. Andrzej Potocki, ed. A. Tymieniecka, Analecta Husserliana: The Yearbook of Phenomenological Research, vol. 10 (Dordrecht: Reidel Publishing Co., 1979), 203.

16 Wojtyła, *The Acting Person*, 203.

throughout the life of the Church. These facts authorize his anthropological project, describing man's complex unity using hylomorphism.

The reason for the correspondence between his philosophical and theological accounts of man is that the natural truths about man revealed by God were also discovered through long and careful observation of and reflection on the visible world. The integration of Christian philosophical and theological anthropology arrived at its most complete form in the thought of St. Thomas Aquinas, and this thought was affirmed magisterially at the Council of Vienne (1312) and the Fifth Lateran Council (1513). John Paul points out that these councils affirm the soul as the form of the body, and that this form is a spiritual, and so immortal, soul.[17]

While one can consider hylomorphism a theory, the reality which it accurately describes is revealed truth. However, John Paul II recognizes that hylomorphism does not go uncriticized in some quarters. He seems to accept this as legitimate as far as it is a criticism of a philosophical system in that he does not try to defend hylomorphism.[18] However, again he does insist on the real existence of the duality of body and soul, which together are seamlessly unified in the person.[19] It is significant to note that John Paul II does not emphasize the faculty of reason, as the manner in which

---

[17] John Paul states:

> It culminated principally in the pronouncements of the Council of Vienne (1312), which calls the soul the "form" of the body: *forma corporis humani per se et essentialiter* (DS 902). As a factor determining the substance of the being "man," the "form" is of a spiritual nature. This spiritual "form," the soul, is immortal. Later, the Fifth Lateran Council (1513) authoritatively stated this—the soul is immortal, in contrast with the body which is subject to death (see DS 1440). The Thomistic school emphasizes at the same time that, by virtue of the substantial union of body and soul, the soul, even after death, does not cease to "aspire" to be reunited with the body. This is confirmed by the revealed truth about the resurrection of the body.

(John Paul II, *A Catechesis on the Creed*, vol. 1, *God, Father and Creator* [Boston: Pauline Books and Media, 1995], 228).

[18] See John Paul II, *God, Father and Creator*. John Paul II's acceptance that hylomorphism is open to criticism as a philosophical system accords with his statement that the magisterium does not "canonize any one particular philosophy in preference to others" (*Fides et ratio*, §49).

[19] He states: "The philosophical terminology used to express the unity and complexity (duality) of man is sometimes criticized. But it is beyond doubt that the doctrine on the unity of the human person and at the same time on the spiritual-corporal duality of man is fully rooted in Sacred Scripture and Tradition. The conviction that man is the 'image of God' because of the soul, has frequently been expressed. But traditional doctrine does not lack the conviction that the body also participates in the dignity of the 'image of God' in

man is made in the image of God, at the expense of the body-soul unity.[20] For example, he states: "Created in the image of God, man is both a corporeal and spiritual being. Bound to the external world, he also transcends it. Besides being a bodily creature, as a spirit he is a person. This truth about man is an object of our faith, as is the biblical truth about his being constituted in the 'image and likeness' of God."[21] Man also reflects the image of God in his body-soul constitution.

In his *theology of the body* catecheses, John Paul makes explicit the manner in which man is similar to God.[22] Certainly he does not consider God to have a body but that does not mean that the fullness of the human person, including his body-soul unity, cannot in some way image God.[23] The possibility that the person, who is a body-soul unity, could image God indicates the depth of his integral view of the human person, as well as his integral vision of the *analogia entis*.[24] It also suggests the dignity with which God endows man. In a later catechesis, he articulates this dignity. He says that it is man, and not the angels, who God put at the center of divine

---

its own way, just as it participates in the dignity of the person" (John Paul II, *God, Father and Creator*, 228).

[20] That is not to say that he does not affirm this traditional Thomist view. He states that "what makes man like God is the fact that—unlike the whole world of other living creatures, including those endowed with senses (*animalia*)—man is also a rational being (*animal rationale*). Thanks to this property, man and woman are able to 'dominate' the other creatures of the visible world (see Gen 1:28)" (John Paul II, Apostolic Letter on the Dignity and Vocation of Women *Mulieris dignitatem* (August 15, 1988), AAS 80 (1988), 1653–1729, §6).

[21] John Paul II, *God, Father and Creator*, 226.

[22] John Paul states that

> of all the "bodies" man came in contact with and conceptually defined, giving them their names (*animalia*), the expression "flesh from my flesh" takes on precisely this meaning: the body reveals man. This concise formula already contains all that human science will ever be able to say about the structure of the body as an organism, about its vitality, about its particular sexual physiology, etc. In this first expression of the man, "flesh from my flesh" contains also a reference to that by which that body is authentically human and thus to that which determines man as a person, that is, as a being that is, also in all its bodiliness, "similar" to God.

(John Paul II, *Man and Woman He Created Them: A Theology of the Body*, trans. Michael Waldstein [Boston: Pauline Books and Media, 2006], 164).

[23] See *Mulieris dignitatem*, §8.

[24] John Paul II follows St. Thomas in this regard. St. Thomas says that while the image of God is more in angels than in man absolutely because angels' angelic nature is more perfect, man is more in the image of God relationally because man proceeds from man in analogy to the Trinitarian processions (*ST* Ia, q. 93, a. 3, resp.). Thus, it necessary to discuss this relational image in the final chapter of part 1.

revelation.[25] This finds its logic in the fullness of divine revelation being the Incarnate Word, the God-Man. The fact that angels are pure spirit who serve God with us and for us, reveals to man the significance of his own nature as a seamless unity of body and spirit in light of the Incarnation.[26]

John Paul II's anthropology focuses on the aspect of hylomorphic theory which states that the soul is the substantial form of the body.[27] The substantial form is an incorporeal substance that is the principle of "act" in the substance. The form actualizes the potency of the matter (the body).[28] Therefore, the soul is the "act" whereby the matter of the body is given its existence,[29] as well as its self-identity, its shape, its self-organizing principle, its animation, and its locomotion. What this means with respect to anthropology is that the human person is a composite being who cannot be reduced to either body or soul but must be taken in his entirety.

The soul gives shape to the body while the body is the medium by which the soul reveals itself, acts, and participates in the created order. The body is also necessary for the action of the intellect.[30] Recall that Wojtyła began his phenomenological study of the person revealed through "act" in *Person and Act* by showing that the "human act" is the visible manifestation of the soul. In fact, it appears that Wojtyła, in large part, justifies his embarking upon a phenomenology of "man-acts" based on the metaphysical notion that the soul is the substantial form of the body.[31] In any case,

---

[25] See John Paul II, *God, Father and Creator*, 303.

[26] John Paul II certainly recognizes that the Incarnation itself reveals to man the dignity of his human nature. However, in this Wednesday audience he indicates that it is man's religious experience of purely spiritual beings in light of the Incarnation that shows to man the significance of his nature. See *God, Father and Creator*, 303.

[27] See Wojtyła, "Thomistic Personalism," 169.

[28] See *ST* Ia, a. 75, a. 2, s.c.

[29] St. Thomas says "in things composed of matter and form, neither the matter nor the form can be designated as that-which-is, nor even can the act of existing be so designated. However, form can be called that-by-which-a-thing-is, or exists (*quo est*), inasmuch as it is a principle of existing. Nevertheless, it is the whole substance which is that-which-is (*quod est*), and the act of existing is that by which the substance is denominated a *being*" (Thomas Aquinas, *Summa contra gentiles* II, 52, cited in *An Introduction to the Metaphysics of St. Thomas Aquinas*, ed. and trans. James F. Anderson [Washington, DC: Regnery Publishing, Inc., 1953], 34; cf. also *ST* Ia, q. 75, a. 4).

[30] *ST* Ia q. 75, a. 2, resp. 3.

[31] This conjecture is partially justified by Karol Wojtyła's preface to the first English translation of *Person and Act* entitled *The Acting Person*. In it he says that "this presentation of the problem [of the person as subject], completely new in relation to traditional philosophy (and by traditional philosophy we understand here the pre-Cartesian philosophy and above all the heritage of Aristotle, and, among the Catholic schools of thought, of

the soul as the form of the body continued to be important for John Paul II in his papal teachings to the very end of his pontificate.

John Paul points to biblical and magisterial statements which correspond to hylomorphism. In his encyclical *Veritatis splendor*, he invokes the "soul as substantial form" in discussing a deficient moral theory.[32] He defends the unity of body and soul as dogmatic by citing the Council of Vienne's hylomorphic-influenced phrase mentioned above in his rejection of the deficient moral theory.[33] Here John Paul II implicitly accepts the modification that St. Thomas makes to Aristotle's hylomorphic theory in order to accommodate it to Christianity; namely, to state that this "form"—the soul—perdures after death.[34] In fact, the author explicitly says that the human self subsists in the soul after death, even though it is separated from the body.[35]

Because the soul is the substantial form of the body and the body is the matter for the soul-form, the soul requires the body to make itself visible, not to mention to exist. The body is necessary for the person in order to express himself in the visible world. Therefore, what one sees expressed through the body, physically, psychologically, emotionally, etcetera, is the visible manifestation of the soul which brings the body into actualization.[36]

St. Thomas Aquinas) has provoked me to undertake an attempt at reinterpreting certain formulations proper to this whole philosophy" (*The Acting Person*, xiii).

[32] In this case it is a "values" oriented theory which rejects natural law as biologism or physicalism.

[33] "It contradicts the *Church's teachings on the unity of the human person*, whose rational soul is *per se et essentialiter* the form of his body. The spiritual and immortal soul is the principle of unity of the human being, whereby it exists as a whole—*corpore et anima unus*—as a person. These definitions not only point out that the body, which has been promised the resurrection, will also share in glory. They also remind us that reason and free will are linked with all the bodily and sense faculties. *The person, including the body, is completely entrusted to himself, and it is in the unity of body and soul that the person is the subject of his own moral acts*" (John Paul II, *Veritatis splendor* [August 6, 1993], *AAS* 85 (1993), 1133–228, §48).

[34] The separation of the human soul from the body does not neatly fit with the hylomorphic theory as proposed by Aristotle. However, Peter Kreeft points out that body-soul separation was not God's original intent for man. Death was due to sin, the latter being an abuse of his freedom. The result is exactly the opposite of Platonist thinking in which the soul is imprisoned rather than freed in death. Kreeft calls this separation "a freak, a monster, an obscenity." Peter Kreeft, *Everything You Ever Wanted to Know about Heaven* (San Francisco: Ignatius Press, 1990), 93.

[35] See John Paul II, *A Catechesis on Salvation History*, vol. 6, *The Trinity's Embrace: God's Saving Plan* (Boston: Pauline Books and Media, 2002), 139–40.

[36] Wojtyła puts it this way:

This, as I will show in the next chapter, is significant for the issue of sex. Neither is the fact that the body reveals the person solely a finding of a particular philosophical system.

John Paul II finds it in biblical revelation, with Adam's exclamation that he found another self in beholding Eve for the first time.[37] This gives the warrant for doing theology via reflection on the human body. John Paul II declares that this should be a surprise to no one. With the Incarnation "the body entered theology . . . through the main door."[38] The expression of the personal self through the body is beyond just a shadowy, exterior expression of a hidden interior. Rather, the body reveals, but does not exhaust, the whole person.[39]

Hylomorphism is also significant for John Paul's expansive phenomenological analysis as it provides the concrete foundation and metaphysical explanation for the results of his phenomenological analysis, which indicates that there is something prior and given to human nature to which he must conform if he is to fulfill himself through his actions. This is essentially his correction of Ockham's reduction of human nature to something which is purely descriptive. Because this Ockhamist reduction is a view that predominates today, hylomorphic theory, as it accurately reflects revealed truth, has many significant implications for the author's thought to which we should now turn.

> The human body forms outwardly a whole that is membered in a specific manner appropriated to man alone. This applies not only to the special distribution of bodily members but also to their mutual coordination in the whole of man's outward form. . . . This outwardly discernible entirety, however, by no means accounts for all the reality constituting the human body, just as it does not in the case of the animal body or of plants. . . . The somatic side of man and his psychical side are strictly interrelated, the relation between them consisting in the fact that the psychical functions are conditioned by the sum total of the somatic functions and especially by some particular somatic functions. The term "psyche" applies to the soul, though not immediately in the metaphysical sense; its first application is in a "physical," or phenomenal, sense. Thus "psyche" and "psychical" apply to the whole range of manifestations of the integral human life that are not in themselves bodily or material, but at the same time show some dependence on the body, some somatic conditioning.

(*The Acting Person*, 201).

[37] See *Man and Woman*, 164.

[38] *Man and Woman*, 221. This theological warrant is not restricted to the discipline of anthropology. It extends of course to other areas. One particularly important area for John Paul II is morality. See *Veritatis splendor*, §50, where he discusses the implications of hylomorphism for the natural law.

[39] See *Man and Woman*, 176.

IMPLICATIONS OF PERSONAL CONCRETENESS

John Paul II presumes the hylomorphic theory throughout his writings and, more importantly, the truth that it describes. One significant implication of hylomorphism is the complex structure of the human person making him at the same time a unity and a duality. He acknowledges that there are those who believe that Scripture emphasizes the unity of the person and agrees that this unity is certainly prominent. However, he points out that Scripture's emphasis on unity is not an exclusivity. Matthew 10:28 is one of several instances in which Scripture is also explicit about the duality of body and soul as constituent aspects of man's unity.[40] He cautions, however, that the soul-and-body duality is not an anthropological dualism in a Cartesian way of thinking but that one should see the relation of the body to the soul as an antinomy.[41] In other words, it is not a pathological separation of two disparate entities but a union of two different realms (corporeal and spiritual) into one complex, seamless unity.

The fact that the soul is the form of the body also has important

---

[40] John Paul says:

> Man is a unit. He is one in himself. But this unity contains a duality. Sacred Scripture presents both the unity (the person) and the duality (body and soul). . . . It is frequently emphasized that biblical tradition stresses especially the personal unity of the human being, by using the term "body" to designate the whole man (see Ps 145:21, Joel 3:1; Is 66:23; John 1:14). The observation is exact. But notwithstanding this, the duality of man is also present in biblical tradition, sometimes very clearly. Christ's words reflect this tradition: "Do not fear those who deprive the body of life but cannot destroy the soul. Rather, fear him who can destroy both body and soul in Gehenna" (Matt 10:28). Biblical sources authorize us to view man as a personal unity and at the same time as a duality of soul and body.

(John Paul II, *God, Father and Creator*, 227–28).

[41] He says:

> Since the subject of discussion is the resurrection of the body, that is, of man in his authentic bodiliness, "spiritual body" should signify precisely *the perfect sensitivity of the senses, their perfect harmonization with the activity of the* human *spirit* in truth and in freedom. The "natural body," which is the earthly antithesis of the "spiritual body," by contrast indicates sensuality as a force that often undermines man inasmuch as, by living "in the knowledge of good and evil," he is often urged or pushed, as it were, toward evil. . . . One cannot forget that what is at issue here is not anthropological dualism, but a basic antinomy. What is part of it is not only the body (as Aristotelian *"hylē"*), but also the soul, or man as "a living soul" (see Gen 2:7).

(*Man and Woman*, 410–11).

implications for many aspects of Church teachings, including her moral teachings, and for an integral theology of grace. For example, hylomorphism helps to articulate a compelling account of morality in the areas of the sanctity of life from conception to natural death as well as for sexual intercourse. Since by definition there would be no human body without the soul, then the philosophical case for personal existence at conception becomes evident.[42] This fits well with available scientific evidence and corroborates the Church's longstanding teaching.[43] Moreover, a moral theory which attempts to delineate absolutely between a bodily act and its moral content can be immediately seen as suspect.

John Paul puts it this way: "*[The] body and soul are inseparable*: in the person, in the willing agent and in the deliberate act, *they stand or fall together*."[44] Given that a person can never be considered an object for use, the unity of the person also indicates that neither can the body be "used," even one's own body, without diminishing the person.[45] Hylomorphism

---

[42] St. Thomas, basing himself on Aristotle's biological theory, thought that the conception process was an extended one (forty days for a male and ninety days for a female) in which the fetus developed through a succession of forms beginning with a vegetative soul and progressing through an animal soul. It was at the end of this conception process in which God immediately created and infused the fetus with a human soul. See Thomas Aquinas, *Commentary on III Sentences* 3:5:2. Resolving the debate over the implications of Thomas's acceptance of Aristotelian biology for abortion is beyond the scope of this paper. However, it seems reasonable to suggest that had St. Thomas known the modern biological description of fetal development, and especially the creation of a unique, personal DNA contemporaneously with the creation of the zygote, he would have revised his thought to hold that conception (and therefore, human "ensoulment") generally occurs at fertilization (pathological abnormalities notwithstanding, e.g., hydatidiform moles). Thomas recognized that the matter must be properly organized prior to the reception of a human soul (*Summa contra gentiles* II, ch. 89), and this did not seem to be the case with the knowledge available to ancient embryology. However, modern microbiology has revealed that the zygote has all of the epigenetic primordia it requires, including that of that of the intellectual organs, in order to develop into a mature person. For a detailed treatment of this issue see John Haldane and Patrick Lee, "Aquinas on Human Ensoulment, Abortion and the Value of Life," *Philosophy* 78 (2003): 255–78.

[43] See John Paul II, Encyclical Letter on the Value and Inviolability of Human Life *Evangelium vitae* (March 25, 1995), *AAS* 87 (1995), 401–522, §60.

[44] John Paul II, *Veritatis splendor*, §49.

[45] Wojtyła states: "Yet, as we know, the human person cannot be an object of use. For the body is an integral part of the person, and thus it cannot be separated from the totality of the person; both the value of the body and the value of sex expressed in the body are based on the value of the person. In this objective relationship, the reaction of sensuality, in which the body and *sexus* appear as an object of possible use, threatens to devalue the person" (Karol Wojtyła, *Love and Responsibility*, trans. Grzegorz Ignatik [Boston: Pauline Books & Media, 2013], 90).

also provides support for the Church's teaching that natural bodily urges are good because they comprise a positive aspect of the somatic structure of human nature. Hylomorphism provides a solid anthropological foundation for understanding concupiscence as a consequence of the fall. It also provides a compelling case for showing why it is the decisions themselves that one makes when moved by concupiscent urges, which are usually problematic.[46]

As a final example, let us look at hylomorphism and grace. In one of John Paul II's later Wednesday audience catecheses he indicates that it is the whole person, body and soul, that is infused and renewed by the sanctifying grace of the Holy Spirit.[47] Western theology has traditionally emphasized the soul as the subject of grace, due in part to hylomorphism's ability to analyze grace's created effects in the soul. However, the implications of that same hylomorphism also point to the reality that it is the whole person, body and soul, who is imbued by grace. This integral view of man and grace is much clearer in Eastern Christian theology. The fourteenth-century Byzantine mystic Nicholas Kabasilas, for example, says that in baptism the believer is united with "the spiritual senses and functions of the body of Christ," which also bring about a change in "the biological dimensions and functions of man into functions of the body of Christ."[48] Christ infuses himself into all of the Christian's "psychosomatic faculties, without confusion but nevertheless in a real way . . . [where] He transforms, refashions and renews our psychosomatic functions, turning them into functions of His own body."[49] While it may not be explicit, hylomorphic theory makes such an integral view of grace implicit in Western theology as well.

A Synopsis of the Metaphysics of John Paul II's Anthropology

John Paul II presupposes hylomorphic theory as his basis for understanding the metaphysical substantiality of human nature. His confidence in the theory's explanatory value is high due to its strong correlation with divine revelation and magisterial teaching, especially in the area of anthropology.

---

[46] See *Man and Woman*, 306–309, and *Veritatis splendor*, §50.

[47] See John Paul II, *The Trinity's Embrace*, 135.

[48] Panayiotis Nellas, *Deification in Christ: Orthodox Perspectives on the Nature of the Human Person*, trans. Norman Russell (Crestwood, NY: St. Vladimir's Seminary Press, 1997), 122.

[49] Nellas, *Deification in Christ*, 123. For more on this, see also 121–25 and 141–42.

This confidence is enhanced by hylomorphism's capacity to explain many other aspects of Church teaching in such areas as morality and theology of grace, to name but two.

The theory provides a system for understanding and discussing the divinely revealed truth that the human person is a unity of a spiritual soul and material body. The soul as the body's substantial form justifies John Paul's phenomenological project as he presents it in *Person and Act* because the soul expresses itself through the body. It also provides the structure for understanding how the human act has an ontological and enduring impact on the human person. John Paul identifies the manner in which the person must engage in these human acts for his proper actualization based on his understanding of the human person as relational. All of these features of the theory will be necessary for John Paul II's account of masculinity and fatherhood because they form the concrete foundation for the person. There is nothing more central than relationality, our final topic in part 1, for the coherence of this account.

CHAPTER 4

Person and Relation

Some contemporary philosophers have come to regard the human person in terms of relationality, though what they mean by relationality is not always the same. Theories are numerous and varied. They range from the advisability of developing interpersonal relationships as a consideration for personal self-improvement to claims that deny personhood can exist outside of relationships.[1] Karol Wojtyła adopts the view of the person as relational in an ontological sense. Thus, he goes well beyond the individualist perspective of the former position, but he does not say that personhood exists only in relationships. In this chapter, we will look at the extent to which he views that relations and relationships ontologically constitute and perfect, respectively, human personhood. We will accomplish this by looking at his early philosophical work and the manner in which Trinitarian theology and Christology influence his anthropology. We will end by clarifying his view of personal relationality through the terms "subsistent" and "subsisting."

EARLY DEVELOPMENT

Karol Wojtyła understood man as one who can never be completely divorced from the communal aspect of his nature because there is an essential correspondence between the subjectivity of the human person and the structure of the human community. Though this correspondence is not explicit in his earliest thought, Wojtyła does refer to the relational

---

[1] For the sake of precision, in this chapter I will follow the convention that views the term "relation" as ontological and innate to the person (such the relation of parent to child, or, in other words, a real relation) and the term "relationship" as a volitional, freely entered into association with another. However, I have not found that Karol Wojtyła makes this distinction.

character of the human person in an early philosophical work on personalism.[2] He asserts that while the human person always remains an individual, he is also a social being.

This innate relationality to others provides a natural inclination to form personal relationships as well as "societies and communities."[3] However, this inclination does not result in mechanistic necessity: rather, rightly ordered relationships are the ground by which human personhood is fulfilled. This is because each person is constituted as personal through freedom and self-determination. Freedom is essential for fulfilling relationships because through one's consent he makes himself who he is, especially in the way he lives his relationships interpersonally. His personhood is, in a sense, in potency, which then must be freely and fully actualized according to the relational structure of the human person.

In his personalist writings, Wojtyła raises the problem of a one-sided emphasis on the individuality of the person. He identifies two poles of this problem: individualism, meaning a radical or atomist individualism, and totalitarian collectivism. The former subordinates the community to the individual desires of the person; the latter subordinates the person to the community in such a way that his value is determined solely in terms of the needs of the collective. His solution to this dichotomous problem is a return to the metaphysics and anthropology of St. Thomas.[4]

Wojtyła shows that in a personalism based on Thomism, the good of the community does have priority, but also that any authentic common good simultaneously promotes the integral good of the person. The true common good will never threaten the good of the person even if it requires at times a "considerable sacrifice of the person."[5] Thomism led Wojtyła already at this early stage to find interpersonal intersubjectivity to be in some way a constituent aspect of the one's personhood. However, he does not explore person and relationality any further at this point. In *Person and Act,* Wojtyła devotes a chapter to relationality in terms of participation. In this work, he delves more deeply into the issues that he only touched on in "Thomistic Personalism." Recall from the above discussion of participation that the person fulfills himself by acting in freedom and truth, in

---

[2] See Karol Wojtyła, "Thomistic Personalism," in *Person and Community: Selected Essays,* vol. 4, trans. Theresa Sandok, O.S.M. (New York: Peter Lang, 1993), 173ff.

[3] Wojtyła, "Thomistic Personalism," 174.

[4] See note 6 in chapter 1 above for more on the specific form of Thomism which forms our author's thinking.

[5] See note 6 in chapter 1.

accord with his interpersonal obligations. This is a key for understanding Wojtyła's theological anthropology.

He further explored this thought at the Fourth International Phenomenology Conference in 1975, held in Fribourg, Switzerland, in a paper reflecting on the last two sections of *Person and Act*.[6] In the paper, Wojtyła specifically looks at the issue of participation in contrast to the Marxist concept of alienation.[7] Of particular interest in his paper is his analysis of the person as a concrete individual in terms of his relation to an "other."[8] Wojtyła argues that the relationship of one person to another does not immediately arise from the essence of human nature but rather that the potency for relationship lies in man's nature.[9] The person must actualize this potency by engaging the other person as another "I." One accomplishes this through the experience of him as another person.[10] When one does this, the "I" participates in the other "I's" humanity. This is Wojtyła's definition of participation.[11]

---

[6] Karol Wojtyła, "Participation or Alienation?," in *Person and Community*, 197–207.

[7] Wojtyła explains that the Marxist concept of alienation is an ambiguous one. He does not attempt to introduce any precision in the definition but implies that it is the disruption of a proper relationship of the human being to some other factor. In general, he says that Marxists understand human beings to be alienated by products of their own making. Of course the emphasis is on alienation of the worker from the fruit of his work, but Wojtyła shows that Marx finds the source of alienation to be the political system, the economic system, property, and religion. For Marxists the resolution to alienation is the transformation and/or annihilation of its structural source. See Wojtyła, "Participation or Alienation?," 205.

[8] Wojtyła states: "It seems that in the very positing of the problem *I-other* (*soi-autrui*) we proceed simultaneously from two cognitive situations. One is the ascertainment of the fact of the existence and activity of a concrete human being, designated by the pronoun I, who exists and acts in common with other human beings. The other is one of them, someone who lives alongside me, and who is both another and one of the others who exists and acts in common with me" ("Participation or Alienation?," 198).

[9] He says: "The universality of the concept 'human being' brings into clear relief the problem of both the potentiality for *I-other* relationships and the need to actualize participation, through which such relationships properly emerge. There is, as we know, an enormous amount of people living and acting in the world, and all of them are apprehended conceptually by anyone who thinks 'human being.' In this concept, however, none of them is yet an *other* in relation to an *I*. The concept 'human being' does not itself create this relationship" (Wojtyła, "Participation or Alienation?," 201).

[10] See Wojtyła, "Participation or Alienation?," 202.

[11] This is significant for fatherhood, as reveals that participation is always interpersonal. Participation is not simply collaborative work, it is the exchange of persons. The implications of this insight for the Catholic social principles of solidarity and subsidiarity are significant. It reveals that they are co-principles, which define the manner

Participation, therefore, is the antithesis of alienation, the latter of which is the denial of the person's right to participation. Later in the paper, Wojtyła discusses this relationship of the *I-other* in terms of a *communio personarum* which he distinguishes from a *communitas* in that the latter encompasses a larger number of persons in a complex web of interrelationships.[12] He deepened these concepts in a much longer article he published two years later.[13]

Person and Act does not provide a "full blown theory of community."[14] Rather, it gives a more fundamental account of the person who is fulfilled qua person, through his existence and through his actions with others.[15] In the later article, Wojtyła addresses the person as both a concrete subject and a relational subject in a more comprehensive manner. This article restates that the person is fulfilled through participation, both interpersonal and social, in the community, but he now explores fulfillment in community in more depth. Wojtyła further distinguishes between society and community.

Society and community are not identical terms; rather, community connotes the specific unity of the "multiplicity of subjects,"[16] while society suggests "the consciousness and lived experience of all its members and also in some sense each of them."[17] The unity of a community "is accidental with respect to each subject individually and to all of them together."[18] Neither a society nor a community itself can be considered a subject. Only an individual subject is a substantial subject (*suppositum*).[19] The operative ideas here are fulfillment, participation, interpersonal relation, and social relation. Let us now turn to an analysis of each of these terms to gain more precision in their meaning.

Fulfillment is described by our author using the Aristotelian-Thomist analysis of potency and act. The human person is a finite being made in the image and likeness of God. God creates man with the potency to

---

of participation in order to maximize the opportunity for interpersonal collaboration toward the common good.

[12] See Wojtyła, "Participation or Alienation?," 204.
[13] See Wojtyła, "Subject and Community," 219–61.
[14] Wojtyła, "Subject and Community," 237.
[15] It provided "the elementary conditions under which existence and activity 'together with others' promotes the self-fulfillment of the human being as a person" (Wojtyła, "Subject and Community," 236).
[16] Wojtyła, "Subject and Community," 238.
[17] Wojtyła, "Subject and Community," 238–39.
[18] Wojtyła, "Subject and Community," 238.
[19] See Wojtyła, "Subject and Community," 238.

achieve a perfection which corresponds to man's creation in God's image and likeness. But Wojtyła is very clear that this actualization must be a proper one, one that is true to the image of the Creator. Man achieves his perfection by the appropriate use of self-determination; in other words, through "man-acts" which are acts of the free will, in accord with truth, and toward the common good. These authentic man-acts actualize the self-possession and self-governance proper to a creature created in the image of Perfection himself.

Wojtyła speaks of this fulfillment of the greater, common good in terms of self-transcendence. In this context, he defines transcendence in contradistinction to modern tendencies to make the concept identical with the person. Thus, transcendence is the rejection of what seems to be a personal good but is really only an apparent good, in preference for the authentic good achieved through discernment of the properly formed conscience and chosen by free will. Fulfillment in community, then, comes by choosing the greater good of the community while maintaining "the irrevocable primacy of the personal subject in relation to community."[20]

As a perfection, this good can only be achieved by the person acting together with others toward a common good. In terms of the community, Wojtyła understands this acting together, or participation, to be one of the necessary elements of community. He carries out sets of analyses which "confirm [Wojtyła] in the conviction that participation should be seen as a property of human beings, corresponding to their personal subjectivity."[21] In addition, he views this participation as "a positive relation to the humanity of others."[22] This analysis reveals two "dimensions" to participation, the interpersonal which he terms the "*I-thou*," and the communal, or the "we."[23]

The interpersonal and communal dimensions are not separate; rather, they are synergistic dimensions of the person found in community participation. Marriage best exemplifies the interpersonal dimension. The social element distinguishes the communal dimension. One can best observe this dimension when married spouses accept the common good of marriage and the family. For our purposes, of particular interest is the way in which Wojtyła characterizes relationality in these two dimensions.

Wojtyła refers to the fact that some say that the "*I*" is in a sense constituted by the "*Thou*."[24] While in this particular statement the "Thou" refers

---

20 Wojtyła, "Subject and Community," 237.
21 Wojtyła, "Subject and Community," 254.
22 Wojtyła, "Subject and Community," 237.
23 See Wojtyła, "Subject and Community," 240.
24 See Wojtyła, "Subject and Community," 241.

to God, and so the "constitution by the Thou" refers to the fact that the human person exists because of his real relation to God, there still is applicability of this idea to relations among human beings.[25] It is clear that he does not consider the human *I-thou* relation to have the same metaphysical weight as man's relation to God.[26] Rather, every individual person is metaphysically constituted in its own *suppositum*.[27]

Nevertheless, in this human *I-thou* relation, the person discovers the lived experience of relation. Moreover, it is in this relation that "both the *I* and the *thou* as another *I* are constituted."[28] It is through consciousness and the experience of the reflexivity of the relation which contains the element "constituting my *I* through its relation to the *thou*."[29]

So there is a sense in which the person is constituted in relation to an *other*, but this does not mean that the relation is essential for the continued existence of the *suppositum*. Unlike the Trinitarian persons, the human person is not one whose subsistence is his relation to another person, but still Wojtyła does see a manner in which interpersonal relations are, in part, constitutive of the person. This is because the Trinitarian persons are the basis for the relationality of the human person, since man is made in the image of a Trinitarian God. This is an essential point for Wojtyła. Therefore, we ought now to explore this Trinitarian foundation for human personhood in more detail.

THE TRINITARIAN FOUNDATION OF PERSONHOOD

John Paul II provides insight into his Trinitarian theology in his Wednesday audience catecheses from January 1985 to August 1986. In these and later catecheses, he follows the traditional Augustinian-Thomist description of God's eternal Generation and Spiration. The Son is the *Verbum*, or interior divine Word, generated or begotten by the Father, who in knowing himself begets the Image of himself. The Father is Father because He begets the Son; the Son is He who is begotten by the Father. The Son, the interior Word, is of the same substance as the Father, so there is one God, one divine nature, but at this point in the description, two distinct persons.

The eternal, divine generation of the Word is a revealed truth, explained in a "well-founded and certain theological doctrine" by the

---

[25] See Wojtyła, "Subject and Community," 261n17.
[26] See Wojtyła, "Subject and Community," 242.
[27] See Wojtyła, "Subject and Community," 248.
[28] Wojtyła, "Subject and Community," 242.
[29] Wojtyła, "Subject and Community," 242.

Fathers and Doctors of the Church.[30] The Holy Spirit then proceeds eternally from the Father and the Son as of one principle. He is the fruit of the total gift of the Father to the Son and, reciprocally, of the Son to the Father. For John Paul II, this is the archetype of the human person who can fulfill himself only through a sincere gift of self.

Because total self-gift is rooted in the essence of the Trinity, being convertible so to speak with the Trinitarian relations, it proves to be fundamental for human interpersonal relations. The human person can only fully perfect himself as created in the image and likeness of God when he totally gives himself to another. Love is the term which describes this total self-gift.

One can understand the depth of archetypal Trinitarian love, of "self-gift," from such a Trinitarian theology. The three divine persons are not individuals, so they are not distinguished with respect to substance, because there is only one God. The Trinitarian persons are distinguished solely in their relations. The Father who begets the Son "is pure Paternity, the Son is pure Sonship, and the Holy Spirit is pure 'Nexus of Love' of the two, so that the personal distinctions do not divide the same and unique divine nature of the three."[31]

The processions are God's eternal act of total self-gift. In fact, "The Holy Spirit is 'Person-Love; he is . . . Person-Gift' (*DViv* 10)."[32] Love is the essence of the Trinitarian relations. The Trinitarian persons subsist in an ineffable unity in which they can only be distinguished by their relations, or in other words, in the manner of their total self-gift to another.[33] One can say the Trinity is Love and so for the human person in whose image he is created, this means that love, or total self-gift, is normative for authentic fulfillment of his personhood.

---

[30] John Paul II, *A Catechesis on the Creed*, vol. 1, *God, Father and Creator* (Boston: Pauline Books and Media, 1995), 170.

[31] John Paul II, God, Father and Creator, 183.

[32] John Paul II, *A Catechesis on Salvation History*, vol. 6, *The Trinity's Embrace*: God's Saving Plan (Boston: Pauline Books and Media, 2002), 86.

[33] The Incarnation and the Passion reveal the total self-gift of the Trinitarian relations *par excellence*. John Paul finds this to be true because the economic missions reveal both processions. See John Paul II, *The Trinity's Embrace*, 175. In a later catechesis he cites the Gospel of John to demonstrate this: "[Jesus] explained to them, 'What I say, I say as the Father told me' (John 12:50). This is an obvious allusion to the eternal utterance whereby the Father generates the Word-Son in the trinitarian life" (John Paul II, *A Catechesis on the Creed*, vol. 2, *Jesus, Son and Savior* [Boston: Pauline Books and Media, 1996], 240). Thus, total self-gift also played a central role in his Christological anthropology.

TRINITARIAN ANTHROPOLOGY: LOVE AND MARRIAGE

John Paul II's anthropology is fundamentally Trinitarian. Piero Coda indicates that this had been the case since the author's participation in writing the anthropological section of *Gaudium et spes*, but that he later developed and deepened it.[34] John Paul summarizes his Trinitarian anthropology in the apostolic letter *Mulieris dignitatem*. Here he concisely describes the implications of the Trinitarian relations for the human person, namely that God has revealed himself to humanity as a tri-unity, a unity in communion. This sheds light on the revealed truth that man is made in the image and likeness of God.

It is significant that Genesis declares that man is created as male and female, in the image of God. Both the man and the woman are like God as persons, that is, they are rational and have the freedom to love by means of the spiritual faculties of intellect and will. Yet they also image God in their bodies, in which the two can be at the same time one "in a communion of love" that has its archetype in the divine *communio*.[35]

So God creates man to be in relationships, like himself, one person with another. The context of the Genesis creation narratives reveals that all human interpersonal relationships have their wellspring in the marital covenant where, in the "unity of the two," man most perfectly images the Trinitarian *communio personarum* through fruitful self-gift. John Paul II states this very forcefully in terms of the way in which human nature is to be understood: "To be human means to be called to interpersonal communion."[36] Applied to the marital *communio*, "The 'unity of the two,' man and woman are called from the beginning not only to exist 'side by side' or 'together,' but they are also called *to exist mutually 'one for the other.'*"[37] But this is a calling, meaning it is something to which one is invited to respond in freedom.

---

[34] Piero Coda, "Per una rilettura dell' 'antropologia trinitaria' di Giovanni Paolo II," *Aquinas* 41 (1998): 641–46. See also John Sikorski, "Towards a Conjugal Spirituality: Karol Wojtyła's Vision of Marriage before, during and after Vatican II," *Journal of Moral Theology* 6, no. 2 (2017): 118–22.

[35] John Paul II, Apostolic Letter on the Dignity and Vocation of Women *Mulieris dignitatem* (August 15, 1988), AAS 80 (1988), 1653–1729, §8. He finds this revealed not only in Genesis but also in the New Testament. Citing Jesus's prayer for unity in the high priestly prayer of John 17, John Paul says that "[Jesus] implied a *certain likeness* between the union of the divine Persons and the union of God's children in truth and charity. This likeness reveals that man, who is the only creature on earth which God willed for its own sake, cannot fully find himself except through a sincere gift of self" (*Mulieris dignitatem*, §7).

[36] *Mulieris dignitatem*, §7.

[37] *Mulieris dignitatem*, §7.

A calling is something that one must hear, freely accept, and then act upon with self-determination and in truth. Fulfillment through self-gift is a potency which the acting person must actualize. Marriage is the first and most fundamental element of this vocation to personal self-fulfillment.[38] John Paul II goes even further. He finds that human fatherhood and motherhood have their origins in the eternal reciprocity and relationality of the Trinity.[39] Thus, the two becoming one, who then become three in the human family, are an analogy, a created reflection of the purely spiritual[40] and eternal Trinitarian processions.[41]

Nachef agrees that this is fundamental. He finds it most relevant that John Paul applies the same total self-gift of the Trinitarian persons to human persons.[42] Divine persons are constituted by the fact that they totally give themselves to one another and by the structure through which they do so. The total self-giving love of the Father is a necessity for the Father's identity as Father. The Son must receive this gift and reciprocate with the same total gift of himself in order to possess his identity as Son. The selfless love that unites Father and Son is itself a person, the Holy Spirit.

This *perichoresis* of total, selfless love distinguishes the persons while it

---

[38] In a sense, marriage is the vocation for all humanity. Not all are called to natural marriage, but all are called into the marital union between the Bridegroom and the Bride, the Church. This will be discussed further in part 2 of this work.

[39] See John Paul II, *The Trinity's Embrace*, 289–90.

[40] Again, John Paul II says that man's body and spiritual soul are "that which determines man as a person, that is, as a being that is, also in all its bodiliness, 'similar' to God" (John Paul II, *Man and Woman He Created Them: A Theology of the Body*, trans. Michael Waldstein [Boston: Pauline Books and Media, 2006], 164).

[41] This is so through the *communion personarum* and through procreation. John Paul states that

> man became the image of God not only through his own humanity, but also through the communion of persons, which man and woman form from the very beginning. The . . . trinitarian concept of the "image of God" . . . is obviously not without significance for the theology of the body but constitutes perhaps the deepest theological aspect of everything one can say about man. In the mystery of creation—on the basis of the original and constitutive "solitude" of his being— man has been endowed with a deep unity between what is, humanly and through the body, male in him and what is, equally humanly and through the body, female in him. On all this, right from the beginning, the blessing of fruitfulness descended, linked with human procreation (see Gen 1:28).

(*Man and Woman*, 46–47, 204–14).

[42] See Antoine E. Nachef, The *Mystery of the Trinity in the Theological Thought of Pope John Paul II* (New York: Peter Lang Publishing, 1999), 218.

assures the oneness of the divine nature. It is not pure consciousness but the concrete divine subjectivity, distinct in each, that constitutes each divine person. Analogously, in man it is the conscious self-determination of the concrete acting person who gives himself in a total self-gift that reveals and makes possible his identity as one made in the image and likeness of God, though he exists as a person prior to and apart from his free acts.

John Paul is consistently integral in his view of the human person and his hylomorphic nature, stating that the latter is a unified body-soul duality. Wojtyła's anthropology is Trinitarian, but it is also christocentric. John Paul II emphasizes that the entire conciliar magisterium[43] was christocentric, and that this christocentrism is profoundly rooted in the Trinitarian mystery.[44] But one cannot view this christocentrism in a Cartesian manner. Given his consistently integrated philosophical and theological thought, certainly one should not expect this.

Nachef explains that John Paul II's theological views are more complex than those of the average academic.[45] This is certainly also the case with his Christology.[46] But as with John Paul's theology in general, so his christocentricity is simultaneously Trinitarian, Eucharistic, ecclesial, and Marian.[47] John Saward is of the same mind. He says that John Paul II exhibits a Catholic christocentrism which is not christomonist.[48] Rather, it is "at once Marian, ecclesial, [and] Eucharistic. Christ's singularity is not solitude."[49]

Christocentrism for John Paul describes more the point of departure rather than the entirety of his theology and anthropology. Christ is the

---

[43] Referencing the Second Vatican Council.

[44] Fernando Bogónez Herreras, "La persona humana en su relación con Dios según la Constitución Pastoral *Gaudium et spes*," *Estudio Augustiniano* 35 (2000): 557.

[45] Nachef states: "In meditating on any theological discipline, John Paul II interweaves trinitarian, christological, ecclesiological, anthropological, soteriological, sacramental, mariological, and social categories of analysis. Whereas academicians are accustomed to a strict separation of the disciplines and their respective methods, the Pope . . . 'shifts methodically from one perspective to another in order to provide multiple viewpoints on a given issue'" (*Mystery of the Trinity*, 9).

[46] Nachef says: "It is true, Christ stands at the center of Pope John Paul II's theological thinking, but this is not as simple as it appears. His first encyclical, *Redemptor hominis*, reveals the main lines of his Pontificate's program as far as theology is concerned. But Christ, as a Divine Person, is part of the Blessed Trinity which constitutes for the Pope the core of the Christian Revelation. He is convinced that Christology and trinitarian theology are two intimately interrelated disciplines" (*Mystery of the Trinity*, 7).

[47] See Nachef, *Mystery of the Trinity*, 176.

[48] See John Saward, *Christ Is the Answer: The Christ-Centered Teaching of Pope John Paul II* (New York: Alba House, 1995), 3.

[49] Saward, *Christ Is the Answer*, 2.

point of departure for theology and anthropology because he is the revelation of the truth that God is a Trinity of persons, a *communio personarum*, and he provides the model for what this means for the human person.

CHRISTOLOGICAL ANTHROPOLOGY: THE PERSON IS FULFILLED VIA A TOTAL GIFT OF SELF

John Paul's theology, and especially his anthropology, is christocentric, but it is christocentric in an integral sense. If the Trinity is the archetype that reveals the truth of man as a created person constituted for a love of total self-gift, Jesus Christ shows us how this love is practically to be lived out by man. Yet, Christ is more than simply the ideal; he is the efficacious ideal whose very life makes possible our "salvific transformation in [him]."[50] This is the author's interpretation of the foundational text from *Gaudium et spes* §22 that says that Christ fully reveals man to himself and makes his supreme calling clear. Christ is our exemplary and efficacious model. As a model, Christ is efficacious because he permits man to enter into the life of the Spirit, and this efficaciousness is key to understanding John Paul II's christocentric anthropology.[51]

In appropriating the saint's exploration of the inner dynamisms of the human person through the relatively new tool of phenomenology, it is important not to misread him in a Pelagian manner. He is particularly interested in man's experience of freedom and those attributes man requires to obtain and remain in this freedom: self-mastery, self-possession, and self-transcendence; freedom though, not as an end but rather as a

---

[50] John Paul II, "Jesus is our Model" (August 17, 1988), in *Audiences of Pope John Paul II* (English) (Vatican City: Libreria Editrice Vaticana, 2014).

[51] He perhaps summarizes best it here:

> For if man is the way of the Church, this way passes through the whole mystery of Christ, as man's divine model. Along this way the Holy Spirit, strengthening in each of us "the inner man," enables man ever more "fully to find himself through a sincere gift of self." These words of the Pastoral Constitution of the Council can be said to sum up *the whole of Christian anthropology*: that theory and practice, based on the Gospel, in which man discovers himself as belonging to Christ and discovers that in Christ he is raised to the status of a child of God, and so understands better his own dignity as man, precisely because he is the subject of God's approach and presence, the subject of the divine condescension, which contains the prospect and the very root of definitive glorification.

(John Paul II, Encyclical Letter on the Holy Spirit in the Life of the Church and the World *Dominum et vivificantem* [May 18, 1986], *AAS* 78 [1986], 809–900, §59).

means to man's final end, which is communion in love.[52] The bulk of his anthropological work looks extensively at these issues, which he describes in terms of original man (man as he was created, prelapsarian) and historical man (postlapsarian, the man of sin) in order to understand the person more deeply.

John Paul's anthropology is thoroughly Catholic. He integrates these phenomenological analyses with his study of redeemed man (man in the life of the Spirit). He skillfully navigates his course through the narrow channel between the opposing heresies of Pelagianism and Quietism; that is, of an exclusive reliance upon one's own efforts at self-mastery and a complete abandonment of one's obligation to develop virtue and to cooperate with grace by actively choosing to love and to reject selfishness.

It is with this in mind, that we need to read his christological anthropology. Christ is both 1) the exemplary model for the human person to whom we must look in order to understand ourselves and to respond authentically to our calling and 2) the one who temporally mediates the grace necessary for personal fulfillment (i.e., holiness) through the Holy Spirit by means of a supernatural ecclesial structure. Christ is the visible manifestation of Trinitarian love. We see in the earthly life of the Incarnate Son, the eternally lived-out love of the divine Son of God.

Christ's entire life, death, and Resurrection reveal to us who we are and how we are to live. We are called to make total gifts of ourselves in everything we do. We must follow the Son by returning ourselves to the Father and by making a gift of ourselves to others. Christ alone satisfies man's vocation, a vocation which originates in the Father's timeless love and whose fulfillment is most perfectly demonstrated in Christ's Passion, where he gave to the Father his complete and total gift of self, becoming "obedient unto death on a cross."[53] Each person can fulfill his vocation only by uniting himself to the one who uniquely and completely responded to the Father's call—Jesus Christ.

Christ reveals to man his likeness to God as a Trinity of persons, and so the model of his life carries implicit obligations within it. These obligations arise from the structure of the person who is made to live in an

---

[52] See John Paul II, Encyclical Letter at the Beginning of His Papacy *Redemptor hominis* (March 4, 1979), *AAS* 71 (1979), 257–324, §10.

[53] See *Redemptor hominis*, 20. Regarding the Christ's singular satisfaction of the Father's love, the author says, "He it was, and he alone, who satisfied the Father's eternal love, that fatherhood that from the beginning found expression in creating the world, giving man all the riches of creation, and making him 'little less than God,' in that he was created 'in the image and after the likeness of God'" (*Redemptor hominis*, 9).

authentic *communio* of persons. John Paul II, drawing from the teachings of the Second Vatican Council, explains that a *communio* is a social structure of persons living in a communion of truth and love.[54] Man images God in both his being constituted as spirit and as social, two characteristics which mutually define and interpenetrate each other. His spiritual constitution gives man the capacity to give himself selflessly, that is, to know and to love. His social constitution arises from this relationality in that love is directed only toward other persons (divine, angelic, and human). Man can therefore only fulfill himself by giving himself away to God and to other persons.[55]

John Paul II finds in the Trinity, revealed in Christ, the ontological structure underlying the constant tradition of the Church that the ultimate Christian vocation is to love one another. One can find the application of *Gaudium et spes* §24 to the Christian life throughout his papal writings. This sincere, total gift of self is a mark of human maturity in which the person expresses himself in freedom grounded in the truth, in love, and in generous service to one's neighbor.[56] This truth of the sincere self-gift is manifested *par excellence* by Christ in his passion and death.[57] This paschal

---

[54] See Karol Wojtyła, *Sources of Renewal: The Implementation of the Second Vatican Council*, trans. P. S. Falla (New York: Harper & Row Publishers, 1979), 61. "Truth and love" here are references to the Trinitarian *communio*; the processions of the eternal Word and the eternal Gift of Love.

[55] John Paul II's lodestar in this anthropology is *Gaudium et spes* §24, a paragraph which is one of his most oft cited texts and one that is crucial for understanding his anthropology. In commenting on this paragraph, the then Archbishop of Kraków clearly spells out this view:

> Man's resemblance to God finds its basis, as it were, in the mystery of the most holy Trinity. Man resembles God not only because of the spiritual nature of his immortal soul but also by reason of his social nature, if by this we understand the fact that he "cannot fully realize himself except in an act of pure self-giving." In this way "union in truth and charity" is the ultimate expression of the community of individuals. This union merits the name of communion (*communio*), which signifies more than community (*communitas*). The Latin word *communio* denotes a relationship between persons that is proper to them alone; and it indicates the good that they do to one another, giving and receiving within that mutual relationship.

(Wojtyła, *Sources of Renewal*, 61).

[56] See John Paul II, Apostolic Exhortation on the Formation of Priests in the Circumstances of the Present Day *Pastores dabo vobis* (March 15, 1992), *AAS* 84 (1992), 657–804 (Boston: Pauline Books and Media, 1992), §44.

[57] See John Paul II, *The Trinity's Embrace*, 107.

gift of self is the new law. For Christians it is the *sine qua non* expression of total self-gift in charity, following the pattern of the crucified Christ.[58]

The marital covenant also demonstrates this call to a total self-gift, as John Paul II deduces from the text of Genesis 2:23–25. The man and woman each give themselves to the other and accept the other as a gift. In looking at it from the perspective of the first woman, in her self-donation she rediscovers herself when she is received and accepted "in the way in which the Creator willed her, namely, 'for her own sake,' through her humanity and femininity; she comes to the innermost depth of her own person and to the full possession of herself when, in this acceptance, the whole dignity of the gift is ensured through the offer of what she is in the whole truth of her humanity and in the whole reality of her body and her sex, of her femininity."[59] This is a reciprocal exchange of whole persons, body and soul, femininity and masculinity. It is an exchange in which each person gives himself and receives the other not as a possession but in purity and innocence, that is, as a gift.[60]

The elements of fatherhood which we will explore in the remainder of this work have now been introduced. The marital covenant is the foundational relationship for the human person, as we will see. It is the foundation for the formation of each person coming into the world, for societal flourishing, and for understanding the human person. Fatherhood in every form has reference to this covenant. Moreover, total self-giving love which has its foundation in the Trinity and is most perfectly manifested in the life of Jesus Christ begins to be understood especially in married life. These truths are essential for understanding the male person—his masculinity and masculinity's fulfillment in fatherhood.

This vocation to salvific love in marriage and parenthood is possible only in Christ. The man of redemption is called to live his entire life like Christ, but he cannot possibly do so without Christ. For his anthropology of redemption, St. John Paul II again returns to Christ. He begins with St. Paul's analogy of Christ as the "new Adam" who has restored man to his lost likeness, after its having been distorted by sin. Following the Council of Chalcedon, it is the very fact that Christ assumed a complete human nature, rather than absorbing it, that man's great dignity has been manifested.[61] He has entered into a new created order through Christ's reforging the broken link in the chain that had previously united man to

---

[58] See John Paul II, *The Trinity's Embrace*, 135.
[59] *Man and Woman*, 196–97.
[60] See *Man and Woman*, 196.
[61] See *Redemptor hominis*, 8.

his Creator.[62] Only in Jesus Christ is man capable of receiving and returning the infinite love of the Father, because Jesus is the personal (hypostatic)
union of God and Man.

Restoration of communion between God and man required the Son's
infinite love to bridge the infinite rupture. Yet, Christ's human love was
also required; it was man who had to return himself to God. In Jesus
Christ we have finite, human love perfectly conformed to infinite, divine
love which allows man to love infinitely.[63] Man united to his Redeemer,
becoming one flesh with him, is inserted into this hypostatic order and
now has the capacity to love perfectly, to love infinitely by following his
Redeemer's example and conforming his love, aided by sanctifying grace,
to divine love. In the order of redemption, man can now fulfill himself by
being transformed in Christ, allowing him to love with Christ's love.[64]

THE HUMAN PERSON, RELATION, AND THE *ANALOGIA ENTIS*

St. John Paul II's broad employment of the analogy of being for understanding the human person is unmistakable, as we have seen. Among
the varied contemporary philosophies of human personhood, there are
two which can contribute to a metaphysical account of St. John Paul's
description of human personhood, particularly as an analogy between the
human and divine persons.[65] The first is the so-called Augustinian view,
in which "person" is primarily relational, and the second is referred to as
the Thomist conception, where "person" is primarily substantial. While
there may be differences of emphasis between them, they are in fact complementary as both (at least implicitly) depend upon the *analogia entis* to
hold that human personhood is at once inherently relational and ontologically permanent. Some employ the term "subsisting relation" for the
human person to identify the analogy (i.e., similarity and difference) from
the divine persons who are "subsistent" relations.[66]

---

[62] See *Redemptor hominis*, 8.

[63] See *Redemptor hominis*, 9.

[64] See *Redemptor hominis*, 10.

[65] See John Grabowski, "Person: Substance and Relation," *Communio* 22 (1995): 139–63,
for a helpful summary of five contemporary philosophies of human personhood.

[66] "Subsisting relation" has a variety of definitions among those who define human personhood in relational terms. The phrase seems to have been coined by Jean Galot, S.J., in
Who is Christ? A Theology of the Incarnation (Chicago: Franciscan Herald Press, 1981),
299. It is meant to be distinguished from the divine persons who are subsistent relations;
the human person rather is a substance which is relational by its very nature. This is

John Grabowski says that Karol Wojtyła is the "best known proponent" of the Lublin school, which looks at the person as subject.[67] In
discussing Wojtyła's *Person and Act*, Grabowski believes that Wojtyła holds
the Thomist understanding of person. In other words, "when applied to
God person denotes subsistent relations which differentiate the Persons
of the Trinity . . . [but for man, personhood] is not purely relational."[68]
According to Grabowski, this approach "still indicates individually subsisting subjects whose unity with one another can provide only an image of
the oneness of nature in the trinitarian communion of Persons."[69] While
Grabowski does not include John Paul II among those who explicitly
indicate that the human person is a "subsisting relation" or a "hypostatic
relation," there are other scholars who are willing to go further.[70]

Mary Shivanandan argues that Wojtyła's anthropological conception
of reflexive consciousness and, as John Paul II, his theological formulation of original solitude together reflect a relational understanding of the
human person that corresponds to the concept of "subsisting relation."[71]
In her review, Shivanandan cites other authors who have the same conception of human personhood, but finds that W. Norris Clarke's rereading of
the Thomist concept of person seems to be the most significant articulation of it. Clarke accords to Étienne Gilson the credit for recognizing that

---

not the more radical relational view of scholars such as Alistair McFadyen, *The Call to
Personhood: A Christian Theory of the Individual in Social Relationships* (Cambridge UK;
New York: Cambridge University Press, 1990); Elaine L. Graham, *Making the Difference:
Gender, Personhood and Theology* (London: Mowbray, 1995), and Vincent Brümmer, *The
Model of Love: A Study in Philosophical Theology* (Cambridge: Cambridge University
Press, 1993) who all seem to deny that one can be a person outside of his relation to
others. Harriet Harris says that "Brümmer and Graham mean . . . [that] persons can exist
only in relation to other persons. Graham goes further than McFadyen or Brümmer by
making a 'non-realist' claim that 'human nature is contingent and contextual'" (Harriet
A. Harris, "Should We Say That Personhood Is Relational?" *Scottish Theological Journal*
51 [1998]: 215).

[67] Grabowski, "Substance and Relation," 154.

[68] Grabowski, "Substance and Relation," 155. This I take to mean that human persons are
not "relations of opposition" as Thomas Aquinas calls the divine persons.

[69] Grabowski, "Substance and Relation," 156.

[70] See Grabowski, "Substance and Relation," 162. However, in private e-mail correspondence he confirmed that he thinks "it is possible to read the pope in these terms though I
don't think that the language is his" (John S. Grabowski, e-mail to author, June 1, 2004).

[71] See Mary Shivanandan, *Crossing the Threshold of Love: A New Vision of Marriage in the
Light Of John Paul II's Anthropology* (Washington, DC: Catholic University of America
Press, 1999), 146. Shivanandan describes a "new view" of person as relation, indicating
that John Paul II shares this conception of the human person.

St. Thomas finds the movement of a being from potency to act to be the source of its fulfillment.[72]

Clarke points to Gilson's statement: "Not: to be, then to act, but: to be is to act. And the very first thing which 'to be' does, is to make its own essence to be, that is, 'to be a being.' This is done at once, completely and definitively. . . . But the next thing which 'to be' does, is to begin bringing its own individual essence somewhat nearer its own completion."[73] Clarke says that the inherent "dynamism of being as overflowing into self-manifesting, self-communicating action, is clear and explicit in St. Thomas."[74] However, thanks to Gilson's insights, one can see the implied "corollary that *relationality* is a primordial dimension of every real being, inseparable from its substantiality. . . . *To be* is to be *substance-in-relation*."[75] Shivanandan finds that John Paul II's anthropological view of the human person corresponds exactly to this Gilsonian-Thomist rereading.

A review of John Paul's writings corroborates Shivanandan's analysis. The human person as a subsisting relation most certainly corresponds with his thinking. Nevertheless, one must add that he is clearly familiar with this terminology for the Trinitarian persons. In his Wednesday catecheses *God the Father and Creator*, he says that the persons of the Trinity are "subsisting" relations who are relational in their very essence. Significantly, here he has the opportunity to draw the analogy between divine and human persons in terms of relationality, but he does not.[76] Rather, he emphasizes human relationality in terms of potency and act.

---

[72] W. Norris Clarke, "Person, Being, and St. Thomas," *Communio* 19 (Winter 1992): 601–18.

[73] Étienne Gilson, *Being and Some Philosophers* (Toronto: Pontifical Institute of Mediaeval Studies, 1952), 184, cited in Clarke, "Person, Being, and St. Thomas," 605.

[74] Clarke, "Person, Being, and St. Thomas," 607.

[75] Clarke, "Person, Being, and St. Thomas," 607.

[76] John Paul II says:

> The relations which distinguish the Father, Son and Holy Spirit, and which really relate them to one another in their same being, possess in themselves all the richness of light and life of the divine nature, with which they are totally identified. They are "subsisting" relations, which by virtue of their vital impulse go out to meet one another in a communion in which each is completely open to the other. This loving communion is a supreme model of the sincerity and spiritual liberty which should characterize human interpersonal relations, which are always so far removed from this transcendent model. In this regard the Second Vatican Council observed: "The Lord Jesus, when he prayed to the Father, "that all may be one . . . as we are one" (John 17:21–22) opened up vistas closed to human reason, for he implied a certain likeness between the union of the divine Persons, and the unity of God's sons in truth and charity. This likeness reveals that man,

Another way of describing relationality is to say that the human person is a metaphysically concrete individual, but one who has a potency to fulfill himself through action. The manner in which he must act in order to fulfill himself is in accord with the Trinitarian archetype (i.e., total self-gift), but his fulfillment is a potency which he must actualize in freedom. Nevertheless, as we have already seen, Karol Wojtyła also presents the relationality of the human person in *Person and Act*, especially in terms of participation. Participation characterizes the person as a relational being who finds his fulfillment as a person not only through his interpersonal relationships but in the way he relates to the rest of creation.

Participation also includes the multiplicity of relations within a society of persons, relations with the subpersonal world, and, of course, most fundamentally in his relationship to God.[77] While this is not explicitly Clarke's *substance-in-relation*, it corresponds to it. But as Wojtyła says here, his primary concern in *Person and Act* (and this is true of his subsequent papal writings also) is the human person who acts (and actualizes) in and through his interpersonal relationships. His project is not to develop further a metaphysical account of the human person. It is not, then, a surprise to find that he relies upon the *ratio* of relation without articulating the metaphysics. Moreover, his discussion of vocation also suggests an affinity with Clarke's formulation .

Before his papacy, Wojtyła placed the person's relationships with others in terms of a potency to which one must freely and authentically respond if he is to actualize this potency of personhood. Authentic relationships should be seen as vocations to which we must respond appropriately. Wojtyła says that "man's vocation as a person in a community constitutes the basis of the reality of the People of God."[78] This calling necessarily conforms to man's structure as a person. The social dimension of the human person resides in man's deepest interiority. It is the human person's innate social dimension that beckons man to communion, that is to a relationship of selfless love (i.e., self-gift) with others. It is innate because man is made in the image of a Trinitarian God who creates his creatures for, and calls them into, an

---

who is the only creature on earth which God willed for itself, cannot fully find himself except through a sincere gift of himself" (GS 24).

(John Paul II, *God, Father and Creator*, 183–84).

[77] See Karol Wojtyła, *The Acting Person*, trans. Andrezej Potocki, ed. A. Tymieniecka, Analecta Husserliana: The Yearbook of Phenomenological Research, vol 10 (Dordrecht, Holland: Reidel Publishing Co., 1979), 175.

[78] Wojtyła, *Sources of Renewal*, 114–15.

analogous family communion.[79] This structure of relationality is rooted in the human person's identity as created in the image of a Trinitarian God.

John Paul explicitly states that in "the human person considered in his 'relationality,' we find a vestige of God's own mystery revealed in Christ as a substantial unity in the communion of three divine Persons."[80] Further, he sees this as the council fathers' thinking, which gave rise to *Gaudium et spes*' declaration that man is the only creature on earth that God willed for his own sake, and so man cannot fully find himself except through a sincere gift of himself.[81]

This relational likeness to God, which constitutes the personal character of the human being, is found in divine revelation (see Gen 2:18) indicating that man is not intended to exist as a solitude. He is made to exist as a unity of the two, meaning he is made to exist in relation to another human person. This primordial relation is fulfilled especially in a mutual relationship of woman and man in marriage. Because man is made in the image of the God of relations, John Paul teaches that this primeval marital union is a proleptic revelation of the triune God who is a living communion of the Father, Son, and Holy Spirit.[82]

John Paul II sees a corollary to the Genesis passage which suggests that the human person is not fully able to realize the potential God has created in him if he remains "alone" (see Gen 2:18). Man can only become who God calls him to become by existing with and for another.[83] The human person simply cannot fully actualize the potency of his personhood for which he was created outside of authentic relationships with others. Other aspects of the Genesis text also show an affinity of John Paul's thought with Clarke's formulation.

In his catecheses, John Paul II repeatedly states man's inability to either live or develop his potential if he fails to relate himself appropriately to others, owing to his innermost personal structure as a social being.[84] He finds the Genesis creation narrative specifies that creation then becomes an indication for the human person of his inherent relationship with the

---

[79] See John Paul II, Post-Synodal Apostolic Exhortation on the Vocation and the Mission of the Lay Faithful in the Church and in the World *Christifideles laici* (December 30, 1988), *AAS* 81 (1989), 393–521, §40.

[80] John Paul II, *The Trinity's Embrace*, 288–89.

[81] See John Paul II, *The Trinity's Embrace*, 289, where he quotes *Gaudium et spes*, §24, which is in turn alluding to Luke 17:33.

[82] See *Mulieris dignitatem*, §7.

[83] See *Man and Woman*, 182.

[84] See John Paul II, *God, Father and Creator*, 232.

world, with another (the man-woman relationship), and with others like them.[85] Man's relational dimension is unique to the human person inasmuch as he is made in the image of God.[86]

Again, all this seems quite compatible with Shivanandan's description of the relational person, even if it does not make explicit use of the term "subsisting" for the relational dimension of human personhood. John Paul rather uses the term "constitutive" for the manner in which relationality impacts the person.[87] It would seem that with regard to the relational character of the human person, the term "constitutive" reasonably indicates the same meaning as the term "subsisting," but without the attending confusion occasioned by the nuanced terminology of "subsisting" used for the human person and "subsistent" for the divine persons. In either case, the theological implications for the human person which St. John Paul II articulates would be the same.

---

[85] See John Paul II, *God, Father and Creator*, 232.

[86] See John Paul II, *God, Father and Creator*, 232.

[87] For example, John Paul II says:

> When God-Yahweh says, "It is not good that the man should be alone" (Gen 2:18), he affirms that, "alone," the man does not completely realize this essence. He realizes it only by existing *"with someone"*—and, put even more deeply and completely, by existing *"for someone."* This norm of existing as a person is demonstrated in Genesis as a characteristic of creation precisely by the meaning of these two words, "alone" and "help." They point out how fundamental and constitutive the relationship and the communion of persons is for man. Communion of persons means living in a reciprocal "for," in a relationship of reciprocal gift. And this relationship is precisely the fulfillment of "man's" original solitude.

(*Man and Woman*, 182). The penultimate sentence above is the English translation for the original Polish: "One właśnie wskazują na to, jak podstawowa i konstytutywna dla osoby jest relacja i komunia osób." Here the Polish term translated in English as "constitutive" is *konstytutywna*. *Konstytutywna* is a feminine singular adjective here, and in this text it modifies *relacja* (relation) and *komunia* (communion). It describes, along with *podstawowa* (rightly translated as "fundamental," "basic," "elementary"), the nature of relation for man. In this sentence, *konstytutywna* defines this relation as being that without which the person is not the same. The degree to which relation constitutes the person must be read within the philosophical framework of John Paul II's thought. We have already seen that he is intimately grounded in a Thomist philosophy of being. In this context, relation takes on ontological significance. "Beings" are what they are and one can know what they are through the identifying features of their nature. Without these "constitutive" features, they cease to "be themselves." From this it is apparent that *relacja* (relation) is an attribute of the being of person (*osoby*), such that in some way relation constitutes the person. In other words, relation is a necessary aspect of a person's intrinsic makeup, lest a person be mistaken for some other being.

Consequently, we see that human persons are analogous to divine persons. However, unlike the divine persons who are subsisting relations, human persons are not relations of opposition. This way of being a relation belongs only to the infinite nature. Still, human personhood belongs to the category of being of relation, the real relations we introduced in the second chapter. These real relations constitute human personhood.[88] Personhood has an ontology that is neither substance nor pure accident but something different, something "quasi-substantial," if you will. There are a growing number of contemporary scholars who also see that this is a necessary consequence of the *analogia entis*. The ontology of human personhood belongs to the category of being of relation, analogous to the divine persons.[89]

RELATION AS A NEW CATEGORY OF BEING IN THE CREATED ORDER

To sum up the relational aspect of personhood, one sees that for John Paul II the acting person is one who ontologically fulfills himself in relation to others, or more precisely, one who fulfills himself through his authentic relationships.[90] He refers to this relational dimension philosophically as participation and theologically as a total self-gift. This relational dimension is a constitutive aspect of man because he is made in the image of

---

[88] See *Man and Woman*, 182.

[89] See, for example, Joseph Ratzinger, "Concerning the Notion of Person in Theology," *Communio* 17 (Fall 1990): 443–47; Galot, *Who Is Christ?*; Angelo Scola, *The Nuptial Mystery*, trans. Michelle K. Borras (Grand Rapids, MI: William B. Eerdmans Publishing Company, 2005), 26–31; Philip A. Rolnick, *Person, Grace and God* (Grand Rapids, MI: William B. Eerdmans Publishing Company, 2007), 194–96; David L. Schindler, "Being, Gift, Self-Gift: Reply to Waldstein on Relationality and John Paul II's Theology of the Body," *Communio* 42 (Summer 2015): 221–51; Clarke, "Person, Being, and St. Thomas," 601–18. However, we should note that rather than an account of relation as a third way of being alongside substance and accidents, Clarke wants to call this new way of being a "system." See W. Norris Clarke, *The One and the Many: A Contemporary Thomistic Metaphysics* (Notre Dame, IN: University of Notre Dame Press, 2001), 135–37.

[90] John Paul II seems to use the terms, "relation," "relationship," "relational," and "relationality" to refer to the category of metaphysical relation and relationship interchangeably. Sometimes he appears to use the terms to indicate both simultaneously. I will continue to make the distinction between relation and relationship. However, I will use the terms "relational" and "relationality" in a similar manner to the author. They will indicate that there is a metaphysical relation which gives rise to the opportunity for a volitional relationship.

the Trinitarian God, and its practical example is manifested in Jesus Christ and, most perfectly, in his paschal self-donation.

From the preceding discussion, one can now see that the action to which each person is called is nothing less than a disinterested love for others. John Paul II's conception of the "human act" is one in which it has an ontological and perduring effect on the human person. Love then, must be ontologically efficacious.[91] This ontological aspect of love should be no surprise given John Paul II's consistent Thomism, his Trinitarian view of the human person, and his integral philosophy. Again, given John Paul's extensive use of the *analogia entis*, it is hard to avoid these implications.[92]

In *Familiaris consortio,* he teaches that man is created in the image of God and so he is called into existence by means of love and is created for love.[93] God's very existence is a communion of love and so man has the inherent capacity, as well as the task and obligation, to live in a communion of love with God and other men. Thus, he finds that every human person has the primary vocation to love, and because he is a hylomorphic (i.e., a composite unity) spirit, he is called to love by means of his body and soul. In this way, the body is incorporated into spiritual love.[94]

Because the Trinity is constituted in love, there can be no other possibility for creatures who are made in God's image and likeness if they are to reach their authentic fulfillment. However, unlike God, for human beings love is not one eternal act. Human love is an *actus humanus*. The human person must freely give his love in repeated, temporal acts of the will. In God, love is his being. For man, love is his calling. Nevertheless, love is an ontological necessity for the fulfillment of the person, but because it is a vocation, each individual can either embrace it in truth or he can reject it.[95]

The significance of relations for the human person can be found in

---

[91] "Only a person can love and only a person can be loved. This statement is primarily ontological in nature, and it gives rise to an ethical affirmation. Love is an ontological and ethical requirement of the person. The person must be loved, since love alone corresponds to what the person is. This explains *the commandment of love*, known already in the Old Testament (see *Deut* 6:5; *Lev* 19:18) and placed by Christ at the very centre of the Gospel '*ethos*' (see *Matt* 22:36–40; *Mark* 12:28–34). This also explains the *primacy of love* expressed by St. Paul in the First Letter to the Corinthians: 'the greatest of these is love' (see 13:13)" (*Mulieris dignitatem*, §29).

[92] For further implications of the *analogia entis* for St. John Paul's account of human personhood, see David H. Delaney, "The Nuptial Mystery, the Sacrament of Marriage and John Paul II's *Man and Woman He Created Them*," *Antiphon* 18, no. 1 (2014): 69–105.

[93] See John Paul II, Apostolic Exhortation on the Role of the Christian Family in the Modern World *Familiaris consortio* (November 22, 1981), *AAS* 74 (1982), 114–37, §11.

[94] See *Familiaris consortio*, §11.

[95] Time and again, John Paul proclaims this truth:

the philosophical discussion of self-fulfillment through participation. It begins with the fact that because he is made in the image of God, man is capable of, and in fact is made for, a relationship with God (*homo est capax Dei*). Man's spiritual nature has the capacity for intellectual knowledge as well as free will and thereby has the capacity for freedom of action. Created in this way, he is in a unique relationship with God from the very beginning.[96] But this relationship is a calling structured by the *analogia entis* in created order, one to which man must say yes or no.

John Paul thus indicates that man has the capacity to accept God and his will along with the capacity to oppose it.[97] This relationship to which man is called is a covenant relationship, a relationship of family unity in and through Christ.[98] This covenant unity, in which man has a family relationship with God, reflects the ecclesial dimension of that relationship. The "essential source" of this unity is the Trinity.[99] It also points to an

---

"This likeness reveals that man, who is the only creature on earth which God willed for its own sake, cannot fully find himself except through a sincere gift of self" [*Gaudium et spes*, §24]. With these words, the Council text presents a summary of the whole truth about man and woman—a truth which is already outlined in the first chapters of the Book of Genesis, and which is the structural basis of biblical and Christian anthropology. Man—whether man or woman—is the only being among the creatures of the visible world that God the Creator "has willed for its own sake"; that creature is thus a person. Being a person means striving towards self-realization (the Council text speaks of self-discovery), which can only be achieved "through a sincere gift of self." The model for this interpretation of the person is God himself as Trinity, as a communion of Persons. To say that man is created in the image and likeness of God means that man is called to exist "for" others, to become a gift.

(*Mulieris dignitatem*, §7). And again: "Yet there is no true love without an awareness that God 'is Love' and that man is the only creature on earth which God has called into existence 'for its own sake.' Created in the image and likeness of God, man cannot fully 'find himself' except through the sincere gift of self. Without such a concept of man, of the person and the 'communion of persons' in the family, there can be no civilization of love; similarly, without the civilization of love it is impossible to have such a concept of person and of the communion of persons" (John Paul II, Letter to Families *Gratissimam sane* [February 2, 1994], AAS 86 [1994], 868–925 [New Hope, KY: Urbi Et Orbi Communications, 1994], §13). This notion of love as an act of the whole person, femininity or masculinity included, which goes to the very core of the human person, will be revisited in parts 2 and 3.

[96] See John Paul II, *God, Father and Creator*, 233.

[97] See John Paul II, *God, Father and Creator*, 234.

[98] See John Paul II, *God, Father and Creator*, 234–35.

[99] John Paul II, *A Catechesis on the Creed*, vol. 4, *The Church: Mystery, Sacrament, Community* (Boston: Pauline Books and Media, 1998), 78.

eschatological dimension which is the simultaneous call to eternal participation in the divine life.[100]

The ontological character of man's personhood and his fulfillment
through man-acts of love (or the contrary choice) in the manner of participation all demand that personhood possess its constitutiveness in some
category of being. Substance and accidents are inadequate to the task.
If person were a substance, it would corrupt the unity of human nature.
Moreover, Chalcedonian dogma prohibits the human person being univocal with the human substance, for this would result in the same error as
the one made by post-Cartesian, hypostatization-of-consciousness philosophers, namely, a form of Nestorianism.

If personhood were accidental, it would undermine the dignity of the
human person. It would be a metaphysical contradiction to assert that an
accident possessed his nature and that all of man's other accidents inhered
in an accident (i.e., the person). Nor can an accident account for the continuity, stability, and concreteness of the person. Finally, it would seem that
accidental being alone is inadequate to account for the ontological change
that comes about through man-acts and the perfection of oneself and one's
eternal beatitude, on the one hand, or his personal annihilation and everlasting damnation on the other. Rather, it would seem the *analogia entis*
points us to the obvious solution.

The analogy of being requires the relational person to exist in a category of being analogous to that of the divine persons. St. Thomas implied
as much, even if he did not pursue the matter in terms of Aristotelian categories. I believe he did not do so because it is obvious that human persons
cannot be relations of opposition among one another; they do not subsist
as such. But then the *analogia entis* recognizes there is not univocity
between created and uncreated relations/persons. The coherency of John
Paul II's compelling anthropology demands "relation" as the person's category of being, a new category in the created order. It also resolves a number
of christological and anthropological perplexities.

---

[100] See John Paul II, *The Church*, 43.

Part Two

SEX DIFFERENCE
AND MASCULINITY

CHAPTER 5

The Body and Sex

Fatherhood is a vocation and state of life for the human male, so it is important that we have an adequate account of John Paul II's view of sex difference in general and of masculinity in particular.[1] We need to include

---

[1] The use of terms to refer to sex difference requires some comment. Possible terms include "sex difference," "sex," and "gender." The most common contemporary term would seem to be "gender." However, this term is not without fatal ambiguities. A brief summary of the etymology of the term will disclose the problem. Webster's Dictionary shows that the term makes its way into modern English from Middle English, having been borrowed from the Old French *gendre*. The Old French word was formed "with an unhistoric -d- from the [Latin] genus, generis" (*Webster's New Universal Unabridged Dictionary, Second Edition* [1983], s.v. "gender"). The *Pocket Oxford Latin Dictionary* (1995) gives the meaning of "genus" as: "birth, descent, origin; offspring; race; kind; family; nation; gender." M. H. Ibrahim says that the Sophists, in the fifth century BC, recognized a tie between the grammatical sense of gender and sex. See *Grammatical Gender: Its Origins and Development* (Paris: Maton, 1973), 15. This was shown in Protagoras's delineation of the masculine, feminine, and neuter genders in Greek. In modern English, its common usage in a sexual context is a relatively recent phenomenon. *The American Heritage Book of English Usage* (1996), s.v. "gender/sex," says that gender was traditionally used primarily in the grammatical sense, but recently has become more commonly used for sex-based categories. It further describes a distinction that has arisen among anthropologists who have been influenced by the feminist discussion. Specifically, the term "sex" is reserved "for reference to the biological categories of male and female and [the term gender for] social or cultural categories." However, *American Heritage* also points out that while a majority agree with this distinction, a sizable minority do not. In general terms, it finds in a survey that about half of their panel of experts follows the above distinction; about a third reverse it, and the remainder allow the terms to be used interchangeably. Some feminist theologians further clarify that the sociological distinction for "gender" is nothing more than a social construct. See, for example, Elizabeth Johnson, *Truly Our Sister: A Theology of Mary in the Communion of Saints* (New York: Continuum, 2003), 20–21. Thus, the ambiguity in meaning, especially in the context of anthropology, which is now heavily influenced by the feminist social construct theory, suggests caution in employing

in this account their interrelationship with human personhood. One of the primary sources for uncovering his understanding of these topics is his Wednesday theology of the body catecheses. While many good summaries of these catecheses are available, a more focused analysis here will provide an outline of John Paul II's view of sex difference and its relation to human personhood.[2] In these catecheses John Paul presents sex difference discovered via the body, in the context of four major horizons. The first of these horizons is the state of original innocence. The significance of this horizon is its ability to expose what authentically belongs to human nature before it suffers the consequences of original sin. This dimension is prehistorical, meaning that only glimpses of it are now possible in lived experience.

By contrast, the second horizon is postlapsarian. John Paul II considers the contrast between the prelapsarian and postlapsarian horizons important because it provides a control in his analysis of lived experience.[3]

---

the term "gender." John Paul II does not appear to observe any distinction between the terms "gender" and "sex." I have not found him to use "gender" in his Wednesday catecheses on his theology of the body. The term John Paul II selects in these catecheses is the Polish *płeć*, rendered in the Italian translation as *sesso*, for which "sex" is the appropriate English translation, and this is what we find in both English translations of *Man and Woman*. However, there is ambiguity here as well. "Sex" in English as we have said, can imply simply the biological aspects of sex difference. Furthermore, "sex" has also relatively recently been employed to refer just to the act of copulation. However, none of these capture the meaning of *płeć*. Rather, *płeć* refers to sex difference. In other words, the Polish word encapsulates all of that which makes the human person a man or woman. However, it does not readily succumb to a biological reduction. Rather, for John Paul *płeć* means the fullness of the human person as male or female, to include every aspect of their physiology, psychology, emotions, etcetera, which is affected by their masculinity and femininity. Because of the attendant ambiguities associated with the terms "gender" and "sex," I will generally employ "sex difference" in referring to that which is meant by the Polish *płeć* when there is a chance for confusion. If it is unambiguous, I will follow the standard of the English translation of the Wednesday catecheses and employ the term "sex."

2 For good general summaries of these catecheses from the perspective of sex difference see Jean-Guy Pagé, "La pensée de Karol Wojtyła (Jean-Paul II) sur la relation homme-femme," *Laval théologique et philosophique* 40, no. 1 (February 1984): 3–29, and Mary Shivanandan, *Crossing the Threshold of Love: A New Vision of Marriage in the Light of John Paul II's Anthropology* (Washington, DC: Catholic University of America Press, 1999), 94–170.

3 I use "control" here in the sense of scientific comparison studies where one establishes a baseline for the normal state of the object under study. One uses the "control" to ensure he knows what is normal and what is atypical in the object of study. In the case of human personhood, the baseline state for what authentically belongs to human nature is prelapsarian man.

In other words, the contrast between prelapsarian and postlapsarian experience is the means by which one can distinguish between that which is authentically human versus that which is a consequence of fallen human nature. The Christian experience, though, which by definition is postlapsarian, is to be distinguished from the postlapsarian non-Christian experience because of the Christian's access to sanctifying grace. This brings us to the third horizon—the horizon of redemption. Christian experience in this horizon is a foretaste of eternal life, to which God calls everyone. The fourth horizon is the eschatological. This is the horizon of the resurrection of the body in which all of the consequences of the fall for the human person and for sex difference are definitively overcome.

In addition to these four horizons, John Paul employs five primary hermeneutical concepts which he uses in order to bring out the significance of personhood and its sex in his analysis of the body.[4] The first three comprise the so-called "original" triptych of original solitude, original unity, and original nakedness. The other two are hermeneutics of the gift and the spousal meaning of the body. We will address the first three in separate sections and the last two under the section on original nakedness. While all five concepts are proper in a certain way to the prehistorical horizon, they can still can be detected by, and all are yet normative for, historical man (i.e., fallen man). However, the effects first of sin and subsequently of redemption have a considerable influence on the way in which one experiences his body and sex. Therefore, we will consider the historical experience of sin and the effects of redemption in a final section. Before beginning an examination of the theology of the body proper, we should briefly describe John Paul's methodology in these catecheses. John Paul II's metaphysics is foundational to his theology of the body. He recognizes the soul to be the substantial form of the body, such that, together, out of the body-soul composite, arises the human person. It is the person who possesses his body-soul unity and who is the acting subject. The body is the visible manifestation of the person who is both body and soul; therefore, we can say that the person expresses himself through the body. John Paul justifies much of his exegetical approach to Genesis, in which he uses a plurality of tools to explore what divine revelation has to say about the human person and his sex, by this fact that the body expresses the person.[5]

---

[4] These are hermeneutical concepts inasmuch as they are ways in which man experiences his body and his sex in relation to the world and to other creatures in the world.

[5] John Paul II often justifies his study of the human person through his body in the biblical texts by means of his phenomenological method (see, e.g., *Man and Woman He Created Them: A Theology of the Body*, trans. Michael Waldstein [Boston: Pauline Books and

The most prominent and, for many, confusing tool in these theology of the body catecheses is his phenomenological method. It is quite apparent in his exegesis that he is phenomenologically analyzing the lived experience of our first parents as mediated by the Genesis narrative. However, he conducts his method in the context of the entire canon of Scripture while drawing upon two thousand years of magisterial teaching.

This approach allows him to find in a phrase like "the man and the woman 'were naked' but still 'did not feel shame,'" an understanding that he is seeing a description of the state of our first parents' consciousness.[6] In other words, he knows from the magisterium certain aspects of the state of original innocence and the consequences of the fall. Using these magisterially taught truths along with theological illuminations of them, he can apply the tools of phenomenology to the inspired description of this primordial event in the Genesis text.[7]

This explains why he can validly come away with more vivid insights than would someone who is employing solely historical critical exegetical methods. Employing his methodology he finds the first parents' experience of conscious is specifically a "reciprocal experience of the body . . . [describing] the man's experience of the femininity that reveals itself in the nakedness of the body and, reciprocally, the analogous experience of masculinity by the woman."[8]

Adam and Eve experience their sex difference and its meaning by means of their bodies. Eventually, the procreative capacity of their bodies will further reveal to them the meaning of their bodies, their entire persons, and their mutual love in the context of parenthood. John Paul says that everyone has the mystery of his own beginning within himself, and

---

Media, 2006], 171f., 175f., 198f.). Hylomorphism, or more particularly, the fact that the body reveals the soul and the person, is fundamental to his rationale (see *Man and Woman*, 171). The hylomorphic rationale for studying the human person and his sex by means of the body logically follows because the body, rather than being simply the disconnected result of random mutations influenced by environmental factors, is a result of the soul giving it its existence, shape, and animation. Therefore, because the body is the visible dimension of the person, it can licitly be used to infer invisible aspects of the person.

[6] *Man and Woman*, 171.

[7] This is not to say that the author necessarily understands Genesis to be a literal recounting of a prehistorical event. In fact, he describes this as a mythological (but not fictional) rendering of an event which expresses a transcendent, universal truth. Therefore, in the Genesis texts, generally speaking, the inspired author is expressing in primitive language, certain truths about God and man. See *Man and Woman*, 138n4.

[8] *Man and Woman*, 171.

that this mystery is tightly connected to his awareness of the procreative meaning of his body.[9] While he admits that Genesis 4:1–2 does not make explicit the relationship between the procreative and spousal meaning of the body, the fact that Adam knew Eve and that she conceived and bore a son shows at the very beginning of his time on earth, man quickly became aware of his body's procreative meaning.

John Paul II finds that "*masculinity contains in a hidden way the meaning of fatherhood and femininity that of motherhood.*"[10] The cited passage comprises a concise summary of John Paul's method for his reading of sex and the body. Namely, it is through a phenomenological study of divine revelation that the author discovers a theology of sex and its significance for the human person.[11] He begins this seminal study with an analysis of Adam's experience of being unique and alone in the world, which John Paul calls "original solitude."

ORIGINAL SOLITUDE

In part 1 we saw that original man experiences original solitude in his naming of the animals (see Gen 2:20). In this event, the man finds that none of the animals is suitable as a "helper." The man discovers that he is different from the animals; in fact, he is different from the entire visible world. He is different in that unlike the animals, he has a unique personal identity which is incommunicable with any other creature. In other words, the man finds that he is not reducible simply to an individual sample from a larger species. In the first man's discovery of original solitude, John Paul finds evidence of the features of personhood we identified in part 1, namely uniqueness, unrepeatability, and incommunicability.

The first man's experience of his original solitude also brings to him the experience of self-knowledge, free will, and self-determination.[12]

---

[9] See *Man and Woman*, 217.

[10] *Man and Woman*, 217.

[11] John Paul makes use of the entire canon of Scripture (yet certainly not *in toto*) in his theology of the body catecheses. However, he does focus on some primary texts, including the Genesis creation narratives (Gen 1–2), the Sermon on the Mount (Matt 5), St. Paul's teachings on the human body (e.g., Rom 8:5–23; 1 Cor 6:13–20; 12:18–25; Gal 5:13–23; Eph 5; 1 Thess 4:3–8; etc.), Jesus's exposition on divorce (Matt 19), the Song of Songs, and Tobit.

[12] In John Paul II's analysis, man's self-knowledge is his understanding of himself "as the first and fundamental manifestation of humanity" (*Man and Woman*, 150). The man comes to this "first self-definition" as he finds himself alone before God (*Man and Woman*, 150). John Paul understands that the man develops this self-knowledge contemporaneously

We identified these same attributes of human personhood, free will and self-determination, in part 1. Man is able to experience these things because he is made in the image of God. Through the man's body, he is aware of being alone. However, original solitude is not solely found through a phenomenological reading of Adam's experience: it is also explicit in the text.[13] God-Yahweh says, "'It is not good that man' (male) 'should be alone; I want to make him a help similar to himself' (Genesis 2:18)."[14] Based on this text, John Paul II calls man's solitude "a fundamental anthropological issue."[15] This implies a second dimension within original solitude.

Original solitude has two dimensions. First, the man is in solitude by virtue of the bodily aspect of his nature which he discovers in his naming of the animals. However, his lack of a suitable partner implies a second dimension resulting from the male-female relationship.[16] John Paul II finds that the man receives early indications of this relationship. The process of naming the animals reveals to the man that he is in some sense a partner with God who allows him the dignity of participating in his dominion over creation. As a partner with the Absolute, the man finds himself in a relationship with Another. But it is precisely as God's partner that the man finds he is alone among the other creatures; there is no other like him. This aloneness, together with his relationship with the Absolute, prepares the man for the discovery of his capacity for a relationship with another human person. The experience of original solitude itself paves the way for a communion of persons. However, this experience of solitude does not belong solely to the man as masculine but also to the woman as feminine.

---

with his discovery of the rest of the world, signified by the naming of the animals. The man becomes conscious of himself as a person who is not like the other animals because he has a unique partnership with God (he is the only creature who participates in the naming of the animals) and because there is none like him among the animals that is suitable as his helpmate. This consciousness of his personhood comes especially through his awareness of his body (see *Man and Woman*, 152f.). John Paul's analysis discovers that the body plays a dual role for the human person. It reveals the man to himself, but it is also the medium through which he expresses himself, and it enables him to act as a person with free will and self-determination. Free will and self-determination carry the same meaning as in *Person and Act*, which was discussed in part 1. While the author seems to use the terms somewhat interchangeably, there is a distinction. He says that free will is a feature of man through which he can choose good or evil. One determines himself as authentically fulfilled or distorted as a person because of the ontological effect of his choices (see *Man and Woman*, 151).

[13] See *Man and Woman*, 151.
[14] Quoted in *Man and Woman*, 146–47.
[15] *Man and Woman*, 148.
[16] See *Man and Woman*, 147.

John Paul says that it is only from within the man and woman's dual solitude that the ability arises for living a special relationship based upon reciprocity.[17] He finds this is indicated by the fact that "the first man ('ādām) . . . is defined as 'male' ('îš) only after the creation of the first woman. Thus, when God-Yahweh speaks the words about solitude, he refers with them to the solitude of 'man' as such and not only to that of the male."[18] Original solitude reveals the person, and so original solitude also opens the way to the discovery of sex difference through the body. The stage is set by the fact that although man is alone as a person, he is open to relationships with others. This is, again, based upon his relationship with the Absolute. The fundamental anthropological "problem" of original solitude can only be answered by another self, a self who is different from the animals or anything else in visible creation.

ORIGINAL UNITY

John Paul calls original solitude an "anthropological issue," but he does not mean thereby that it is entirely a problem to be eliminated. His aloneness in the body is a fact of his nature. However, since the dimension of original solitude arises from being made for others (and, in particular, he is made for the male-female relationship), the apparent problem of aloneness can be resolved in what the author calls the key concept of "original unity." John Paul shows that, as with original solitude, one also finds original unity in the book of Genesis. God-Yahweh, seeing that it is not good that the man is alone, puts him into a deep sleep. While the man is asleep, the woman is created from a rib removed from the man so that man wakes up male and female. John Paul II points to the fact that he is the 'ādām (man-inclusive) before the sleep but afterward he is 'îš (man-male) to the 'iššāᵇ (woman). John Paul explains that this deep sleep has the biblical connotations of non-being, indicating that the Genesis narrator is suggesting that man ('ādām) is being returned to the moment of creation.[19]

---

17 See *Man and Woman*, 163.

18 *Man and Woman*, 147.

19 See *Man and Woman*, 159. John Paul II explains in an endnote that the Hebrew term for sleep, *tardemah*, "appears in Sacred Scripture when, during deep sleep or immediately afterward, extraordinary events are about to happen (see Gen 15:12; 1 Sam 26:12; Isa 29:10; Job 4:13; 33:15)" (*Man and Woman*, 159n14). However, in this case the author believes that God brings about a "re-creation" of humanity. In describing "non-being" in the context of sleep in Genesis 2:23 he theorizes: "Perhaps, . . . the *analogy of sleep* indicates here not so much a passage from consciousness to subconsciousness, but a specific

Solitary man emerges from this moment as a dual unity of man and woman. John Paul finds that when he wakes, the man exhibits almost jubilation for the first time. Previously there was no reason for joy, at least among his relationships with the animals, because there was not yet another like him. But now there is delight in finding a "second self." John Paul II finds this ebullience manifested in the words spoken by the man upon seeing the woman.[20] In this text we see the body revealing the person, and here the body also reveals him as male and female. There are two ways, two complementary ways, of being a body—as a male and female.[21] They are complementary not just in a physical sense, but they are two complementary dimensions of self-consciousness and self-determination. These are simultaneously two complementary modes of being aware of the body's meaning.[22] This complementarity is an important aspect of the man-woman relationship, a relationship which has its origins in the Trinity.

We saw in part 1 that the basis for the relationality of the human person is located in the fact that man is made in the image of the Trinitarian God.[23] He is a *communio personarum*.[24] In God, the divine relation is the

---

return to non-being (sleep has within itself a component of the annihilation of man's conscious existence), or to the moment before creation, *in order that the solitary 'man' may by God's creative initiative reemerge from that moment* in his double unity as male and female" (*Man and Woman*, 159). For further development of this idea, see Deborah Savage, "The Nature of Woman in Relation to Man: Genesis 1 and 2 Through the Lens of the Metaphysical Anthropology of Aquinas," *Logos* 18, no. 1 (Winter 2015): 71–93.

[20] See *Man and Woman*, 161.

[21] See *Man and Woman*, 166.

[22] See *Man and Woman*, 166.

[23] As noted earlier, the term "relationality" reflects the fact that the human person is relational. In other words, man exists in relation to others and is created for volitional relationships. The definitions for the terms "relation" and "relationship" from part 1 continue to apply throughout this work.

[24] John Paul in fact believes that man reflects the image of God more in a unity of persons than in solitude:

Man became the image of God not only through his own humanity, but also through *the communion of persons*, which man and woman form from the very beginning. The function of the image is that of mirroring the one who is the model, of reproducing its own prototype. Man becomes an image of God not so much in the moment of solitude as in the moment of communion. He is, in fact, "from the beginning" not only an image in which the solitude of one Person, who rules the world, mirrors itself, but also and essentially the image of an inscrutable divine communion of Persons.

(*Man and Woman*, 163). At first, this might seem to contradict St. Augustine (see *De trinitate* XII, 8–9) and St. Thomas (see *ST* Ia, q. 93). However, this is not necessarily the

same as the divine essence.[25] Furthermore, each relation which signifies the person (i.e., paternity, filiation, procession/spiration), is a divine person. The Father is his paternity, the Son his filiation.[26] The divine persons are subsistent relations. Subsequently, the revealed analogy between God and man implies that, for John Paul, relation in some manner constitutes what it means to be a human person. He finds this implication demonstrated in the Genesis text in which he discovers the concept of original unity. Sex difference is the foundation for the discovery of this complementary relationality.[27] John Paul II finds in the biblical formulation of Genesis 2:23 that the woman as feminine and the man as masculine discover themselves as such in the presence of one another. The subsequent verse shows that this gift of sex difference allows the man and the woman to become "one flesh" through their bodies.[28]

In marriage, they become a *communio personarum* through the body. The marital *communio* is a reflection of the Trinitarian *communio*, in whose image man—male and female—is made. The spouses most intimately and completely manifest this *communio* in marital intercourse that is open to procreation.[29] However, John Paul makes it clear that this unity

---

case. St. Augustine rejects marriage as an analogy in the context of his "mental image," where he was looking for an absolute image of God in terms of substance and processions. Thus, only non-substantial distinctions within one monolithic substance would suffice. However, John Paul II is not working in terms of an analogical processional model, per se. He is thinking relationally in terms of fruitful love in a communion of persons. St. Thomas on the other hand, would seem to explicitly agree with John Paul II. In his reply to article 3 in the above citation from the *Summa*, St. Thomas says that while angels are more perfect images of God than man is absolutely, man is more perfect an image relatively, in that man proceeds from man by begetting.

25 See *ST* Ia, q. 28, a. 2.

26 See *ST* Ia, q. 33, a. 2, resp. obj. 1.

27 John Paul says: "On the level of man and in the reciprocal relationship of persons, sex expresses an ever-new surpassing of the limit of man's solitude, which lies within the makeup of his body and determines its original meaning" (*Man and Woman*, 167).

28 NB recall that John Paul II's use of the term *płec*, which in English is rendered "sex," does not draw a separation between a person's biological dimension and his psycho-social and spiritual dimensions. The author's philosophy of the concrete totality of the person sees all of these as unified, comprising the entire person.

29 I should note that the intimacy of Trinitarian love can be expressed in every human relationship ordered by selfless love. It can be expressed in the various manners appropriate to each particular relationship and through a continuum of degrees of intensity. However, in marriage the intimacy of Trinitarian love is expressed uniquely and more fully than in any other human relationship. It is expressed in every action throughout the marriage to the degree it conforms with selfless love. This is because the mode and degree of intimacy of persons necessary for procreative knowing and loving exclusive to marriage is

is not simply a biological necessity. Rather, if it is to reflect authentically its archetype—the Trinitarian *communio*—each person must freely and continually consent to the *communio* with the entirety of their persons. It is the whole person, in his self-possession, self-determination, and free will, who is called into this *communio personarum*.[30]

Another feature of original unity is that it is both a duality and a complementarity. It is a duality in that it is formed through a unity of two individual persons who lose nothing of their concrete individuality. It is a complementarity because both bring something to the unity that fulfills the other, and that the other did not possess in his individuality.[31] This *communio personarum* is based upon the complementarity of sex difference and is most fully expressed in marital intercourse that is open to fruitfulness, and so it also implies parenthood.

John Paul II indicates this when he says that "the unity about which Genesis 2:24 speaks ('and the two will be one flesh') is without a doubt expressed and realized in the conjugal act. The biblical formulation . . . indicates sex, that is, masculinity and femininity, as that characteristic of man—male and female—that allows them, when they become one flesh, to place their whole humanity at the same time under the blessing of fruitfulness."[32]

Mary Shivanandan provides a helpful summary of the author's view of the interplay among the body, sex, and parenthood in this *communio*

---

intimately bound to the complementarity of the couple who are united in their oath of commitment to the meaning of marriage. This complementarity and their mutual oaths to marriage permeate the entirety of their persons, and so permeate each and every act of selfless love. However, the fullness of expression of Trinitarian love is unique to marriage because this relationship alone can reflect the total self-giving love, which can bear fruit in the creation of a new person. This third person as the fruit of intimate knowing, borne as love, is objectively the fullness of the reflection of the Trinitarian archetype. But this is not to say that one may reduce the reflection to the marital act, though it may not be separated from it. That the marital act is a *sine qua non* for marital consummation reflects its uniqueness in manifesting Trinitarian love. The marital act is essential to completing the uniting of the spouses in marriage and so a marriage is consummated only through the marital act. The tradition of the marital debt suggests that while not strictly essential to the continuing life of a marriage, it is still of primary importance for flourishing marital intimacy when it is possible. Nevertheless, to say that the Trinitarian archetype is expressed and manifested most fully in the marital act need not imply that the intimacy of marital love is diminished in any way in the multitudinous manners of love expressed visibly or interiorly between spouses outside of the marital act.

[30] See *Man and Woman*, 167–69.

[31] John Paul II's understanding of complementarity will be further discussed later in the next chapter.

[32] *Man and Woman*, 167.

112

personarum: "John Paul II discerns in the biblical narrative different levels or layers of man's being, the deepest of which is his creation in the image of God, made visible in the body, then the duality of sex and lastly physical fertility. . . . Fertility is part of [the person's] bodily dimension in this world (although it will not be a factor in the eschaton) and implies an opening to parenthood."[33]

Original solitude identifies key features of the individuality of the human person, while original unity indicates the significance of his relationality. Original solitude reveals the human person, and this person always remains in some sense in solitude, even when in a unity of persons.[34] As a unity, there is no confusion or conflation of individual, concrete persons into a single person. Thus the dimension of original solitude which arises from human nature, particularly because of man's body, always remains.

Original unity indicates that relation to and relationship with others is part of what it means to be a human person. This is most intimately manifested in the marital *communio personarum*, itself uniquely reflective of the Trinitarian *communio personarum* in marital intercourse which is open to fruitfulness. Original unity is ordered by masculinity and femininity and implies fatherhood and motherhood. Prelapsarian man experienced this marital *communio personarum* in a way that is now irretrievable. John Paul II discusses this in the third panel of his triptych, "original nakedness."

ORIGINAL NAKEDNESS

The body reveals the person, his sex, and God's call to form a *communio personarum*, all of which together imply a call to fatherhood and motherhood. The primordial experience of the body reveals another dimension of personhood. John Paul II discovers original nakedness in the verse "and the man and his wife were both naked, and were not ashamed" (Gen 2:25). Original nakedness is descriptive of the condition of the first parents' consciousness whereby they reciprocally experience each other's masculinity and femininity in their bodies.[35] It is indicates the state of consciousness in which the man and woman "see and know each other . . . with all the peace of the interior gaze, which creates precisely the fullness of the intimacy

---

[33] Shivanandan, *Threshold of Love*, 105.
[34] Man's solitude, again, is an inherent result of his being a body (see *Man and Woman*, 167f.).
[35] See *Man and Woman*, 171.

of persons."[36] Their experience of original nakedness revealed to them another important aspect of the relational person, which John Paul II calls the "spousal meaning of the body."[37]

Original nakedness describes the fact that the spousal meaning of the body was immediately evident to man in the horizon of original innocence. The spousal meaning of the body is closely associated with the *communio personarum* and its analogy to the Trinitarian processions.[38] John Paul states that the communion of persons "means living in a reciprocal 'for,' in a relationship of reciprocal gift. And this relationship is precisely the fulfillment of 'man's' original solitude."[39]

This is a gift of the whole self, arising from love, and to which the body is a witness.[40] The body's masculinity and femininity is the first and primary sign of the body's meaning in terms of fruitful self-donation and man's awareness of this fruitful self-donation in terms of a gift.[41] John Paul takes care to point out that the awareness of this gift comes from the fact that they were naked.[42] In other words, it is the visible, genital complementarity of masculinity and femininity, which is the first source of this awareness.[43] But the spousal meaning of the body also encompasses the free giving and reception of each other as whole persons. A prerequisite of this freedom is self-mastery and self-possession.[44]

Before the advent of concupiscence, a consequence of the fall, man was free of concern with respect to the way he regarded, and was regarded by, others. Concupiscence changes this situation irrevocably. John Paul II calls the resulting threat "immanent shame."[45] After the fall, the man becomes reductive in his look at the body of the woman and vice versa. This look

---

[36] *Man and Woman*, 178.

[37] See *Man and Woman*, 178ff.

[38] See *Man and Woman*, 183ff.

[39] *Man and Woman*, 182.

[40] See *Man and Woman*, 183.

[41] See *Man and Woman*, 183.

[42] See *Man and Woman*, 185; here he cites Genesis 2:25.

[43] John Paul II's hylomorphic anthropology rescues this paraphrase from the charge of reductionism. Because the soul is the form of the body, the soul expresses its masculine or feminine aspects, which are in the spiritual realm, as bodily masculinity or femininity. In other words, the body can legitimately express the fullness of personhood, including body and soul, though it does not exhaust the mystery of the person. Thus, it is legitimate for him to assert that the body in its sex is the first indication of the complementarity of the other person, as masculine and feminine, without limiting complementarity to the body.

[44] See *Man and Woman*, 186f.

[45] *Man and Woman*, 242ff.

tends to objectify the body and therefore the person, and to reduce the other to his or her sexual value.

In the state of original innocence this reduction does not occur. One sees the other through the body to be another self, one who is created by God for his own sake.[46] In this horizon of innocence there is a mutual experience of the person through the body due to the person's complete freedom arising from his self-possession and self-mastery. Because of this freedom, the spousal meaning of the body is thereby manifested in the free and sincere gift of self to the other, in love. This dimension allows for the simple manifestation of the body's spousal meaning.[47] This meaning is that the body, and so the person, is apposite for love.

In the horizon of original innocence, man participates in God's vision in that he sees and accepts the other as a person through his or her body. The man and woman can serenely look upon each other without the temptation to reduce the other to his or her sexual value. They can know each other in the authentic intimacy of persons precisely because in this state, there is no threat in the body to seeing and accepting the entirety of the other person.[48] Each person sees and accepts the other as a subject, as another self, and not an object. This is possible because, as John Paul describes it, there is a "perfect system of powers" within the person.[49] There is not yet a disruption between the corporeal faculties, such as the various appetites, and the spiritual faculties of the soul.

The phrase "perfect system of powers" describes the situation of man prior to concupiscence. Concupiscence is man's experience of the manifold imperfections in this system of powers after the fall. It forever changes the way each person experiences the other sex in his naked body. John Paul II summarizes the spousal meaning of the body in terms of original nakedness in the following statement: "The original meaning of nakedness corresponds to the simplicity and fullness of vision in which their understanding of the meaning of the body is born from the very heart, as it were, of their community-communion. We will call this meaning 'spousal.'"[50]

John Paul II uses the phrase "hermeneutics of the gift" to express

---

[46] See *Man and Woman*, 195.

[47] John Paul II says: "The human body, with its sex—its masculinity and femininity—seen in the very mystery of creation, is not only a source of fruitfulness and procreation, as in the whole natural order, but contains 'from the beginning' the 'spousal' attribute, that is, *the power to express that love in which the human person becomes a gift* and—through this gift—fulfills the meaning of his being and existence" (*Man and Woman*, 185–86).

[48] See *Man and Woman*, 178.

[49] See *Man and Woman*, 391ff.

[50] *Man and Woman*, 178.

the depth and truth found in the concepts previously discussed: original solitude, unity, and nakedness.[51] Hermeneutics of the gift arises from man's creation in the image of a Trinitarian God, and with the Trinitarian processions in which each person subsists in the total gift of himself to another divine person. Total self-gift establishes the archetype for authentic anthropology because man is made in the image of total self-gift. The gift of creation arises from an overflowing of this divine self-giving. The heart of the mystery of creation is the fact that creation *ex nihilo* presupposes creation as a gift. Consequently, the gift archetype also extends into all of creation. The world is a gift to man and, conversely, because man is made in the image of God, man is a gift to the world.[52]

John Paul also sees in the Genesis text the discovery by the first man and woman that they are gifts to each other. The body, in its masculinity and femininity, their bodily sex, indicates to them that they are to be self-gifts to one another. Therefore, it is through the body that man is made aware of the gift and is open to its acceptance. This offering and acceptance of the self as a gift must be made freely and disinterestedly, and it must be mutual. While the hermeneutics of the gift is most perfectly expressed in marriage, it also applies to other relationships. For example, the child is a gift from God, he is a gift in himself, and he is also a gift of the spouses to each other. This hermeneutics of the gift is briefly articulated in *Gaudium et spes* §24, but John Paul II deepens and expounds upon it in his theology of the body. It is a key concept for his entire theological anthropology.

Perhaps it would be helpful here to summarize the interplay among these five concepts. Original solitude and original unity are concepts proper to the first man and woman, but they still have application for Christian anthropology. They are not now experienced in the way that was possible before sin, but with effort, one can still partially glimpse them in the experience of historical man.[53] Nevertheless, original nakedness was lost with the fall and will never again be experienced.[54] But the spousal

---

[51] See *Man and Woman*, 179.

[52] See *Man and Woman*, 181.

[53] John Paul II clearly sees that the capacity to overcome concupiscence requires sanctifying grace, and thus to consistently glimpse the spousal meaning of the body requires a "life according to the Spirit" (see *Man and Woman*, 358). However, he seems to think that historical man prior to the horizon of redemption (and therefore before access to sanctifying grace) also had at least some capacity to partially glimpse the spousal meaning of the body through his own efforts (see *Man and Woman*, 202, 216, 258, 259–60).

[54] This will be true even in the eschaton and is due to the fact that original nakedness is

meaning of the body "*has not been totally suffocated . . . by concupiscence, but only habitually threatened.*"[55]

The body's spousal meaning is still operative in fallen man, but now one must discern its presence and meaning through the distorting lens of concupiscence. In fact, John Paul argues that historical man's experience of shame is a testament to the endurance of the spousal significance of the body.[56] In a manner similar to the body's spousal meaning, in this dispensation of redemption, one can achieve the demands of the "hermeneutics of the gift" only with difficulty, but the ability to achieve it is necessary because it is fundamental to man's fulfillment as a person. Concupiscence's broad and insidious effects on the human person impel John Paul to emphasize that the experiences of historical man remain under the influence of sin.

THE HISTORICAL EXPERIENCE OF SIN

In the horizon of original innocence, man, as male and female, experienced a purity of heart and did not give rise to the easy reduction of another person to a mere object. John Paul II states that original man and woman "had the reciprocal *awareness of the spousal meaning of their bodies*, in which the freedom of the gift is expressed and *the whole inner richness of the person as subject is shown.*"[57] However, with the fall man enters a new state of existential experience. They are "two antithetical situations, . . . two different states of human nature, '*status naturae integrae*' (state of integral nature) and '*status naturae lapsae*' (state of fallen nature). . . . [This] has a fundamental significance for the theology of man and for the theology of the body."[58] This point is significant. If Christian anthropology is to avoid

---

primarily prelapsarian man's experience of the body before his knowledge of shame. While in the eschaton there will certainly be no concupiscence, the eschatological experience will still be distinct from original nakedness. In the eschaton there will be the knowledge of "shame" overcome by grace rather than the experience of original nakedness when shame was completely unknown. In this way, shame is indeed, an insuperable barrier (see *Man and Woman*, 199).

[55] *Man and Woman*, 258.

[56] "Historical man" is roughly equivalent to the "man of concupiscence" (see *Man and Woman*, 265). Both terms refer to man in his fallen state, but the author uses the former to refer to postlapsarian man in his fallen experience, while the latter is used primarily in the context of man as subject to sexual concupiscence.

[57] *Man and Woman*, 202.

[58] *Man and Woman*, 140–41.

false conclusions, it must take into consideration that historical man's experiences are an amalgam of authentic and fallen experiences.

In addition to a change in the disposition of forces within man, sin has altered the relationship between God and man, as well as between man and creation. Original sin's altering of these relationships must be viewed in terms of man being created in the image and likeness of God. From such a reference, one sees sin as the mystery of man's descent into "non-likeness" to God. This non-likeness presents itself as evil throughout world history.[59]

Because sin is non-likeness to God, it deforms the operation of the proper order of creation, especially in man who is created in his image and likeness.[60] Sin has the effect of reducing the human person, restricting and even preventing his personal fulfillment.[61] Sin especially distorts the relationship between man and woman.[62] As a result, it requires significant effort on the part of woman and man if they are to reconstruct the meaning of mutual, total self-gift.[63] We must be attentive to the effects of the insuperable barrier sin introduced, and which now divides man from original innocence.[64] What was lost was man's ability for effortless, disinterested self-gift. What we now experience is almost a different relation between the body-soul in which such giving comes only with considerable effort. One must understand this difference if he is to follow John Paul's exegesis of original man's experience in the state of original innocence found in the Book of Genesis.[65]

Original sin changes the interior experience of both the man and the woman because original grace has been lost.[66] John Paul II finds the *dis-graced* body-soul union acknowledged in Adam's words: "I was afraid, because I was naked" (Genesis 3:10).[67] Man's first sin inaugurates a new experience, that of shame.[68] Shame is primarily the experience of fear with respect to the body. Yet, it is a composite experience of fear, an inclination

---

[59] See John Paul II, Apostolic Letter on the Dignity and Vocation of Women *Mulieris dignitatem* (August 15, 1988), AAS 80 (1988), 1653–1729, §9.

[60] See John Paul II, *A Catechesis on the Creed*, vol. 2, *Jesus, Son and Savior* (Boston: Pauline Books and Media, 1996), 19.

[61] See *Mulieris dignitatem*, §9.

[62] See *Mulieris dignitatem*, §10.

[63] See *Man and Woman*, 216.

[64] See *Man and Woman*, 199.

[65] See *Man and Woman*, 198–99.

[66] See *Man and Woman*, 202.

[67] See *Man and Woman*, 243–44.

[68] *Man and Woman*, 238–46. John Paul II distinguishes two types of shame: cosmic and immanent. The former is a fear created by man's ruptured relationship with creation. The

to protect oneself, and the urge for authentic communion with another. It is fear that one's integral value as a human person is threatened by the other because one feels the almost insuperable temptation to do just that to him. At the same time, it is an unarticulated inclination to protect oneself from such a reduction by separating oneself from the other. And the experience is also one of the natural urge for authentic communion, that is, through a selfless, reciprocal gift with the other. Shame, therefore, is foundational for developing an ethos for all interpersonal relationships, and this is especially true for relationships between men and women.[69]

So while shame is first a negative experience, it has a positive purpose. To some degree, it motivates one to actions which militate against the proclivity to objectify the other sex. In other words, shame evokes a derived need for corporeal privacy.[70] One of its manifestations is sexual modesty, which is a conclusion also drawn in the Pauline epistles.[71] However, the author is careful to note that shame is not a positive ontological change to human nature. Rather, it is due to the deprivation of grace and its resulting effects in the spiritual realm.[72] Man needs shame as a sort of remedy to the sexual objectification of one person by another which occurs in the age of concupiscence. When one consents to this inclination to objectify another, reducing him to his sexual value, it is called lust.

Concupiscence in this context is the proclivity toward objectifying the other, that is reducing him to his sexual value.[73] Again, John Paul II

---

latter is the shame I will discuss here, the fear that the other person will see one as an object rather than as a person.

[69] See *Man and Woman*, 173–74. See Karol Wojtyła, *Love and Responsibility*, trans. Grzegorz Ignatik (Boston: Pauline Books & Media, 2013), 158–77, for a more fully developed discussion of the experience of shame, which is used throughout these Wednesday audiences. Even though approximately two decades separate the initial appearance of these two works, *Love and Responsibility* still represents John Paul's thinking about shame.

[70] See *Man and Woman*, 368ff.

[71] John Paul writes: "Shame seems to be at the . . . basis of what the Apostle says in 1 Corinthians: 'Those members of the body that we think less honorable we clothe with the greater reverence, and our unpresentable members are treated with greater modesty' (1 Cor 12:23). Thus one can say that from shame is born 'reverence' for one's own body, a reverence that Paul asks us to keep (1 Thess 4:4)" (*Man and Woman*, 347).

[72] See *Man and Woman*, 250ff.

[73] See *Man and Woman*, 244. John Paul II distinguishes between biblical (or theological) concupiscence and psychological desire. The former is a state that is due to man's fallen nature. It is not sinful in itself, but when it rises to the level of an intentional act in which the person gives his consent to the inclination, it becomes morally sinful. The latter is an appetitive response of one person to the sexual value of another person of the opposite sex; i.e., sexual desire. The desire is prior to conscious willing. There is no free will

uses his phenomenological analysis of the Genesis text to reveal that concupiscence has entered the world, and that shame arises because of it.[74] Concupiscence attacks postlapsarian man's self-gift, threatening to deprive him of the dignity he finds in his sincere self-giving. To the degree one gives into this temptation, he degrades his authentic participation in a mutual gift of persons by means of his bodily masculinity or femininity.

Concupiscence breaches the dimension of mutual self-giving and challenges the truth that God willed each person for his own sake. Giving into concupiscent temptation is lust, which means one succumbs to a depersonalized objectification of the other by means of that person's body.[75] Lust means that a person as a subject has been replaced by his objectified body. Sexual objectification reduces one person to just a body for another, male for female and female for male.[76] Such a reduction eviscerates the male and female relationship of its fullness. It no longer expresses a full, personal, selfless communion. Reduction means that the complementary relationship is now unilaterally established by sex difference.[77] Lust means a loss for the person.

Historical man no longer possesses the same interior freedom for self-giving that he experienced in the state of original nakedness. It is not that the freedom is lost, but exercising this freedom becomes a task, and for most it can be an arduous one. Because the spousal meaning of the body is associated with this freedom, one can experience it only when he masters and possesses himself. Because self-control can overcome a concupiscent desire, it shows that man's reduction of another person to a sexual object is willful. Consent to reduction is not the same as being unaware of the sexual value of the other. The mystery of the person is infused with his sex; the two cannot be separated, and so to appreciate a person necessarily includes being aware of his sex. Lust is free consent to the reduction of the other for the satisfaction of one's own sexual desires.[78]

This interiority of lust, rooted in the person's free will, has many implications for interpersonal relationships, including changing "the very

---

involved in the experience of psychological desire. Psychological desire existed even prior to the fall but did not lead to temptation until the arising of biblical concupiscence.

[74] See *Man and Woman*, 242. He says: "The words of Genesis 3:10, 'I was afraid, because I am naked, and I hid myself,' confirm the collapse of the original acceptance of the body as a sign of the person in the visible world."

[75] See *Man and Woman*, 259.

[76] See *Man and Woman*, 259.

[77] See *Man and Woman*, 259.

[78] See *Man and Woman*, 287–88.

intentionality of the woman's existence 'for' the man";[79] the reduction of "the wealth of the perennial call to the communion of persons, the wealth of the deep attraction of masculinity and femininity, to the mere satisfaction of the body's sexual 'urge'";[80] the distortion of "the other person ... [to] an object for the possible satisfaction of his own sexual 'urge'";[81] and the loss of the "*character of communion of persons in favor of the utilitarian function.*"[82] The antithesis of biblical concupiscence is purity in thought and deed, and especially sexual purity. One can overcome the effects of biblical concupiscence with purity, but one can achieve purity only via a habitual exercise of free will in cooperation with grace, in favor of the spousal meaning of the body.[83]

Original sin ruptures relationships. John Paul II turns again to Genesis to explain the effects of original sin on relationships. The effects begin with man's relation to creation. These include man's need to "toil" for his subsistence (see Gen 3:17–19), the multiplication of pain in childbirth (see Gen 3:16), and the entry of death into the world (see Gen 3:19).[84] Not only is man's relation to creation changed but "division and rupture" extend to his interpersonal relationships. Experience confirms for us that our sin has damaged relationships within the family, in the professional environment, and in the social milieu.[85]

Of particular significance is the effect of this damage to the relationship between man and woman which he studies in the Genesis story of the fall, taking special notice of the passage "*Your desire shall be for your husband, and he shall rule over you*" (Gen 3:16). Here God warns the couple that their communion is now under continual peril due to the consequences of their original sin. The woman faces greater disadvantage in the newly deficient state in which they find themselves because the man will too often succumb to temptations to use his masculine gifts for self-serving interests. He will tend to use his greater strength to dominate his wife. John Paul is firm on the point that God is not commanding the man to rule over the woman but rather that he is warning them of the

---

[79] *Man and Woman*, 298.

[80] *Man and Woman*, 298.

[81] *Man and Woman*, 298.

[82] *Man and Woman*, 298.

[83] See *Man and Woman*, 342ff.

[84] See *Mulieris dignitatem*, §9.

[85] See John Paul II, Apostolic Exhortation on Reconciliation and Penance in the Mission of the Church Today *Reconciliatio et paenitentia* (December 2, 1984), *AAS* 77 (1985), 185–275, §13.

challenges they will face. The man's misuse of his gifts will undermine the experience of stability and equality in the relationship.[86]

Sin, via concupiscence, introduces instability in the exercise of relational equality between the husband and wife. This instability is a threat to the authentic expression of their complementary gifts, which is required for an authentic communion of persons. If one side dominates, the relationship is put in imbalance. While the woman may feel the disruption more deeply when the man dominates her, the man also suffers the attenuation of his dignity in his very act of domination. John Paul implies that the man less often realizes his loss of dignity, which bodes ill both for marriage and for society. Because the man is less likely to recognize that a problem exists, he is less likely to address it.

While Genesis 3:16 refers immediately to marriage, it also contains an implicit wider reference to the manifold spheres of public life. One finds the effects of ruptured interpersonal relationships between the sexes in all circumstances in which women are put at a disadvantage or discriminated against because of their femininity. These consequences logically follow because Revelation itself testifies to the fact that both man and woman derive their dignity and, therefore, their equality from the same source.[87] Whether it is in marriage or society, the fact that both man and woman are made in the image of God militates against any sort of injustice.

Any breach of the marital relationship has an impact at the level of the person's sex and so it impacts one's entire personhood as a man or as a woman. With the advent of sin, what had been the locus of complementary unity—their sex difference—now is experienced, and even understood, as a factor in "the mutual opposition of persons."[88] Their sex which is the very source of man's and woman's ability to become a *communio personarum* is now experienced as an obstacle. John Paul II sees this in the woman and man's hiding their nakedness from one another after the fall, almost instinctively manifesting shame.[89]

This concealment of the sexual attributes which determine them as male and female "shows the fundamental lack of trust, which already in itself points to the collapse of the original relationship 'of communion.'"[90] Cosmic shame or fear replaces the unconditional trust underlying the

---

[86] See *Mulieris dignitatem*, §10.
[87] See *Mulieris dignitatem*, §10.
[88] See *Man and Woman*, 248.
[89] See *Man and Woman*, 243, in which he comments on Gen 3:7.
[90] *Man and Woman*, 249.

mutuality of the male-female relationship found in original innocence.[91] Their sex which once revealed one person to the other now becomes the cause, or at least the focal point, of the opposition between man and woman, husband and wife.

Shame is revealed in the man's and the woman's almost instinctive desire to cover their bodies' sexual differences. John Paul's phenomenological analysis detects, along with shame, a sort of alienation of the person from his own body and from sex. While shame gives rise to interpersonal alienation based upon sex difference, this opposition does not annihilate conjugal union and its procreative fruits. However, it does import into this union the negative ramifications of concupiscence.[92]

Sex difference may be a source of conflict for historical man, but the fall does not destroy the possibility of a true *communio personarum*. Concupiscence makes authentic *communio* more difficult to achieve, but the capacity for experiencing the full communion of original innocence has been irretrievably lost.[93] The mutual alienation historical man now experiences called shame, reciprocally felt by each sex, can only be properly understood from the perspective of original innocence.

In the original state it was the sexed body that enabled and revealed through the conjugal act, the unity that man and woman could achieve as spouses becoming "one flesh" (Gen 2:24).[94] The body of historical man, in its sexuality, still bears witness in and through sexual shame, to the loss of the primordial conviction that the body and its sex is "'that substratum' of the communion of persons."[95] While this witness is the function of shame, it does not always protect against lust. When lust does occur, it manifests itself in ways which differ for the sexes.

Even if Scripture hints that the man is more susceptible to lust in a certain sense, the woman is equally susceptible to concupiscent desires. They both are also subject to shame. While shame reaches to the depths of both men and women, they experience it differently.[96] Because they experience concupiscence and shame differently, their experiences of the marital relationship and its distortions in the dominion of sin similarly differ. These differences are important for understanding sex difference and the relationships between man and woman, especially in marriage.

---

[91] See *Man and Woman*, 250.
[92] See *Man and Woman*, 251–52.
[93] See *Man and Woman*, 246–48.
[94] See *Man and Woman*, 246–48.
[95] See *Man and Woman*, 248.
[96] See *Man and Woman*, 255.

Lust contributes to the urge for the man dominate the woman. The woman, because of her experience of domination, responds with a desire to modify the natural structure of the union in order to free herself from the man's dominance. More precisely, if the man's inclination to domination triumphs, the result is that the union deteriorates into one of possession rather than one of mutual, disinterested gift of self. In response, the woman will be tempted to take on a comparable disposition in an attempt to dominate the man, ending in instability and conflict.[97] This in turns leads to a direct threat to the woman's femininity. John Paul warns that even in rightfully opposing unjust male domination, women must not try to remedy the situation by adopting masculine modes of behavior. To do so will lead to woman's deformation and loss of authentic femininity.[98]

The fact that a woman can "deform and lose" an aspect of her constitution as a person already strongly suggests that sex difference must have an essential relation to the "being" of the human person.[99] Here, however, the author points to the threat particularly to the woman, due to her reaction to the masculine threat of domination. This seems to be due to the fact that power is usually met with power, and so the woman, in her own defense, is likely to adopt the same disordered masculine manifestations of power which are used against her. Rather than domination, the ethos established by the Creator requires a reciprocity between wife and husband. The husband is to offer himself to his wife and in turn respond by receiving her as the gift of a whole person, in the image of the *communio personarum*. Therefore, living in accord with this ethos is the only way that the man and the woman in the marriage covenant will perfect themselves.[100]

John Paul II shows that the paschal event provides a remedy for the

---

[97] See *Man and Woman*, 254.

[98] See *Mulieris dignitatem*, §10.

[99] John Paul II's view of sex difference and personhood is shared by Paul Evdokimov, an Orthodox theologian who finds that Marxist attempts to masculinize women were actually attempts to create new anthropological types beyond male and female (see Paul Evdokimov, *Women and the Salvation of the World* [Crestwood, NY: St. Vladimir's Seminary Press, 1994], 267). The integrated nature of Orthodox thinking is in agreement with John Paul's integral view of the human person and sex difference. Paradoxically, though, in rejecting the idea that sex difference is essential for human personhood, Elizabeth Johnson accuses John Paul of dualism. She believes that the idea originates from John Paul II's "new version of gender dualism" (Johnson, *Truly Our Sister*, 62). I will address her criticism when analyzing the adequacy of John Paul II's theology of fatherhood in part 4.

[100] See *Mulieris dignitatem*, §10.

fallen state and so Christ's redemption of mankind is of great significance for historical man.[101] The problem for historical man is that the body is no longer subject to the spirit as it was before the fall. In fact, the body seems to have within it "a constant hotbed of resistance against the spirit."[102] Concupiscence puts at risk one's moral integrity, an integrity grounded in the human person's constitution. Bodily concupiscence is a particular threat to one's self-mastery and self-possession, but it is through these that one forms himself as a human person. Therefore, concupiscence poses an ongoing danger to one's personal flourishing. "[T]he man of concupiscence does not rule his own body in the same way, with the same simplicity and 'naturalness' as the man of original innocence. The structure of self-possession, which is essential for the person, is in some way shaken in him to the very foundations."[103]

With the fall, appetites and emotions now compete with reason for satisfaction. Christ has provided a remedy for this, a gift, which one must accept in order to receive. But although this gift of sanctifying grace does not remove the problem of concupiscence. It does provide the capacity to overcome it.[104] So even in the horizon of redemption "the discovery of the spousal meaning of the body was to cease being for [man and woman] a simple reality of revelation and of grace. Yet, this meaning was to *remain as a task given to man by the ethos of the gift*, inscribed in the depth of the human heart as a distant echo, as it were, of original innocence."[105] Thus, concupiscence still poses a problem for seeing the spousal meaning of the body, but one that can now be overcome by achieving self-mastery through one's cooperation with grace.[106]

---

[101] John Paul II begins his discussion of this new horizon from Christ's words in the Sermon on the Mount: "Everyone who looks at a woman lustfully has already committed adultery with her in his heart" (Matt 5:28) (see *Man and Woman*, 322). He seems to present the "ethos of redemption" as temporally prior to the paschal event. However, as John Paul discusses "The Resurrection of the Body as a Reality of the 'Future World,'" he makes it clear that this dispensation is based upon man's access to grace. Only grace can make living in accord with this new ethos possible (see, e.g., *Man and Woman*, 355, 391ff.). John Paul does not mean to imply that the ethos of redemption, preached by Christ prior to his redemptive death and Resurrection, was possible prior to the sending of the Holy Spirit. While he is not always explicit about this, there is no evidence that he claims this new "ethos of redemption" is possible outside of man's renewed access to habitual grace.

[102] *Man and Woman*, 244.

[103] *Man and Woman*, 244.

[104] John Paul is clear that one never definitively overcomes concupiscence; it is always lurking, and so man is always in need of temperance and continence in order to master himself.

[105] *Man and Woman*, 202.

[106] See *Man and Woman*, 258.

The human heart is still the "battlefield between love and concupiscence."[107] Repeatedly succumbing to concupiscent desire results in lust becoming a vice. Vice reveals that the more the person allows concupiscence to dominate his free will, the less that person is sensitive to the body's spousal meaning.[108] This seems to be the lot of the man of concupiscence. Nevertheless, "*redemption restores*, in a sense, at its very root, *the good* that was essentially 'diminished' by sin and its heritage in human history."[109] Therefore, for those who are "in Christ," the reciprocal antagonism between man and woman due to original sin "is essentially overcome."[110] However, John Paul is explicit that this definitive overcoming in Christ must be realized in each human person by means of his cooperation with grace.

Cooperation with grace includes "the imperative of self-mastery, the necessity of immediate continence and habitual temperance. . . . The ethos of redemption is realized in self-mastery, that is, in the continence of desires."[111] Temperance is the means to self-mastery and the actualization of self-mastery is a prerequisite for the experience of freedom of the gift and of the spousal meaning of the body.[112] The ability to experience the freedom of the gift in this new horizon leads the author to declare that one receives, in a sense, himself and his body back again through his incorporation into Christ's redemption.[113]

The Son of God united a human body and soul to himself, and thereby raised the dignity of the body to a previously unattained level. This dignity, conferred through Christ's Incarnation and manifested *par excellence* in his resurrection, brings a new obligation to the new ethos—the obligation to cooperate with grace. John Paul illustrates this obligation by reference to Paul's exhortation to the Corinthians: "You were bought at a great price" (1 Cor 6:20).[114] It is a grave obligation to cooperate with the precious grace which he "bought" for each person. The Christian cooperates through his efforts to grow in virtue in order to arrive at the purity of heart demanded by this ethos of redemption.

---

[107] *Man and Woman*, 258.

[108] See *Man and Woman*, 258.

[109] *Mulieris dignitatem*, §11.

[110] *Mulieris dignitatem*, §11.

[111] *Man and Woman*, 324. By "self-mastery" John Paul means a habit, which has become part of the person through temperance and repeated acts of self-control, whereby the person has gained the freedom to act according to his reason.

[112] See *Man and Woman*, 324.

[113] See *Man and Woman*, 350.

[114] See *Man and Woman*, 350.

John Paul reminds us that this new horizon of redemption does not completely return man to original innocence. That has been forever left behind.[115] However, the new ethos which Jesus preached in his Sermon on the Mount is a summons to discover the manner of its recovery.[116] The human person cannot return to a prelapsarian experience because concupiscence remains. Nevertheless, he can experience authentic freedom of the gift because it has been made accessible by grace and self-mastery. John Paul sees Christ's call in the Sermon on the Mount as an appeal to the "man of concupiscence" to recall the "man of original innocence."[117] He considers this to be a realistic invitation on Christ's part.

The way to purity of heart is not through the abolition of conflict between man's concupiscent desires and his free will. Rather, "the inner man must open himself to life according to the Spirit, in order to participate in the evangelical purity of heart: in order to find again and realize the value of the body, freed by redemption from the bonds of concupiscence."[118] God has created man for purity of heart, and as such, this purity of heart is rooted in the interiority of the human person. Christ's call to a purity of heart is normative. Given John Paul II's hylomorphic vision of man's complex unity, it is no surprise that the body is fundamentally implicated in this call because the whole person, male and female, is called to fulfill himself through a sincere gift of self.

Man's freely given total self-gift is possible only for the one who achieves self-mastery and self-possession, and so one can achieve purity only through a mature temperance which the whole person has cultivated. It is in this manner that the mutual relations of woman and man, down to the way they look at each other, can be authentically recovered according to the spousal meaning of the body.[119] This is spiritual maturity, which is the fruit borne of cultivating a pure heart through temperance. Self-mastery is a task for the human spirit, and so the body in its sexuality is likewise a task. The task is to discover the spousal meaning as it is rooted in the body and sex, by means of a pure heart.[120]

The horizon of redemption will eventually give way in the eschaton, to the final resurrection. This final horizon also provides insight into the meaning of the human person and his body. John Paul explains that the

---

[115] See *Man and Woman*, 323.

[116] See *Man and Woman*, 323.

[117] See *Man and Woman*, 358.

[118] *Man and Woman*, 358.

[119] See *Man and Woman*, 359.

[120] See *Man and Woman*, 361.

body and spirit will regain their perfect harmony in the unity of body and soul only in the eschaton. The disruption of concord that historical man experiences between the material and spiritual aspects of his unified nature will finally come to an end. The eschatological unity of body and soul means that the spirit will have dominion over, and completely permeate the body. Furthermore, the spirit's "forces" will wholly permeate the body's "energies."[121] But John Paul clarifies that one cannot read this as a "definitive victory of the spirit over the body."[122] To do so would be to view the eschaton through a dualist anthropological hermeneutic.

Those with a dualist anthropology assert that human nature is the imprisonment of the soul by the body. John Paul by contrast, describes the eschaton as a return to the harmony that was disrupted in the dis-grace of original sin. So "the resurrection will consist in the perfect participation of all that is bodily in man in all that is spiritual in him. At the same time, it will consist of a perfect realization of what is personal in man."[123] The harmonization to be experienced in the eschaton will be the final perfection of grace acting on and throughout the human person and his nature.

This is what John Paul II calls divinization. Man is divinized by grace, which is nothing less than partaking of the divine nature (2 Peter 1:4). This fruit of face-to-face communion with God permeates the entirety of the human person, body and soul. John Paul emphasizes that this permeation of man with God happens to the subject (i.e., the person) because the reception of grace is the fruit of an encounter of the human person with the divine person of Jesus Christ.[124] The final state of saved man arises necessarily from John Paul II's integral anthropology. It is not just the soul which is "divinized" but the entirety of the human person, which includes both the spiritual and material aspects of man's unified nature.[125]

---

[121] See *Man and Woman*, 391.

[122] *Man and Woman*, 392.

[123] *Man and Woman*, 392.

[124] "*God's self-communication in his very divinity*, not only to the soul, but *to the whole of man's psychosomatic subjectivity*. We speak here about 'subjectivity' (and not only about 'nature'), because that divinization should be understood not only as an 'interior state' of man (that is, of the subject) able to see God 'face to face,' but also as a new formation of man's entire personal subjectivity according to the measure of union with God in his trinitarian mystery and of intimacy with him in the perfect communion of persons" (*Man and Woman*, 392–93).

[125] Divinization (also termed deification or *theösis* from the Greek) has been emphasized in the East without cease; however, we have seen great increase of interest in this topic among Catholic theologians in the West since the advent of St. John Paul II's pontificate. Whether or to what degree the late Pope contributed to the retrieval of divinization in

A THEOLOGY OF THE BODY

John Paul II's theological anthropology as it relates to sex difference is foundational for his account of sex difference and fatherhood. We have seen that Scripture reveals aspects of man's constitution in original solitude. He is a metaphysically concrete individual made for relationships. The body is the visible expression of the entire person. It is the medium through which one discovers every personal attribute. One aspect of original solitude is an anthropological problem. It indicates man is meant for a union with another person, a state John Paul calls "original unity."

Original unity shows that sex difference is the foundation for man's awareness that he is meant for union with another, and bodily sex is the visible manifestation of sex difference (i.e., the whole person as male or female). Original unity implies the fundamental nature of masculinity and femininity, of fatherhood and motherhood, for human personhood. Sex difference plays a key role in man's full awareness of himself as a person. In fact, the Genesis text's focus on man as male and female, indicates that one cannot be a human person without being either a female or a male person.

Original unity also shows the fundamental complementarity of man and woman. They are two complementary ways of being a person. The experience of original nakedness provides more insights into the manner and meaning of the unity to which God calls man and woman in marriage. These insights include the spousal meaning of the body which indicates how fundamental sex difference is for personal identity and for the marital relationship between man and woman. Thus, sex difference has fundamental importance for marriage, family, and society. To understand himself, therefore, a man must understand his masculinity and his calling to fatherhood.

The hermeneutics of the gift is another insight gained from the experience of original nakedness. The hermeneutics of the gift shows how interpersonal relationships are to be conducted, through a sincere gift of oneself. The historical experience of sin reveals the challenges historical man faces in living up to his calling to marriage and family life. The horizon of redemption provides the ultimate resolution to the problem of sin and concupiscence.

John Paul's theology of the body provides a basic understanding of his

the consciousness of the West, I will leave to others. Nevertheless, John Paul's emphasis on divinization is an important and fascinating topic and still can do much to aid dialogue between the Orthodox East and the Catholic Church. For a more detailed treatment of John Paul II's thought on divinization, see David V. Meconi, "Deification in the Thought of John Paul II," *Irish Theological Quarterly* 71 (2006): 127–41.

view of sex and human personhood and points the way for study of his larger corpus of writings on these matters. John Paul indicates that sex difference is fundamental to what it means to be a human person. A closer look at his anthropology in terms of the meaning of sex difference is now needed in order to provide more precision about the manner in which sex difference relates to personhood. Complementarity and relationality are two additional aspects of sex difference which need further explication. Finally, his theology of the body also indicates the importance of sex difference for the calling to marriage and parenthood. We will address these matters in the remaining chapters of part 2.

CHAPTER 6

Sex and Human Personhood

John Paul II's theology of the body identifies several important aspects of sex difference in its relation to personhood which require further exploration. In this chapter we will take a look at John Paul II's broader corpus of writings to gain a more precise understanding of the manner in which he finds that sex difference impacts human personhood. First, we will look at the basic differences between men and women in his thought. From these differences, we will be able to identify the most significant features of sex difference, including the significance of sex difference for personhood—or sex's *constitutiveness*, the complementarity of sex difference and, ultimately, sex difference as relation.

MASCULINITY AND FEMININITY

Using the Genesis creation narratives, John Paul II shows that God's plan for creation was to create man in his image. Specifically, man's image is found in human nature's male and female duality.[1] These texts further help to explain the fact that each sex in this duality of humanity complements the other. This complementarity shows that man and woman are meant to be a unity of two persons in marriage, the foundational communion of persons upon which every higher level of social community depends. Sexual complementarity is also a sign of the interpersonal *communio* of love that is the Trinity.[2] This duality has practical implications

---

[1] See John Paul II, *Man and Woman He Created Them: A Theology of the Body*, trans. Michael Waldstein (Boston: Pauline Books and Media, 2006), 237.

[2] See John Paul II, Post-Synodal Apostolic Exhortation on the Vocation and the Mission of the Lay Faithful in the Church and in the World *Christifideles laici* (December 30, 1988), *AAS* 81 (1989), 393–521, §52. Of course the revelation through bodily complementarity that man and woman are made for one another in marriage does not exhaust the meaning

for the person and society because it derives from the Trinitarian relations, and so it interpenetrates the entirety of the human person.

We also might note that the author often and emphatically repeats that God made man as male and female and only as male or female; this continues to be significant for him. He states that there can be no human person who is not either male or female. There are indeed personally devastating conditions in which the body does not conform with the person's authentic sex difference.[3] Nevertheless, he is clear that theology and biology corroborate that such disorders do not indicate the existence of any other sexual state of human personhood.

His theology of the body shows this theologically, while with regard to biology he argues that the disorder of "so-called hermaphroditism" does not invalidate this truth any more than any other disorder would disprove that there is an underlying order that has gone awry.[4] For Wojtyła, sex difference performs an all-encompassing constituting function for the human person—for his orientation and for his interior development. As pope, he continued to profess the same conviction that it is a "fundamental fact of this existence of man in every stage of his history . . . that God 'created them male and female'; in fact, he always creates them in this way, and they are always such."[5] The human person has always been and will always be

---

of sexual complementarity. In fact, we shall see that one's sex difference is fundamental in shaping the manner in which one experiences and acts within the world. Sex difference arises from the personal fruitfulness of the Trinitarian *communio* and so its meaning cannot be separated from its reflection in marital fruitfulness. Nevertheless, it is lived out in everything the person does, with some areas of life more significantly linked to sex difference than others such as parent-child relationships, sibling relationships, consecrated life, and spiritual parenthood.

[3] Now called "disorders of sex development" (DSD) by the medical community, or intersex conditions colloquially and by others such as sociologists and gender theory activists; see Margaret Schneider et al., *Answers to Your Questions about Individuals with Intersex Conditions* (Washington, DC: American Psychological Association Office of Public Communication, 2006), https://www.apa.org/topics/lgbtq/intersex.pdf.

[4] See Karol Wojtyła, *Love and Responsibility*, trans. Grzegorz Ignatik (Boston: Pauline Books & Media, 2013), 31. Wojtyła of course accepts as real the condition in his time referred to as hermaphroditism, today understood to be a variety of disorders increasingly referred to collectively as DSD or intersex conditions, as mentioned in the footnote above. These conditions are not simply disorders of the body, but due to the constitutiveness of sex difference, they profoundly affect the entire person. Understanding the truth of sex difference is essential to developing effective pastoral approaches to assisting those suffering from these disorders. We will discuss this matter further in chapter 14.

[5] *Man and Woman*, 200.

either male or female. Each and every individual human person will ever-lastingly retain his or her given sex.

In his apostolic letter *Christifideles laici*, John Paul links sex difference to God's plan for each person, which has been permanently inscribed into the essence of the human person from "the beginning." Sex difference is, therefore, an essential aspect of that which makes up the human person at his deepest level.[6] While the full meaning of sex difference is deeply interior to the human person, helping to form his psychology, his emotions, and, indeed, the entire mystery of his personhood, it also has empirical manifestations. Therefore, John Paul commends the study of the human person and sex difference to the human sciences and theological disciplines to find and clarify the specific gifts of femininity and masculinity. However, he warns that the findings of science will be partial and incomplete, so while they can contribute to our understanding, they can never justify any redefinition of sex difference. The final and fullest meaning of sex difference is to be found in the deepest and immutable realities of the human person revealed by God.[7]

John Paul II is adamant that women and men are equal both at the level of creation and at the level of grace. At the level of creation, they both find their dignity in the fact that they are made in the image of God.[8] Since God creates them as equals, it follows that both have equal access to his grace.[9] By the fact of their baptism and confirmation, both men and women share in Christ's threefold mission as Priest, Prophet, and King. Hence, they are both given the task and the ability to fulfill the Church's primary mission that has been given to all Christians.[10] This equality and overlap of responsibilities does not, however, obviate vocations, roles, and responsibilities particular to the one or the other of the two sexes. For reasons I will address in part 3, John Paul pays explicit attention to women in his pontificate while his treatment of men is in general more oblique. He affirms the particular dignity of femininity, finding that this is especially apparent given that God chose to assume "human flesh from the Virgin Mary."[11]

Feminine dignity brings with it the entrustment of two significant tasks. The first is the charge of manifesting and defending the full dignity

---

[6] See *Christifideles laici*, §50.

[7] See *Christifideles laici*, §50.

[8] See *Christifideles laici*, §50.

[9] See *Christifideles laici*, §50.

[10] See *Christifideles laici*, §51.

[11] John Paul II, Apostolic Exhortation on the Role of the Christian Family in the Modern World *Familiaris consortio* (November 22, 1981), *AAS* 74 (1982), 114–37, §22.

of conjugal life and motherhood. The second is the mission to ensure the moral life of the culture in which they live.[12] These tasks derive from the gifts proper to femininity. These gifts are not based solely on biology but rather flow from the fullness of the feminine person. The man also has particular tasks that correspond to his masculine gifts. Interestingly, one of man's more significant tasks is his role in marriage. John Paul analyzes the text of Genesis 2:23–25 to find that it "shows precisely the man's responsibility in welcoming femininity as a gift and in receiving it in a mutual, two-sided exchange."[13] One of man's more fundamental tasks as a husband is to understand, appreciate, and appropriately treat the gift of his wife as a female person. Implicit in this masculine task is the call to all men to respect all women in all aspects of society. It is implicit because marriage and the family are society's fundaments.

As with the analogy between divine and human personhood,[14] John Paul II views sex difference to be derived from something of God's perfection based on the revelation that he is made, man and woman, in God's image. He further clarifies that with respect to sex difference, this analogy of man with God focuses on the "'unity of the two' in a common humanity. This 'unity of the two,' which is a sign of interpersonal communion, *shows that the creation of man* is also marked by a certain likeness to divine communion ('*communio*')."[15] This explains the normativity of sex difference in the marital *communio personarum* as well as the fact that human fatherhood and motherhood are both derivative of God's fatherhood.[16] However,

---

[12] See *Christifideles laici*, §51. Of course, he does not mean to imply that masculinity has no responsibilities here. Rather, he wants to emphasize that these particular tasks require the sort of leadership connatural to femininity and its proper genius.

[13] *Man and Woman*, 261. John Paul uses the term "receive" with regard to femininity here to emphasize that the husband does not own his wife as a female person, which includes her body and its sexuality, in the sense of a one-sided, authoritarian relationship. In other words, John Paul uses the term "femininity" as a synecdoche to refer to the entire female person, but with a special emphasis on her sex and bodily sex. The context of this quote reflects the effect of the fall and of concupiscence on the relationship between husband and wife. One of the results of the fall is the propensity for the husband to consider his wife and her body to be property rather than a gift of a person. The interpersonal "grammar" which establishes a person as a gift in marriage requires a mutual, total self-donation of each of the spouses to the other. Because they are to be given and received as gifts, persons can never be owned or viewed as the property of another.

[14] See Karol Wojtyła, "Thomistic Personalism," in *Person and Community: Selected Essays*, vol. 4, trans. Theresa Sandok, O.S.M. (New York: Peter Lang, 1993), 166.

[15] John Paul II, Apostolic Letter on the Dignity and Vocation of Women *Mulieris dignitatem* (August 15, 1988), AAS 80 (1988), 1653–1729, §7.

[16] See John Paul II, *A Catechesis on Salvation History*, vol. 6, *The Trinity's Embrace: God's*

John Paul II does not explicitly relate the Trinitarian relations to sex difference as have some theologians.[17] Features particular to each human sex

Saving Plan (Boston: Pauline Books and Media, 2002), 289–90.

[17] I have in mind here the work of Hans Urs von Balthasar, who finds that the eternal
Trinitarian processions have analogical expression in sex difference. Balthasar summarizes
this analogy in saying that

> the divine unity of action and consent . . . is expressed in the world in the duality
> of the sexes. In trinitarian terms, of course, the Father, who begets [the Son and]
> who is without origin, appears primarily as (super-) masculine; the Son, in con-
> senting, appears initially as (super-) feminine, but in the act (together with the
> Father) of breathing forth the Spirit, he is (super-) masculine. As for the Spirit, he
> is (super-) feminine. There is even something (super-) feminine about the Father
> too, since . . . in the action of begetting and breathing forth he allows himself to
> be determined by the Persons who thus proceed from him; however, this does
> not affect his primacy in the order of the Trinity. The very fact of the Trinity
> forbids us to project any secular sexuality into the Godhead (as happens in many
> religions and in the Gnostic *syzygia*). It must be enough for us to regard the
> ever-new reciprocity of acting and consenting, which in turn is a form of activity
> and fruitfulness, as the transcendent origin of what we see realized in the world
> of creation: the form and actualization of love and its fruitfulness in sexuality.

(Balthasar, *Theo-Drama: Theological Dramatic Theory*, vol. 5, *The Last Act*, trans. Graham
Harrison [San Francisco: Ignatius Press, 1998], 91). Although John Paul is not as explicit
as Balthasar, there are certain affinities between John Paul's and Balthasar's thinking,
both in general and in this matter specifically. To begin with, Balthasar was living when
John Paul referenced him, albeit in a footnote, in his apostolic letter *Mulieris dignitatem*
(see §27 and §27n55). It is quite unusual for living theologians to be cited as authori-
ties in papal documents, and this certainly connotes a familiarity with, and great respect
for, Balthasar. Secondly, John Paul seems to be employing Balthasar's Petrine and Marian
ecclesial models (see *The Office of Peter and the Structure of the Church* [San Francisco:
Ignatius Press, 1986]) in the above footnote from *Mulieris dignitatem*. Indeed, much of
Balthasar's Marian model is consonant with John Paul II's Marian writings, especially the
significance of Mary's fiat (see Balthasar, *Office of Peter*, 208ff.; *Mulieris dignitatem*, §19).
Both have an integral view of the human person as a unity of body and soul and both
express this in a similar manner. For example, John Paul finds that the physical makeup of
the woman's body reflects aspects of her spiritual makeup in the way that she can "create
a space" within her to receive as a gift the fruit of the love between her husband and
herself (see John Paul II, Letter to Families *Gratissimam sane* [February 2, 1994], AAS 86
[1994)], 868–925 [New Hope, KY: Urbi Et Orbi Communications, 1994], §11). Here
John Paul depicts the wife-mother "making space for the other" in terms of her baby
during pregnancy. This has a great affinity with Balthasar's Marian view of the Church
(which the author cites in *Mulieris dignitatem*) in which he depicts a significant aspect
of the Church's femininity in human, maternal terms—namely in her womb's accommo-
dation for her children. He refers to the Church as "primarily an open womb" (*Office of
Peter*, 185). She "gives birth to her children in baptism [but] does not release them from
her body but on the contrary accepts them into her body" (*Office of Peter*, 190). In her

reflect the manner in which each participates in divine perfection. John Paul provides copious characteristics which he associates particularly with femininity.[18]

John Paul II states that women possess "humble initiative, respect for individuals without seeking to impose a way of seeing things, [and] the invitation to repeat the same experience as a way of reaching the same personal conviction of faith."[19] He says that a woman "has an understanding, sensitive and compassionate heart that allows her to give a delicate, concrete style to charity."[20] This corresponds with the fact that "[i]t is commonly thought that *women* are more capable than men of paying attention *to another person*."[21] John Paul also believes women to have "a special *sensitivity which is characteristic of their femininity*,"[22] and this is reflected in the way that the women of the Gospel respond to Jesus in his preaching, at the Cross, and at the tomb. These feminine capacities which are amenable for relationships with others make women especially well-suited to the vocations to holiness, marriage, and family.

The feminine response of faith reflects "a true resonance of mind and heart."[23] The feminine mind is more intuitive than a man's, and this makes her "more open to revealed truth, more able to grasp the meaning of events and to accept the Gospel message."[24] These gifts prove to make the women

---

body, she "carries, bears and rears her children" (*Office of Peter*, 184). Additionally, they both see the Marian dimension of the Church as reflecting the receptivity of femininity (see *Mulieris dignitatem*, §29; *Office of Peter*, 184–190). More to the point, John Paul II declares that human fatherhood and motherhood have their basis in the divine begetting, and like Balthasar, John Paul is careful to eliminate any reversal of the analogy. In other words, they both are careful to reject projecting any sense of bodiliness into the Trinitarian begetting. Paragraph eight of *Mulieris dignitatem* is very similar to the above quote from the *Theo-Drama*. If John Paul II is indeed sympathetic to Balthasar's view of the manner in which the processions are expressed in human sex difference, the fact that he does not explicitly adopt it in its entirety could suggest a reticence to imply magisterial endorsement of a relatively new theological theory.

[18] Lisa Sowle Cahill criticizes these as "gender stereotypes." She specifically points to feminine characteristics of nurturing, loving, and compassion as exemplified by the Virgin Mary (see "Accent on the Masculine," in *Considering* Veritatis Splendor, ed. John Wilkins [Cleveland, OH: The Pilgrim Press, 1994], 59). I will address this criticism in the part 4.

[19] John Paul II, *A Catechesis on the Creed*, vol. 4, *The Church: Mystery, Sacrament, Community* (Boston: Pauline Books and Media, 1998), 489.

[20] John Paul II, *The Church*, 490.

[21] *Mulieris dignitatem*, §18.

[22] *Mulieris dignitatem*, §16.

[23] *Mulieris dignitatem*, §15.

[24] John Paul II, *The Church*, 489.

following Christ stronger than even the apostles in moments of danger, because "those who love much succeed in overcoming their fear."[25] John Paul "sees in the face of women the reflection of a beauty which mirrors the loftiest sentiments of which the human heart is capable: the self-offering totality of love; the strength that is capable of bearing the greatest sorrows; limitless fidelity and tireless devotion to work; the ability to combine penetrating intuition with words of support and encouragement."[26]

A woman's feminine structure is marked by the "readiness to accept life which marks her 'ethos' from the 'beginning.'"[27] This openness to a new person is a special aspect of femininity associated with a woman's unique role and vocation as a mother.[28] In fact, motherhood is the source of a special moral and spiritual strength proper to femininity, derived from "her awareness that *God entrusts the human being to her in a special way.*"[29]

These feminine features, which reflect participation in God's perfection, are also fittingly found in the created order in other things such as human relationships with God throughout salvation history,[30] in ecclesial structure,[31] and in soteriology.[32] They all reflect an active receptivity to the offer of a gift. Furthermore, John Paul II points to femininity as a symbol for Old Testament Jerusalem. It is a symbol which continues into the New Testament, where the feminine image is applied to the heavenly Jerusalem: the "feminine symbol represents the face of the Church in her various aspects as betrothed, bride and mother, thus stressing a dimension of love and fruitfulness."[33] This relational analogy also depicts God as the Bridegroom to the Church-as-Bride, and is operative in both Old and New Testaments. John Paul declares that this analogy articulates the spousal aspect as well as the uncreated quality of God's love in analogy with human marital love, but as with all theological analogies, there is always a greater difference.[34]

---

[25] *Mulieris dignitatem*, §15.

[26] John Paul II, Encyclical Letter on the Blessed Virgin Mary in the Life of the Pilgrim Church *Redemptoris mater* (March 25, 1987), *AAS* 79 (1987), 361–433, §§46–47.

[27] *Mulieris dignitatem*, §14.

[28] See *Mulieris dignitatem*, §18.

[29] *Mulieris dignitatem*, §30.

[30] See, e.g., Ezek 16:8–63 for a negative sense in which Israel fails to give herself totally to God as a faithful bride.

[31] See *Redemptoris mater*, §46.

[32] See Ephesians 5:21–25 in which the Church is required to subject herself to Christ the Bridegroom who gives up his life for his Bride, the Church.

[33] John Paul II, *Trinity's Embrace*, 443.

[34] See *Mulieris dignitatem*, §25.

It is important to recall that theological analogy is based upon the fact that God creates *ex nihilo*, and so all creation necessarily reflects the perfection of God. As God is infinite, finite creation's reflection of the infinite perfection means that the difference is much greater than the similarity.[35] Even so, the ecclesial spousal relationship still has the capacity to reveal additional attributes of femininity. John Paul II goes to the fifth chapter of the epistle to the Ephesians and finds that when Paul "calls Christ 'the Bridegroom' and the Church 'the Bride,' he indirectly confirms through this analogy *the truth about woman as bride*. The Bridegroom is the one who loves. The Bride is loved: *it is she who receives love, in order to love in return*."[36] The masculine Bridegroom is the one who makes the first offer of love. The feminine bride is the one who responds by accepting the love and in returning that love the interpersonal exchange becomes fruitful. In the case of the Church, this fruitfulness is the holiness of her members. We begin to see that feminine receptivity has a divine archetype, manifested in God's relationship to man.

The Blessed Virgin Mary holds a central place in John Paul II's theology. She is the symbolic link between the Church and humanity in the sense that her exemplary femininity provides the model for the feminine aspects of the Church. She also provides the model not only for women in their feminine vocations but also for men as members of the Church.[37] Mary's openness to receiving God's love and her response with the fullness of her person is the model for all humanity. But in a special way, this reflects the "genius" of femininity.[38] John Paul finds Mary's emblematic

---

[35] See *Mulieris dignitatem*, §8.

[36] *Mulieris dignitatem*, §29.

[37] See *Mulieris dignitatem*, §4. Many feminists reject the Virgin Mary in the manner in which Catholic tradition has espoused her as an example for women. Cahill says that when John Paul II presents Mary as emblematic of femininity, "he fails to ask critically whether stereotypical definitions of 'feminine nature' . . . [which] chase after a romantic ideology of mother-love—are part of the problem [of discrimination against women]" ("Current Theology, Notes on Moral Theology: 1989: Feminist Ethics," *Theological Studies* 51 [1990]: 58). Elizabeth Johnson says that in "picturing Mary as the most perfect of women, the patriarchal marian tradition functions paradoxically to disparage all other women" (*Truly Our Sister: A Theology of Mary in the Communion of Saints* [New York: Continuum, 2003], 23). Phyllis Kaminski calls this an abstraction and idealization of women which is a move "to confirm the traditional patriarchal values and to limit women's special dignity to her role in the private sphere as mother." Phyllis H. Kaminski, "'Reproducing the World': Mary O'Brien's Theory of Reproducing Consciousness and Implications for Feminist Incarnational Theology," *Horizons* 19, no. 2 [1992]: 254. I will assess these charges in part 4.

[38] See *Mulieris dignitatem*, §§30-31.

example most perfectly manifested in her fiat, resulting in the fruitfulness of the Incarnation.[39] The fruitful gift of the Incarnation in turn reveals to her the ultimate meaning of her femininity.

Mary's Magnificat reveals her recognition of the gifts which make up her femininity that include her creation as an end—a person for her own sake—and which allow her to discover herself through her sincere and total self-gift.[40] What the Blessed Virgin discovers is that her femininity is made for, and perfected in, her open, free reception of God's offering of his gift of love. This receptivity is fructified in the gift of a person borne out of love. Receptivity, love, and their resulting fruitfulness are dimensions necessary for each person individually and are characteristic of the Church.[41] Nevertheless, they are primarily feminine-spousal in quality. This is an "*active* receptivity" which defines the feminine mode in complementarity.[42]

Femininity has been associated with receptivity since Aristotle. Feminine receptivity was necessary for his metaphysical account of the origination of males and females. While sex difference appears to be in some ways an absolute difference, at the same time it has to be accidental to human nature if the male and female are to be of the same species.[43] His solution was to identify masculinity and femininity as contrary principles at the origin of procreation.[44] The male is the active principle because his seed generates in another as the efficient cause of generation. The female receives the male seed and provides the matter of generation which takes place within her.

Feminine receptivity is situated in the metaphysical co-principles of potency and act, which describe the dynamism of being. Potency (*dunamis*) is receptive of act (*energeia* and *entelecheia*) and so this potency (or passivity) is the contrary of act. Therefore, femininity is associated with matter, potency, and receptivity. Likewise, masculinity is associated with form, act, and initiative. Passion or passivity are simply terms used in the context of the receptive contrary of act.

This metaphysical description of sex difference was adopted by St. Thomas and prevails in the scholastic tradition.[45] Karol Wojtyła was

---

[39] See *Mulieris dignitatem*, §§4–5.

[40] See *Mulieris dignitatem*, §11.

[41] See John Paul II, *The Church*, 118; and *The Trinity's Embrace*, 444–45.

[42] See Wojtyła, *Love and Responsibility*, 94: "A woman seems more passive, although in another way she is more active. In any case, her role and responsibility will be different from the role and responsibility of a man."

[43] See Aristotle, *Metaphysics* X.9–10.

[44] See Aristotle, *On the Generation of Animals* I.2.

[45] See David L. Schindler, "Catholic Theology, Gender, and the Future of Western

formed by this tradition. In fact, he uses language that evokes just this Thomist-Aristotelian view, saying, "Although it is true that man is the creator of life, this life is created within the woman."[46] He accepts femininity as receptive because he finds it in accord with Christian revelation, magisterial teaching, the Thomist patrimony, and reason, all of which are confirmed by his phenomenological analysis. But as we have seen, his phenomenology infuses into Thomist metaphysics the dynamisms of conscious human experience. So we see that John Paul II adds "active" to feminine receptivity for the woman because she is a person who fulfills herself through conscious, free act. While she is metaphysically ordered to receptivity, we have seen that in John Paul II's anthropology, one must choose and act in order to fulfill himself.

John Paul II refers to the relationship among femininity, receptivity, and love in a text quoted earlier: "The Bride is loved: *it is she who receives love, in order to love in return*."[47] He finds that this phrase has meaning that extends beyond marital spousal relationships. It has a universal meaning that applies to every woman in her relations with all other men and women, regardless of her race, nationality, creed, culture, age, education, spiritual or physical state, marital state, etcetera. This is because it has to do with her very femininity, which one can begin to see for John Paul, is deeply rooted in the person's being.

In the context of Ephesians 5, he associates the feminine primacy in the receptivity of love with what he calls "a special kind of 'prophetism' that belongs to women in their femininity."[48] Here he finds that the

---

Civilization," *Communio* 20 (Summer 1993): 240). For a more complete analysis of the history of the relationship between receptivity and femininity, see Prudence Allen, *The Concept of Woman*, vol. 1, *The Aristotelian Revolution, 750 BC–AD 1250* (Grand Rapids, MI: William B. Eerdmans Pub., 1997), and *The Concept of Woman*, vol. 2, *The Early Humanist Reformation, 1250–1500* (Grand Rapids, MI: William B. Eerdmans Pub., 2002).

[46] Pope John Paul II/Karol Wojtyła, *The Way to Christ: Spiritual Exercises*, trans. Leslie Wearne (NY: Harper Collins, 1984), 56.

[47] *Mulieris dignitatem*, §29.

[48] *Mulieris dignitatem*, §29. I will discuss the ideas of primary and secondary sex-difference-based characteristics when I treat sex difference's complementarity. "Prophetism" here is undoubtedly what John Paul refers to in *Man and Woman* (534–38) as a "prophetism of the body." This is an analogy with the Old Testament prophets who spoke God's truth to his people. Because the body expresses the soul (and so the whole person), the body "speaks" the truth of the soul; it "speaks" the interiority of the person. The truth which the body speaks is especially spoken through its masculinity and femininity, its sex. "It speaks with the mysterious language of the personal gift" (*Man*

analogy of the Bridegroom and Bride speaks about Christ's love for each and every human person, male and female. However, appealing to "the biblical analogy and the text's interior logic, it is precisely the woman—the bride—who manifests this truth to everyone."[49] Therefore, there is a "prophetic character" to femininity itself which reveals Christ's love. It is a love mediated through the Holy Spirit and offered to every person.

John Paul says that the Virgin Mother is the "highest expression" of this prophetic femininity.[50] The love she receives and gives in return is connected to the very core of her femininity. So much so that he calls this particular mode of sincere self-gift an "ontological affirmation [which] also indicates the ethical dimension of a person's vocation. *Woman can only find herself by giving love to others*."[51] The Blessed Virgin's motherhood is one of the most significant characteristics of her femininity, which is the fruit of her particular gift of self. A distinctive and unrepeatable relationship between the mother and her child is always established by the fact of motherhood.[52] This unique relationship might be summed up in the word "entrusting."

Mary's entire life, from her *fiat mihi* to her acceptance of the Beloved Disciple as her son at the foot of the Cross, is a magnificent demonstration of trust. Joyce Little explains that it is in her ability to trust that John Paul finds the importance of Mary, and of all women.[53] The ability to trust can be said to be synonymous with the prophetic character of femininity. The copious features of femininity and their relation to love, which John Paul II identifies in his papal writings, suggest that for him the manner in which women love is one of the most significant features of femininity. Namely, feminine love is a trusting love marked by a hierarchy which entails first an active reception of the offer of love and then a return of love. John Paul's discussion of features of masculinity is not as plentiful, nor as explicit. There are few attributes associated with masculinity that John Paul explicitly identifies. Nevertheless, John Paul understands sex

---

and Woman, 536). In the above context, John Paul is referring to the witness the body "speaks" about sex difference.

[49] *Mulieris dignitatem*, §29.

[50] *Mulieris dignitatem*, §29.

[51] *Mulieris dignitatem*, §30. By "this particular mode of sincere self-gift," he means the feminine reception and subsequent return of love.

[52] See *Redemptoris mater*, 45.

[53] See Joyce Little, *The Significance of Mary for Women* (Washington, NJ: AMI Press, 1989), 5ff. Originally published in the Proceedings of the Thirty-Ninth National Convention of the Mariological Society of America held at Christ the King Seminary, East Aurora, NY, June 1–2, 1988.

difference, as with all created perfections, to be analogously derivative of some perfection in God. Though he is not explicit about aligning anything of God to sex difference, he says it is associated in some manner with the Trinitarian relations, implicitly in the first procession.[54] For example, he says that that the eternal, divine generation is the absolute model of human generation.[55] Nevertheless, one must also contend with his assertion that "divine fatherhood does not possess 'masculine' characteristics in a physical sense."[56]

It is important to note here that he excludes masculine characteristics from divine fatherhood only in the "physical sense." This is an obvious Christian dogma and leaves open the possibility of making analogical correlations between God as Father and masculine characteristics. In fact, he does go on to make it clear that both masculinity and femininity, as well as fatherhood and motherhood, are created analogies of the divine archetype which he finds in the divine relations of paternity and begetting.[57]

John Paul II further confirms this when he states that biblical anthropomorphisms treating of God's love for man "attribute to him both 'masculine' and 'feminine' qualities."[58] Unfortunately, this makes finding analogies which are proper to masculine characteristics difficult without his explicitly identifying them. Even so, John Paul's understanding of the complementarity and the relationality of sex difference do permit some extrapolation of masculine attributes based upon explicitly identified feminine characteristics.

Because the bride is the one who is loved, the man (bridegroom) would be the one first to offer love, and when it is accepted, to receive the love that is returned. A second and more profound characteristic of authentic masculinity would be the implication that a man has the need to be trusted and the need to learn trust. This can be inferred from the observation that trust is inherently interrelational. Indeed, relationships of intimacy

---

[54] See John Paul II, *Trinity's Embrace*, 289–90.
[55] *Mulieris dignitatem*, §8.
[56] See *Mulieris dignitatem*, §8.
[57] "Every element of human generation which is proper to man, and every element which is proper to woman, namely human 'fatherhood' and 'motherhood,' bears within itself a likeness to, or analogy with the divine 'generating' and with that 'fatherhood' which in God is 'totally different,' that is, completely spiritual and divine in essence; whereas in the human order, generation is proper to the 'unity of the two': both are 'parents,' the man and the woman alike" (*Mulieris dignitatem*, §8).
[58] *Mulieris dignitatem*, §8. He cites Is 42:14; 46:3–4; 49:14–15; 66:13; Ps 131:2–3; Hos 11:1–4; and Jer 3:4–19 as examples. These show God's love and concern as a bridegroom and a father but also as a mother.

demand trust. Due to the fall, trust is now a process that begins by initiation of an offer of the gift of oneself in truth and the active acceptance of this gift by the receptive partner. Trust increases and the relationship matures as this "gift in truth" and its "active receptance" demonstrate a long-term, consistent pattern of truthful reciprocity.

Yet, the initiating of the gift of oneself in truth comes with the risk of rejection, which can reveal the man's need to be trusted.[59] Lawrence Porter points out another inferred masculine characteristic based on John Paul's anthropology. Using much the same approach as we do here, Porter states that the masculine "'personal structure' exhibits a far less innate, overt or pronounced, capacity for the other, whether that be human or divine."[60] This attenuated capacity for the other would be neither a strength nor a weakness if it is a valid characteristic. Rather, it would simply imply a different way of approaching interpersonal relationships. These characteristics will be explored further in part 3 of this study.

We have identified characteristics of femininity and masculinity in this section in the process of understanding the manner in which sex relates to human personhood. The significance John Paul II attaches to the distinctly feminine manner of love is indicative of more than an accidental association between sex difference and human personhood. While the relation is not yet precisely described at this point, it seems that for John Paul II, sex—masculinity and femininity—is rooted in the person's being. This follows from personhood's origin in God's perfection (i.e., the *analogia entis*). We are now prepared to provide a more precise description of sex difference in its connection to human personhood which John Paul describes as "constitutive."

---

[59] A psychological manifestation of this would follow John Paul's anthropology, perhaps manifested by the so-called "fragile male ego." Cathleen Kaveny sees this as a fear on the part of the male that his female mate's strength reduces his masculinity (see "What Women Want: 'Buffy,' the Pope and the New Feminists," *Commonweal* 130 [November 7, 2003]: 18–24). Presuming the need for trust, if there is such a thing as a fragile male ego, if it is proper to call it fear for his masculinity, one could understand this as a deeper recognition on the man's part that the woman's show of strength could communicate a lack of trust in him, such as his inability to be an adequate husband or father who can provide for her and her children's security or material needs.

[60] Lawrence B. Porter, "Gender in Theology: The Example of John Paul II's *Mulieris dignitatem*," *Gregorianum* 77 (1996): 112.

Sex Difference as a Constitutive
Aspect of the Person

John Paul II states that "sex . . . in some way is 'constitutive for the person' (not only 'an attribute of the person')."[61] From what we already have seen, it is apparent that "constitutive" refers to the human person's ontology, to his very essence.[62] However, we still need a clearer understanding of the ontology of sex difference. The first step toward clarity is a review of John Paul's metaphysics and approach to hylomorphism in particular. We will draw on our discussion of hylomorphism in chapter 3 to investigate the constitutiveness of sex difference for personhood.

Wojtyła finds an "especially profound analysis of the human soul" in St. Thomas's metaphysics.[63] Thomas holds that the soul is the human being's substantial form. For Wojtyła this fact is key for understanding the uniqueness of the human person because the fundamental faculties (i.e., the rational faculties) of the human person are actualized through the body-soul unity. The soul relies on the cognitive and appetitive senses of the body in order to actualize the faculties of intellect and will. The body is not simply a shell in which dwells the soul. Rather, the body is integral to what it means to be human.

Hylomorphism in turn implies a necessary association between sex difference and human personhood, since the soul is the form of the sexed body, and so sex difference must originate, in some manner, in the soul. Aristotle, however, realized a nature's relationship to sex difference had to be accidental to avoid speciating males from females. Consequently, he developed a less than satisfactory account, making sex difference a biological accident.[64] Soteriology deepens this requirement, otherwise Christ's Atonement would have reconciled only males with God.[65] There is a more satisfactory account of the ontology of sex difference.

---

[61] *Man and Woman*, 166. "Sex" is the English rendering of *sesso* in the original Italian.

[62] Elizabeth Johnson criticizes John Paul II for his ontological view of sex difference, saying that it results in dualism which "cleaves the human race into two radically different types of persons—men who have a masculine nature and women who have a feminine nature" (Johnson, *Truly Our Sister*, 48; see also 61ff.). I will assess this criticism in part 4.

[63] Wojtyła, "Thomistic Personalism," 168.

[64] D. C. Schindler shows that to separate sex difference from the soul by placing it in the body alone as Aristotle did, requires gender to have the status of a "contingent aberration" (D. C. Schindler, "Perfect Difference: Gender and the Analogy of Being," *Communio* 43 [Summer 2016]: 205). This results in a logical contradiction. He calls St. Thomas Aquinas's effort to overcome it by appealing to God's Providence unconvincing. Indeed, something so fundamental that it is necessary to constitute the human person cannot also be a defect of his human nature.

[65] St. John Damascene says that "the Word of God assumed a body and an intellectual and

We saw in chapter 4 that the human person belongs to the category of being of relation. Personhood is that in which the rational human nature subsists; it is the relational subject who possesses his nature. Therefore, the demands of hylomorphic theory, anthropology, and soteriology that sex difference be essential to personhood while remaining accidental to human nature do not have to rely on the categories of substance and accidents alone.[66] Sex difference can be essential to personhood because a person, being a relation, can have an essence that is not substance. So, sex difference is essential to personhood because the person is distinct but is not separate from its nature, that is, its unity of body and soul. Sex, more than any other hylomorphic attribute, is determinative of the person as manifested throughout his body-soul. I argue that this is what John Paul means by the term "constitutive." A broader survey of his writings will support this assertion.

We saw in chapter 5, John Paul II's discovery of original solitude in the Genesis creation narratives. One dimension of original solitude is the lack of a certain completeness of the man. John Paul's analysis shows how the creation of the woman, who is a helpmate and companion to the man, overcomes this deficient situation. Her creation introduces a communion between the man and woman, which reflects the Trinitarian *communio*. The man and woman see in their bodies that they are made for this communion.

They see in the sex of their bodies the fact that they are made to complement and fulfill one another through fruitful, life-giving love. This spousal communion is a foretaste of the final unity of mankind with the divine community of persons for which the human person was created. The woman, the only other one in creation who is like the man, is also made in the image and likeness of God and is the only other in whom, and with

---

rational soul. . . . The whole was united to the whole, that He might bestow salvation on me wholly; for what was not assumed is not curable" (*De fide orthodoxa* iii, 6, quoted in *ST* III, q. 5, a. 4, resp.).

[66] John Grabowski employs this concept with its associated terminology in his article "The Status of the Sexual Good as a Direction for Moral Theology," *The Heythrop Journal* 35 (1994): 25–28. In a later article (cited earlier) he explains that "the term 'essential' . . . need not be restricted to the person understood substantially—one can also speak of the essence or being of a relation" (John Grabowski, "Person: Substance and Relation," *Communio* 22 [1995]: 139–63). Here he follows Joseph Ratzinger and Jean Galot who, he explains, argue that "essence," deriving from the Latin *essentia*, refers to the *esse* or being of a thing and not necessarily to its substance. Given that "relation" is an ontological category of being in addition to substance and accident, relation can also have an essence. As can be inferred from the discussion in part 1, this seems to describe John Paul II's philosophical position.

whom, the deficiency associated with original solitude can be overcome. Man and woman are created to complement and complete each other.[67]

While this complementarity is first evident in the body, sexual complementarity interpenetrates every aspect of the spiritual organism and, more than anything else, constitutes the identity of the person. While sex expresses itself in almost every aspect of the biological-hylomorphic organism, it transcends biology and interpenetrates the dimension of spirit. John Paul demonstrates this in commenting on the Blessed Virgin's Magnificat: *"He 'has done great things for me': this is the discovery of all the richness and personal resources of femininity,* all the eternal originality of the 'woman,' just as God wanted her to be, a person for her own sake, who discovers herself 'by means of a sincere gift of self.'"[68]

Here two factors stand out. First, John Paul considers the Blessed Virgin's femininity to constitute the manner by which she makes a gift of herself, and this gift necessarily originates in the human spirit (though it incorporates the whole organism). Second, it is in giving herself by means of her femininity that she fully realizes her "self," her personhood. Her personhood and its fulfillment are inseparable from her femininity. In a similar statement, the author more explicitly illustrates the relationship of sex difference to personhood: "In this broad and diversified context, a woman represents a particular value by the fact that she is a human person, and, at the same time, this particular person, by the fact of her femininity."[69]

Sex difference is foundational for personal identity and so it is likewise foundational for the ordering of intersubjective relations. John Paul declares that all aspects of social life are "marked by this primordial duality."[70] This rootedness of sex difference in personal identity and social order is what he means by "constitutive," which is consonant with the view that sex difference is essential to personhood.[71]

My contention that there is an identity between the concept that "sex

---

[67] Of course, man and women complete each other only in an advised sense. They are not ends for one another, much less means. They are partners in assisting one another in the task of salvation. God is man's end and so in an absolute way of speaking, only God completes man.

[68] *Mulieris dignitatem,* §11.

[69] *Mulieris dignitatem,* §29.

[70] Letter to Families, 6.

[71] This assertion is contested by many feminist writers; however, they vary in their approach to the manner in which sex difference is related to personhood. See John Grabowski, "Theological Anthropology and Gender Since Vatican II: A Critical Appraisal of Recent Trends in Catholic Theology" (Ph.D. diss., Marquette University, 1991), 82–95, for a helpful summary. I will assess this in part 4.

difference is essential to personhood" and John Paul's idea that sex difference is, in part, constitutive of personhood is further supported by a closer look at the passage just cited. John Paul says "the function of sex [that is, being male or female], which in some way is 'constitutive for the person' (not only 'an attribute of the person'), shows how deeply man, with all his spiritual solitude, with the uniqueness and unrepeatability proper to the person, is constituted by the body as 'he' or 'she.'"[72] The sex of the body visibly manifests the sex of the person and is responsible in a fundamental way for personal identity.

The body reveals and, in part, constitutes the person as "he" or "she." Sex difference permeates and transcends biology and penetrates all aspects of the human person. John Paul II says there is a simultaneity between personhood and the sexed body. One cannot deal with sex without also dealing with the entire human person.[73] To attempt such would destroy the integral anthropology presented in the Genesis creation narratives, for they show one must understand sex in terms of reciprocal gift.[74]

Sex difference not only expresses the spousal gift of the person, it is the very expression of man as a person. Sex difference establishes the manner in which human personhood mediates reciprocal, interpersonal self-giving, and its structure indicates that both human personhood and sex difference are fundamentally relational. Before looking at the relationality of sex difference, let us look at its role in constituting the concrete, individual human person. Sex difference is constitutive for bodily identity, and in fact it is constitutive for the identity of the entire human person. It is necessary to establish the concrete, unique, and unrepeatable person.[75]

Furthermore, sex difference and its inherent complementarity is the substratum which permits the intimate "knowing" proper to the *communio personarum* of the marital covenant. The fruit of this interpersonal knowledge is another person, a child. All of this indicates that John Paul II's

---

[72] *Man and Woman*, 166.

[73] For an important account of the metaphysics of sex difference, see D. C. Schindler, "Perfect Difference," 194–31.

[74] See *Man and Woman*, 182–83.

[75] "Sex is not only decisive for man's somatic individuality, but at the same time it defines his personal identity and concreteness. And exactly *in this personal identity and concreteness as an unrepeatable feminine or masculine 'I,' man is 'known when the words of Genesis 2:24 come true*: 'the man will unite with his wife, and the two will be one flesh.' The 'knowledge' about which Genesis 4:1–2 and all subsequent biblical texts speak reaches the innermost roots of this identity and concreteness, which man and woman owe to their sex. Such concreteness means both the uniqueness and unrepeatability of the person" (*Man and Woman*, 208).

thought on sex difference and personhood corresponds to what is meant by the idea that sex difference is essential to personhood. But he also shows that sex difference is not alone in establishing man's personal structure. For example, he states: "The fact that man is a 'body' belongs more deeply to the structure of the personal subject than the fact that in his somatic constitution he is also male or female."[76]

Initially, it could appear that this statement undermines all we have shown John Paul having said about the relation of sex difference to personhood. However, there is nothing about the term "more deeply" that implies either that sex difference is unnecessary or that an "unsexed" body is a possibility. Rather, it is an assertion that men and women share a common nature.

Hylomorphism indicates that the body-soul unity is the fundament of man's nature. A person is not (fully) human without his body-soul nature. One can find the reason that John Paul II emphasizes the priority of the body from the context of the quote, which is that man's original solitude is rooted in the body. He uses this insight of hylomorphism to show that the body, which is the source of solitude, goes more deeply into one's personal structure than differences of sex, which is the source of original unity.[77] Thus, he can say that "the meaning of original solitude . . . is substantially prior to the meaning of original unity."[78]

Nevertheless, while other constitutive aspects of the person that are essential to human personhood may not be at the same fundamental level as those of the body and soul, it does not follow that these aspects are unimportant, much less expendable. Sex difference may rightly be called a secondary factor to the structure of personhood, but the human person would still be annihilated without this "secondary" factor. It is an error to

---

[76] *Man and Woman*, 157.

[77] Admittedly, John Paul II does not explicitly state his assumption of hylomorphism in this context. Rather, he uses his analysis of the Elohist text of Genesis 1 in comparison to the Yahwist text of Genesis 2 to justify his assertion about the body's priority over sex difference in the structure of the person. However, in an earlier Wednesday catechesis he states that (at least) Genesis 1 provides "an incontrovertible point of reference and solid basis of a metaphysics and also for an anthropology" (*Man and Woman*, 137). He makes explicit that the context is the scholastic idea that "the good is convertible with being," but clearly he is not hesitant to discover findings from philosophy also revealed in the inspired texts. Then the assumption that hylomorphism is the metaphysical language which most aptly explains what John Paul finds in his biblical analysis is in line with his methodology outlined in the first part and with his explicit statements in his theology of the body catecheses.

[78] *Man and Woman*, 157.

assume that for John Paul, anything other than primary features are dispensable. This type of thinking is foreign to his integral thought.

John Paul clearly sees sex difference penetrating to the innermost depths of the human person. He declares that it was "the Creator's decision that the human being should always and only exist as a woman or a man."[79] In this, he is explicit about sex difference's depth and permanence for human personhood. One can see permanence in that sex difference perdures in the eschaton, though its meaning will be understood more completely than on earth. The person will be wholly spiritualized in the final resurrection. But this is not to say that John Paul envisions eternal life without a corporeal body. In fact, he explicitly rejects this theory, saying that it would make the resurrection meaningless.[80]

This new spiritualized life will be one with sex difference remaining at the core of personal identity but without exclusive marriage or procreation. This reveals that marriage and procreation are not originating factors in the meaning of human femininity or masculinity. Rather, marriage and procreation are the concrete, historical manifestations of a much deeper meaning.[81] The concrete reality that is lived in the body manifests the spousal meaning of the body and shows that man is created as a person in order to be able to answer the call to live his life in a *communio personarum*. This earthly *communio* is a foreshadowing of the ultimate, divine *communio* to which God calls every human person.

The preceding discussion has already indicated sex difference's profound role in concretizing and giving personal identity to the human person. However, considering John Paul II's Thomism, the question remains of the manner in which sex difference relates to the soul. Because the soul is the substantial form of the body, the constitutiveness of sex difference requires that it have some sort of manifestation in the soul. St. Thomas dealt with the differences in sex while maintaining the unity of human nature in a common substantial form by adopting Aristotle's view that females are "misbegotten males."[82]

---

[79] *Mulieris dignitatem*, §1.

[80] See *Man and Woman*, 389.

[81] See *Man and Woman*, 399.

[82] See *ST* Ia, q. 92, a. 1., ad. 1. I would argue that St. Thomas had no intention of demeaning women with this unfortunately translated phrase. The Latin term is *occasionatus*. In fact, *occasionatus* has the sense of "happening by chance." Thomas says that while with respect to her particular nature, the female is unable to actualize the potency of the sperm to become a male; therefore with respect to universal nature the female sex must be considered intended by God and not something accidental. (For a discussion of the distinction

While John Paul II does not explicitly address St. Thomas's theory of sex difference, he also does not follow Thomas in the Aristotelian theory as to how two sexes arise from a single type of form. John Paul recognizes that the intimate interrelationship of sex difference and personhood cannot be accounted for with that theory. He is confident in affirming its essential character for personhood without feeling obligated to articulate explicitly a metaphysical account for it. This is not unlike the early Church's experience in proclaiming the revealed truth about the Incarnate God while working out its Trinitarian and christological accounts.

John Paul II expresses this confidence when he asserts that "it cannot be denied that the feminine soul has a particular capacity to live in a mystical spousal relationship with Christ and thus to reproduce in herself the

---

between particular and universal nature in this context, see Michael Nolan, "What Aquinas Never Said about Women," *First Things* [November, 1998]: 11–12.) The female sex was intended by nature, under God's design, for procreation. Thomas's acknowledgement that the first woman was made directly by God (see *ST* Ia, q. 92, a. 4) and that both male and female bodies will be resurrected (*ST* IIIa, q. 81, a. 3) together indicate that the phrase cannot be taken to indicate that the female sex is in any way deficient, since according to Thomas only a positive good can be created by God and will exist in the eschaton. In other examples of apparent deprecation of femininity one must also take into consideration these statements and his metaphysics. For example, St. Thomas's assertion that women are passive in procreation (see, e.g., *ST* Ia, q. 92, a. 1, resp.) is simply the alignment of femininity with the receptive "matter" and masculinity with the active "form," following Aristotle. As discussed above, Aristotle came to this assignment by correlating observation with his metaphysics. Thomas's assertion that males possess more of the "good of reason" and that women are more susceptible to concupiscence (*ST* IVa, q. 62, a. 4, resp. obj. 5) derive from medieval biology and correspond with this metaphysics. Because men and women have the same "form," it is the matter/body which causes the differences between male and female potency. Therefore, women have the same ultimate capacities as men for reason but the "good of reason" or the ability to use reason is more limited in women because they are more subject to concupiscence due to their bodily makeup (i.e., they have more abundant bodily "humors" than men [see *ST* IVa, q. 62, a. 4, resp. obj. 5]). Nevertheless, St. Thomas admits that these "biological facts" are not absolute. With respect to reason, he says that some women possess a firm judgment of reason despite the greater difficulty they have in combating passions in order to exercise their reason (see *ST* IIa-IIae, q. 156, a. 1, resp. obj. 1). With respect to moral virtues, some women also display greater virtue than men, despite greater difficulties due to concupiscence. He says that some women have demonstrated more courage than men in spiritual combat (see *ST* IIIa, q. 72, a. 8, resp. obj. 3). Moreover, he states that "sometimes a woman is found to be better than many men as regards the soul" (*ST* IVa, q. 39, a. 1, resp. obj. 1). The failure to take into consideration St. Thomas's metaphysics explains the confusion of some who suggest that St. Thomas was inconsistent in describing women as inferior in one place and exalting the Virgin Mary above even the angels in another (see, e.g., Johnson, *Truly Our Sister*, 24).

face and heart of his bride, the Church."[83] Here he suggests that there is something sex-specific about the soul. Some further texts support this interpretation of the phrase "feminine soul." In John Paul II's theology of the body catecheses, he discusses the husband's knowing of his wife: "It seems as if the specific determination of the woman, through her own body and sex, hides what constitutes the depth of her femininity."[84]

The depth of the woman's femininity is not exhausted by her body. Sex difference must also have some manifestation in her soul. John Paul shows this in his discussion of the woman's reception of the man as a gift: "The man, therefore, not only accepts the gift, but at the same time is welcomed as a gift by the woman in the self-revelation of the inner spiritual essence of his masculinity together with the whole truth of his body and sex."[85] Here the author refers to the spiritual essence of masculinity. He indicates that sex differences are in some way rooted in the soul, which would be expected from hylomorphism since the soul is the substantial form of the body.[86] This is necessary if they are constitutive of personhood.[87] While he does not provide us with an explicit metaphysical account for this, we can infer one.[88]

---

[83] John Paul II, *The Church*, 608. The English "feminine soul" is a translation of the original Italian *l'anima femminile*.

[84] *Man and Woman*, 210. This "knowing" is in the sense of the conjugal union in which husband and wife become "one flesh" (204–208).

[85] *Man and Woman*, 197.

[86] Perhaps someone might raise, as difficulty with this assertion, a statement from his first book in which he says that "[s]piritual fatherhood and motherhood is a distinctive characteristic of a mature interior personhood of a man and a woman. This spiritual fatherhood is much more similar to spiritual motherhood than bodily fatherhood is to bodily motherhood. The sphere of the spirit stands beyond the scope of sex" (Wojtyła, *Love and Responsibility*, 246). We will address this text in part 4.

[87] It is consistent as long as sex difference is not in the substantial category of being.

[88] One possible reconciliation might be a theory which prescinds from Balthasar's "(super-) masculinity" and "(super-) femininity" as modes of love in the Trinitarian persons (see footnote 17 in this chapter). The Father has both "(super-) masculinity" and "(super-) femininity," as does the Son. However, for the Father the former is primary and the latter is secondary. For the Son this is reversed. David Schindler expounds upon Balthasar's thought that this is analogically reflected in the human person (see "Future of Western Civilization," 200–39). He indicates that the difference between St. Thomas's and Balthasar's approaches is that St. Thomas aligns masculinity with act and femininity with potency. Balthasar anchors both in different modes of "act." For Balthasar, the primary male mode is an initiating act of love. The woman's primary mode is a receptive act of love. The woman secondarily then returns this love and the man secondarily receives it. In this case, both masculine and feminine souls, which are substantial forms, would have all that is necessary to human nature. They simply possess it differently. In this reading of

John Paul understands that men and women must be of the same species. He repeatedly calls man "a double unity as male and female."[89] Divine revelation discloses the fact that woman and man (male) equally share the same nature. The taking of the rib from the first man is an "archaic, metaphorical and figurative way of expressing the . . . homogeneity of the whole being of both [man and woman]."[90] This bodily homogeneity is certain regardless of the binary modality of man, which arises because of sex differences.[91] "Masculinity and femininity express the twofold aspect of man's somatic constitution. . . ."[92] So there is no question about a common human nature in his thinking. But again, we must remind that the author does not provide a philosophical account explaining the manner in which sex difference constitutes a somatic duality, penetrates the entirety of the person, and still maintains the unity of human nature.

Nevertheless, John Paul II's "constitutiveness" of sex difference can be shown to be coherent if we consider personhood and sex difference both to be in the category of being of relation, with sex difference specifying the manner in which the person complementarily expresses love, whether as initiating or as actively receptive.

SEX DIFFERENCES AND COMPLEMENTARITY

Karol Wojtyła explains sexual differentiation to be not simply difference but complementary difference.[93] In *Love and Responsibility*, Wojtyła notes that a prima facie observation of sex reveals that each sex manifests attributes the other does not. Yet, a closer evaluation of just the anatomical features of each sex reveals a reciprocal complementarity ordered to procreation. Additionally, sexual attraction, which he calls the "drive to mutual completion," indicates that the opposite sex has a reciprocal value for each

---

Balthasar, the theory seems quite consonant with John Paul II's morphology of the *communio personarum*–gift in his theology of the body catecheses, and which he succinctly summarizes in *Mulieris dignitatem*: "When the author of the Letter to the Ephesians calls Christ 'the Bridegroom' and the Church 'the Bride,' he indirectly confirms through this analogy *the truth about woman as bride*. The Bridegroom is the one who loves. The Bride is loved: *it is she who receives love, in order to love in return*" (*Mulieris dignitatem*, §29). We will say more about this when we discuss sex difference as relation.

[89] *Man and Woman*, 159.
[90] *Man and Woman*, 160.
[91] See *Man and Woman*, 161.
[92] *Man and Woman*, 165.
[93] See *Christifideles laici*, §50.

sex, intrinsically linked to procreation.[94] However, complementarity goes much deeper than the science of biology alone can reveal.[95]

Wojtyła points out that the complementarity of the sexual urge is found in the makeup of the human psyche. The man's psychic structure orients him to analysis, moving him to want to study and disclose the mystery of the woman. Conversely, a woman's psychic structure inclines her to want to preserve the mystery of persons. The man's more analytical proclivity causes him to focus on the woman and the urge in terms of the fruit of pleasure, while she will tend to consider such intimacy with the man in terms of a more integral emotional gratification she experiences as affective love. Their complementary difference places different responsibilities on each for the mutual maintenance of purity.[96]

This analysis illustrates differences between the way men and women experience and manifest love, but that in their very differences, they complement one another. Wojtyła makes it a significant point of note that both the man and the woman are complementarily active but in different modes, such that one's activeness complements the other. Because both are active, their roles and responsibilities must differ, or they would naturally conflict. It

---

[94] See Wojtyła, *Love and Responsibility*, 32. Another example of this is that

> [t]he sexual drive expresses itself in this vitality in such a way that the organism possessing masculine properties "needs" an organism possessing feminine properties in order to achieve the proper effect through being joined to it—the effect in which the sexual vitality of the body finds its natural consummation. For the sexual vitality is by nature disposed toward reproduction, and the other sex serves this end. This disposition in itself is not to consume, since nature does not have only use for an end. Hence, this is simply a natural disposition in which an objective need of a being comes to light.

(*Love and Responsibility*, 89).

[95] Cahill rejects the idea of complementarity as an effort "to advance hierarchically ordered links between reproductive characteristics and social roles" ("Feminist Ethics," 50). Johnson calls it a "sexist theology" (*Truly Our Sister*, 51). George Tavard provides insight into the feminist rejection of this concept when he says that if Christian anthropology rightly sees "manhood and womanhood as distinct complementary ways of being that cannot be reduced to one or the other" then a good case can be made for two functions in the Church (George Tavard, "A Theologian Responds to Margaret Farley," in *Women and Catholic Priesthood: An Expanded Vision*, ed. Anne Marie Gardiner [New York, Paramus, Toronto: Paulist Press, 1976], 54). Christine Gudorf believes complementarity to be problematic because it leaves each person incomplete outside of marriage. She finds this in conflict with the Church's position on consecrated celibacy (see Christine Gudorf, "Encountering the Other: The Modern Papacy on Women," *Social Compass* 36, no. 3 [1989]: 301). We will look at criticisms of complementarity in part 4.

[96] See Wojtyła, *Love and Responsibility*, 94.

might be noted that the above passage corresponds well with the Balthasarian model of complementarity of masculine and feminine love discussed earlier.

John Paul finds integral sexual complementarity to be revealed in Scripture and manifested in the created order. He applies his phenomenological hermeneutic to Genesis 2:23 to find Adam's "words of gladness and also of enthusiastic rapture . . . on seeing a being essentially like himself. The diversity and, at the same time, the psycho-spiritual complementarity are at the origin of the particular richness of humanity, which is proper to the descendants of Adam through their entire history."[97] This verse shows John Paul that in coming to understand sex difference, Adam and Eve find that as man and woman they are almost "two 'incarnations' of the same metaphysical solitude before God and the world."[98] Human beings share at the most fundamental level a common human nature, while at the same time man and woman are so structured in their personhood and complementary differences that they possess the potency for a remarkable unity in the dimensions of their individual persons and natures.

John Paul II sees the fact that God creates man as male and female (Gen 1:27) as a positive revelation of complementary sex difference which interpenetrates all aspects of human life. He sees that the sacred author seems to be declaring that both man and woman bear within themselves the source of their equality—their creation in the image of God. But in addition to their shared human nature, she also bears God's image in her feminine genius. He refers to this as "equality in diversity."[99]

Complementarity implies equality in diversity. It also implies that personal fulfillment requires each sex to understand what fulfillment means for its particular genius. Much earlier, in his letter *Mulieris dignitatem* (On the Dignity and Vocation of Women), John Paul II says this even more emphatically. He argues that the personal resources of men and women are equal but different. Furthermore, both sexes need to understand that

---

[97] John Paul II, *A Catechesis on the Creed*, vol. 1, *God, Father and Creator* (Boston: Pauline Books and Media, 1995), 231.

[98] *Man and Woman*, 166. For scriptural treatment of masculine and feminine complementarity based upon St. John Paul II's thought, see Deborah Savage, "Woman and Man: Identity, Genius and Mission," in *The Complementarity of Women and Men*, ed. Paul C. Vitz (Washington, DC: Catholic University of America Press, 2021), 89–131.

[99] See John Paul II, *The Church*, 480, in which he cites CCC §369. The term is "*uguaglianza nella diversità*" in the official Italian in which the audience was delivered (see https://www.vatican.va/content/john-paul-ii/it/audiences/1994/documents/hf_jp-ii_aud_19940622.pdf). He also says that this has significance for the woman in that she can find her perfection only by embracing her femininity and so it is important for women and for society to recognize women's particular equality in difference.

these personal resources establish a complementary metaphysical structure by which each may achieve their personal fulfillment. Though this text is addressed especially to women, both men and women can overcome the effects of original sin and its contribution to their interpersonal conflicts by understanding and living in accord with their sexually differentiated structure because this structure is established by the divine archetype in whose image they are created.[100] In a word, the consequences of failing to recognize the ramifications of complementarity—that the gifts of each sex are different—can include the loss of the ability to overcome the discord between husband and wife introduced by concupiscence.[101]

John Paul II describes complementarity in relational terms. The fact that man was created male and female shows man that God made him to become a communion of persons, for from the core of man's essence he is created as a social being.[102] Man cannot reach his potential—and in fact he cannot live—without relationships of love with others. He finds this relational character reflected in the Genesis command to subdue the earth.[103] Creation itself suggests that man is created for relationships with other human beings, especially in the marital relationship, and he is created for a relationship with the world as well.

John Paul II characterizes complementarity as the reciprocal relation between the two sexes.[104] In the matter of reciprocal relations, he again reminds us that man is also made in the image of God.[105] He goes so far as to say that this fact is a call to exist for another.[106] By this he means that through his relationships lived rightly as male or female (and only as such), can man achieve the fullness of his personhood. The human person

---

[100] See *Mulieris dignitatem*, §10.

[101] John Paul II's reference to these differences could suggest that one sex is deprived of some "resource" of human nature which the other sex possesses. If this is the case, then it could be a serious problem for John Paul's anthropology because it would seem to cleave human nature into separate species. I will address this issue in part 4.

[102] See *Gaudium et spes*, §12.

[103] See John Paul II, *God, Father and Creator*, 232

[104] See John Paul II, *God, Father and Creator*, 232.

[105] See John Paul II, *God, Father and Creator*, 232. One might ask whether John Paul believes that there is complementarity in the Trinitarian relations. The referenced text seems to suggest that John Paul II thinks that there is something analogous to complementarity in the Trinity, as would his commitment to the *analogia entis*. Any Trinitarian complementarity would have to be relational and would be found in the relations of Paternity and Filiation.

[106] John Paul says: "To say that man is created in the image and likeness of God means that man is called to exist 'for' others, to become a gift. This applies to every human being, whether woman or man, who live it out in accordance with the special qualities proper to each" (*Mulieris dignitatem*, §7).

has a potency for fulfillment which he achieves only in authentically actualizing, by means of a sincere self-gift, his relationships with others. But this fulfillment is a potency in personhood which the person actualizes through free will rather than through some sort of fulfillment of the person's incomplete human nature.[107] But for his fulfillment to be realized, the free choices he makes must accord both with his human nature and his sex difference, because both reflect how he images God.

John Paul affirms the reciprocity of complementarity again in discussing the prelapsarian communication between the first woman and man through the spousal meaning of their bodies. He says that before the fall, man and woman each had the capacity for interpersonal communication in the fullness of their humanity. This communication was marked by their complementary sex difference which allowed them to form an authentic communion of persons by means of total self-gift. The prelapsarian state permitted them to understand the fullness of meaning of their persons in their bodies, through their complementary reciprocity.[108]

This notion of complementarity has obvious importance for marriage and the family, and because the family is the nucleus of society, complementary relationality also influences fulfillment of society and the life of the Church. Thus, the author finds complementarity also to be an aspect of ecclesial mission. Without the complementary vocations, roles, and tasks of men and women, John Paul says that the Church cannot carry out her mission. This is especially true of men and women's mutual cooperation in collaboration with the Church, in married life, and in "the family which is 'the first, primordial expression of the social dimension of the person' (CL 40)."[109]

Complementarity, seen in relational terms, demonstrates that diversity need not imply mutual opposition. Very much to the contrary, complementarity as an attribute of relationality reveals diversity as necessary for mutual fulfillment. John Paul II finds relational complementarity indicated in the first biblical creation account when God tells the man and woman to be fertile and multiply in order to fill the earth and to exercise dominion over it. He finds this task can be fulfilled only through their cooperation in employing the mutually complementary gifts of masculinity and femininity.[110] Rather than opposition, complementarity implies

---

[107] See, e.g., John Paul II, *The Trinity's Embrace*, 287, and *The Church*, 480.
[108] See *Man and Woman*, 178ff.
[109] John Paul II, *The Church*, 500.
[110] See John Paul II, *The Church*, 480.

the demand for cooperation. This is demonstrable from reason as well as evident in divine revelation. For example, God says that it is not good that man is alone; he needs a fit "helper."

The man cannot complete his task as man without an adequate "helper." This helper must be one who can complement the gifts given to the man. John Paul points out that in Genesis 2:21–22, God calls the woman into being from Adam's rib in order to resolve the problem of the man's relational insufficiency in his solitude. Consequently, the Genesis text shows that they are necessary for each other's individual vocation and each other's personal fulfillment.[111] The sharing of the same nature, indicated by the rib, and the completion of the man by the woman demand the acknowledgement of the man and woman as equals. John Paul II argues, therefore, that mutual opposition between the man and woman is incompatible with the call to personal fulfillment.

As suggested above, equality is yet another aspect of complementarity. Complementarity begins with a unifying nature, and so men and women must be equal in some ways. However, one must not mistake equality of nature with the absolute sameness of men and women.[112] John Paul warns that the woman will perfect herself in a manner different than the man. She must not lose what is unique to her as a woman. Her perfection is to be found through her femininity, perfecting herself as a woman who is equal to but also different from a man.[113]

The contemporary confusion of equality with an overall sameness presents a serious threat, pressuring women in the name of equality to masculinize themselves and thereby lose themselves. Of course, the same thing is true of men who would adopt feminine manners, but John Paul appears

---

[111] See John Paul II, *God, Father and Creator*, 223.

[112] While "equal" can mean "same," even in its etymological origins it can also connote similarity as well as justice and fairness. In its modern usage, since the time of the French Revolution, it has come to be used to emphasize the just recognition of every person's dignity, rights, and opportunities. Yet, even at the time of the Rights of Man, this notion of equality began to imply that a homogenizing sameness must be imposed irrespective of real differences, in order to achieve in practice the just recognition of rights and opportunities. With time, this rejection of real differences has become more pronounced and irrational, leading some today to assume the definition of "equal" as meaning "the same." John Paul II accepts the use of "equality" to describe men and women. He grounds it in their common human nature, saying they both possess it to the same degree (see *Mulieris dignitatem*, §6). He acknowledges their equality in matters that apply to our common human nature. He reserves calling men and women different for matters that apply to their unique, complementary differences.

[113] See John Paul II, *The Church*, 480.

to see the former to be a greater risk as women move more into their rightful places in society. To counter this problem, he emphasizes the need to recognize woman's equality with man coextensively with her diversity.[114] The recognition of equality in diversity is the remedy for the homogenizing societal trend which tries to locate the basis of masculine and feminine equality in an androgenizing sameness in which each sex is demanded to emulate the other to the detriment of both.

The proper understanding of masculine and feminine equality and difference is a concern for broader society as well as for the life of the Church. Equality must first be understood as an equality of dignity. John Paul II is emphatic that women have the same dignity as men.[115] He says, "'God created man in his own image, in the image of God he created him; male and female he created them' (Gen 1:27). The man and the woman were created with equal dignity as persons, as units of spirit and body. But they are also differentiated by their psycho-physical structures."[116] He finds even in the biblical names for man and woman a relationality which suggests complementary equality.[117] The proper character of the relationship between the woman and the man is revealed in a lexical analysis of Genesis 2:18, and of the term "helper." This term does not connote a servile relationship but rather a collaborative one. The statement that she is a "helper fit for him" indicates that the collaborative capacity of the woman with the man rises from the fact that she perfectly complements him. They are both self-determining persons who share a common nature, a nature which is constituted by two sexes with equal dignity and complementarily different gifts.[118]

---

[114] This could apply to men welcoming women for the first time into a role or task traditionally dominated by men. Men should not engender the expectation that the woman perform in the same manner as would a man. Similarly, a woman must be careful not to adopt masculine traits which would be a danger with solely masculine role models. We will look at specific differences between male and female traits in the part 3.

[115] For example, see *Mulieris dignitatem*, §§6, 12, 16, 19; John Paul II, Encyclical Letter on the Value and Inviolability of Human Life *Evangelium vitae* (March 25, 1995), *AAS* 87 (1995), 401–522, §35; *The Church*, 479; *Familiaris consortio*, §19; *Christifideles laici*, §§20, 50; Post-Synodal Apostolic Exhortation on the Consecrated Life and Its Mission in the Church and in the World *Vita consecrata* (March 26, 1996), §102.

[116] John Paul II, *God, Father and Creator*, 231.

[117] We discuss below the Hebrew *iš* (male) and *iššiah* (female).

[118] See John Paul II, *The Trinity's Embrace*, 288. John Paul is not specific in this text with respect to the areas of collaboration between man and woman, but since this is in the context of the Genesis text one should probably read this as a general collaboration in their task of establishing dominion over the earth.

Complementarity between men and women indicates unity in their common human nature but diversity in their personal structure as male and female persons. Unity of nature points to their equality in dignity, but their differences due to sex suggest diversity in the manner in which each sex acts and reaches personal fulfillment. We are still left with the question of the category of being by which we classify sex differences. We have seen that John Paul II implicitly understands the human person, in analogy to the divine persons, to exist in the category of being of relation. Let us now turn to his writings that reveal the same is true for sex differences.

Sex Difference and Relationality

To understand how John Paul II views sex difference in a relational sense requires a short review of his metaphysical thinking. In the Thomist metaphysical system there are two ways of "being" in the created order: substances and accidents. Substances exist by themselves, they subsist. Accidents exist only in the substance in which they inhere. Relation is one of nine categories of accidents but there are other relations. Relations can be either "real" or "logical." Real relations have accidental being.[119]

Logical relations, on the other hand, exist entirely in the mind. While St. Thomas does not explicitly accept created persons as relations, we showed in chapter 4 that St. John Paul II does implicitly do so. Our description of sex difference to this point suggests that to be consistent, it must also have ontological being in the category of a real relation. However, we must ask whether sex difference is nothing more than an accident, which is Aristotle's and Thomas's thinking. Or does sex difference exist in itself in the category of being of relation as is the case for personhood?[120]

---

[119] See Mark G. Henninger, S.J., *Relations: Medieval Theories, 1250–1325* (Oxford: Clarendon Press, 1989), 19–23.

[120] We do not have the space to develop this point here, and it would go well beyond a direct treatment of John Paul II's thought to do so, but I should point out that it is not necessary for sex difference as a relation to be either an accident (real relation) or to exist in the category of being of relation in a mutually exclusive manner. I suggest that at least in some cases it must be both because it is necessary for metaphysical coherence. Just as a person (who is a created relation) exists always and only as possessing his nature (angelic or human), other created relations must necessarily exist always in a substance. The presence of a relation in a substance would need to manifest its presence. It would seem that this manifestation explains at least some accidents which inhere in a substance. In this way, certain relations could change the essence of the subject, registered as an accident inhering in the subject's substantial form, without introducing substantial change in the subject. This provides an account of the deeper metaphysical reality of our discussion

159

John Paul II confirms that sex difference is relational from an etymological analysis of the Hebrew terms for "man" and "woman." If sex difference had the being of a substance, it would rupture the homogeneity of human nature, for then each sex would comprise a separate species of humanity.[121] When we say sex difference is accidental with respect to human nature, it is not to say that it is unimportant. St. Thomas categorizes accidents as either essential or accidental.[122] Essential accidents are attributes which are inseparable from the nature or essence of the thing under consideration. Accidental accidents are separable from the subject. Thus for human nature, sex difference is an essential accident, which is called a property. A human person must have sex difference, but the sex difference can be either male or female.

While sex difference is accidental to human nature, it is not accidental to human personhood. Sex difference is foundational in establishing personal identity; in fact, it is essential to human personhood. Sex difference is also fundamental for interpersonal relationships and as a relation it sets the framework for these relationships.[123] John Paul II's analysis of Scripture shows sex difference as necessarily relational and essential for relationships. While he does not develop the matter in metaphysical terms, his analysis permits us to inquire about sex difference's metaphysical

---

of the interplay of relation and substance in personhood and personal fulfillment in chapter 4.

[121] John Paul II does use language in at least one place that might call this statement into question. In speaking about man's part in a mutual gift of the whole person, he says: "The man, therefore, not only accepts the gift, but at the same time is welcomed as a gift by the woman in the self-revelation of the inner spiritual essence of his masculinity together with the whole truth of his body and his sex" (*Man and Woman*, 197). The phrase "spiritual essence of his masculinity" (*spirituale essenza della sua mascolinità*) may be taken in the metaphysical sense of "substantial existence," but it is not clear that he means it in this way. For example, it could be that he is using a synecdoche in which "masculinity" is referring to the entirety of his spiritual personhood. However, it is more likely that John Paul does not see essence as necessarily synonymous with substance. For example, Grabowski finds that both Galot and Ratzinger indicate that essence is not necessarily to be equated with the substance of a thing but primarily refers to its "being" (See Grabowski, "Person: Substance and Relation," 158n79), as we discussed earlier in this chapter.

[122] See St. Thomas Aquinas, *Commentary on Aristotle's Metaphysics*, trans. John P. Rowan (Chicago: Henry Regnery Company, 1961), bk. 4., lesson 1, 534–47.

[123] Sex difference as a relation that instantiates the person-relation as male or female together with its accidental manifestation in the human substance, alone provides a coherent account for the immutability of sex difference while permitting a unity of nature between male and female persons.

foundations. It seems to me that his analysis demonstrates why we must hold that sex difference to be in the category of being of relation.

John Paul II's analysis of the terms for "man" and "woman" in the second chapter of Genesis helps to elucidate the manner in which sex difference is relational. He says: "The Bible calls the first human being "man" ('ādām), while from the moment of the creation of the first woman, it begins to call him "male," 'îš, in relation to 'iššā^h ("woman," because she was taken from the male = 'îš)."[124] The very names indicate the woman's relation to the man is based necessarily on a difference in sex.[125] He finds that in addition to etymology, the sequence of the Genesis texts can be significant for the meaning of sex difference. For example, John Paul finds it is important "that the first man ('ādām) . . . is defined as a 'male' ('îš) only after the creation of the first woman."[126]

John Paul believes that the Genesis narrator implies that one can only understand the two sexes in terms of each other. They have a relational essence. This is what John Paul means in discussing Genesis 2:23 when he states that "femininity in some way finds itself before masculinity, while masculinity confirms itself through femininity."[127] Scripture manifests this relationality through the means of the body. That is to say, the relationality of sex difference gives rise to the relationship of the marital covenant.

The body, including sex difference, expresses the person and, therefore, it expresses the fullness of one's humanity.[128] The corporeal manifestation

---

[124] *Man and Woman*, 139.

[125] The objection might be raised that this is reading too much into the text. In response, I would suggest that John Paul recognizes the modern nominalist presupposition that words are arbitrarily applied to whatever they describe. But he also understands this was not part of Hebrew thinking. As was true with Aristotle, the Hebrew mind understood words to be dianoetic. In other words, words are signs that transcend themselves and are able to make their referent intelligible (see John L. McKenzie, "Aspects of Old Testament Thought," in *The New Jerome Biblical Commentary*, ed. Raymond E. Brown, Joseph A. Fitzmyer, and Roland E. Murphy [Englewood Cliffs, NJ: Prentice Hall, 1990], 1291b ff.). Therefore, it would be all too hasty to dismiss out of hand, this etymological insight as a facile interpretation.

[126] *Man and Woman*, 147.

[127] *Man and Woman*, 166.

[128] This is perfectly coherent from the standpoint of an integral notion of the human person but may pose some problems for those who possess Cartesian presuppositions in their anthropology. In other words, this will make no sense for those who reject Thomist metaphysics, which leaves them with an anthropology in which the spiritual realm, if it exists at all, is entirely independent from the material realm. Aside from the inherent problems of the system itself, imposing Cartesian anthropological assumptions on biblical thought is anachronistic and results in a distorted reading of Scripture.

of sex difference's relationality is most perfectly visible in the concrete case of the marital covenant.[129] Marriage is the context for John Paul's comment that the body expresses femininity "for" masculinity and vice versa. It is the sexed body that reveals complementary reciprocity, and it is this complementarity that provides the structure for a fruitful, living, giving communion of persons. Inasmuch as masculinity and femininity are the primordial signs of a self-giving that is creative.[130] In this way, the meaning of the body within marriage reveals an even greater meaning for sex differ- ence for the person. It is a witness of one person's relation to another and the call to a sincere relationship based on a gift of the self, which John Paul repeatedly refers to as a "communion of persons."

Man's vocation to communion has its source in the love which is the Trinity. The Trinitarian *communio personarum*, the archetype and *telos* for man, has its most perfect corporeal witness through sex difference in marriage. The body, through its sex, becomes the substrate by which the husband and wife form their irrevocable communion.[131] John Paul repeat- edly makes it clear that it is the complementarity of masculine and feminine anatomy which reveals sex difference's deepest meaning.[132] This view that the body in both its structure and its actions can reveal the deepest meaning of sex difference and its complementarity is coherent only when one keeps in mind John Paul II's commitment that the soul is the substan- tial form of the body, along with its attendant hylomorphic implications.

Divine revelation, especially sacred Scripture, shows John Paul II that sex difference, as a relation, establishes the framework for interpersonal relationships. This is particularly the case between a husband and wife. The complementary relationality of sex difference is apparent in Scripture and visibly manifest through the structure and actions of the person and his body. The primary mechanism integrating these insights into a coherent anthropology is John Paul's hylomorphic metaphysics. These facts provide us the framework we will need for developing a deeper understanding of masculinity and fatherhood.

---

[129] John Paul indicates this in the context of original innocence: "The sentence: 'Both were naked, the man and his wife, but they did not feel shame,' expresses precisely such inno- cence 'in the reciprocal experience of the body' an innocence that inspires the inner exchange of the gift of the person, which concretely realizes the spousal meaning of mas- culinity and femininity in their reciprocal relation" (*Man and Woman*, 195).

[130] See *Man and Woman*, 183.

[131] See *Man and Woman*, 231.

[132] See *Man and Woman*, 367–68, 372.

RELATIONAL COMPLEMENTARITY: MASCULINE AND FEMININE MODES OF PERSONAL CHARACTERISTICS

Complementarity is best accounted for in the context of the category of being of relation. This will play a large role in the extraction and synthesis of John Paul II's theology of fatherhood. Therefore, we will need a model from which we can identify complementary masculine characteristics based upon the corresponding feminine characteristics which John Paul II explicitly identifies. In order to develop such a model, we should look at a cross section of texts illustrating the complementarity we have just explored. Following the logic of his anthropology will help to illuminate his understanding of complementarity. John Paul's understanding of sex complementarity begins with creation and the fact that man and woman are both fully human, both made in the image of God.[133] Both men and women share the same human nature. Further, he states that God has ordered everything in creation in such a way that man, male and female, is called to have dominion over the earth and to subdue it.[134]

Man's dominion over creation is an integral process which embraces every human being throughout all time, and so each person is called to take part in this dominion through his work. The process of dominion is not simply external, but it also takes place *"within each human being, in each conscious human subject."*[135] Here there is a sense in which all things in creation equally apply to men and women. But at the same time, there are two key points of John Paul's anthropology which suggest an important distinction in the manner in which they apply. First, man is unified in terms of nature, in the category of substance. But at the same time, he is a duality, in terms of sex difference, giving rise to personal diversity, both of which are in the category of relation. Personhood, with its sex, is the source of man's diversity.

John Paul habitually highlights man's dual unity because he is convinced that God's ordering of things is inextricably linked to the fact that he was created male and female, and that as male and female, man also is in God's image.[136] The second important point is the interiority of action,

---

[133] John Paul considers this "the basis of all Christian anthropology" (*Mulieris dignitatem*, §6).

[134] See John Paul II, Encyclical Letter on Human Work *Laborem exercens* (September 14, 1981), AAS 73 (1981), 577–647, §4.

[135] *Laborem exercens*, §4.

[136] See *Laborem exercens*, §4. For example, he emphasizes humanity's "dual unity" in the Wednesday catecheses published in as his theology of the body and in *Mulieris dignitatem*, but one can find this idea throughout most of his anthropologically oriented writings.

specifically in this case, that of work. We saw in part 1 that this interior aspect of personal, free human acts has a lasting and ontological character. John Paul also is convinced that there is a manner of acting which is proper to each sex. One must carry out free, personal acts in a manner which is in accord with the created order. From the very beginning man is called to exercise dominion over creation, yet he is called to do so as a male or female.

God has ordered creation in such a way that the two sexes approach this exercise of dominion in a different but complementary manner. In our previous sketch of the structure of complementarity we noted that each sex has all the characteristics proper to humanity, but there are still sex-specific characteristics. Many of these sex-specific characteristics are present in the other sex but exist in a complementary manner. These characteristics arise from the soul, the body's substantial form, which is also, as we have said, "act." Sex difference, then, can be understood as the expression of different modes of act which are manifested by the soul.

In the masculine mode, an initiating love predominates, and in the feminine mode, an actively receptive love prevails. But men also have a secondary receptive love and women have a secondary initiating love. In this way the characteristics referred to above, orient each sexed person toward a certain manner of acting which is in accord with their sex.[137] This sexual structure establishes one's appropriate manner of acting and is important for self-fulfillment. John Paul explains that each person is called by God to fulfill a personal calling, which in general terms is the same for men and women.

The universal human vocation is to perfect oneself in love through sincere self-giving. However, the manner in which this self-giving is to be expressed will differ between men and women.[138] The manner will be similar because both the man and the woman are human persons possessing composite natures of body and soul, with the same general vocation to love.[139] The manner of love differs in the mode of giving and receiving. The context of the great mystery (Ephesians 5:21–33) most eloquently illustrates their complementary manner of expressing love in terms of their vocation.[140] There are manifold additional examples that show complementarity between men and women is fundamental in John Paul II's view.

---

[137] The characteristics orient the person, but they do not determine his choosing for him. He always possesses free will.

[138] See *Familiaris consortio*, §22.

[139] See Letter to Families, §20.

[140] See Letter to Families, §20. Even for consecrated celibacy, Ephesians 5 is normative. In

Both man and woman are called to reciprocally give themselves to each other and, as husband and wife, to their children.[141] This is a call to authentic family life. John Paul consistently roots this vocation in divine revelation as part of the Creator's plan—the One who created them male and female. Authentic family life is anchored in the "'unity of the two' ... the prime community of persons, source of every other community, and ... [the] 'sign' of that interpersonal communion of love which constitutes the mystical, intimate life of God, One in Three."[142] Both the man and the woman equally have this vocation to fulfill the responsibilities of Christian family life in the realm of conjugal relations, as well as in maternity and paternity. Together, through mutual self-gift, they not only satisfy the requirements for a fruitful conjugal life, but also through this giving they fulfill the needs of their children by means of the different, complementary gifts which a father and mother synergistically provide.[143]

Man and woman, as a couple, are similarly called to share in the mission of the Church—the building up of the kingdom of God—by following the pattern of the community established in their family life. This mission is due to the fact that the family is the foundational community upon which larger communities are built. The family participates in the Church's mission by the self-giving love shared *"between husband and wife and between members of the family*—a love lived out in all its extraordinary richness of values and demands: totality, oneness, fidelity and fruitfulness—that the Christian family's participation in the prophetic, priestly and kingly mission of Jesus Christ and of his Church finds expression and realization."[144] The common denominator in all of John Paul II's writings on the complementary nature of vocation is that man and woman are to accomplish these tasks as a feminine-masculine duality, in a reciprocal gift as husband and wife, and as mother and father, as a complementary unity.

Complementarity is most apparent in conjugal life. The fruitful conjugal life is authentic only if the man and woman live it out by loving each other in the manner of reciprocal, free self-giving in the marital covenant. Authenticity requires the complementarity of a man and woman through which they become co-creators with the Creator, whose overflowing

---

chapter 8, we will see that John Paul II understands celibacy as a witness to the ultimate meaning of Christ's spousal union with his Church. The consecrated person reveals the perfect eschatological communion of persons in which all the saved will participate.

[141] See *Familiaris consortio*, §22; Letter to Families, §20.

[142] *Christifideles laici*, §52.

[143] See *Christifideles laici*, §52.

[144] *Christifideles laici*, §52.

love enriches and enlarges his family.[145] Once again, we cannot overstate the fact that complementarity is not simply biological, though it cannot be separated from it. The two great dangers into which contemporary minds often fall are either mistaking biology as all-determining, on the one hand, or else considering it to be of no significance for the person, on the other; ironically, frequently they do so simultaneously. In accordance with the Trinitarian archetype of self-giving love, the spouses' fecund love must extend beyond procreation. The fruit of this marital love permeates the spouses' moral, spiritual, and supernatural lives, and through this, it provides the means by which they mediate this life to their children and, through their children, to both the world and the Church.[146] In procreation, the structure of complementarity is most evident. This is to say, procreation reveals differences which together form a purposeful unity. But there also is a spiritual fecundity arising out of genital love.

This fecundity is an overflowing of the love which is most perfectly and complementarily expressed in the conjugal relations of husband and wife. In other words, the unity expressed and achieved in the conjugal life is the source of the fruitful love which nurtures the spouses' children. Fruitfulness is not simply psychological but also is metaphysical, because of the sacramental nature of marriage and the grace which the husband and wife mediate to each other in marriage, and especially in the covenantal act of intercourse.[147] Thus, all aspects of marital fruitfulness are ordered to the spouses' complementarity.

Natural fatherhood and motherhood generally result from the fruitful conjugal life, but they are also vocations and tasks which require great effort. They are tasks entrusted to a woman and a man in which both must cooperate in complementary ways.[148] The complementarity of these vocations has its foundation in the source of both motherhood and fatherhood—God's fatherhood (see Ephesians 3:14–16). John Paul reads this pericope from Ephesians to reveal the meaning of human fatherhood and motherhood. Hence, these vocations cannot simply be reduced to sociological constructs; they have a divine archetype.[149] Revelation likewise gives warrant to his assertion that the man and woman in their vocations both reflect God's fatherhood, but differently.[150]

---

[145] See Letter to Families, §16.

[146] See *Familiaris consortio*, §28.

[147] See *Familiaris consortio*, §33.

[148] See Letter to Families, §7.

[149] See Letter to Families, §6.

[150] See Letter to Families, §16.

Both the mother and father share the responsibility for raising, forming, and educating their children. These tasks are "rooted in the primary vocation of married couples to participate in God's creative activity: by begetting in love and for love a new person who has within himself or herself the vocation to growth and development, parents by that very fact take on the task of helping that person effectively to live a fully human life."[151] The education of children begins with the mutual gift of the parents to each other and to the child, through which they communicate to a newborn baby their mature humanity. The parents' reciprocal self-gift is fundamental to the child's healthy upbringing. There is also reciprocity between parents and children; children also nourish their parents. As for the child, it is through the parents, the mother and father together, that he first experiences the love and providence of God's fatherhood. This experience, provided by the parents together, is needed to enable the child to grow up with the confidence and tranquility necessary for a healthy life.[152]

On the other hand, the newborn gives himself and the "newness and freshness" of the humanity he has brought into the world to his parents.[153] This gift helps the parents to continue to deepen their love for each other and their children by means of their children's gift of existence and personhood, which the children give back to them. Again, for John Paul, this mutual, reciprocal nourishment (between spouses, parent to child, child to parent) is not simply meeting a bodily, psychological, or emotional need. It includes these but given the integrated nature of the person, it includes the entire person, body and spiritual soul.

Of significance here is the necessity that *both* parents mediate and witness to God's fatherhood. This obligation is rooted in the very structure of man as male and female. Since human motherhood and fatherhood are different ways of participating in divine fatherhood, and since each possesses a complementary aspect of this participation, both parents must bring their unique gifts to the formation of the child. The fundament of what they bring in fatherhood and motherhood is their sincere, disinterested self-gift, modulated by their feminine and masculine genius, respectively.

This capacity for sincere self-giving has its roots in God's gift of himself as Creator and Redeemer of man, a gift given in the grace of the Holy Spirit. Without sanctifying grace, a couple cannot grasp the full

---

[151] See *Familiaris consortio*, §36.
[152] See *Familiaris consortio*, §41.
[153] See Letter to Families, §16.

meaning of marriage and family, authentically live out the marital vocation, or achieve their authentic meaning.[154] The vocation to total self-gift requires the grace that heals, elevates, and perfects fallen human nature. In cooperation with this gift, the parents acquire the capacity to faithfully respond to their vocation, a capacity that exists in virtue of the parents' participation in God's unique goodness. Each participates in a manner particular to his sexually defined vocation.[155] This participation illuminates God's commandment to honor one's father and mother, and it bestows upon them the obligation to witness to this goodness in such a way that they merit the honor and love of their children.[156]

It is through the mutual honor shared between the parents themselves and between them and their children that they bear witness to God's goodness and command the honor from their children that the children require in order to flourish. These callings, tasks, and obligations can be summed up in the requirement of self-gift; that is, in the parents' complementary gift of love.[157] This complementary self-giving love is so rooted in the meaning of the sexed human person and his marital vocation that John Paul II argues that "*motherhood necessarily implies fatherhood,* and in turn, *fatherhood necessarily implies motherhood.* This is the result of the duality bestowed by the Creator upon human beings 'from the beginning.'"[158]

AN INTEGRAL ACCOUNT OF JOHN PAUL II'S COMPLEMENTARITY

Having examined John Paul II's view of complementarity, we still require a model informed by our account to more precisely explain how complementarity is manifested in each sex and how it influences the physiological, emotional, psychological, spiritual, and other dimensions of the integral person. This model will eventually be needed to infer masculine features through complementarity with reciprocal feminine features, as many more of his writings address femininity and motherhood than masculinity and fatherhood.

John Paul II does not provide a detailed articulation of the integral person we require in order to determine the masculine complements to the plethora of feminine attributes and tasks he presents. However, he provides

---

[154] See Letter to Families, §11.
[155] See Letter to Families, §15.
[156] See Letter to Families, §15.
[157] See Letter to Families, §22.
[158] Letter to Families, §7.

enough of an account that it is possible to flesh out such a description. Active receptivity, especially a receptive love, is a primary feminine characteristic. It is the woman who first receives love and the man who first offers his love. This supports the inference drawn from John Paul's acceptance of a form of scholastic thought in which the woman is receptive and the man's complement is initiative.[159]

We have seen that Hans Urs von Balthasar espouses a Trinitarian anthropology, which begins with this idea of the man as the initiator and the woman as receptive. William May describes an anthropology similar to Balthasar's, but his is intended to be descriptive of John Paul's anthropology with respect to complementarity. For May, the key feature of John Paul II's account of femininity is interiority. A woman tends to take in and to integrate her experiences within her. Women, in general, manifest this tendency in response to their experiences. May points out that this integration includes the manifold aspects of a woman's experiences (mental, bodily, emotional). The predominant masculine features are the complements to the feminine. Therefore, unlike a woman, a man tends to be more exterior, associating more with his actions themselves than incorporating them into his entire being as does she. He is inclined to respond in a diffuse and differentiated way.[160]

We might note that May's articulation of complementarity does not make these characteristics exclusive to each respective sex. Rather, in terms of giving and receiving, he says that while both men and women give in a receiving way and receive in a giving way, the masculine structure is ardently inclined toward the former and the feminine structure toward the

---

[159] While receptivity and initiative may be closely linked with Aristotelian biology, they are not based solely upon it. Rather, John Paul II can maintain these notions because he finds them in Scripture (see, e.g., Eph 5) and in human experience. Furthermore, Aristotle did not arrive at the consequence that woman is receptive and man is active as a result of his biology or metaphysics; rather, he built a biology from these observations (see Allen, *The Concept of Woman*, 1:89–103). Thus, the overturning of Aristotelian biology does not require John Paul to abandon valid insights which may have been originally tied to a now-antiquated understanding of biology.

[160] See William May, "The Mission of Fatherhood," *Josephinum Journal of Theology* 9, no. 1 (2002): 48–49. May subsequently compares his system to John Paul II's *Mulieris dignitatem*, §18, to find a correspondence of the text of that paragraph to his description (see May, 50). The fact that May's system correlates well with *Mulieris dignitatem* is not surprising. John Paul's integrated, hylomorphic anthropology naturally leads to May's findings; see also William E. May, "Marriage and the Complementarity of Male and Female," *Anthropotes: Rivista sulla persona e la famiglia* 8, no. 1 (1992): 41–60.

latter.[161] One could say that there is a particularly masculine way for a man to be integrative, and a feminine way for a woman to go out of herself. May provides a general description of how initiating and receptive love manifest and affect the masculine and feminine person. However, we need a yet more detailed account.

Manfred Hauke provides the detail we require. Hauke shows that many aspects of masculine and feminine physical characteristics also correspond to the main features of interiority and exteriority.[162] Quoting Philipp Lersch, Hauke says that looking at the physiology of the act of coitus, the woman has the natural role of receiving and assimilating. Lersch calls this a "centripetal" process. In other words, feminine physiology is such that it directs inwardly that which comes to her from the without, "toward the center of life."[163] The man, on the other hand, has a "centrifugal" function by which he directs outwardly, away from this vital center of life.[164] He describes this physiological insight in terms of primary sex characteristics, the genitalia.

Hauke goes on to show how secondary sex characteristics, such as skeletal structure, musculature, adipose tissue distribution, epidermal texture, and so on are all organically integrated in such a way that they support the purpose of the primary sex characteristics. This support is not limited to the act of coitus but rather extends to the attributes needed for gestation—subsequent nurturing of children and assisting in the flourishing of the family. Masculine secondary sex characteristics all serve to facilitate the man's extending himself out into the world. He does this in a way that Hauke explains to be the overcoming and conquering of space.[165] Female sex characteristics, by contrast, converge in such a way that the woman is more strongly directed toward the inside. For both sexes, there is a psychosomatic integration of these functions which is not limited to physiology. This certainly accords with John Paul's integral, hylomorphic understanding of human nature and the human person.

Hauke also studies body dynamics, psychological development,

---

[161] See May, "Marriage and the Complementarity," 47.

[162] See Manfred Hauke, *Women in the Priesthood? A Systematic Analysis in the Light of the Order of Creation and Redemption*, trans. David Kipp (San Francisco: Ignatius Press, 1988), 85–120.

[163] Hauke, *Women in the Priesthood?*, 86, citing Philipp Lersch, *Vom Wesen der Geschlechter*, 4th ed. (Munich and Basel: n.p., 1968), 25.

[164] Hauke, *Women in the Priesthood?*, 86, citing Philipp Lersch, *Vom Wesen der Geschlechter*.

[165] Hauke, *Women in the Priesthood?*, 86, citing Philipp Lersch, *Vom Wesen der Geschlechter*, 88.

differences in experiencing the world—including religious experience and differing world visions. He calls the terms that generally describe the differences between men and women "summary forms." These are "centrality" for women and "eccentricity" for men.[166] Like John Paul II, Balthasar, and May, he says these are the dominant modes for each sex. In other words, each sex has the features of the opposite sex, but they function in a secondary manner. Hauke's model provides a more specific way of describing masculine and feminine characteristics. This centrality-eccentricity model fits quite nicely the data from John Paul II in terms of what he says about women and mothers. Let us take some examples in order to demonstrate their correspondence.

John Paul states that women possess "humble initiative, respect for individuals without seeking to impose a way of seeing things, [and] the invitation to repeat the same experience as a way of reaching the same personal conviction of faith."[167] The invitation to reach the same faith describes the feminine acceptance of something from the outside followed by her integrating it into herself. The fact that she invites reflects the feminine manner of manifesting initiative. Her desire not to impose suggests a reticence to go outside of herself as her primary mode of acting.

As stated in the beginning of this chapter, John Paul II says that a woman "has an understanding, sensitive and compassionate heart that allows her to give a delicate, concrete style to charity."[168] Understanding requires the incorporation and integration of what is given to the woman. Sensitivity is an integral response not just to information but to the entirety of the other person.[169] The ability to pay attention to another person corresponds to the feminine structure of an active receptivity. It is also integrative because it is a concern for the whole person rather than one's primary attention being paid to certain dominant aspects of the person or situation. A woman is structured to receive the entirety of another person and to integrate him into her presence.

John Paul's depiction of motherhood also suggests that the centrality-eccentricity model is correct. He emphasizes that the two primary vocations of women are motherhood and virginity. Empirical analysis "confirms that the very physical constitution of women is naturally

---

[166] See Hauke, *Women in the Priesthood?*, 86, citing Philipp Lersch, *Vom Wesen der Geschlechter*, 96.
[167] John Paul II, *The Church*, 489.
[168] John Paul II, *The Church*, 490.
[169] See *Mulieris dignitatem*, §18.

disposed to motherhood."[170] This includes her psychological constitution, because in John Paul's anthropology the material and the spiritual may be called distinct but they can never be separated. He says: "Motherhood as a *human* fact and phenomenon, is fully explained on the basis of the truth about the person. Motherhood *is linked to the personal structure of the woman and to the personal dimension of the gift.*"[171] Motherhood also "implies from the beginning a special openness to the new person: and this is precisely the woman's 'part.' In this openness, in conceiving and giving birth to a child, the woman 'discovers herself through a sincere gift of self.' The gift of interior readiness to accept the child and bring it into the world."[172]

In the preceding texts, John Paul describes the woman's entire makeup as oriented in a receptive manner in order to bring a baby to life from within herself. This also corresponds well with Hauke's account. John Paul II also says that due to her feminine structure the mother is well suited to the domestic life. Anticipating objections, he makes it clear that women have the same rights as do men to contribute to various public functions. He argues that societies must be structured in such a way that women are not penalized for staying at home for the formative years of child rearing. He says women must be able to enter, or reenter, public life after having raised children without having to start from the beginning because of their time in the home. Nevertheless, he also eschews the mindset that honors women more for their work outside the home than within it.[173]

One cannot accuse John Paul of limiting a woman's place to the home. On the contrary, he says that a woman's presence in all aspects of public life is necessary. However, he is clear that during the phase of a family's life when children are young, the mother plays a primary role in their nurturing. The Western proclivity to take domesticity as a pejorative descriptor would appear to justify John Paul II's concern about society's anti-domestic mentality. Domesticity can be described as integrating and nurturing from within the womb of the home. This characteristic of interiority is also in line with Hauke's model. Many other texts demonstrate similar characteristics of interiority, integrativeness, and receptivity.

Let us summarize those places in which we have seen him illustrate these attributes. John Paul II says that a characteristic of femininity is a

---

[170] *Mulieris dignitatem*, §18.
[171] *Mulieris dignitatem*, §18.
[172] *Mulieris dignitatem*, §18.
[173] *Familiaris consortio*, §23.

special sensitivity to others, particularly seen in the women-disciples' response to Jesus's preaching,[174] which reflects an authentic "resonance of mind and heart."[175] This is so because the feminine mind is more intuitive and better able to receive and accept the meaning of the Gospel message.[176] These gifts of femininity allowed those women to exhibit greater courage than the apostles demonstrated in times of danger.[177] He sees reflected in the feminine countenance the most sublime manifestations of fulfilled humanity: total selfless love, strength to bear the greatest of sorrows, complete faithfulness and devotion, tender solicitude for others, an openness to accept life, and an innate orientation to the vocation to motherhood which comes from an interior awareness that it is a divine calling.[178]

Hauke's centrality-eccentricity account is consonant with John Paul II's integrated anthropology. This assessment is validated by May's evaluation of a similar account against the text of *Mulieris dignitatem*. For that reason, we shall carefully employ the account of the integral person we get from May and Hauke in the analyses of John Paul II's writings which can shed light on his view of fatherhood that we will undertake in part 3.

A Synopsis of Sex Difference and Human Personhood

John Paul II's view of sex difference has several significant features for this study: it is in part "constitutive" of human personhood, it is the basis for complementarity, and it is metaphysically relational. John Paul II uses the term "constitutive" to indicate that sex difference is essential to human personhood while remaining accidental to human nature. He finds the constitutive attribute of sex difference in the example of the Virgin Mary, who fully realizes her personhood by means of her femininity. An analysis of Genesis 2 indicates that sex difference plays an irreplaceable role in establishing personal identity. It is also confirmed in the fact that sex difference both endures in the eschaton and also is somehow manifested in the spiritual soul.

The complementarity between men and women indicates unity in their common human nature and diversity of their personal structure. Thus, complementarity presupposes the distinctions between person and

---

[174] *Familiaris consortio*, §16.
[175] *Familiaris consortio*, §15.
[176] John Paul II, *The Church*, 489.
[177] *Mulieris dignitatem*, §15.
[178] *Redemptoris mater*, §46; *Mulieris dignitatem*, §§14, 18, 30.

nature. The unity of nature indicates that men and women are equal in dignity, but their sex-derived differences (which are in the relational category of being) indicate that there is an innate framework for interpersonal relations, and that they reveal a pathway to personal fulfillment. These differences also provide a structure for interpersonal relationships which is necessary for the healthy growth of marriage, family, society, and ecclesial life. Furthermore, complementarity shows that one must not absolutize equality in all things belonging to human nature to eliminate the differences belonging to person-sex difference. Finally, complementarity implies relationality, or relations and relationships between the sexes.

We also saw that sex difference is a real relation (accident) and a relation as a category of being (two manifestations of the same essence) which establishes the framework for interpersonal relationships, which include marriage, family, and broader society. Therefore, sex difference is fundamental for understanding vocations. However, before looking at sex difference and vocation, an important prerequisite is an analysis of John Paul II's writings on the significance of Christ's masculinity. This is needed because "Christ reveals man to himself" (GS §22), so the importance John Paul places on Jesus's masculinity should reveal additional insights into sex difference and perhaps vocation.

CHAPTER 7

Sex and the Incarnation

John Paul II says that Scripture reveals the significance of Jesus's masculinity for his mission with his articulation of the nuptial mystery. He begins by showing that the Old Testament depicts God as the Spouse of Israel, as the Bridegroom to the Bride-Israel. In the proclamation of the prophets, Yahweh, Israel's covenant name for God, is commonly presented as Israel's Bridegroom, especially in Isaiah, Hosea, and Ezekiel. The relational image of Bridegroom is formed around the love which unites God to Israel, his Bride, revealing the spousal dimension of the covenant. The proclamation of the covenant's spousal dimension is predominant over all others as salvation history nears the advent of the Messiah. Israel's disobedience to the covenant, especially through idolatry, is portrayed in terms of the adultery of the Bride Israel against her divine Spouse.[1]

John Paul believes that this marital bond presented by the prophets not only reveals to Israel a unique facet of Yahweh's relationship with them, it also prepares the way for revealing Christ's spousal bond with the New Testament Church, the New Israel. Jesus is the fulfillment of this Old Testament promise of the Bridegroom coming to redeem his Bride.[2] The fulfillment—the consummation—is when the marriage is sealed through Christ's blood on the Cross.[3] The foundation laid by the Old Testament prophets, John the Baptist proclaims to be fulfilled in Jesus Christ. Citing John 3:28–29, John Paul finds it significant that in clarifying for his followers that he is not the Christ, John the Baptist portrays himself

---

[1] See John Paul II, *Man and Woman He Created Them: A Theology of the Body*, trans. Michael Waldstein (Boston: Pauline Books and Media, 2006), 273.

[2] See John Paul II, Letter to Families *Gratissimam sane* (February 2, 1994), AAS 86 (1994), 868–925 (New Hope, KY: Urbi Et Orbi Communications, 1994), §19.

[3] See John Paul II, *A Catechesis on the Creed*, vol. 4, *The Church: Mystery, Sacrament, Community* (Boston: Pauline Books and Media, 1998), 103.

as the "best man," as the one who prepares the way for the Bridegroom and rejoices that he has arrived. Thus, the entire self-understanding of the Baptist's mission is oriented toward the Bridegroom.[4]

John Paul also points to the manner in which Jesus confirms the Baptist's legitimate proclamation of the Gospel as a firm indicator of Jesus's own self-identity. Namely, Jesus confirms himself as the Bridegroom and Messiah promised by the Old Testament prophets. This confirmation can be found in the imagery Jesus uses of himself directly when he tells the Pharisees that his disciples cannot fast as long as the Bridegroom is with them (Matt 9:15; see also Mark 2:19–20), and indirectly in the parable of the ten lamp-carrying maidens who went out to wait for the Bridegroom (Matt 25:1).[5] Jesus maintains this association in his wedding feast parable (Matt 22:2) in which he compares the reign of God to a king who gave a wedding feast for his son.[6]

Finally, Jesus confirms his identity as the Bridegroom promised by the prophets in the warning of Luke 12:35–38, in which he uses the parable of the servants who must watch and wait for their master to return from a wedding. John Paul II asserts that Jesus's self-identification as the Bridegroom definitively interprets the meaning of his entry into history. Jesus comes to consummate the nuptial mystery into which he invites humanity just as foretold by the prophets of old. This marriage consummates Yahweh's covenant, the New Covenant, with his people.[7]

All of this makes it significant that Jesus inaugurated his public mission with his first sign at the wedding feast in Cana (see John 2:1–11).[8] John Paul sees the Cana imagery as closely related to Jesus's identity as the Bridegroom. The story is replete with the message that the Bridegroom has come to save his Bride. In this way John's all important "hour" documents the beginning of the work of redemption.[9] The imagery of the water made wine together with the hour bring into view the paschal event, which is not complete until Christ's glorification. Moreover, it is through Mary's effective intercession that Jesus discloses that he is the Messiah who has come to save his Bride. John Paul finds that it is in Jesus's encounter with the

---

[4] See John Paul II, *The Church*, 108–109.

[5] See John Paul II, *The Church*, 109–11, 565.

[6] See John Paul II, *The Church*, 109–10.

[7] See John Paul II, *The Church*, 565. For a more complete review of the nuptial mystery, see David H. Delaney, "The Nuptial Mystery, the Sacrament of Marriage and John Paul II's *Man and Woman He Created Them*," *Antiphon* 18, no. 1 (2014): 69–105.

[8] See John Paul II, *The Church*.

[9] See John 7:30; 8:20; 12:23–27; 13:1; 17:1; 19:27, in which Jesus refers to his "hour."

betrothed couple at Cana that he begins his mission as the Bridegroom. In this way, Cana inaugurates the incipient wedding feast of the Kingdom of God (see Matt 22:2).[10]

John Paul II also notices that in the Old Testament, the analogies of Yahweh's spousal love for, and marriage to, Israel appear only in the context of Yahweh as Israel's *Redeemer*.[11] This analogy of spousal love emphasizes a particular facet of God's gift of himself to man. This self-gift is the love that saves man from the spiritual death he has endured since the sin of his first parents. The Bridegroom's love is the love which brings salvation. It is the radical gift of God's own Being, uncreated grace in the form of participation in the divine nature, which alone has the power to overcome death. When the prophets present Yahweh's love as a paternal love, it is a love of compassion.

When the prophets depict God's love as spousal love, it takes on the character of God giving himself as a gift to Israel in the manner of a Redeemer.[12] John Paul finds the New Testament fulfillment of the promised Bridegroom most profoundly articulated by the Pauline great mystery, which is the image of Christ's marriage to his Church found in Ephesians chapter 5. This marital image draws together those dimensions professed by the Old Testament prophets, namely, the redemptive and spousal dimensions of love. Christ makes himself the Bridegroom by giving himself up on the Cross for his Bride, the Church (see Eph 5:25).[13]

There is one vitally important aspect of this redemptive event of which John Paul does not want us to lose sight. This is the connection between self-sacrificial love and Christ's mission as Bridegroom.[14] John Paul draws this connection from Ephesians 5, showing that "through a total gift that springs from love, [Christ] *formed* the Church *as his body* and continually builds her, thus becoming her head. As head, he is the Savior of his body and, at the same time, as Savior, he is the head. As head and Savior of the Church, he is also Bridegroom of his Bride."[15] Thus, the great mystery makes the imagery of the wedding feast at Cana explicit. The key text which reveals the mystery is that in which Jesus gives himself for his

---

[10] See John Paul II, *A Catechesis on Salvation History*, vol. 6, *The Trinity's Embrace: God's Saving Plan* (Boston: Pauline Books and Media, 2002), 21.

[11] See *Man and Woman*, 498.

[12] See *Man and Woman*, 501.

[13] See *Man and Woman*, 527ff.

[14] See, for example, Letter to Families, §22.

[15] *Man and Woman*, 478. See also John Paul II, Apostolic Letter on the Dignity and Vocation of Women *Mulieris dignitatem* (August 15, 1988), AAS 80 (1988), 1653–1729, §23.

bride, the Church.[16] It is in this Pauline phrase that John Paul sees redeeming love transformed into spousal love. When Jesus gives himself for his Bride, he at once is united to her, as the husband with his wife. Here the nuptial mystery, the wedding feast of the Lamb (see Rev 19:7), is hidden within the mystery of the redemption of the body.[17] In this way, John Paul II demonstrates that the wedding feast prominent throughout the Gospels is not mere symbolism. The feast is ineluctably connected to the Church's sacramental life. The Bridegroom's wedding feast is the Eucharist, the "Sacrament of Redemption."

John Paul II believes Scripture makes it clear that the images of Christ as the Bridegroom, the Eucharist as the wedding feast, and the Church as Bride are not simple metaphors conceived solely in the minds and culture of the apostolic authors. Beginning with the Gospels' institution narratives, which form the heart of the Paschal mystery, the deeper ontology of the divine spousal relationship with the Church becomes apparent. These narratives (e.g., Luke 22:19–20) limpidly manifest God's spousal love in the giving up of Christ's body and the pouring out of his blood. This is the sacrifice of the Cross, the total gift of self, which reveals the meaning of God's love for humanity—spousal, redeeming love. In this way, the—the

---

[16] John Paul believed that the truth of the "great mystery" is gravely threatened today. In his Letter to Families he lays out the danger:

> Modern rationalism does not tolerate mystery. It does not accept the mystery of man as male and female, nor is it willing to admit that the full truth about man has been revealed in Jesus Christ. In particular, it does not accept the "Great Mystery" proclaimed in the Letter to the Ephesians, but radically opposes it. It may well acknowledge, in the context of a vague deism, the possibility and even the need for a supreme or divine Being, but it firmly rejects the idea of a God who became man in order to save man. For rationalism it is unthinkable that God should be the Redeemer, much less that he should be "the Bridegroom," the primordial and unique source of the human love between spouses. Rationalism provides a radically different way of looking at creation and the meaning of human existence. But once man begins to lose sight of a God who loves him, a God who calls man through Christ to live in him and with him, and once the family no longer has the possibility of sharing in the "Great Mystery," what is left except the mere temporal dimension of life? Earthly life becomes nothing more than the scenario of a battle for existence, of a desperate search for gain, and financial gain before all else. The deep-seated roots of the "Great Mystery," the sacrament of love and life which began with Creation and Redemption and which has Christ the Bridegroom as its ultimate surety, have been lost in the modern way of looking at things. The "Great Mystery" is threatened in us and all around us.

(*Letter to Families*, §19).

[17] See *Man and Woman*, 478.

Eucharist—becomes the sacrament of the Bridegroom and his Bride. Thus, the Eucharist makes present and temporally applies the grace of Christ's redemptive act.[18]

The symbols of the Bridegroom and his spousal love, definitively actualized in the Eucharist, derive from God's ordering of creation, and this arises from his own Being.[19] This entire reality comes about in creation only as a result of Jesus's enactment in history of God's spousal love. The sincere gift of self which the Son eternally offers to the Father is visibly manifested on the Cross and sacramentally made present in the Eucharist. The Paschal Lamb's marriage supper (see Rev. 19:7) is liturgically celebrated throughout time in the Eucharist. It visibly expresses and makes concrete God's marriage covenant with his people in the Church.[20] Through this sacramental action, Christ the Bridegroom really becomes present among his people and manifests the communion of the Church with God and of her members with one another.[21]

In John Paul II's view, the imagery of Bridegroom and Bride is not accidental to the fact that in God's created world, the bridegroom is male and the bride is female. For John Paul, isolating the sex of the body from the meaning of the whole person as male or female would be to fall either into nominalism or into a modern Cartesian rationalism.[22] Rather, inasmuch as Christ explicitly connected the apostolic priestly service to the Eucharist

---

[18] See *Mulieris dignitatem*, §26.
[19] See Letter to Families, §18.
[20] See John Paul II, *The Church*, 62–63.
[21] See John Paul II, *The Church*, 126.
[22] This isolation would be nominalism if it rests on the presupposition that we cannot know anything beyond the physical world. It would be Cartesian rationalism if it rests on the assumption that the body, its appearance and its features, takes its shape independently of the soul. This type of rationalism introduces a dualism between body and soul. John Paul II consistently attributes the modern dualism between body and soul to Descartes's rejection of metaphysics. Elsewhere he summarizes this view:

> St. Paul's magnificent synthesis concerning the "great mystery" [Eph 5:31–32] appears as the compendium or *summa*, in some sense, *of the teaching about God and man* which was brought to fulfillment by Christ. Unfortunately, Western thought, with the development of *modern rationalism*, has been gradually moving away from this teaching. The philosopher who formulated the principle of "*Cogito, ergo sum*," "I think, therefore I am," also gave the modern concept of man its distinctive dualistic character. It is typical of rationalism to make a radical contrast in man between spirit and body, between body and spirit. But man is a person in the unity of his body and his spirit. The body can never be reduced to mere matter: it is a *spiritualized body*, just as man's spirit is so closely united to the body that he can be described as *an embodied spirit*.

when he instituted the latter, it is eminently reasonable to conclude that Jesus simultaneously intended to reveal the meaning of the spousal relationship between man and woman. The marriage covenant between a man and woman therefore is willed by God in the mystery of redemption as well as in the mystery of creation.

John Paul finds that it is with the Eucharist that Christ shows his redemptive act—the love of the Bridegroom for the Church, his Bride. Moreover, he finds that this spousal love based upon sex difference is clear and unambiguous when, in ministering the Sacrament, it is a man who performs the priestly act *in persona Christi*. He goes on to say that this confirms St. Paul VI's declaration *Inter insigniores*, which authoritatively taught that only men may be ordained as priests.[23] Thus, John Paul declares that Christ's appearance as Bridegroom in reference to the Church as Bride has an essential connection to what it means to be masculine and what it means to be feminine, respectively. This marital understanding of the Eucharist conforms well with John Paul's integral view of the human person, the fact that sex difference is in part constitutive of human personhood, the essential relationality of sex difference, and Christ's masculine Incarnation.[24]

Given John Paul II's thought on sex difference and complementarity, it is not surprising that he sees *"all human beings—both women and men—are called* through the Church, *to be the 'Bride' of Christ, the Redeemer of the world.* In this way 'being the bride,' and thus the 'feminine' element, becomes a symbol of all that is 'human,' according to the words of Paul: 'There is neither male nor female; for you are *all one* in Christ Jesus' (Gal 3:28)."[25] This is understandable only if John Paul recognizes that each

---

(*Letter to Families*, §19).

[23] See *Mulieris dignitatem*, §26.

[24] From what was said in part 1, clearly John Paul rejects any view that would claim Jesus Christ to be a human person. However, in joining to himself the fullness of human nature, which the author says can only concretely exist as male or female, the Son's divine hypostasis has to have hypostatically joined to himself the masculine sex as well. As sex difference perdures in the eschaton, Christ maintains his masculine identity. To attribute to him androgyny or hermaphroditism would annihilate the continuity of his human identity in the same way that it would annihilate the personal identity of a human person. In fact, the destruction of Christ's masculinity would annihilate his very humanity.

[25] *Mulieris dignitatem*, §25. Later in the exhortation John Paul puts human-divine relationality in terms of the great mystery:

It expresses at the same time the "Great Mystery" described in the Letter to the Ephesians: *the bride united to her Bridegroom*; united, because she lives his life; united, because she shares in his threefold mission (*tria munera Christi*); united

human person, man and woman, has all that it means to be human. The defining difference between each sex is the primary mode of relating in love. The woman-bride first receives love and then returns it.

Men certainly have the capacity to receive love. In the relationship between husband and wife, the husband is the first to offer love, but he is then to receive it. However, in relation to God, a man must relate in a primarily receptive way; even though receptivity is secondary for his sex in human interpersonal relationships. All of humanity is primarily receptive in relation to God. This is why it is symbolized by femininity in the corporate image of the Church as Bride.[26] From this perspective the feminine symbols of Mother Church and of the Virgin Mary as the exemplar of the Church and the fullness to which it is called, are certainly apt.[27] Additionally, just as the Blessed Virgin symbolizes all humanity but also

---

in such a manner as to respond with a "sincere gift" of self *to the inexpressible gift of the love of the Bridegroom,* the Redeemer of the world. This concerns everyone in the Church, women as well as men. It obviously concerns those who share in the ministerial priesthood, which is characterized by service. In the context of the "Great Mystery" of Christ and of the Church, all are called to respond—as a bride—with the gift of their lives to the inexpressible gift of the love of Christ, who alone, as the Redeemer of the world, is the Church's Bridegroom. The "royal priesthood," which is universal, at the same time expresses the gift of the Bride.

(*Mulieris dignitatem,* §27).

[26] This is consonant with the widely acknowledged phenomenon in which women seem to be more "religious," on average, than are men. Balthasar finds a primacy of "feminine receptivity" not only in humanity but in all created being. He says that "competent biologists have expressed the view that the basic embryonic structure of all living beings, including man, is primarily feminine, and the subsequent differentiation of the male arises from a tendency toward extreme formulations, while the development of the female shows a persistence in the original balance" [citing a 1974 article by Adolph Portmann] (Hans Urs von Balthasar, "A Word on Humanae Vitae," in *New Elucidations* [San Francisco: Ignatius Press, 1986], 213–14, quoted in David L. Schindler, "Catholic Theology, Gender and the Future of Western Civilization," *Communio* 20 [Summer 1993]: 256). It is perhaps valid to suggest that the assertion that "males are feminine in relation to God" appears to be in some tension with the author's dictum that the "body reveals the person." In other words, one might ask where in the body is the human male's receptivity to God manifested? John Paul makes it clear that the body reflects the complementary relation between men and women. I suggest that the body only manifests complementarity for other hylomorphic beings. Furthermore, man has a real relation to God, but God's relation to man is only logical. In other words, man's relation to God is not strictly complementary. Regardless, even if it were complementary, it is not clear how the body would manifest receptivity to an incorporeal Being, much less an infinite one.

[27] See Second Vatican Council, Dogmatic Constitution on the Church *Lumen gentium* (November 21, 1964), §§14, 63.

has a particular meaning for women, so does Christ's love as Bridegroom have a particular application to men.[28]

John Paul II uncovers a masculine thread in terms of relation throughout salvation history. This thread starts from the beginning when God first loved us (see 1 John 4:19) and leads all the way to the Incarnation of the Son of God as a human male. This thread seems to be based upon God's love as it is understood in terms of the processions. The Father takes the initiative, the source of divinity and the initiator of Trinitarian love. Since the Trinitarian missions reveal the processions, it follows that the Son, the Bridegroom, must be a male who reveals his Father's love for his Bride, the Church.[29] Christ comes as a male because he reveals and effects divine love in its created pattern of human, male love.[30]

The Son, the redeeming Bridegroom foretold by the Old Testament prophets, reveals to man the Father's initiating love and offers it to those willing to receive it. He singularly expresses this self-giving, redemptive love in his Passion and death, and he sacramentally renews it in the

---

[28] It would not be correct, then, to say that men are called to be both bride and bridegroom, at least not in the same sense. The Bride is the symbol of the Church, which is a corporate personality (see John Paul II, "Analogy of Spousal Love Indicates the Radical Character of Grace," general audience [September 29, 1982], L'Osservatore Romano Weekly Edition in English, October 4, 1982). A man is one member of this corporate personality of the Church, so he cannot be "the" Bride; nor, for that matter, can a woman. While individually and collectively he relates to God in a feminine manner, he still responds as a human male but in a manner which requires him to subordinate his primarily initiating love to God's initiating love. Moreover, a male person cannot symbolize the femininity of the Church, which is primarily her receptive relation to God. Only a female person, solely because of her femininity, can symbolize the feminine Church and so can be called a bride. However, the male person, because of his masculinity, can symbolize the Bridegroom. Thus, John Paul's statement that all human persons are called to be the "Bride of Christ . . . [because they] are all one in Christ Jesus" (Mulieris dignitatem, §25) is to be understood in the context of their receptive response to God's initiating love, as faithful members of the Church.

[29] For the author's assertion that the missions reveal the processions, see John Paul II, A Catechesis on the Creed, vol. 1, God, Father and Creator (Boston: Pauline Books and Media, 1995), 175.

[30] This seems to be what John Paul II's following assertion indicates, which conforms with our earlier discussion of Balthasar's Trinitarian theology. "The Bridegroom—the Son consubstantial with the Father as God—became the son of Mary; he became the 'son of man,' true man, a male. The symbol of the Bridegroom is masculine. This masculine symbol represents the human aspect of the divine love which God has for Israel, for the Church, and for all people. . . . Precisely because Christ's divine love is the love of a Bridegroom, it is the model and pattern of all human love, and men's love in particular" (Mulieris dignitatem, §25).

Eucharistic sacrifice. His redemptive-spousal love is poured out upon all entering his Bride, the Church. This is the foundation for understanding the great mystery of Ephesians 5, which uncovers an important aspect of masculinity with particular implications for Christian husbands.

Jesus thereby reveals important aspects of masculinity which bear on men's roles, tasks, and vocations. First of all, all men are made for selfless giving of themselves in the way of initiating love. Initiation is risky because when one offers himself to another he can be rejected. The Cross reveals the extreme among possibilities of such rejection. Yet the risk is necessary in order to become what a man is made for. He must be willing to suffer loss to gain himself. Jesus's example is necessary for the man of concupiscence, whose masculine gifts themselves can incline him to the misuse of these gifts of initiative for possessing and controlling others, and to use others for his own sake.

Jesus's example of tender, fatherly solicitude for his children is *par excellence*, the example of the masculine genius.[31] Men might live this out by increasing their awareness of others they encounter, developing habits of inquiring about their well-being, preparing to sacrifice his own immediate concerns for the sake of helping another in a need for which he is able to assist, and being ready to offer encouragement for others when they are suffering.

In marriage, Jesus shows that men relate (ontologically) to their wives in the manner revealed by Christ's relation to the Church. They are called into a like relationship of love for their wives; that is, they are called to love their wives as Christ loved the Church. This is the husband's masculine manner of loving. John Paul says that "the husband's love for his wife is a participation in Christ's love for the Church."[32] Christ was first to love, and so the husband must follow this example. Husbands must love their wives with a total self-giving love; they must emulate the initiating love of the Bridegroom for his Bride.

However, in relation to God, men must subordinate this primary mode of love to God's initiating love. The profound depth to which sex difference penetrates into the interior structure of the human person, who is an acting person, suggests that one should also expect sex difference to have a significant influence on vocation. The significance of Jesus's masculinity confirms this influence. In the next chapter, we will investigate John Paul's understanding of the relationship between sex difference and vocation.

---

[31] E.g., in his healing of Simon's mother-in-law (Mark 1:31), of the leper (Mark 1:41), of the paralytic (Mark 2:5), and of the woman with the flow of blood (Matt 9:22).

[32] John Paul II, *The Church*, 114.

CHAPTER 8

Sex and Vocation

Let us look at the issue of vocation in two steps. In this chapter the scope will be limited to a study of the consequence of sex difference on the person's vocation in John Paul II's thought. We will again take up the issue of vocation in part 3 as it relates to fatherhood. For the chapter at hand, the starting point in coming to understand how sex difference relates to vocation in John Paul's thought must begin with the basis for understanding human personhood—the Trinitarian relations. Man made in the image of God is one of the primary hermeneutical keys for understanding John Paul II's anthropology. A consequence of this is another key, namely, that man can only fulfill himself through a sincere gift of self. John Paul indicates that these two keys provide an "essential indication of what it means to be human, while emphasizing the value of the gift of self, the gift of the person."[1] This total gift of self is necessary for fulfillment as a human person; but to give oneself as a gift one needs another.

Sex difference is a fundamental constituent in determining the manner in which a person must live out her or his vocation of total self-gift. There is a masculine way and a feminine way of giving oneself not only in marriage but in every aspect of life. This is not well received today for the fear that acknowledging such differences threatens equality between men and women. Therefore, the assertion of one's personal value necessarily requires the denial of any sex-based vocations or roles in society, in religion, or in the family. One can find this attitude in some forms of modern feminism, such as so-called radical feminism.

Some feminists, in the extreme, would deny sex-based vocations or roles even in the face of the evidence of biology. For example, some deny

---

[1] John Paul II, Apostolic Letter on the Dignity and Vocation of Women *Mulieris dignitatem* (August 15, 1988), AAS 80 (1988), 1653–1729, §18.

that motherhood is necessarily tied to female biology. Many others certainly deny sex-based roles and vocations in other aspects of the temporal sphere, and for those feminists who consider it, they likewise deny such in the realm of the spiritual life.[2] Critiques from these feminists, which implicate John Paul's view of sex difference, include arguments that giving sex difference a constituting role for the person contradicts Scripture (e.g., Galatians 3:28), that it constitutes a dualism which leaves men and women only half human, that it is simply rationalizing unjust stereotyping, and that it reduces men and women to their biology. We will take up these critiques in part 4.

John Paul II's understanding of the constitutive role sex difference plays in the interior structure of human personhood provides an important corrective for all forms of androgenizing equality. Recall his admonition in this regard: "In the name of liberation from male 'domination,' women must not appropriate to themselves male characteristics contrary to their own feminine 'originality.' There is a well-founded fear that if they take this path, women will not 'reach fulfillment,' but instead will *deform and lose what constitutes their essential richness*."[3] This quote also emphasizes the person-constituting role of sex difference. Of course, the same is true of men who reject their masculine identity. This suggests particular vocations and associated roles that are proper to women, together with distinct vocations and roles for men.

John Paul II identifies two dimensions of a woman's primary vocation—virginity and motherhood—that arise from her femininity.[4] He speaks of virginity as the vocation of a chaste bride of Christ living out a life of spiritual motherhood. This is significant in light of the hylomorphic foundation of his anthropology, because hylomorphism implies that the spiritual aspects of personhood give shape to the biological aspects of the body and, in turn, the bodily aspects reciprocally foster the spiritual.

In the case of feminine personhood, her body indicates that her potential for motherhood is integral to her personal identity.[5] This can be shown

---

[2] For a helpful review, see John Grabowski, "Theological Anthropology and Gender since Vatican II: A Critical Appraisal of Recent Trends in Catholic Theology" (Ph.D. diss., Marquette University, 1991), 70–95. In part 4, I will address specific challenges from representatives of these thinkers which might seem to undermine the coherence or adequacy of the author's theology of fatherhood.

[3] *Mulieris dignitatem*, §10.

[4] See *Mulieris dignitatem*, §17.

[5] It is helpful to know that he classifies feminine virginity as spiritual motherhood for a fuller sense of the meaning of this claim.

from the text of Genesis 4:1 where the term "knowledge" serves to reveal the mystery of femininity via motherhood. Applying this same principle to masculine personhood, one can see that the masculine mystery is similarly manifested in the generative and fatherly meaning of the man's body.[6] The man's body thus reveals his basic vocation to be a spiritual and biological fatherhood.

The biblical concept of "knowledge" provides further insight through its relation to "begetting." This can be seen by comparing the terms used in the early chapters of Genesis.[7] Here, knowledge and begetting apply to both the man and the woman, but they do so differently. Women and men differ in their physical, psychological, and emotional makeup. In his theology of the body catecheses, John Paul shows a woman to be constituted differently than a man, a difference that penetrates to the deepest levels of her being.[8] The outward manifestation of this constitution, in her gross anatomy, reveals only a portion of this difference. Interiorly, this difference can be summed up in the unique potency of femininity, namely, motherhood. The complement of this is true for men and fatherhood. The fruit of knowledge is that to which the vocations of fatherhood and motherhood point.

The man and woman transcend themselves by their mutual knowledge through the medium of their very bodies, in begetting a child. Through the body itself the spouses move beyond the objectivity of body. They recognize in the marital act that they are not encountering simply a thing. Rather, they discover each other as subjects, as persons, through their mutual self-giving. The body mediates their knowing one another, a knowledge that is primarily achieved through the body's sex. The spouses discover what John Paul calls the "'pure' subjectivity of the gift," through

---

[6] See John Paul II, *Man and Woman He Created Them: A Theology of the Body*, trans. Michael Waldstein (Boston: Pauline Books and Media, 2006), 210–11.

[7] John Paul II ultimately defines knowledge as a concrete experience of intimate, disinterested self-gift—love. He says: "Beyond the frontiers of history, then, the full, shining epiphany of the Trinity awaits us. In the new creation God will give us the intimate, perfect communion with him that the fourth Gospel calls 'eternal life,' the source of a 'knowledge' which in biblical language is precisely a communion of love: 'This is eternal life, that they know you, the only true God, and Jesus Christ whom you have sent' (John 17:3)" (John Paul II, *A Catechesis on Salvation History*, vol. 6, *The Trinity's Embrace: God's Saving Plan* [Boston: Pauline Books and Media, 2002], 353–54). In marriage, the spouses express this intimate love most perfectly in the marital act of sexual intercourse (see *Man and Woman*, 204–208).

[8] See *Man and Woman*, 194ff.

their reciprocal, marital knowledge.[9] Mutual self-fulfillment through marital knowledge is the fruit each spouse experiences by subjecting himself to the grammar of the body, a grammar associated with the language of the gift.[10] In women, John Paul asserts, "'Knowledge' conditions begetting."[11]

There is a proper relational ordering in this knowing, an ordering which is given by sex difference. John Paul II says that "'knowledge' indicates, on the one hand, [that there is] he who 'knows' and, on the other, she who 'is known' (or vice versa)."[12] This mutual, reciprocal knowledge reveals a gift which is fruitful, but there is a hierarchical structure to the giving. In the reciprocal knowing of the spouses, a third person arises (or at least may arise). This is procreative love by which the two cooperate with God in his plan of creation. Here one can see that knowledge in the biblical sense means that biological determination is not something passive. Rather, it is a capacity for active cooperation with God by means of the personal faculties of self-consciousness and self-determination. Moreover, it also necessitates a personal awareness of the meaning of the body and its sex in the context of motherhood and fatherhood.[13]

The body reveals a vast array of deeply interior facets of the human person along with his or her sex and vocation. But because the body does nothing in isolation from the soul, the whole human person is implicated in the physical structure and actions of the body. Thus, the acting person freely acts through his male or female body in the manner appropriate to his sex. The appropriate manner of free acts, depending upon discernment and intention, can be called a vocation. It is called a state in life when one

---

[9] *Man and Woman*, 211. In other words, gifts can only be given in freedom and only subjects (i.e., persons) have freedom.

[10] The grammar of the body indicates that the gift can only be discovered when it is a free and total self-gift (it is "total" in the marital act, which by definition is marital only when it is open to procreation).

[11] *Man and Woman*, 211. The assertion that "knowledge conditions begetting" seems to evoke the Trinitarian processions, in which the Son is known by the Father as a Word, the interior *Verbum*, his only begotten Son. They reciprocally know each other through the unity of Love, who is a third person. The quote in note 7 above, in which the author defines "knowledge" as intimate love further supports this contention that the knowledge between the spouses in marriage is analogous to the knowledge among the Trinitarian persons in the processions.

[12] *Man and Woman*, 211.

[13] See *Man and Woman*, 212. This further implicates the begetting of a child as a participation in (or at least analogy to) the processions; particularly his reference to the production of a third person as the fruit of the mutual self-gift of the two spouses.

answers the vocational call. Let us now briefly look at three vocations: marriage, consecrated celibacy, and parenthood.

MARRIAGE

Christ's love for his Church brings to fulfillment God's spousal love for man. God reveals his spousal love for mankind through the analogy and symbolism of the marriage covenant between a husband and wife. The third hermeneutical key—that Christ reveals man to himself—means for John Paul that Ephesians 5 is key text for understanding marriage. The analogy of the relationship between Christ and his Church and between the spouses in human marriage are reciprocally illuminative.[14] The mystery of Christ's relation to the Church sheds light on the relationship between husband and wife in the marriage covenant. In turn, the lived experience of the couple united in marriage, to the extent they live this life authentically, can also shed light on the mystery of the Church's spousal relationship with Christ.

The analogy between human marriage and Christ's love for his Church means that marital love must be transformed until it corresponds with Christ's redemptive, spousal love. For this reason, the marital covenant is authentic to the Christian vocation when it manifests the love that the Bridegroom, Jesus Christ, bestows upon his Bride, the Church. Christ pours out his spousal love upon the Church, bringing salvation to her. Christian marital love is authentic to the degree the spouses manifest exteriorly *and* effect interiorly Christ's love of total self-gift.[15] Only in this way does their spousal love manifest and effect redeeming, salvific love. Authentic marital love is a calling to Christian spouses and their acceptance of that vocation renders it an obligation.[16]

The Ephesians marital analogy is unique among biblical marital analogies in its emphasis on the call to total self-gift. This is its most distinctive element. Here, self-gift has a radical, immutable character. Even though God's total gift of himself cannot be received by creatures in the totality of his simple, infinite nature, we can still say God's radical for man is given as a total self-gift in that the Incarnation permits those in a state of grace to become partakers in the divine nature (see 2 Peter 1:4). This partaking is man's incorporation into the Trinitarian *communio*, which is the archetype

---

[14] See *Man and Woman*, 476.

[15] See *Man and Woman*, 476.

[16] See *Man and Woman*, 477.

and source of human spousal love.[17] Therefore, Christian spousal love must be rooted in the total gift of self which has its source in the sharing of divine life received through sacramental grace. Trinitarian self-gift arises from the concomitant divine will in the divine processions, but for human spouses sincere self-gift is a moral calling. The spouses cannot fulfill themselves if they reject this call, but refusal is possible because self-giving means it must be freely given.

John Paul II finds that sex difference itself is a sacramental sign within the marriage covenant. He concludes this based upon Matthew 19:4, which indicates that from the beginning, the sex difference of the body is purposed to make visible what is not visible, namely, the spirit. The conjugal union of husband and wife is the act through which the makeup of sex difference reveals the fullness of the person of each spouse to the other in a sort of sacramental sign.[18] In this covenantal union, they become one flesh. So sex difference reveals the profound interior unity of the husband and wife in the fullness of their persons, and it points toward the spouses' sacramental unity which is established in Christ. John Paul often refers to Genesis 2:24 to illustrate the unity of these insights, saying that: "In marriage man and woman are so firmly united as to become to use the words of the Book of Genesis—'one flesh' (Gen 2:24)."[19]

It is important to clarify that this unity through flesh does not extinguish the dual subjectivity of the two spouses.[20] Obviously they remain physically individual and they also remain two separate human personal subjects. Their unity is a moral rather than substantial unity. Nevertheless, their unity of flesh indicates that they both equally share not only the mandate but also the ability to live together in truth and love.[21] This is a capacity proper to the human person, indicating that that capacity carries with it both a corporeal as well as a spiritual dimension.

The body is the medium by which the spouses have the predisposition to form a marital communion of persons. And this communion is possible because they are created in the image and likeness of a God who is a *communio personarum*. Thus, the moral dimension of man's likeness necessitates

---

[17] See *Man and Woman*, 501.

[18] See *Man and Woman*, 306–307.

[19] John Paul II, Letter to Families *Gratissimam sane* (February 2, 1994), AAS 86 (1994), 868–925 (New Hope, KY: Urbi Et Orbi Communications, 1994), §8.

[20] See *Man and Woman*, 480ff., 484–85.

[21] By "truth and love," John Paul means the marital communion's exclusiveness, irrevocability, and sincere self-giving nature which reflect that of its archetype.

his living this union of flesh and spirit in truth and love. Only in this way is it possible to actualize the maturity proper to man's divine likeness.[22]

The mandate of spousal unity in truth and love is revealed in the great mystery of Ephesians 5. The capacity for this Christian union is made possible only through grace, access to which is only by virtue of the paschal event.[23] Therefore, marriage between baptized persons becomes "a real symbol of that New and Eternal Covenant sanctioned in the blood of Christ."[24] In the sacrifice of the Cross, Christ unites himself with his Bride, the Church, as her Savior. This same total-self-giving is the vocation of the spouses. It is only the grace given in the Sacrament of Matrimony that gives the spouses the ability to overcome concupiscence and so love one another as Christ loves the Church. This sign is rooted in sex difference, as sex difference is the basis of the analogical symbol of Bridegroom-Bride.

The sanctifying Christian *communio personarum* of the marriage covenant is grounded in sex difference.[25] However, in the historical experience of sin, false views of the human person and his sex have arisen, and in recent years these now threaten to undermine the authentic marital *communio*. One such widespread but superficial view of sex is that in which love is reduced to an erotic experience and ends in the woman's surrendering of her body to the man. There is an authentic surrender in the marital act, but it is the mutual surrender of each spouse, one to the other, and their mutual, reciprocal acceptance of the fullness of the other person.[26]

Even so, this mutual surrender must not become reciprocal sexual exploitation, which is too often the case when sexual intercourse is reduced to a deficient erotic and strictly corporeal exchange. In such mutual use, each tries to possess the other's body and person for the purpose of extracting the maximum sexual pleasure, control, and/or an illusory sense of self-fulfillment. On the contrary, mutual fulfillment is possible only through the reciprocal, total self-gift expressed in the marital covenant.

---

[22] See Letter to Families, §8.

[23] See Letter to Families, §8.

[24] John Paul II, Apostolic Exhortation on the Role of the Christian Family in the Modern World *Familiaris consortio* (November 22, 1981), *AAS* 74 (1982), 114–37, §13.

[25] *Familiaris consortio*, §19.

[26] The distorted emphasis on the surrender of the woman is common because it is she who surrenders first to the man's invitation in acts of love. Overlooked and so usually not actualized is the man's requirement for reciprocal surrender to the woman. This one-sided focus on feminine surrender helps to make room for social acceptance of the common sort of sexual decadence that almost always comes at the immediate expense of women. St. John Paul's introduction of mutual submission can be an important remedy to this problem (for more on this, see the discussion in chapter 13).

Outside of the simultaneous structure of marriage and total self-gift, love becomes impossible and sexual intercourse degenerates into use. Authentic love cannot survive in such cases even if the use is simultaneous and mutual, because authentic sexual love must correspond with its divine archetype. Sexual intercourse is authentic only as a marital act open to fruitfulness in total self-giving love.[27]

Total self-gift is the only way spouses can avoid the lot of fallen man, in what otherwise would be at best a mutual exploitation of each other's bodies and persons. Mutual exploitation degrades the entire personhood of each.[28] The required elements necessary for sincere self-gift include the free, reciprocal giving and accepting of the other as a full human person, body and soul.[29] To achieve this virtue, the couple must develop the aptitude for the authentic expression of love as a gift into a stable proficiency.[30] This is perhaps not a romantic turn of phrase, but it reveals the reality that the habitual practice of self-mastery and self-possession are necessary in order to give oneself as a gift, since one cannot give that which he does not first fully possess. A precursor to this habitual exercise of self-mastery is the requirement to understand the value of the human person.

Wojtyła says, "Only that woman is capable of truly giving herself who is fully convinced about the value of her person and of the value of the person of the man to whom she gives herself. And only that man is capable of fully receiving the self-giving of a woman who is thoroughly conscious of the greatness of this gift—and he cannot possess such awareness without the affirmation of the value of the person."[31] Both women and men must understand that the whole person, which includes his or her sex, is of incomparable value if giving and accepting a person as a gift is to be possible. Men and women then have specific vocational requirements which they must achieve if they are to fulfill their call to marriage.

Celibacy

As with the section above on marriage, it is not my purpose here to discuss all aspects of the vocation to celibacy but rather to address briefly the

---

[27] See Karol Wojtyła, *Love and Responsibility*, trans. Grzegorz Ignatik (Boston: Pauline Books & Media, 2013), 210–13.

[28] They degrade themselves as persons through a free act in which they treat each other as objects. Thus, rather than fulfilling themselves through their sincere self-gift they diminish themselves and the other through a sinful act of selfishness.

[29] See Wojtyła, *Love and Responsibility*, 107–12.

[30] See Wojtyła, *Love and Responsibility*, 111.

[31] Wojtyła, *Love and Responsibility*, 111.

significance of sex difference for the celibate vocation. Contrary to some popular assumptions, celibacy is not a rejection of the gifts proper either to sex difference or to bodily sex, but rather it is a profound affirmation of them. The consecrated life carries with it a spousal meaning in which the consecrated persons give witness to the Church's call to complete devotion to her Spouse. It also gives witness to the eschatological meaning of sex difference and sexual intercourse. In other words, consecrated celibacy presages the profound, perfect, and universal intersubjective unity that all will share with one another in the eschatological unity in Christ.[32] The body and its sex provide concrete expression and foreshadowing of the eschatological unity which all united in the Church will share in the beatific vision. But the *communio personarum* of the marital covenant does not objectively achieve the excellence to which consecrated celibacy more perfectly witnesses. On the other hand, the objective superiority of celibacy for the sake of the kingdom does not either denigrate marriage or negate the subjective superiority of this state for those who are called to it.[33] In fact, John Paul understands that these two vocations are necessary complements to one another.[34]

Because authentic consecrated life is inextricably linked to its spousal dimension, the author believes that this aspect has a special meaning for women. In the consecrated life, women's spousal relationship with Christ manifests their primary mode of loving which belongs properly to their femininity. John Paul says that women "find [in the spousal dimension] their feminine identity and as it were discover the special genius of their

---

[32] See *Familiaris consortio*, §§16ff.; Post-Synodal Apostolic Exhortation on the Consecrated Life and Its Mission in the Church and in the World *Vita consecrata* (March 26, 1996), §§3ff., 16ff.; *Man and Woman*, 267ff.

[33] See *Man and Woman*, 426ff. Bishop Karol Wojtyła provides more insight into his view of the objective superiority of consecrated celibacy in a 1961 article published in the magazine *Przewodniku katolickim*, which was later translated into Italian and republished in *Bellezza e spiritualità dell'amore coniugale*, ed. Ludmiła Grygiel, Stanisław Grygiel, and Przemysław Kwiatkowski (Siena: Edizioni Cantagalli, 2009). He explains the superiority in terms of the consecrated state being ordered to the pursuit of perfection through the evangelical counsels of poverty, chastity, and obedience. This system of life favors the attainment of perfection, though it does not guarantee it. Nor does the married state prevent a Christian couple from attaining perfection, though the natural order of marriage does not in itself provide a system of life ordered to the attainment of Christian perfection. Nevertheless, the grace provided by the Sacrament of Marriage raises the natural state to one that does indeed call the couple to assisting one another to the pursuit of perfection and indeed makes it attainable (see Wojtyła, *Bellezza e spiritualità*, 52–55).

[34] See *Man and Woman*, 429ff.

relationship with the Lord."[35] This inherent aspect of femininity seems to enable women to conform more readily to a relationship of surrender to God than is generally the case for men.

What is it about femininity that provides this predisposition? In language which appears to be in concert with the earlier explication of the primacy of femininity for human-divine relationality, John Paul II explains that it is the spousal receptivity of the bride. The Blessed Virgin exemplifies this receptivity as an image of the Church as Bride. He points to Mary's vigil with the apostles in the upper room awaiting the day of Pentecost (see Acts 1:13–14) as a sign of this image. Mary is an image of the Bride, the Church, anxiously awaiting the arrival of her Bridegroom, prepared to accept his gift to her.

John Paul says, "In Mary the aspect of spousal receptivity is particularly clear; it is under this aspect that the Church, through her perfect virginal life, brings divine life to fruition within herself."[36] This helps to explain why the consecrated life has always been seen primarily in terms of Mary, the Virgin and Bride. Virginal love has a special kind of fruitfulness. It is the wellspring which brings about and nurtures divine life within us. Consecrated people, especially women, thus follow in Mary's footsteps, manifesting spiritual fruitfulness in their receptivity to the Word. By this, they contribute to the development of a renewed humanity, especially through the variety of forms of Christian service. Thus, the appropriate symbol for man making a receptive, active, loving response of "yes" to Christ's initiative of love is found in feminine exemplars. These include the Virgin Mary and the spousal aspect of consecrated celibacy in which the consecrated woman is the bride of Christ.

Men, in their masculinity, can also aspire to this primarily feminine mode of love without the danger of deforming themselves through some kind of feminization, because the man is not relating to another human person but to God.[37] On the other hand, one can find a masculine mode of

---

[35] *Vita consecrata*, §34.

[36] *Vita consecrata*, §34.

[37] Wojtyła says the sphere of the spirit is beyond sexual differences (see *Love and Responsibility*, 246). See also *Mulieris dignitatem*, §8. John Paul also says that men also express spiritual motherhood but in a manly way. This he calls spiritual fatherhood. See Letter to Priests for Holy Thursday 1988, §4, in *Letters to My Brother Priests: 1979–2001*, ed. James Socías (Chicago: Scepter Publishers, 2001), 146; see also Letter to Priests for Holy Thursday 1979, §8. These statements seem contradictory to Wojtyła's hylomorphic anthropology and could undermine its coherence. Therefore, I will evaluate them further in part 4.

celibate love and activity in the hierarchical aspect of the Church.[38] In the end, consecrated celibacy is a vocation which complements and supports marriage through the very renouncing of it for the sake of the kingdom of God, the true eschatological end to which marriage itself points and finds its sacramental meaning. The vocation to the consecrated life highlights an important truth about the human person. If man has the potency to give himself to God as a gift for the sake of the kingdom of heaven, one may deduce from this the freedom of the gift in the human body. One can find in his body its fully spousal meaning.[39] As with marriage, celibacy is also associated with parenthood.

PARENTHOOD

Parenthood is a vocation that flows out of marriage and celibacy alike. What I will term "natural parenthood" is a vocation which arises from marriage and is ordered to, but may or may not include, biological parenthood. Natural parents and adoptive parents, as well as celibate "parents," are called to spiritual parenthood. Marriage necessarily differs in some respects from celibacy in the manner in which each manifests spiritual parenthood, but there is also some overlap. Central to this overlap is the fact that sex difference establishes the way in which one lives out his parenthood. More obvious is the correlation of natural parenthood to sex difference, but there is also a correlation between sex difference and spiritual parenthood. Let us first look at natural parenthood.[40]

With natural parenthood the mutual gift of the spouses to one another, which forms a communion of persons, overflows into "a communion of parents."[41] Therefore, a constituent aspect of parenthood must necessarily include sex difference. This communion of parents together with their children becomes the most fundamental expression of the social dimension of the human person. God did not create man to be a solitude. Rather, he created him from the beginning as male and female, forming a primordial bond of man and woman which constituted the first human communion

---

[38] See *Vita consecrata*, §34.

[39] See *Man and Woman*, 190.

[40] Most of what John Paul II says of natural parents is also true of adoptive parents. While their child may not be the product of their love in the biological sense, he can be such in every other way to the degree they conform to the Trinitarian archetype. Though contemporary circumstances dictate that it must also be said that this holds only for authentic, sexually complementary, married parents.

[41] Letter to Families, §11.

of persons.[42] Marriage and the family form interior and exterior networks of interpersonal relationships. Interfamilial relationships include married life, fatherhood, motherhood, filiation, and fraternity.

Parents together are responsible for nurturing their children as a human family and as part of the Church, which itself is the family of God. They do this through education into human society, as well as catechesis and rebirth into God's family. The hermeneutical principle that man is made in the image of God who is a communion of persons, justifies this integral view of life. The Trinitarian *communio* forms the basis of communion within marriage and the family. The fact that the family is a product of the overflowing love between the spouses derives from this inner mystery of God and "conforms to the innermost being of man and woman."[43]

All authentic aspects of family life which have their foundation in the Trinitarian mystery therefore must be integrated by means of the gifts proper to motherhood and fatherhood, the gifts which correspond to their sexes.[44] One can see this correspondence of sex difference to parenthood in the body. This is manifested throughout Scripture, particularly in the case of motherhood.[45] However, one must not take this in a narrow, solely biological sense. Rather, the body manifests a deeper, spiritual reality which is the manner in which a woman loves. As a mother, she loves with a specifically feminine form of creative love. There is to this a male counterpart.

John Paul II's integral anthropology shows that what is expressed

---

[42] See John Paul II, Post-Synodal Apostolic Exhortation on the Vocation and the Mission of the Lay Faithful in the Church and in the World *Christifideles laici* (December 30, 1988), *AAS* 81 (1989), 393–521, §40.

[43] See Letter to Families, §8.

[44] See *Familiaris consortio*, §§15, 19.

[45] The whole exterior constitution of woman's body, its particular look, the qualities that stand, with the power of a perennial attraction, at the beginning of the "knowledge" about which Genesis 4:1–2 speaks ("Adam united himself with Eve"), *are in strict union with motherhood*. With the simplicity characteristic of it, the Bible (and the liturgy following it) honors and praises throughout the centuries "the womb that bore you and the breasts from which you sucked milk" (Luke 11:27). These words are a eulogy of motherhood, of femininity, of the feminine body in its typical expression of creative love. And in the Gospel these words refer to the Mother of Jesus, Mary, the second Eve. The first woman, on the other hand, at the moment in which the maternal maturity of her body revealed itself for the first time, when she "conceived and bore," said, "I have acquired a man from the Lord" (Gen 4:1). . . . These words express the whole theological depth of the function of begetting-procreating. The body of the woman becomes a place of the conception of the new human being.

(*Man and Woman*, 212).

in the body reflects something deeply interior to both the spirit and the person. Likewise, it will be manifested in acts peculiar to the duality of persons, as male and female. The biological complementarity of the body reveals that there is also a spiritual complementarity between the husband and wife, and so one finds complementary manners for expressing love. To the woman's receptively creative love corresponds the masculine initiating, creative love.

The complementary masculine and feminine forms of love give rise to the particular roles men and women have in procreation proper to their sex, and extend beyond conception and pregnancy. We will treat this in detail in part 3, but what is important for this chapter is that the parents' complementary roles elicit an awareness that the meaning of procreation is to be found in human life received as a gift in order to be given as a gift. They are able to recognize that the child born as a result of their mutual self-gift is a gift for them, which also flows from them. Even more so, in raising children by word and example the parents must cultivate in them gospel values which will allow them also to live life as a gift.[46] These responsibilities of natural parenthood that John Paul describes, suggest that there is not a rigid delineation between what one could consider natural and spiritual parenthood.

In fact, spiritual parenthood is an integral aspect of natural parenthood. Likewise, the author does not delineate roles between celibate spiritual parenthood and natural spiritual parenthood. It seems that any differences originate more in what is proper to the particular relationship between "parent" and "child" than in the fact that the parenthood is specifically celibate or natural. Finally, the distinction between spiritual fatherhood and motherhood is less defined than that between the fatherhood and motherhood which result from the biological aspects of their sex differences.[47] For example, with regard to the spiritual fatherhood of priests, John Paul also refers to the fact that he has a role to fulfill as a spiritual mother.[48]

---

[46] See John Paul II, Encyclical Letter on the Value and Inviolability of Human Life *Evangelium vitae* (March 25, 1995), *AAS* 87 (1995), 401–522, §92.

[47] For example, John Paul says that "spiritual fatherhood and motherhood is a distinctive characteristic of a mature interior personhood of a man and a woman. This spiritual fatherhood is much more similar to spiritual motherhood than bodily fatherhood is to bodily motherhood. The sphere of the spirit stands beyond the scope of sex. Having in mind his spiritual fatherhood with respect to Galatians, the apostle Paul did not hesitate to write: 'My children, to whom I give birth suffering. . . .'" (Gal 4:19)" (Wojtyła, *Love and Responsibility*, 246).

[48] Specifically, he says: "Through his celibacy, the priest becomes the man 'for others,' in a

Sex difference provides an inherent framework not only for the vocation to and roles within marriage but also for parenthood and celibacy. Thus, there are particular vocations and roles based upon sex difference. Feminine and masculine bodies help in discovering a person's primary vocation. For women, John Paul finds that this is motherhood and virginity, and for men it is fatherhood. In John Paul's anthropology, one can now see why and how men's vocation to fatherhood is based upon their masculinity.

---

different way from the man who, by binding himself in conjugal union with a woman, also becomes, as husband and father, a man 'for others,' especially the radius of his own family: for his wife and, together with her, for the children, to whom he gives life. The priest, by renouncing this fatherhood proper to married men, seeks another fatherhood and, as it were, even another motherhood, recalling the words of the Apostle about the children whom he begets in suffering [see 1 Cor 4:15; Gal 4:19]" (John Paul II, *Letters to My Brother Priests, 1979–2001* [Princeton, NJ: Scepter Publishers, 2001], 19).

Part Three

FATHERHOOD

CHAPTER 9

Fatherhood as a Vocation

FATHERHOOD AND THE UNIVERSAL VOCATION

Fatherhood is the vocation to which God calls every human male, as we will see. We have just seen that sex difference, masculinity and femininity, is the foundation for each person's vocation. In this chapter, we see that fatherhood characterizes how each man is to pursue his vocation. This begins with the universal Christian vocation to holiness, which is one's perfection in selfless love. This universal calling is possible only for those united to Christ in the power of his Holy Spirit.[1] Because it is a calling, every person must be free to accept or reject it. He can work for holiness, or he can refuse. Holiness brings with it the implication of an axiological requirement.[2] Wojtyła boils this down to the obligation to "be good as man—do not be bad as man."[3] Embedded within this succinct phrase is the fact that man has an ontological structure that defines his good. To act

---

[1] See John Paul II, Post-Synodal Apostolic Exhortation on the Vocation and the Mission of the Lay Faithful in the Church and in the World *Christifideles laici* (December 30, 1988), *AAS* 81 (1989), 393–521, §16.

[2] John Paul II uses "axiological" to refer to a moral requirement derived from an analysis of the value associated with that requirement. This reflects Max Scheler's influence on his thinking, who emphasized value over against Kant's locating moral requirements in terms of duty. Lawler points out that Wojtyła criticized the Kantian emphasis on duty alone as a sort of legalism, not completely unlike some of the legalism that had crept into Catholic piety and moral theology by his formative years. However, unlike Scheler's subjectivist view of value, Wojtyła locates value in the authentic good which has its source in God. See Ronald Lawler, *The Christian Personalism of Pope John Paul II* (Chicago: Franciscan Herald Press, 1982), 58–60.

[3] Karol Wojtyła, *The Acting Person*, trans. Andrezej Potocki, ed. A. Tymieniecka, Analecta Husserliana: The Yearbook of Phenomenological Research, vol. 10 (Dordrecht, Holland: Reidel Publishing Co., 1979), 168.

in accord with this given structure is to "be good as man." To act contrary to this structure is to "be bad as man."

Clearly, John Paul rejects Hume's "is-ought" dichotomy, or at least the contemporary instantiations of this claim.[4] In fact, he argues that the ontological and axiological structures of the human person are integrated in an essential way. In this way, man can be said to "create" himself, so to speak, as a good or bad person, as holy or evil, through his actions. Holiness establishes the overarching structure for human action being the universal human vocation. Every other more specified calling or vocation can be subsumed into this general calling. Everything else that one can call a vocation, such as marriage, fatherhood and motherhood, consecrated celibacy, the priesthood, and so on, are particular instantiations of living out this fundamental calling to the good.

This primary vocation arises from the fact that man is made in the image of God, and so he reflects the *communio personarum*. This Trinitarian archetype establishes the structure by which man fulfills his vocation to holiness and his particular vocation. A man acts in accord with the way he is created and realizes his human potential when he responds to the particular demands of his vocation by offering himself as a gift, by which he makes a "sincere gift of himself" (GS §24). This is also the manner in which all derivative vocations must be lived out if they are to be authentic responses to vocation. Self-giving is the definition of the human person, which not only corresponds to a foundational, biblical truth about man created in the image of God but also provides the essential hermeneutic for interpreting the human person.[5] Consequently, it is not surprising that those things which John Paul refers to as vocations are all implicated in service.

The call to serve is decisively intertwined with being a Christian. Jesus's admonition to his disciples in the washing of the feet indicates to John Paul that service constitutes the basis for life in the kingdom of God.

---

[4] See David Hume, *A Treatise of Human Nature: Being an Attempt to Introduce the Experimental Method of Reasoning into Moral Subjects*, book III, *Of Morals* (Oxford, UK: Clarendon Press, 1896), 469–70. In a short passage, Hume argues that the normal mode of moral reasoning proceeds from the way God has ordered something, an "is," proceeding to some obligatory manner of behavior because of which, an "ought," without any intervening argumentation. He says that this should not be permitted. Rather, he argues that it is necessary to present an argument from the fact that something is to the obligation that arises from it. This has come to be referred to as "Hume's Law" and is often paraphrased something along the following lines: an "is" does not mean an "ought."

[5] See John Paul II, Apostolic Letter on the Dignity and Vocation of Women *Mulieris dignitatem* (August 15, 1988), AAS 80 (1988), 1653–1729, §18.

He says that "to serve . . . means to reign."[6] Vocation is to be answered in complete freedom by a sincere gift of self in a form of service that is uniquely chosen by God for each Christian. When John Paul II uses the term "vocation" he presupposes the freedom of the individual to say "yes" or "no." A free response is essential for any human act (*actus humanus*) and particularly for an act of love. His anthropology assumes vocation as normative for the fulfillment of the person. Personal fulfillment, of course, ultimately means the person's perfection in holiness. An authentic response in freedom through disinterested self-gift has a lasting, ontological effect on the person who is called.

Each human being derives his dignity from his having been made in the image of God. Because his vocation derives from God, no one can achieve his vocation or fulfill himself apart from union with God.[7] Though, union with God is not automatic. It is a result of a gift, but this gift of union comes in degrees that correspond to one's cooperation with God's gift. Because of man's fallen state, the realization of one's capacity for sincere self-giving demands he overcome temptations arising from concupiscence, a pathway John Paul calls self-transcendence. Self-transcendence comes about through one's cooperation with grace in concrete acts of selfless love toward others.

No man can give himself as a gift to an abstract idea or utopian ideal. He can only give himself to another person. Among human persons, this gift is given in a provisional way. Man can give himself totally only to God. Only God has the right to a total and complete gift of self in an absolute sense, and God alone has the capacity to fully accept our gift. Sin is the alienation that man experiences from God when he refuses to transcend himself and to dwell in true human communities that organize themselves toward their finality in God. Fatherhood demands that men especially be attentive to the task of self-transcendence.

John Paul often uses the term "state" in a way that seems to overlap with "vocation." Distinguishing the two terms reveals again his emphasis on responding in freedom for personal fulfillment. For John Paul II the Christian vocation is the calling to become holy by freely responding, in a sincere gift of self, through a person specific means of service. He talks about "states of life,"[8]

---

[6] *Mulieris dignitatem*, §5.
[7] See *Mulieris dignitatem*, §5.
[8] *Christifideles laici*, §§52, 55-56; John Paul II, Apostolic Exhortation on the Role of the Christian Family in the Modern World *Familiaris consortio* (November 22, 1981), *AAS* 74 (1982), 114–37, §§1, 50.

the "lay state,"[9] the "clerical state"[10] or "consecrated state,"[11] and the "religious state."[12] He also mentions the "married state,"[13] the "conjugal state,"[14] and the "baptismal state."[15] Many of these states are sacramental and have an ontological character to them, such as the states achieved through Baptism and Holy Orders. Other states one enters through vows or promises.

When he discusses these states, it is in the context of the attributes, tasks, and roles of those who are living in them, either because of the reception of a sacrament or the profession of an intention. Thus, for John Paul, states of life are, at least ideally, the result of one's free, affirmative response to God's beckoning to a vocation. The distinction between vocation and state is the distinction between a calling and the free acceptance of the call. Three of these vocation-states deserve short mention here because of their relationship to fatherhood: marriage, celibacy, and parenthood. In part 2, we analyzed them from the perspective of sex difference; here we will look at them more precisely as vocations to fatherhood.

Marriage and Fatherhood

John Paul characterizes marriage as a vocation, the calling of a particular man and a particular woman to follow Christ irrevocably united as a couple and by serving his kingdom with the love proper to husband and wife.[16] Marriage reflects the Christian vocation to the degree that it manifests the spousal love that Jesus Christ the Bridegroom has for his Bride the Church, and with which the Church reciprocates. It is manifested when the spouses show one another self-sacrificing love that is sacramentally transformed into a redemptive love—that self-same love with which God has loved man from eternity in Christ.[17] Marriage is a path to holiness

---

[9] *Christifideles laici*, §§2, 35, 55-56.

[10] *Christifideles laici*, §6.

[11] John Paul II, Apostolic Exhortation on the Formation of Priests in the Circumstances of the Present Day *Pastores dabo vobis* (March 15, 1992), *AAS* 84 (1992), 657–804 (Boston: Pauline Books and Media, 1992), §81.

[12] *Christifideles laici*, §9; John Paul II, Post-Synodal Apostolic Exhortation on the Consecrated Life and Its Mission in the Church and in the World *Vita consecrata* (March 26, 1996), §§20, 60.

[13] *Familiaris consortio*, §§1, 49, 56; *Vita consecrata*, §62.

[14] *Christifideles laici*, §17.

[15] *Christifideles laici*, §23.

[16] See *Familiaris consortio*, §1.

[17] See John Paul II, *Man and Woman He Created Them: A Theology of the Body*, trans. Michael Waldstein (Boston: Pauline Books and Media, 2006), 476–77.

for those who are so called because it both points to and participates in Christ's love for his Bride, the Church.[18] Jesus most dramatically manifests his love in his Passion and death, when he gives himself up for his Bride.

In marriage, the spouses are united and vivified by this love which is the source and basis for their own. This love is raised to a sacrificial level through grace by virtue of the sacramental nature of the Church. In fact, spouses are only able to serve Christ's kingdom by means of their cooperation with the grace of the sacraments.[19] This grace is a prerequisite for an authentic Christian marriage. The husband and wife mediate to one another the grace necessary for holiness by responding to their vocation to the great mystery: "'Husbands, love your wives, as Christ loved the Church and gave himself up for her' (Eph 5:25)."[20] They further their sanctification through their affirmative response to the task of procreation. This response manifests a love which is not turned inward. Rather, through their gift of self, they transcend themselves and so they find that their love overflows into openness to new life. By cooperating with sanctifying grace, they are able to experience the sanctifying love which provides them the means to contribute to the growth of Christ's Bride.[21]

Men who are called to the Christian vocation of natural fatherhood are first called to marriage. Christian marriage is itself a state, which symbolizes and uniquely participates in the most perfect act of human selfless love, the Cross. John Paul certainly does not reduce it to a means to fatherhood, but he does recognize that it prepares a man for fatherhood. Indeed, beginning with the consummation of the marriage, the man engages in his first act of natural fatherhood. The marital act is ordered to be an act of responsible parenthood and responsible fatherhood, which is both an expression of selfless love for his wife and his active openness to the possible fruit of a child.[22]

The degree to which the man transcends himself and selflessly gives himself to his wife will likely correspond to his ability to love and nurture his children. The man's task to master himself and purify his initiating love for his wife and his children is a serious one. It forms the heart of the

---

[18] See John Paul II, *A Catechesis on the Creed*, vol. 4, *The Church: Mystery, Sacrament, Community* (Boston: Pauline Books and Media, 1998), 501.

[19] John Paul II, *The Church*, 49.

[20] John Paul II, *The Church*, 501.

[21] See John Paul II, *The Church*, 503. See also Karol Wojtyła, "Pastoral Reflections on the Family," in *Person and Community: Selected Essays*, vol. 4, trans. Theresa Sandok, O.S.M. (New York: Peter Lang, 1993), 348.

[22] See *Man and Woman*, 625ff.

message of the great mystery to the husband.[23] And because it is a sacrament, it provides the grace necessary for the man to love his wife as Christ loves the Church, and to prepare him to give his masculine love to his children in a self-transcending manner. When a man accepts entrance into the state of Christian marriage, he must know the entirety of what he is accepting, the vocation to self-transcending love as a husband and father.

CELIBACY AND FATHERHOOD

John Paul II links the vocation and state of consecrated celibacy very closely to marriage. One can authentically understand feminine consecrated virginity only in reference to marital love. Spousal love is of such a kind that two persons become gifts to one another.[24] In consecrated celibacy, the Christian gives visible witness, by means of her body, to the Christian hope and vigil for the eschatological wedding supper of the Lamb.[25] The celibate makes herself a gift to her divine Spouse by freely choosing this vocation. This spousal image gives celibacy a particular meaning for women.[26]

This is why the Christian tradition has always seen Mary as the ideal of consecrated virginity, since Mary is both Virgin and Bride. Mary reveals to mankind the fruitfulness of virginal love. It is a love that nurtures the interior begetting and growth of God's love within his children's hearts. Christians have always been encouraged to model their lives after the Blessed Virgin Mary. Consecrated virgins especially are able to live their lives in solidarity with Mary by manifesting their spiritual fecundity through their receptivity to the Word, and thereby to cooperate in the growth and sanctification of the Church.[27]

While celibacy is intimately tied to marriage, it is also a calling to renounce marriage for the sake of the kingdom of heaven. John Paul understands both of these vocations to reveal the same truth about human nature. By the fact that the Christian has the ability to make himself a gift for the kingdom of God, he demonstrates the existence in the human body, a freedom of the gift. In other words, the body has a spousal meaning.[28] Fundamental to consecrated celibacy is the free choice in favor of self-giving. John Paul clarifies that celibacy does not equate to the choice

---

[23] See *Man and Woman*, 465ff.

[24] See *Mulieris dignitatem*, §20.

[25] See *Familiaris consortio*, §16.

[26] See *Vita consecrata*, §34.

[27] See *Vita consecrata*, §34.

[28] See *Man and Woman*, 190.

to simply remain unmarried. This is because this consecration is not first saying no. Rather, even more, it is the emphatic response of "yes," in full freedom, to the spousal order, that is, to the total gift of self in an exclusive and irrevocable manner to the divine Bridegroom.[29]

Celibacy is also a vocation of service to the Church. The consecrated life is a vital constituent of the mission of the Church, belonging to the very heart of the Church. This is so because it makes the core of the Christian vocation visible. Speaking corporately, this vocation is one in which the whole Church labors as Bride for final communion with her Spouse.[30] Through this way of life, which is working for increasing perfection in one's union with Christ, one surrenders his whole life to Jesus and to the service of his kingdom through imitation of him.[31] But it is a special vocation in which those who are called to it by a special initiative of the Father receive the grace of the Holy Spirit needed to live this image of Christ in such a radical way.[32]

One important aspect of this service is as a witness to and model of Jesus and his life. Through one's total obedience, complete chastity, and radical poverty in which he has nothing which he can call his own, one gives living expression to the gospel in a most radical way.[33] This way of service is divine because the God-Man embraced this manner of living while he was on earth. It is for this reason that the Christian tradition lauds the consecrated life as an objectively superior vocation.[34] Another duty of those living the consecrated life is that of showing that the Son of God Incarnate is the end to which all creation is drawn.[35] They do this by conforming their whole being to Christ in such a way that it is clear they have fully committed themselves to achieving perfection in love, but a perfection that will only finally be eschatologically achieved.

In fulfilling this duty, consecrated persons manifest themselves as eschatological icons of the spotless Bride, a time in which the Church will finally be able to love her Bridegroom perfectly.[36] It should be clear that far from denigrating marriage, this state extols it. The consecrated person proleptically participates, with her body, in the final resurrection.

---

[29] See *Mulieris dignitatem*, §20.

[30] See *Vita consecrata*, §3.

[31] See *Vita consecrata*, §14.

[32] See *Vita consecrata*, §14.

[33] See *Vita consecrata*, §18.

[34] See *Vita consecrata*, §18.

[35] See *Vita consecrata*, §18.

[36] See *Vita consecrata*, §§7, 26.

Through this heroic witness, consecrated virginity keeps in the Church's consciousness the full mystery of marriage and protects it from diminution or impoverishment.[37] John Paul argues that the promise of celibacy or virginity actually permits the consecrated person a more direct participation in the mystery of marriage, and more specifically, participation in the marriage of Christ to his Church.[38] Since marital love unites one with Christ via a human union, it is a mediated union. With consecrated virginal love, there is no mediating structure.

Virginal love proceeds directly to an immediate union with Christ, "a truly complete and decisive spiritual espousal."[39] This is a truer witness to the eschatological union man will experience in the beatific vision. John Paul says that "this immediate union with the bridegroom is an anticipation of the life of heaven, which will be characterized by a vision or possession of God without intermediaries."[40] This immediacy is the source of the profound happiness of consecrated life. It is the purpose of our beatific union with the Church's Bridegroom.[41] This eschatological sign is most perfectly manifested in the virginity and divine motherhood of Mary. She receives this gift from God as the fruit of her total gift of self to him. "This gift is the beginning and the prototype of a new expectation on the part of all. It measures up to the Eternal Covenant, to God's new and definitive promise: it is *a sign of eschatological hope*."[42] Celibacy is not unrelated to parenthood; rather, there is a significant overlap between the two vocations.

Men who are called to consecrated celibacy are called to a fatherhood that is purely spiritual. They set aside natural fatherhood for the sake of giving themselves to Jesus and his Church in Christian witness through their particular masculine gifts. While consecrated celibacy in holy orders more clearly manifests spiritual fatherhood, consecrated men who are not called to holy orders are also called to express their spiritual fatherhood through this state, even if they cannot be signs of it. In the next chapter, we will take up this matter of spiritual fatherhood and its significance for men in a state which is a sign of the virgin bride and spiritual motherhood.

---

[37] See *Familiaris consortio*, §16.

[38] See John Paul II, *The Church*, 566.

[39] John Paul II, *The Church*, 566.

[40] John Paul II, *The Church*, 567.

[41] See John Paul II, *The Church*, 566.

[42] *Mulieris dignitatem*, §20.

PARENTHOOD OF FATHERS

Here we will only briefly look at parenthood as a vocation, as the remainder of part 3 is devoted to the extraction and explication of John Paul II's theology of human fatherhood. In concert with his anthropology, John Paul sees that the entire structure of the feminine person is oriented toward the vocation to motherhood.[43] Men also have the personal structure necessary for their vocation to fatherhood. However, their fallen state seems to affect this vocation in certain ways more deeply than it does women (though it can affect women more deeply in other ways). For example, men have a need for assistance from their wives in learning to be effective fathers.[44]

It is important to note that parenthood is a vocation, something that can be freely accepted or rejected. The authentic vocation of parenthood goes beyond simply biological parenthood; it extends to all aspects of the formation of the child.[45] It is also an internal attitude by which the

---

[43] See *Mulieris dignitatem*, §§18, 30.

[44] See *Mulieris dignitatem*, §18. John Paul is clear that concupiscence affects both men and women, but it does so in different manners (see *Man and Woman*, 260–61). John Paul II finds theological justification for this difference in Gen 3:16 where the man is the one who is more likely to dominate the woman (see *Man and Woman*, 261). The implication is that the effect of concupiscence on the man's masculine constitution makes him more susceptible than a woman is to viewing a woman as an object to possess for the sake of pleasure rather than as a person-gift: "The woman in particular is in danger of becoming a mere object of enjoyment for the man" (211; see also 99). In the same work, his view of the man's psycho-physiological structure could explain his understanding of Genesis 3:16. He says:

> The very structure of the masculine psyche and personality is such that it is more speedily forced, as it were, to reveal and objectify what is hidden in love for the person of the other sex. This is linked to the rather more active role of a man in this love, and also has a bearing on his responsibility. Concerning a woman, however, sensuality is, so to speak, concealed and hidden in affectivity. And therefore she is "by nature" more inclined to consider as a manifestation of affective love what a man already clearly recognizes as an activity of sensuality and a wish to use. Hence, evidently a certain psychological divergence exists in the scope of a man's and a woman's participation in love. A woman seems more passive, although in another way she is more active. In any case, her role and responsibility will be different from the role and responsibility of a man.

(Karol Wojtyła, *Love and Responsibility*, trans. Grzegorz Ignatik [Boston: Pauline Books & Media, 2013], 94). In *Mulieris dignitatem,* §18, John Paul does not explicitly tie to concupiscence the man's need to learn his fatherhood from his wife, but given his interpretation of Genesis 3:16 it seems reasonable to infer that concupiscence is at least part of the problem.

[45] See Wojtyła, *Love and Responsibility*, 245–46.

self-giving love the parents express for each other transcends their union and overflows to their children. It is a vocation which depends upon love elevated by the grace of the Sacrament of Matrimony for its success. Additionally, it involves the whole person and so each parent, the father and mother together, must give the whole of themselves in fulfilling the calling.

Men and Fathers' Vocation to Support and Defend Women and Motherhood

Elaborating on the manner in which John Paul sees that this applies to fatherhood is the remaining task. We can begin by looking at some specific ways in which men are called to exercise their gifts of masculinity and fatherhood by supporting and defending women in their femininity and motherhood. John Paul II considers the prevailing loss of a sense of the real genius of femininity and motherhood in society as one of the most urgent problems to be addressed. Therefore, he gave considerable attention to helping restore the authentic meaning of femininity and motherhood in his magisterial corpus.

Many commentators suggest that John Paul II focuses on women and motherhood while completely neglecting men and fatherhood. If so, he would seem to be missing the mark with respect to the acknowledged crisis in marriage and family life. More explicitly, in 2004, then-Cardinal Joseph Ratzinger said that the current crisis in the family is a crisis of fatherhood.[46] Ratzinger is not alone in his diagnosis. David Blankenhorn, in his book *Fatherless America*, shows how one can correlate the US national trend of increasing societal ills with the increase in fatherless households.[47]

---

[46] Ratzinger says: "Human fatherhood gives us an anticipation of what [God the Father] is. But when this fatherhood does not exist, when it is experienced only as a biological phenomenon, without its human and spiritual dimension, all statements about God the Father are empty. The crisis of fatherhood we are living today is an element, perhaps the most important, threatening man in his humanity. The dissolution of fatherhood and motherhood is linked to the dissolution of our being sons and daughters" (Cardinal Ratzinger on the dangers of biotechnology at the Cathedral of Palermo to the Theology Faculty of Sicily during the inauguration of the Third Diocesan Week of Faith; excerpted from the "Insidious Threat to Sense of Fatherhood," *Zenit*, March 15, 2000; this article is no longer available from Zenit's website.

[47] Blankenhorn shows that the problem of fatherless households has grown significantly since 1960. In 1995 about 40 percent of all children in the US were living without their biological fathers. While divorce and remarriage account for the majority of cases, 40 percent of these children live only with their mothers. Almost one-third of these cases

In the United States, a variety of organizations have been formed, aimed at addressing the specific problem of absentee fathers. Some of these include the National Center for Fathering founded by Ken Canfield, and the National Fatherhood Initiative headed by Don Eberly. Evangelical Protestants formed a movement called Promise Keepers, whose aim is to redress the loss of the father's role in family life by educating and motivating men to live up to their obligations as men and fathers. Similarly, the Knights of Columbus provide a Catholic response to the crisis with their fatherhood initiative called Fathers for Good.

In this context, John Paul's apparent lack of attention to men and fatherhood might seem all the more worthy of criticism. However, I do not believe that John Paul II was ignorant of this problem.[48] Rather, it would

---

are due to men fathering children out of wedlock; two-thirds are due to the father voluntarily leaving due to divorce or separation/abandonment. Only 7 percent of these cases are involuntary due to the death of the father. Thus, fatherless households, due to the father being involuntarily separated, are certainly much less than 17 percent of all households. The result is that for more than 34 percent of all households, the biological father is voluntarily absent for a significant portion of his children's childhood. In contrast, the mother is absent in less than 8 percent of all cases. Blankenhorn cites study after study linking male youth crime, emotional and behavioral problems, and social maladjustment to fatherless households. In fact, the most significant indicator of crime in a neighborhood is the percentage of households without the biological father present. While violence and crime are the main results of boys being raised without a father, for girls juvenile and single motherhood become the problems. For example, girls in single-parent homes (87 percent of which are fatherless) are 53 percent more likely to marry as teenagers, 111 percent more likely to have children as teenagers, 164 percent more likely to have a child out of wedlock, and 92 percent more likely to divorce. These facts help to perpetuate further societal problems, since women living with men who are not their husbands are four times more likely to experience abuse than is a wife at the hands of her husband. In addition, children in fatherless households are at a significantly higher risk of sexual abuse. Finally, children are six times more likely to live in poverty if they live only with their mother (see David Blankenhorn, *Fatherless America: Confronting Our Most Urgent Social Problem* [New York: Harper-Collins Publishers, 1995], 9–62).

48 This would seem to be indicated by his comment about the link between sin and fatherhood: "As we know from Revelation, in human history the 'rays of fatherhood' meet a first resistance in the obscure but real fact of original sin. *This is truly the key for interpreting reality*. Original sin is not only the violation of a positive command of God but also, and above all, a violation *of the will of God as expressed in that command. Original sin attempts, then, to abolish fatherhood*, destroying its rays which permeate the created world, placing in doubt the truth about God who is Love and leaving man only with a sense of the master-slave relationship" (John Paul II, *Crossing the Threshold of Hope*, ed. Vittorio Messori, trans. Jenny McPhee and Martha McPhee [New York, NY: Alfred A. Knopf, Inc., 1994], 227–28). His reference to the "rays of fatherhood" intone the derivative human fatherhood which is always under attack due to sin. However, he also gives

appear that he found the crisis of fatherhood itself to be a symptom of a more fundamental problem. John Paul states: "Who can deny that our age is one marked by a great crisis, which appears above all as a profound '*crisis of truth*?' A crisis of truth means, in the first place, a *crisis of concepts*. Do the words 'love,' 'freedom,' 'sincere gift,' and even 'person' and 'rights of the person,' really convey their essential meaning?"[49]

It is first a loss of the meaning of the human person that has led to the crisis in marriage and family and, therefore, in society. I would argue that John Paul aims his approach at addressing the crisis of contemporary family life from another direction, dictated by his anthropology. Let's look at his writings which, at least indirectly, address the rationale for choosing women and motherhood as his point of departure for family life to see what I mean. Such an approach can help men and fathers to exercise more effectively their vocation vis-à-vis women and motherhood.

Perhaps the most explicit explanation for John Paul II's focus on women and motherhood that one can find is in his series of essays published in *Crossing the Threshold of Hope*. Here he argues that for liberal societies, the twentieth century has been marked by a growth in a type of feminism that arose in reaction to the lack of respect women have experienced. He contrasts this lack of respect with his experience as a youth in Poland in which the culture held women in very high regard, especially those women who were mothers. His experience from his youth corresponds with revealed truth, he argues. These truths are to be found in the faith of the Church which has always respected women and the mystery of motherhood. This respect is particularly visible in the tradition of the spousal love of Christ for his Church. He laments that modernity has eroded this great tradition

---

explicit reference to the problem of the absent father in *Mulieris dignitatem*, §14: "How often is [the mother] abandoned with her pregnancy, when the man, the child's father, is unwilling to accept responsibility for it? And besides the many 'unwed mothers' in our society, we also must consider all those who, as a result of various pressures, even on the part of the guilty man, very often 'get rid of' the child before it is born" (no. 14). In his Apostolic Exhortation on the laity he again refers to the missing father: "Man himself—husband and father—can be helped to overcome forms of absenteeism and of periodic presence as well as a partial fulfillment of parental responsibilities—indeed he can be involved in new and significant relations of interpersonal communion—precisely as a result of the intelligent, loving and decisive intervention of woman" (*Christifideles laici*, §51).

[49] John Paul II, Letter to Families *Gratissimam sane* (February 2, 1994), AAS 86 (1994), 868–925 (New Hope, KY: Urbi Et Orbi Communications, 1994), §13.

and has led modern civilization to justify treating women as, first of all, objects of pleasure under the guise of their liberation.[50]

John Paul admits that his upbringing may have influenced his view of women and motherhood. However, he is clear that his theological anthropology arises not from a nostalgic, romantic idealization of women but rather from divine revelation itself.[51] The lack of respect accorded to women is a significant problem affecting societal health. This problem continues unabated, with the perennial predilection of men to view women essentially as objects of pleasure resulting in practices injurious to women's dignity. These practices include sexual tourism and trafficking in young girls, as well as mass sterilization, and a variety of other forms of violence to women.[52]

Respect for the dignity of women is one of John Paul's major focuses in *Mulieris dignitatem* because he finds it to be a key concern for the sake of women as well as for larger society. His Christian anthropology demands that women be accorded the same respect as men because their personal dignity derives from the same source; namely, that both are made in the image of God. He lays much of the blame for the objectification of women at the feet of men and their selfishness, men both past and present.[53]

The problem of men's objectification of women is further exacerbated by a modern mentality which reduces the human person in general to a commodity of trade, a means of productivity, or even simply a path to selfish pleasure. This ubiquitous manner of thinking further attenuates the Christian message of human dignity. It seems that women are usually the first victims of this mentality.[54] For this reason, his focus on women begins with his concern for their dignity as persons.

In many of his writings, he addresses himself directly to women. He believes that women must take responsibility for the task of promoting their rightful dignity. Likewise, the task to advocate for their rightful

---

[50] See John Paul II, *Threshold of Hope*, 216–17.

[51] This charge has been leveled against John Paul II's theology of women and motherhood. See, e.g., Lisa Sowle Cahill, "Notes on Moral Theology: Feminist Ethics," *Theological Studies* 51 (1990): 58. I will assess this criticism in part 4.

[52] See John Paul II, *A Catechesis on Salvation History*, vol. 6, *The Trinity's Embrace: God's Saving Plan* (Boston: Pauline Books and Media, 2002), 288.

[53] See John Paul II, *The Church*, 479. Though, it must be countered that women can also cooperate in their own objectification (see Carrie Gress, *The Anti-Mary Exposed: Rescuing the Culture from Toxic Femininity* [Charlotte, NC: TAN Books, 2019]). John Paul II is clearly aware of this, telling women they must not be complicit in anything that attacks their dignity; see John Paul II, *The Church*, 479.

[54] See *Familiaris consortio*, §24.

role in the Church and society belongs first to women themselves.[55] He considers it their "duty to demand respect for their nature as persons, not descending to any form of complicity with what demeans their dignity."[56] The latter part of this quote contains an important point. Women must recognize their equal dignity as persons, but as *feminine* persons. Thus, they must also carefully avoid participation in all activities which degrade their femininity.

This includes activities such as pornography and participation in media which portray women as objects of pleasure.[57] However, it extends to a misguided response in which women reject their femininity as a weakness which facilitates their oppression, opting instead for masculine forms of behavior.[58] Along similar lines, he writes to men as well. They also have a solemn duty to fight the mentality which treats women as objects.[59] He saw this as a serious problem from his pastoral work. In fact, as the Auxiliary Bishop of Kraków, during a retreat for college students given in 1962, he addresses the men in a surprisingly explicit fashion about this fallen masculine predilection, which gives them the stronger desire for sexual relations.[60] This results in their being the primary instigators of sexual relations outside of marriage. He also warns them that their fallen inclination to conquer, to take, and to use also inclines them toward an unwillingness to take responsibility for their actions. He tells men that this is where Christ makes great demands on them, to take responsibility and to master themselves, or they will likely follow this fallen path. Men must strive for perfection and follow Christ so that they have the strength to give of themselves and to be able to support women in their greater inclination toward chastity.

John Paul also addresses himself to the whole Church—both laity and clerics, women and men—to promote the rights and dignity of both women and men for their own good, for the good of the family, and for the good of society.[61] John Paul's concern for the effects of the diminution of women as persons also reflects a concern for the family and larger society as well. He sees women themselves as key in helping to overcome

---

[55] See *Christifideles laici*, §49.
[56] John Paul II, *The Church*, 479.
[57] See John Paul II, *The Church*, 479.
[58] See *Familiaris consortio*, §23.
[59] See John Paul II, *The Church*, 479.
[60] John Paul II, *The Way to Christ: Spiritual Exercises*, trans. Leslie Wearne (NY: Harper Collins, 1984), 54–57.
[61] See *Christifideles laici*, §49.

family and social problems that result primarily from the objectification of women. He identifies two essential functions for which he believes women must take the lead. The first of these is the task of restoring the full truth and dignity to conjugal life and to motherhood. John Paul agrees that a crisis in modern times is the absent, or only occasionally present, husband and father. But there are new possibilities today for women to understand these fundamental Christian values better and so to help these absentee men to overcome their deficiencies in meeting parental responsibilities. Women's wise and loving but decisive intervention can help involve these men in deeper more committed marital communion.

The second task is that of helping to ensure that culture is returned to its moral center, a center necessary for the cultivation of the dignity of the person and for promoting healthy social life.[62] This admonition is addressed to everyone because all share in the responsibility for these tasks, but in different ways. Nevertheless, John Paul assigns to women a leading role. Women can even be instrumental in helping to overcome the problem of men deserting their wives and young children, as well as the problem of men failing to take full responsibility for raising their children. John Paul's anthropology tells him that women's very constitution makes their prominent role essential to solving the problems plaguing marriage, family, and society.

John Paul locates the problem of paternal absenteeism particularly in society's loss of respect for both conjugal life and motherhood. John Paul asserts that men's selfishness is a primary cause of the prevalent disregard for women's dignity. This might seem to attribute all of the responsibility for societal ills to men, but I have not found John Paul II to be one-sided.[63] He also hints that women, too, have participated in some measure, at least by not accomplishing their two major tasks. However, this is not a matter of distributing blame but rather one of identifying problems and solving them by accomplishing the tasks appointed to one according to one's feminine or masculine gifts. Women's feminine characteristics, in general, enable them to be first to recognize the full dignity of both conjugal life and motherhood, and enable them to demand that men also acknowledge this dignity. This presumably begins with their refusal to engage in conjugal relations outside of the marital covenant.

Within marriage, the wife must ensure that she is not objectified in conjugal relations with her spouse. Indeed, John Paul says that through

---

[62] See *Christifideles laici*, §51.
[63] See John Paul II, *The Church*, 479.

the woman's "intelligent, decisive and loving intervention" the man, who for various reasons would not otherwise, can come to know and embrace the gift of an authentic interpersonal communion with his wife.[64] This first task is inextricably linked with the second task, that of assuring that culture does not fall into moral relativism, especially in the sexual sphere. Again, John Paul takes pains to ensure that his audience understands that these truths about women and their particular gifts are not simply derived from a time long past but rather rest upon the order of creation and are likewise divinely revealed.

John Paul identifies some of a woman's particular gifts in his analysis of Genesis 2:18. While everyone is entrusted to each and every other human being, man is entrusted in a special way to woman.[65] This special entrustment arises from the woman's experience of motherhood, which provides her with "a *specific sensitivity* toward the human person and all that constitutes the individual's true welfare, beginning with the fundamental value of life."[66] Her sensitivity is due in part to the intimacy she experiences with the baby in her womb. John Paul says: "'This unique contact with the new human being developing within her gives rise to an attitude toward human beings—not only toward her own child, but every human being—which profoundly marks the woman's personality.' A mother welcomes and carries in herself another human being, enabling it to grow inside her, giving it room, respecting it in its otherness."[67]

John Paul II finds that even though the man may faithfully share in the responsibilities of parenthood, nevertheless he "always remains 'outside' the process of pregnancy and the baby's birth; in many ways he has to *learn* his own *'fatherhood' from the mother*."[68] Thus a woman, because of her feminine constitution, is in many ways more directly disposed to the tasks required for a healthy family and society than is a man.

Women learn first that authentic human relations must be grounded in an acceptance of the other person because of his personhood rather than

---

[64] John Paul II, *The Church*, 479.

[65] See John Paul II, *The Church*, 479.

[66] John Paul II, *The Church*, 479.

[67] John Paul II, Encyclical Letter on the Value and Inviolability of Human Life *Evangelium vitae* (March 25, 1995), *AAS* 87 (1995), 401–522, §99.

[68] *Mulieris dignitatem*, §18. John Paul's statement is supported by others. For example, John Miller writes that "due to the marginality of males in the reproductive process, fathering is a cultural acquisition to an extent that mothering is not" (John Miller, *Calling God "Father": Essays on the Bible, Fatherhood, and Culture* [New York: Paulist Press, 1999], 11). Miller then goes on to buttress this claim by using historical, cultural, and sociological arguments.

for utilitarian or superficial aesthetic reasons. Because women learn this first, they also are the primary teachers of this insight. John Paul argues that this is the essential contribution that women make not only to human society at large but also to the Church. Without this contribution, positive cultural change is not possible.[69] A woman's gifts better enable her to take a leading role in combating the dehumanizing effects of the amoral application of science and technology in a society which tends to consider only utilitarian goals.[70]

One must keep in mind that John Paul does not discern these characteristics and tasks solely on the basis of biology. Rather, biology reveals the feminine soul and so it provides insights about that which is invisible. Consequently, John Paul arrives at the above characteristics and tasks based upon the whole of that which comprises the entirety of the feminine person.[71] In so doing, he finds that women occupy a unique and decisive place in transforming culture in virtue of their feminine gifts. But unlike the more common strains of feminism that argue for similar goals sans a concern for their femininity, he advocates for a "new feminism."

This new feminism refuses to succumb to the enticement to follow the pervasive and problematic models of male domination as is common with so-called radical feminism. Rather, it acknowledges and affirms the true genius of femininity in all corners of societal life. It champions authentic femininity as it works to overcome every form of violence and inequity toward and abuse of women.[72] Hence, John Paul again emphasizes that

---

[69] See *Evangelium vitae*, §99.

[70] See *Christifideles laici*, §51.

[71] Some accuse John Paul II of "biologism" for his use of the physical make-up of the person to understand his interiority. Benedict Ashley attributes the terms "biologism" or "physicalism" to Charles Curran. These terms are applied by Curran to the use of insights derived from the body for discerning the morality of human acts. Curran claims the fallacy of Thomists is in trying to ascertain the morality of human acts by determining the teleology of various bodily parts. He claims that this approach succumbs to the Stoic reduction of human morality to the teleology of animal instincts. Ashley agrees with Curran that one must reject the Stoic reduction but argues that Curran's complete separation of human morality from the teleology of the human body falls into Platonic dualism. See Benedict Ashley, *Theologies of the Body: Humanist and Christian* (Braintree, MA: The Pope John Center, 1985, repr. 1995), 369–70. John Grabowski is concerned in an analogous manner that discerning attributes of the whole person from biological appearance and function "runs the risk of physicalism . . . or . . . a meta-physicalism" ("Mutual Submission and Trinitarian Self-Giving," *Angelicum* 74 [1997]: 501n30). Whether John Paul's approach succumbs to either of these concerns will be assessed more fully in part 4.

[72] See *Evangelium vitae*, §99.

women and men have particular ways of acting that are in accord with their sex difference. This is, for him, a fundamental truth.

From what has been said, it might be argued that John Paul is decidedly one-sided in his program for family and cultural renewal. But it would not be accurate to say that he places the responsibility solely, or even primarily, at the feet of women. He charges women *and* men, including the Church hierarchy, with the responsibility for restoring the Christian view of the dignity of women, marriage, and motherhood in contemporary society. He finds it both necessary and urgent that concrete steps be taken to make it possible for women to participate in every aspect of public life, including as decision-makers, especially in matters that directly concern women themselves.[73]

Still, in some ways one could say that men's role in this matter is supportive in order to enable women to help in the restoration of the family and culture. Certainly, women must have a leading role in this cultural transformation because it will come about through recognition, by both men and women, of true feminine genius. As a result, women must labor to make visible their authentic feminine identity. This role is theirs in virtue of the gifts inherent to femininity.

John Paul II identifies many reasons for women to take a leading role in this endeavor. For example, he is concerned that the value of motherhood has been assailed by those who consider it regressive for women to be encouraged to embrace a primary vocation to motherhood. This, they say, restricts a woman's personal development and denies them their freedom to pursue more personally enriching endeavors.[74] This ideology has led many women to believe that they must give up, or at least subordinate the importance of motherhood, if they are to fulfill themselves. This diminution of the appreciation of the value of motherhood is especially damaging to the woman herself, as well as to society.

It is contrary to the structure of femininity to make an activity such as a profession the goal rather than to allow her to fulfill her personhood through service to others, especially to her child, in a feminine manner. Women who can experience and appreciate motherhood are the most credible witnesses to its value and dignity. Presumably, because of their ability for undivided attention to this concern, John Paul turns to consecrated women as a source of leadership for finding new efforts to cultivate family and social life, as well as Christian belief and morality.

---

[73] See *Vita consecrata*, §58.
[74] See John Paul II, *The Church*, 493.

Women's leadership is especially needed in all matters which relate to the dignity of women and respect for human life. In these matters, women have a unique and decisive role to play both in the arena of thought as well as that of action.[75] This new feminism is authentic feminism because it appreciates the value of women's differences. It is in contrast to those older forms which, in some measure or another, tend to reject femininity as an exploitable weakness.[76] For this reason, only this new, authentic feminism will be capable of leading the way to a renewal of society.

John Paul also looks to consecrated women to help educate contemporary women about the truth of their feminine vocation.[77] The self-awareness by women of the irreplaceable gift of femininity will have the effect of influencing men to reconsider their predominantly one-sided view of the world. This includes their masculine self-understanding, historical hermeneutics, and the way they tend to organize ecclesial life, religious life, society, the economy, and political structures.[78]

John Paul II emphasizes that an important aspect of men's vocational responsibilities as men and fathers is to collaborate with women in their task as women and mothers. Their masculine gifts are indeed ordered to these in roles of supporting and defending. This begins with the foremost problem which is the attack on the feminine person in terms of the sex trade. Men are the primary producers and consumers of activities that reduce, objectify, and abuse women. To begin with, men must express their masculine gifts and spiritual fatherhood by overcoming temptations to participate in this horrific commodification of women. They must also be active in supporting efforts aimed at stopping pornography and other sex trades, eliminating gratuitous sex from popular media, and helping people free themselves from the grip of these destructive activities.

Men also need to learn more about what it means to be a man and father, and to be more docile to learning those things which women and mothers can teach them, such as love and solicitude for others. He can

---

[75] See *Vita consecrata*, §58.

[76] Of course, not every older form of feminism rejects feminine differences as weaknesses. Some feminists tend to emphasize sexual differences in order to extol women as psychologically and morally superior to men (see Paul Vitz, "The Fatherhood of God: Support from Psychology," *Josephinum Journal of Theology* 9, no. 1 [2002]: 76).

[77] See Vitz, "The Fatherhood of God," 76.

[78] See *Vita consecrata*, §57. The Pope's reference to men's revaluation of the way they organize ecclesial life cannot refer to the Church's hierarchical structure which he acknowledges as divinely mandated (see, e.g., John Paul II, Encyclical Letter on Commitment to Ecumenism *Ut unum sint* [May 25, 1995], §§89–95). Rather, it must refer to those aspects of the Church's life which the Church has the authority to alter.

learn these things in all his opposite-sex relationships, even as he observes women and mothers from the time he is a child with his own mother, as he observes the motherhood of women in his life, including that of his sisters, and if he is called to marriage himself, from observing his wife.

Men also must be proactive in helping to form a "new feminism" in which they collaborate with women to reimagine and rebuild societal structures that allow women to contribute their gifts to society according to their feminine genius, which again, they have the obligation to understand if they are to assist in this effectively.

CHAPTER 10

The Fatherhood of God

For Karol Wojtyła, all human fatherhood, as well as motherhood, is a participation in the fatherhood of God. His writings on God's fatherhood, then, should provide material for developing an analogous theology of human fatherhood. In fact, Cardinal Wojtyła provides the justification for this approach himself in his play *Radiation of Fatherhood*. In the play, he suggests that the authentic role of human fatherhood radiates to man from God the Father as revealed through Jesus Christ, his Son. The father in the play, Adam, is perhaps the antithesis of what a father is called to be in light of man's reflection of the Father as revealed through the Son.[1]

Adam learns that a man is called to be a child,[2] brother,[3] bridegroom,[4] and finally father through suffering and death-to-self in the image of the self-giving love of the Trinity as revealed and expressed *par excellence* in Christ's Passion and death.[5] Scholars may not often recognize Jesus

---

[1] See Karol Wojtyła, *Radiation of Fatherhood*, in *The Collected Plays and Writings on Theater: Karol Wojtyła*, trans. Bolesław Taborski (Berkeley: University of California Press, 1987), 336. In his commentary on this play in the cited work, Bolesław Toborski says that the father character is perhaps both the original Adam of Genesis as well as historical man who has succumbed to concupiscence and become a fallen father.

[2] See Wojtyła, *Radiation of Fatherhood*, 339, 362. Of course, becoming a child does not properly belong to God the Father but rather presents the proper disposition a human father must have in his relationship with God if he is to authentically radiate divine fatherhood in his individual vocation.

[3] See Wojtyła, *Radiation of Fatherhood*, 363.

[4] See Wojtyła, *Radiation of Fatherhood*, 360.

[5] See Wojtyła, *Radiation of Fatherhood*, 362–64. Francis Martin appears to agree with this: "Thus, the radiation of Fatherhood is in Jesus, uniquely the One who is 'poor and brokenhearted and trembles at my word' (Is 66:2), who, because he does nothing but what he sees the Father doing (see John 5:19), is the Son in whom the Father is well pleased (see Matt 3:17). This Jesus, the perfect child of the Father, is himself the Father

explicitly as a father figure, but he himself indicates that he reveals the Father,[6] justifying Wojtyła's presentation of Jesus as a father. Because the title "father" in the spiritual sense is applied in the first place to God the Father,[7] it is not surprising that Jesus does not explicitly refer to himself as a father, but he does in fact accept his fatherly role.[8] For example, he addresses his disciples as children,[9] and he addresses both the woman with the hemorrhage and the Canaanite woman as "daughter."[10]

The New Testament provides additional indications of Jesus's fatherhood. We might take as an example the messianic title Father-Forever given in Isaiah 9:6. While the title is not explicitly cited in the New Testament, the surrounding context is referred to frequently.[11] Additionally, the Epistle to the Hebrews ties the theme of Jesus's brotherhood and fatherhood together in combining two scriptural testimonies: "'I will proclaim thy name to my brethren, in the midst of the congregation I will praise you' [Ps 22:22].... And again, 'Here am I, and the children God has given me' [Isa 8:18]" (Heb 2:12–13). While he understands the significance differently, James Swetnam also sees this transition: "Jesus moves subtly but unmistakably from 'brother' of Abraham's spiritual children in 2, 10–12 to one for whom these brothers are 'children' (*paidia*) in 2,13b–18."[12]

---

of the human race, the New Adam, who as the Child and Bridegroom of the New Eve, has made of her the gathering place of the radiation of Fatherhood." Francis Martin, "*Radiation of Fatherhood*: Some Biblical Reflections," *Josephinum Journal of Theology* 9, no. 1 (2002): 38.

6 See, for example, John 14:19.

7 See Rom 1:7; 15:6; 1 Cor 1:3; 15:24; 2 Cor 1:2; Gal 1:3; Eph 1:2; 5:25; 6:23; Phil 1:2; 2:11; Col 1:2; 2 Thess 1:2; 2 Tim 1:2; Titus 1:4; Phlm 3; Jas 1:27; 1 Pet 1:2; 2 John 3.

8 Here we should address a common objection: it is true that Jesus forbids his disciples, in Matt 23:8–10, from calling anyone "father," except for his heavenly Father. Some would therefore rule out any spiritual fatherhood except for that of God the Father. However, Jesus's hyperbole cannot be a compelling argument against calling Jesus, or any other man, for that matter, father. First, the passage does not limit the restriction of "father" to the realm of spiritual fatherhood: thus this prohibition should also apply to natural fathers if we are to take it literally. Furthermore, the New Testament provides a plethora of examples in which the term "father" is applied to men as spiritual fathers (see Luke 14:26; Acts 7:2; 21:40; 22:1; Rom 4:16–17; 1 Cor 4:14–15; 1 Thess 2:11; 1 Tim 1:2; Titus 1:4; Heb 12:7–9; Phlm 10; 1 John 2:13–14). Therefore, this verse does not negate the possibility that Jesus can be seen as a father.

9 See Mark 10:24; John 13:33; 21:5.

10 See Matt 9:22; Mark 5:34; Luke 8:48; and Matt 15:28, respectively.

11 See Matt 4:15–16; Luke 1:78–79; 2 Cor 4:6; 1 Pet 2:9; John 1:45; Eph 2:14.

12 James Swetnam, S.J. "The Structure of Hebrews: A Fresh Look," *Melita Theologica* 41, no. 1 (1990): 32.

John Paul II is on solid ground with his assertion that the Son reveals the fatherhood of God.

Karol Wojtyła provides an outline of his thinking in *Radiation of Fatherhood*, whereby one might extract an analogical theology of human fatherhood from divine fatherhood.[13] We will follow his method laid out in this early play. Let us first look to his writings on God's fatherhood. Next, we will investigate his writings which describe Jesus's revelation of this fatherhood. Finally, we will review his writings dealing with Jesus as an exemplar for human fatherhood. These texts viewed through the lens of John Paul II's anthropology will reveal an analogical theology of human fatherhood. At the same time, because both motherhood and fatherhood have their foundation in the fatherhood of God, there must be reasonable grounds for assigning attributes proper to human fatherhood (i.e., exclusive of motherhood).

GOD THE FATHER

God is Father from all eternity. John Paul II asserts this many times in following the Trinitarian theology explicated especially by St. Augustine of Hippo and St. Thomas Aquinas. His description of divine fatherhood then is no surprise. The Father is without origin, the font of all divinity, and the absolute principle of Trinitarian life. The three persons are a unity in their common, full possession of divine nature. However, citing the Fourth Lateran Council, John Paul clarifies that "the dynamism of reciprocal relations . . . have their source and foundation in the Father. 'It is the Father who generates, the Son who is begotten, and the Holy Spirit who proceeds' (Fourth Lateran Council: *DS* 804)."[14] We can see here that fatherhood means relation; in fact, divine fatherhood is the Origin of the Trinitarian relations. The Father's essence is his fatherhood. He is distinguished as a

---

[13] It might be argued that this play is very early and may not necessarily reflect the author's later thought. However, in reflections published in the book *Crossing the Threshold of Hope*, John Paul II seems to suggest that the concepts from *Radiation of Fatherhood* were still operative in his thought later in his life. He speaks of the rays of God's fatherhood radiating down on man and all of creation, an image which evokes his main theme of *Radiation of Fatherhood* (see *Crossing the Threshold of Hope*, ed. Vittorio Messori, trans. Jenny McPhee and Martha McPhee [New York, NY: Alfred A. Knopf, Inc., 1994], 227–28).

[14] John Paul II, *A Catechesis on Salvation History*, vol. 6, *The Trinity's Embrace: God's Saving Plan* (Boston: Pauline Books and Media, 2002), 183.

person by his relation to his Son—as Father, for he eternally generates the Word, his Son.[15]

The Father begets the Son by giving his whole self, such that Father and Son are intimately united in a union of love that is a person, the Holy Spirit.[16] This is the definition of love, the Love that is God (see 1 John 4:8).[17] The begetting of the Son is also called "generation," and generation explains the reciprocity of the relations of paternity and sonship.[18] But God the Father is the Origin, and being innascible, it is he who "must take the initiative" in self-giving because by definition everything originates from him.[19] His fatherhood belongs to the inner life of the Trinity. Divine fatherhood is a subsisting relation characterized by total self-gift to another. Of course, we know all of this, we know who the Father is only by the definitive revelation of Jesus Christ, his Son.[20]

Yet, John Paul also suggests that the Father is such, more than just concomitantly. He is also Father by choice; that is, he chooses to be a Father to his creatures.[21] God demonstrates his freedom as Father by entering

---

[15] As is his practice with everything, he is careful to ground these aspects of God's fatherhood in Scripture:

> "Blessed be the God and Father of our Lord Jesus Christ" (Eph 1:3). Paul's words are a good introduction to the newness of our knowledge of the Father as it unfolds in the New Testament. Here God appears in his trinitarian reality. His fatherhood is no longer limited to showing his relationship that characterizes his inner life; it is no longer a generic feature of God, but the property of the First Person in God. In his trinitarian mystery, God is a Father in his very being; he is always a Father, since from all eternity he generates the Word who is consubstantial with him and united to him in the Holy Spirit, "who proceeds from the Father and the Son."

(John Paul II, *The Trinity's Embrace*, 178).

[16] See John Paul II, *A Catechesis on the Creed*, vol. 1, *God, Father and Creator* (Boston: Pauline Books and Media, 1995), 162. Here we discuss the begetting of the Son in terms of love, something with which some might quibble. It is true that the generation of the Word is the divine act of intellect, and love is the divine act of the will, but the act of intellection cannot be separated from the act of love in God as it would in creatures, for God is simple. In God there is one eternal act distinguished only in relations: God's knowing is his loving.

[17] See John Paul II, *The Trinity's Embrace*, 210–11.

[18] See John Paul II, *God, Father and Creator*, 161.

[19] Of course, St. Thomas's doctrine of remotion requires that we remove any created implications in the phrase in quotations, which would include change, causation, or any other suggestion of potency or actualized potency.

[20] John Paul II, *God, Father and Creator*, 162.

[21] The author is not suggesting a distorted sense of divine freedom whereby the Father

into a covenant with Israel. He reveals himself as Father in commanding through Moses that Pharaoh let Israel, God's "firstborn son" (Exod 4:22–23), go into the desert to serve him. On the basis of the covenant, one can see that this is volitional fatherhood grounded in creation's mystery. This scriptural image of divine fatherhood in which the Father calls Israel his firstborn son highlights God's unique relationship of fatherhood.[22] Isaiah calls God, Israel's Father, Israel, who is the work of the potter's hands (Isa 63:16; 64:8).[23]

John Paul notes that the revelation of God's fatherhood to Old Testament Israel was gradual and incomplete. Israel's acknowledgment of this relationship was under the constant threat of idolatry, ever condemned by the prophets (see, e.g., Jer 2:27). In assessing the Old Testament revelation of God's fatherhood, he observes that God was more often presented as Father in terms of his covenant relationship with Israel than simply with his creative work. The dominant aspect of this relationship was Israel's experience of God's paternal solicitude in his saving actions on behalf of his covenant people.[24]

Israel also came to see God as a father through analogy with public figures, especially those who had religious functions. These included priests (see Judg 17:10; 18:19; Gen 45:8) and prophets (see 2 Kgs 2:12).[25] While the character of God's fatherhood is revealed indistinctly in the Old Testament, it is made explicit in the New Testament through Jesus's direct revelation of his Father and through the first disciples' experience of the Father's love. The Father's love is his essence.[26] It "is a disinterested love. It aims solely at this: that the good comes into existence, endures and develops according to its own dynamism."[27] John Paul illustrates the implication of this otherwise affectively stark, philosophical statement. This is to be found in Jesus's new, full interpretation of the Old Testament prescription to love in terms of God's fatherhood and covenant sonship.

When Jesus commands the love of enemies as well as friends, he is doing so after the example of the Father who sends the rain and commands

---

could choose not to beget the Son. He freely chooses to be Father in his offer of a covenant relationship with mankind.

[22] See John Paul II, *The Trinity's Embrace*, 176.

[23] See John Paul II, *God, Father and Creator*, 156–57.

[24] See John Paul II, *The Trinity's Embrace*, 172–73.

[25] See John Paul II, *The Trinity's Embrace*, 175.

[26] See John Paul II, Encyclical Letter *Dives in misericordia* (November 30, 1980), *AAS* 72 (1980), 1177–1232, §6.

[27] John Paul II, *God, Father and Creator*, 208–209.

the sun to shine on the just and the unjust, on the good and the evil (see Matt 5:43–45; CCC §2784).[28] All believers have available to them the experience God's fatherly love. One need look no further than the Father who is rich in mercy, who reveals this merciful love by sending his only Son to be crucified and to rise again from the dead that we might, after our earthly journey, join him at the Father's right hand by means of our insertion into the hypostatic order.[29] The covenantal relationship which God has entered into with mankind is key in John Paul II's writings that concern the Father's attributes.

The second installment of John Paul II's Trinitarian trilogy of encyclicals is *Dives in misericordia*. This encyclical focuses on God the Father and his mercy. John Paul considers the mercy of the Father to be an attribute of central concern for contemporary man.[30] This is true for many reasons, including the fact that it is a central point of Christ's messianic mission because he reveals the Father, who is Love.[31] Kenneth Schmitz nicely summarizes John Paul's depiction of the Father's mercy as love's second name in this encyclical, when he argues that God's fatherhood is organically structured by his paternity, that is, his relation as Father. He says that the Father expresses unmerited love and mercy to his rebellious children because of his *hesed*, his faithfulness to his very Being. His gratuitous love and mercy flow from his authority because he alone is uniquely Author; he is the Unoriginate Source of Being which is Love. Love is revealed in the mystery of redemption as mercy; in the eschaton, mercy will be revealed to have been love.[32]

The Father reveals his love and mercy through his Son. In his very person, Jesus makes the "Father of mercies" visible to man. In a certain sense, in Christ, mercy becomes Incarnate.[33] John Paul II takes the parable of the prodigal son as best revealing the Father's love and mercy. This is most especially true when viewing the parable from the context of Old Testament Israel's manifold covenant transgressions, each loss of grace, and every single sin.[34] This reveals the identity of the Father's mercy and his

---

[28] See John Paul II, *The Trinity's Embrace*, 195.

[29] See John Paul II, *The Trinity's Embrace*, 228–29.

[30] See *Dives in misericordia*, §1.

[31] See *Dives in misericordia*, §13.

[32] "See Kenneth Schmitz, "Who Has Seen the Father," *Josephinum Journal of Theology* 9, no. 1 (2002): 67.

[33] See *Dives in misericordia*, §2.

[34] See *Dives in misericordia*, §5.

love. John Paul says that as Jesus presents this parable, one can discern that mercy expresses the love the New Testament calls *agape*.[35]

This disinterested love is the merciful love of a father.[36] But the Father's merciful love is not restricted to this New Testament parable. Jesus also reveals mercy as forgiveness through his many works and words. This mercy is set in relief against the penchant some Jewish religious leaders demonstrated for disingenuous rigor, which Jesus always opposes. In these pericopes, Jesus manifests how deep the mercy of the Father is for his children.[37] In essence, God reveals his fatherhood as merciful love bestowed upon Israel and upon each individual.[38]

Gerard Beigel uncovers another paternal attribute as he performs a detailed analysis of John Paul II's presentation of a bilateral link between God and humanity through God's merciful love of man.[39] Beigel discovers that for John Paul, the meaning of mercy belongs to the essence of paternal solicitude as revealed in the parable of the prodigal son. Mercy is the enduring character of the father that he shows toward his son and by which he draws his son toward the good, toward a repentance that restores him to his father.[40] God the Father's offer of merciful love beckons his children to repentance and reconciliation. This is the archetype for human paternal love in which merciful paternal love of initiation can draw an estranged child to conversion.

Another of the Father's attributes tightly connected to his mercy is his fidelity. The Father's unwavering fidelity is especially remarkable when, again, considering man's myriad infidelities. He is a Father who is always faithful to his promises. This fidelity is also brought out in the parable of the prodigal son. The father is shown to continue to be faithful to the love that he has always poured out upon his son, even in the presence of the son's infidelity to his sonship. One sees this paternal fidelity first in the father's haste to welcome his son home after his son had frittered away his

---

[35] See *Dives in misericordia*, §6.

[36] However, John Paul also indicates that the Father's merciful love, in its reality, transcends the love of both human fatherhood and motherhood (see John Paul II, *The Trinity's Embrace*, 255). The hands of the father in the parable are the hands of both a mother and a father. In the way that the love is manifested in the parable, the father's embrace resembles that of a mother (see *The Trinity's Embrace*, 255).

[37] See John Paul II, *The Trinity's Embrace*, 254.

[38] See John Paul II, *God, Father and Creator*, 158.

[39] See Gerard Paul Beigel, "'The Person Revealed in Action': A Framework for Understanding How Social Justice is an Essential Part of the Gospel in the Teaching of Pope John Paul II" (Ph.D. diss., The Catholic University of America, 1994), 141–65.

[40] See Beigel, "Framework for Understanding," 151.

wealth. But a deeper expression can be found in the father's joy at the son's return and his desire to share this joy with everyone else through a most generous gesture, a feast on the fatted calf. This fidelity, even in the face of his elder son's bitter opposition, is the father's faithfulness to the very being of a father. Fidelity to one's character is known as *hesed* in the Old Testament.[41] In this parable, paternal *hesed* is manifested as compassion for his son.[42]

The fidelity of God the Father is first a fidelity to himself. He cannot act other than in accord with his nature which, as Schmitz points out, is love, mercy, and all good. However, in terms of the parable, the father's fidelity is also rooted in love for his son. The father focuses not on the squandering of the son's ill-obtained patrimony but on the fundamental goodness of his son's humanity that has been saved through his repentance. This is merciful love; love that immediately rushes to accept a repentant child because the child has chosen the Good. The son has chosen to match his likeness to the dignity he has because he was made in the image of God. This reading of the parable reveals that fatherhood means fidelity, a fidelity to fatherhood itself, and therefore to fatherly mercy and love.

Initiative is another attribute of God's fatherhood. John Paul does not mention the father's initiative in running out to meet his repentant son as an analogy for the initiative of God the Father. However, he does acknowledge God the Father's initiative, which is rooted in the Trinitarian relations and manifested to mankind in his relationship with his creation.[43] The Father manifests his love for man by taking the initiative in creation and in redemption. The Father exercises initiative in gathering together the lost and making them his children through their incorporation into his only-begotten Son.[44] This initiative, a fruit of his love, is most ineffably demonstrated in his Son's Passion and death. The Father takes the initiative and first loves us and so allows his only Son, his most cherished treasure, to suffer and die at the hands of ungodly men.[45]

A final attribute of the Father that John Paul describes is that as a Father he maintains covenant-family unity.[46] Again, in reference to the

---

[41] *Hesed* is variously translated as merciful love, faithful love, fidelity, loving-kindness, steadfast love, grace, mercy, faithfulness, goodness, or devotion.

[42] See *Dives in misericordia*, §6.

[43] See John Paul II, *The Church*, 78, and *The Trinity's Embrace*, 364.

[44] See John Paul II, *The Trinity's Embrace*, 364.

[45] See John Paul II, *The Trinity's Embrace*, 70.

[46] I mean to indicate by the term "covenant-family unity" that God's covenantal relationship with Israel, fulfilled in the New Testament Church, is one of family, which has its

parable of the prodigal son, he explains the cultural significance of the younger son's request for his inheritance. In Jewish culture at the time of Jesus, the common practice was for the sons to work in the father's house until the father died. It was only after the father's death that the sons would divide and take possession of their inheritance. In Jesus's parable, the younger son's brazen demand for his share of the patrimony is an unabashed refutation of family unity and paternal authority. This is the rebellion of an ungrateful son who cares nothing for the pain that his actions cause his father.[47]

The father's response when he sees his son still far off is that of a father who is always ready to accept the return of a repentant child. He is ready to gather him back into the family fold. In the human dimension, fatherhood serves this unifying role, but John Paul finds this is also translated into God's functioning in this same role as guarantor of covenant communion. In the Pentateuch, the knowledge of God as a father indicates the source of the covenant: "'Is he not your father, who created you, who made you and established you?' (Deut 32:6)."[48] The prophets reflect this same belief that God as a father maintains communion among all those with whom he has sworn a covenant: "'Have we not all the one Father? Has not the one God created us?' (Mal 2:10)."[49]

In this survey, we see several attributes of God's fatherhood: 1) Fatherhood is relational. In fact, it is a relation by which the Father is distinguished from the other two persons of the Trinity. The derivative relationality of human fatherhood and motherhood, which is based on this, was indicated in part 2. This is an important attribute of human

---

source of unity in the father. In the Old Testament, the idea of covenant is inextricably linked with family. W. Brueggemann says that

> in the world of Biblical faith, the family is the primary unit of meaning which shapes and defines reality. . . . Of course, the family in that context is not the nuclear family, for that is unknown and unthinkable in the ancient world. Rather family consists in the network of interrelations of the extended family that should be thought of as clan or tribe. . . . Biblical faith is essentially covenantal in its perception of all reality. . . . The family is first of all a community of covenant-making, covenant-keeping, covenant-breaking and covenant-renewing. That is its principal mark, for being human is primarily concerned with effective covenanting.

(W. Brueggemann, "The Covenanted Family," *JCSI* 14 [1977]: 18–23).

[47] See John Paul II, *The Trinity's Embrace*, 254–55.
[48] John Paul II, *The Trinity's Embrace*, 187.
[49] John Paul II, The Trinity's Embrace.

fatherhood but as I have indicated, relationality is shared by human father-hood and motherhood. 2) The Father generates the Son; in this he takes the initiative. These are analogous attributes proper to masculinity as we have already shown. 3) The Father is faithful. 4) The Father manifests his fatherhood through a merciful love which draws his children to repen-tance. 5) The Father maintains covenant-family unity. These are the major attributes of God's fatherhood. The plan of *Radiation of Fatherhood* indi-cates we should next take up an analysis of Jesus's revelation of the Father.

JESUS REVEALS THE FATHER

The fact that Jesus Christ reveals the fatherhood of God is fundamental to Karol Wojtyła's plot in *Radiation of Fatherhood*. His approach follows the patristic Trinitarian theology in which the economic Trinity reveals the immanent Trinity. This theology remains an important part of John Paul's thought in his papal writings and is essential for understanding his biblical exegesis in these matters.[50] For example, John Paul says that Jesus expected that his disciples, whom he had taken into an intimate association with himself, should have realized that to see him was to see his Father.

John Paul notes that the Son's radiation of the Father is demonstrated in his rebuke of Phillip. "Precisely because of this intimacy, Philip should have understood that the Father's face was revealed in Jesus: 'He who has seen me has seen the Father' (John 14:9). With the eyes of faith the disci-ple is called to discover the invisible face of the Father in Christ's face."[51] In fact, only the Son is capable of revealing the Father because only he has seen the Father (see John 1:18).[52] All of this is to say that Christ's disclo-sure of God's fatherhood continues to be essential for the task of extracting a theology of fatherhood from John Paul's papal writings. With that in mind, we will now spend some time surveying these writings for the attri-butes of God's fatherhood that Jesus reveals.

John Paul II in fact believes that many of the Father's attributes are revealed through Christ. Jesus reveals the Father's mercy, love, and faith-fulness through the parable of the prodigal son. He reveals the Father's merciful, redeeming love especially in his Cross and Resurrection. The Father's initiative of love and forgiveness is also revealed in the paschal

---

[50] See *Dives in misericordia*, §2.
[51] John Paul II, *The Trinity's Embrace*, 17.
[52] See John Paul II, *A Catechesis on the Creed*, vol. 2, *Jesus, Son and Savior* (Boston: Pauline Books and Media, 1996), 202.

event, through which the Son restores covenant communion. However, a more complete survey of these papal writings will determine whether he mentions any other significant divine paternal attributes.

John Paul proffers a caution of which one must be aware before embarking on such an analysis. He warns that on various occasions, that there are certain aspects of Jesus's relationship with his Father which are unique to the divine Father-Son relation. For example, the Gospels indicate that Jesus made an important distinction between his divine sonship and the sonship his disciples shared through him. In discourse with his disciples, Jesus never calls God "Our Father." Rather, in order to emphasize the distinction, he always says "my Father" and "your Father."[53]

In teaching the disciples how to pray, Jesus does use the phrase "Our Father," but this is a prayer that obviously excludes Jesus himself, as he would not have prayed for any of his trespasses to be forgiven.[54] Jesus also makes this distinction in the context of his Ascension. He says here that he is ascending to "my Father and your Father, to my God and your God" (John 20:17). John Paul understands this to signify that Jesus is emphasizing an exclusive, inimitable relationship with the Father that not even his disciples can share. "In Matthew's Gospel alone Jesus calls God 'my Father' seventeen times. The fourth evangelist will use two different Greek words, one—*hyios*—to indicate Christ's full and perfect divine sonship, the other—*tekna*—to refer to our being children of God in a real but derivative way."[55]

There is another term which illustrates this relational uniqueness. The word *abba* is a word taken from family life which indicates a close, loving communion between father and child. In fact, John Paul imagines that when Jesus's listeners heard him speak of God in these terms, that they must have been full of amazement; perhaps they were even shocked. This is because a son or daughter of Abraham would never call God *Abba*. "An Israelite would not have used [Abba] even in prayer. Only one who regarded himself as Son of God in the proper sense of the word could have spoken thus of him and to him as Father—Abba, or my Father, Daddy, Papa!"[56] There is no Gospel text in which Jesus advocates that his disciples pray using the term *Abba*.

John Paul explains that this is because *Abba* refers exclusively to the

---

[53] See Matt 5:48; 6:8–9; 7:21; Luke 11:13.
[54] See John Paul II, *The Trinity's Embrace*, 179.
[55] John Paul II, *The Trinity's Embrace*, 335; see also *Jesus, Son and Savior*, 147.
[56] John Paul II, *Jesus, Son and Savior*, 170.

consubstantial relation of the Son to the Father.[57] Of course, there are two places in the Pauline epistles (Rom 8:15–17; Gal 4:6–7) in which Paul calls God "Abba, Father." St. Paul is using this term in a derivative sense. In these passages, the inspired writer attributes our sonship to a participative sonship. We are adoptive sons of the Father in Christ and through the Holy Spirit.[58] These insights give rise to an important caveat. While some aspects of Jesus's relationship with his Father may directly apply to human fathers, others, if they apply at all, will be applicable only in a derivative sense.

One can look especially to John Paul II's encyclical *Dominum et vivificantem* to find the focus of Jesus's mission described as revealing his Father. In Jesus's response to the seventy-two disciples upon their return from their mission (see Luke 10:1ff.), he rejoices in God's fatherhood both because it has been appointed to him to reveal it and also because this fatherhood has been bestowed upon men.[59] It is his mission to reveal the Father and effect his will for man. Jesus exhibits sincere satisfaction in his accomplishment of this mission. In another place, John Paul says that Jesus's task of revealing the Father is his essential mission.[60]

It is not solely the person of the Father but also his attributes that Jesus reveals. Love is the attribute that underlies and unifies all of these revealed attributes. In his first encyclical, *Redemptor hominis*, John Paul seems to equate God's fatherhood with a self-giving love. Here he admonishes his readers never to forget that Jesus became man's reconciliation with the Father. Only the Son was capable of satisfying the eternal love of the Father. Out of this overflowing love God created the world, bestowing upon man all of creation's wealth, making him in his image and likeness.[61] Moreover, God's fatherly love was never withdrawn, even when man repeatedly rejected it by breaking the first series of covenants. Though Israel was unfaithful, God continued to offer her his merciful love. Christ's entire life reveals his Father's ineffably mysterious, eternal love, beginning with his Incarnation, continuing into his public life, and *par excellence* in

---

[57] See John Paul II, *Jesus, Son and Savior*, 172.

[58] See John Paul II, *The Trinity's Embrace*, 343.

[59] See John Paul II, Encyclical Letter on the Holy Spirit in the Life of the Church and the World *Dominum et vivificantem* (May 18, 1986), *AAS* 78 (1986), 809–900, §20. John Paul II follows the Vulgate in identifying the number of disciples as seventy-two. However, the textual evidence is ambiguous with various ancient sources testifying to both seventy and seventy-two disciples (see Barbara Aland, Kurt Aland, et al., eds., *The Greek New Testament*, 4th rev. ed. (Stuttgart: United Bible Societies, 1994], 242n1).

[60] See John Paul II, *Jesus, Son and Savior*, 360.

[61] See John Paul II, John Paul II, Encyclical Letter at the Beginning of His Papacy *Redemptor hominis* (March 4, 1979), *AAS* 71 (1979), 257–324, §9.

his Cross. Jesus reveals the love that reconciles man to God and offers him the possibility of sonship in the Son.[62]

In his second encyclical, *Dives in misericordia*, John Paul continues this theme. Again, Christ reveals the Father and his love.[63] The crucified Son shows the presence of God's fatherly love among us. This love will overcome all the evils of the world.[64] Jesus also reveals that God's bond of love with mankind surpasses in intimacy his bond with the rest of creation.[65] This is demonstrated by man's new capacity for participation in Trinitarian life which Christ won for us. Jesus makes visible the eternal and total self-gift of the Father.[66]

Indeed, Christ's entire messianic mission, culminating in his crucifixion, death, and Resurrection, manifests the Father's fidelity to his fatherhood and to his love.[67] Everything of Christ's life, gospel, Passion, death, Resurrection—in a word, his entire life and mystery—testifies to the mercy of God.[68] This revelation is mediated by the life of the Church. Her purpose is to direct herself, and so her members, to Jesus's very heart. In drawing close to him and his Sacred Heart, the Church professes the Father's merciful love witnessed by his Son. This profession John Paul finds to be "the central content of the messianic mission of the Son of Man."[69]

There is no doubt, then, that John Paul II places Jesus's revelation of the person and attributes of the Father in a central position of importance. The final step in our analysis of God's fatherhood is to finish following the outline of *Radiation of Fatherhood*, and to look at those writings of John Paul II which recount Jesus as the model for human fathers.

JESUS AS EXEMPLAR FOR HUMAN FATHERHOOD

We have already discussed the image of Jesus as the Bridegroom with a focus on his masculinity. We should now turn to the Bridegroom image as an example for husbands and fathers. Albeit in an indirect manner, John Paul II indicates that Jesus is the visible exemplar of human fatherhood. Just as Jesus's mission is to reflect the Father, John Paul says in *Familiaris consortio*

---

[62] See *Redemptor hominis*, §9.
[63] See *Dives in misericordia*, §1.
[64] See *Dives in misericordia*, §7.
[65] See *Dives in misericordia*, §7.
[66] See *Dives in misericordia*, §7.
[67] See *Dives in misericordia*, §15.
[68] See *Dives in misericordia*, §13.
[69] *Dives in misericordia*, §13.

that human fathers have the same responsibility to reflect the fatherhood of God.[70] This implies Jesus is the role model for human fathers, but he is more explicit when drawing from Ephesians 5 and the great mystery. This should be no surprise. Marriage is, after all, where human fatherhood authentically begins and so the great mystery appropriately provides the foundation for a theology of human fatherhood.

Among the many Old Testament descriptions of Yahweh's covenant relationship with Israel, they are spousal or marital only when God is presented as Redeemer.[71] When Yahweh's love is presented as a paternal love, the love is a love of mercy and compassion. When his love is spousal, it is a gift of himself.[72] The words of the great mystery in which Paul says Christ gave himself up for his Church (Eph 5:25) comprise the key text which transforms redeeming love into spousal love.[73] In fact, this binds together the spousal and redeeming dimensions of Yahweh's relationship with his people.[74] Christ reveals the Father's paternal, compassionate love through his redeeming spousal love.

We have already seen John Paul's view that the Bridegroom image is purposefully masculine because it manifests God's initiating love; a love which is redemptive and finally spousal.[75] John Paul writes: "Precisely because Christ's divine love is the love of a Bridegroom, it is the model and pattern of all human love, men's love in particular."[76] The great mystery demands, then, that a man's love for his wife and family must imitate Jesus's archetypal spousal love which he manifested in his *salvific* life and death. It must be a complete and radically disinterested gift of himself with its end, the salvation of his wife and family.[77]

We have seen that teaching men this lesson is of particular concern for John Paul, because the man of concupiscence must learn to give himself, to overcome his selfishness and lack of willingness to commit to another. For this reason, the emphasis of the great mystery lesson for the husband is to love his wife as Christ loves his Church. This is what Christ teaches and

---

[70] See John Paul II, Apostolic Exhortation on the Role of the Christian Family in the Modern World *Familiaris consortio* (November 22, 1981), *AAS* 74 (1982), 114–37, §25.

[71] See John Paul II, *Man and Woman He Created Them: A Theology of the Body*, trans. Michael Waldstein (Boston: Pauline Books and Media, 2006), 498.

[72] See *Man and Woman*, 501.

[73] See *Man and Woman*, 478.

[74] See *Man and Woman*, 352.

[75] See John Paul II, Apostolic Letter on the Dignity and Vocation of Women *Mulieris dignitatem* (August 15, 1988), AAS 80 (1988), 1653–1729, §25.

[76] *Mulieris dignitatem*, §25.

[77] See John Paul II, *The Church*, 114.

demands of the husband and father. Such masculine love is even possible only because the Christian "husband's love for his wife is a participation in Christ's love for the Church."[78]

Christ reveals the Father's love by manifesting his merciful, compassionate love as a redeeming love. This redemptive love is fused with a spousal love, a total self-gift, by Christ's complete self-offering on the Cross. Moreover, Jesus is the masculine Bridegroom because he makes visible the Father's divine, paternal, initiating love: it is he who first loved us.[79] John Paul elsewhere characterizes the masculine initiative of love through the fact that the husband "is above all, *he who loves* and the wife, on the other hand, is *she who is loved*."[80] In his anthropology, this initiating love is made visible through the body.

One can see in the spousal meaning of the body that the husband's body initiates the gift whereas the wife's receives it. The body reveals this initiating-receptive relation in conjugal love, a consequence of his hylomorphic anthropology in which the human body makes visible a spiritual reality. Because the body manifests the soul, the configuration and function of the sexual organs point to a deeper reality about men and women. The man's body-soul unity, his whole person, takes the initiative in this intimate act.

Even beyond sexual intercourse, the husband has the task of taking the initiative in loving his wife and family in a disinterested and self-giving way, as John Paul II's model of the Father as revealed in Christ indicates. This characteristic of initiative which fills the whole masculine person is in concert with the great mystery in which Christ first loves his Bride. In the latter analogy, the husband is head of his wife and family which also implies the man's initiative. Initiative provides the husband and father with a requisite attribute needed to accomplish the task of family leadership.

A man's initiating love places on the husband certain obligations toward his wife and family. These obligations can be seen arising from Ephesians 5:25–26 and they point to the husband's obligation to give himself up for his wife's, and also his family's, sanctification.[81] Beyond the sanctification of his wife and family, the husband also must be solicitous for the welfare of his wife's entire being because of Christ's model of love for his Church. "It commits him to desire her beauty and at the same time

---

[78] John Paul II, *The Church*, 115.
[79] See *Mulieris dignitatem*, §25.
[80] *Man and Woman*, 485.
[81] See *Man and Woman*, 481–83.

to appreciate this beauty and to care for it."[82] Because this is a beauty of the entire person, it includes a visible, physical beauty. There must be a concern on the part of the husband to find everything that is good and beautiful in his wife. This survey of the background texts has provided copious material for the task of extracting John Paul II's theology of men and fatherhood, by analogy from the fatherhood of God.

---

[82] See *Man and Woman*, 484.

CHAPTER 11

Natural Human Fatherhood

We are now ready to extract John Paul II's theology of masculinity and fatherhood from his writings, using the groundwork previously laid in our survey of personhood, complementary sex difference, and masculinity. We will first revisit the analogy between human fatherhood and divine fatherhood to determine which divine attributes can legitimately be applied to human fathers and in what manner. Where possible, attributes unique to human fatherhood will be distinguished from attributes applying to both fatherhood and motherhood. Where the distinction is not explicit, I will use Wojtyła's anthropology and the insights gained from Wojtyła's play, *Radiation of Fatherhood*, as hermeneutical keys. Second, we will evaluate Christ as exemplar using much the same approach as with the divine-human analogy. Third, will be an investigation of St. Joseph's example of fatherhood to discern the meaning and attributes of fatherhood. Finally, we will extract an implicit theology of masculinity and fatherhood from John Paul's more explicit theology of women and motherhood. Here I will use the insights from May and Hauke, which we have shown to correspond to our author's anthropology. The principle of complementarity discussed earlier will figure prominently in extracting the theology of fatherhood from his texts on women.

However, prior to beginning let us define natural fatherhood. For our purposes, natural fatherhood will encompass the everyday roles, responsibilities, and experiences of fatherhood by the husband and father in a nuclear family. Again, those things which apply to natural fathers also apply to adoptive fathers, except for discussions about conception and pregnancy.

A Theology of Natural Fatherhood by Analogy with God's Fatherhood

John Paul II understands analogy in a manner equivalent to St. Thomas Aquinas.[1] When comparing anything created to God, one must realize that the difference is much greater than any likeness.[2] Thus, one must not push analogies too far; one must consider the limitedness of creation and creatures and the simplicity of God in pursuing analogies. Nor can one immediately assume that a particular divine paternal attribute is correlated uniquely to human fatherhood; it may also apply to motherhood. Therefore, any attribution not explicitly said to be unique to human fatherhood will require sufficient rationale to authorize such a conclusion.

Earlier I justified my basic approach to extracting a theology of fatherhood from writings on the fatherhood of God by showing that Karol Wojtyła advocated this approach in *Radiation of Fatherhood* and that John Paul II continued to do so in his papal writings. Specifically, in that play he showed that human fatherhood is a participation in (or radiation of) divine fatherhood, which is made visible in God's Son, Jesus Christ. This ultimately entails self-gift to the point of suffering and regularly to death-to-self in imitation of Jesus. This is a death which passes through the suffering and death of the Child—the Son, so as to become a child of the Father and thereby to be able to radiate the Father's paternity as does his Son. In *Radiation of Fatherhood*, one can find both explicit and inferred human paternal roles, tasks, and attributes in Wojtyła's thinking. I will not attempt to summarize or analyze the entire play. Other competent efforts are already available.[3] Rather, I will provide the context as necessary for each particular issue.

The basic theme of the play is the struggle of the protagonist, Adam,

---

[1] The definition of theological analogy was codified at the Fourth Lateran Council in 1215: "Between the Creator and the creature so great a likeness cannot be noted without the necessity of noting a greater dissimilarity between them." Henry Denzinger, *The Sources of Catholic Dogma*, trans. Roy Deferrari (Saint Louis, London: B. Herder Book Co., 1957), 171. Originally published in Latin as *Enchiridion symbolorum*, 30th rev. ed. (Freiburg: Herder & Co., 1954).

[2] See John Paul II, *A Catechesis on the Creed*, vol. 1, *God, Father and Creator* (Boston: Pauline Books and Media, 1995), 145.

[3] See, e.g., Bolesław Taborski, introduction to *Radiation of Fatherhood*, in *The Collected Plays and Writings on Theater: Karol Wojtyła*; trans. Bolesław Taborski (Berkeley: University of California Press, 1987), 323–31; Kenneth Schmitz, *At the Center of the Human Drama: The Philosophical Anthropology of Karol Wojtyła / Pope John Paul II* (Washington, DC: Catholic University of America Press, 1993), 19–29; Schmitz, "The Passage of Love: Wojtyła 's *Radiation of Fatherhood*," *Communio* 22 (1995): 99–106; and

with his vocation to fatherhood. Adam, as with the other two characters, is identified as an archetype. Adam represents everyman in his struggle with his desire for solitude and anonymity. Adam considers the responsibilities of fatherhood a burden which he cannot bear, and he fears that he cannot live up to its calling. This struggle seems to suggest the struggles of historical man with the central themes of original solitude and original unity.

Adam's struggle is the struggle of the man against concupiscence, which is an obstacle to his vocation to a familial communion of persons. It is the struggle of the husband-father to fulfill himself through a sincere (disinterested) gift of himself. Kenneth Schmitz wonders if in Adam's struggle with his desire for solitude there are seeds of the first Adam's original solitude.[4] This struggle with fatherhood, which demands that Adam become a child in imitation of the Child Jesus, lasts throughout all three acts of the play.

Wojtyła's focus is on Adam's struggle to overcome his inclination to turn inward in selfishness, which draws him away from his vocation to fatherhood. To overcome this, Adam must give himself first to the Father, in image of the Incarnate Son, and thereby radiate divine fatherhood. Deriving his fatherhood from God's, man must live it by giving himself in love, but this opens man to the risk of suffering. Adam recognizes that this is a vocation which demands that he give all of himself and he fears he is not up to the task. He does not want to suffer.

Adam is mature enough to be able to distinguish the authentic vocation of fatherhood from simple biological fatherhood. He protests to God that "I could not bear fatherhood; I could not be equal to it. . . . I later said to Him, complaining, 'You could have left me in the sphere of fertility (I would have somehow reconciled myself to nature) without placing me in the depths of fatherhood to which I am unequal! Why did you plant it in the soil of my soul? Was it not enough that You had it in Yourself?'"[5] Schmitz observes in Adam's recognition of the authentic vocation to fatherhood his admission that it is not possible to fulfill his vocation simply through physical reproduction. For even in Adam's self-imposed loneliness, he can still procreate. Rather, Adam sees and rebels against his obligation to acknowledge, choose to accept into his life, and give himself

---

Francis Martin, "*Radiation of Fatherhood*: Some Biblical Reflections," *Josephinum Journal of Theology* 9, no. 1 (2002): 22–41.

[4] See Schmitz, "Passage of Love," 103.

[5] Wojtyła, *Radiation of Fatherhood*, part 1, section 2, "The Analysis of Loneliness," 336.

to the child he has begotten.[6] Yet, he knows the great calling to fatherhood is still written into his masculine soul.

Francis Martin believes Wojtyła portrays Adam's sin as rejecting his sharing in God's fatherhood. Martin says that on a deeper level, one can see that this is Adam's "refusal to live in the world of trusting receptivity."[7] The Adam of the play is an archetype who also represents the first Adam. One can find Martin's view of Adam's sin confirmed by John Paul II in a later manuscript. He says, in language evocative of the play, that original sin was the attempt to abolish the rays of fatherhood.[8]

Martin further assesses this crisis of fatherhood to be in reality a crisis of childhood. Citing Adam's recognition that God did not want him to be a father without being a child, Martin argues that the link between childhood and fatherhood is clear.[9] This crisis of childhood is at root a revolt against God as Father. Martin states: "Because men refuse to enter into the movement of love that will enshrine their freedom and make them, in the unimaginable power of love as a gift, the 'equal' of the Father, they remain perpetual adolescents, not childlike enough to become fathers. They are unwilling to accept the terrible discipline of being a child, so that they too, like Jesus, may radiate the mystery of the Father."[10]

Adam wrestles with his vocation in a way that does not seem to be as much of a problem for women. It is likely that this has to do with feminine makeup and its amenability to her vocation, even in a fallen state. The woman in the play is the archetype for everywoman, for the Church, and for the Blessed Virgin Mary, but Schmitz observes that it is not always clear who she represents at any one time.[11] In one passage, the woman as mother seems to suggest, as John Paul II does in *Mulieris dignitatem* §18, that she must teach Adam to be a father.

She says in response to Adam's recoiling at the prospect of the suffering which is entailed in fatherhood: "Do not be afraid. This must hurt. It is a pain like the pain of birth. A woman knows infinitely more about giving birth than a man. She knows it particularly through the suffering that accompanies childbearing. Still, motherhood is an expression of

---

6   See Schmitz, "Passage of Love," 103.
7   Martin, "Some Biblical Reflections," 25.
8   See John Paul II, *Crossing the Threshold of Hope*, ed. Vittorio Messori, trans. Jenny McPhee and Martha McPhee (New York, NY: Alfred A. Knopf, Inc., 1994), 227–28.
9   See Wojtyła, *Radiation of Fatherhood*, part 1, section 4, "Between Meeting and Fulfillment," 339.
10   Martin, "Some Biblical Reflections," 39.
11   See Schmitz, "Passage of Love," 99.

fatherhood. It must always go back to the father to take from him all that it expresses. In this consists the radiation of fatherhood."[12] The man shares in God's fatherhood, the divine archetype that formed his masculine, personal constitution, but the effect of the fall on his masculine gifts requires him to look to his wife to help him to discover and experience of the gifts of fatherhood.

This discovery and experience are things the concupiscent man will try to resist, but it is, in part, through the help and encouragement of his wife, by seeing his fatherhood expressed in a maternal way through his wife's motherhood, that he will succeed in overcoming his resistance. Wojtyła expresses this in the play when the woman archetype shows Adam that the path to radiating fatherhood is through dying like the Incarnate Child, but he will not listen. She explains that he can see his fatherhood embodied in her motherhood, but he refuses look, retreating inward upon himself instead.[13]

It is not clear whether the woman-mother speaking to Adam is his wife, the Church, or the Blessed Virgin Mary. Perhaps she could be seen as a synthesis of all three. However, these and other passages do seem to indicate a particular and consistent weakness, in Wojtyła's view, of the man in his ability to fulfill his vocation to fatherhood that the woman does not generally experience. The remedy is that the man must learn his vocation from the woman. But even in Adam's refusal, the mother still sees that he is made to be a father. Thus, his major task is to overcome his concupiscence and to accept the radiation of fatherhood; to become a child, a son in the Son, to suffer as did the Bridegroom, and so to become an authentic human father.[14]

Adam recognizes that he is called to transform himself and to be transformed into an image of the Bridegroom, to be a child and then a father. He admires Christ the Bridegroom but fears he cannot imitate him.[15] Through the character Adam, Wojtyła unveils what will become his later emphasis on the great mystery for men. This mystery brings with it the requirement of husbands and fathers to take Christ as their model and goal, which is to imitate the Bridegroom. But in Wojtyła's anthropology, this is more than mere emulation. As Adam says, it is a personal transformation. For Wojtyła, as he shows in *Person and Act*, through one's man-acts one ontologically

---

12. Wojtyła, *Radiation of Fatherhood*, part 1, section 5, "Mother," 341.
13. See Wojtyła, *Radiation of Fatherhood*, part 3, section 2, "Radiation and Dying," 362–63.
14. See Wojtyła, *Radiation of Fatherhood*, part 3, section 2, "Radiation and Dying," 362–63.
15. See Wojtyła, *Radiation of Fatherhood*, part 3, section 2, "Radiation and Dying," 362.

changes who one is. Adam understands that knowledge, in the sense of cognitive appropriation, is insufficient. Action is also required in order to transform himself, though of course it is not purely human action but transformation through cooperation with grace.[16]

In summarizing roles and attributes from the play, the role concupiscence plays in man's vocation to fatherhood takes center stage. The special difficulty of the man in combating concupiscence, in a way that threatens his achieving authentic fatherhood, is of primary concern. The man's loss of original grace seems to be more debilitating for the man's vocation than is the case for the woman, at least in this fundamental matter. He now needs his wife to help teach him to become an authentic father. His vocation also demands his willingness to imitate Christ, to become an obedient child, and to be willing to enter into suffering in order to become a father. This imitation is nothing other than a total and sincere gift of himself first to God, and then derivatively to his wife and to his family.

In his papal writings, John Paul also makes some explicit statements about the analogy between God's fatherhood and human fatherhood.[17] John Paul identifies some explicit ways in which a human father is called to bear witness to and participate in divine fatherhood. Human fathers have the role of fostering unity and harmony in the development of individual family members and of the family as an organic whole. Fathers must cooperate with their wives in the education and formation of their children. This is especially important to remember when it comes to formation of children in the faith, which includes helping them to experience a deep unity with Christ and his Church in the life of the family.[18] This is especially important for young boys to see demonstrated by their fathers.[19]

---

[16] See Wojtyła, *Radiation of Fatherhood*, part 3, section 2, "Radiation and Dying," 363.

[17] We should note that the analogy goes both ways. Not only can one learn what authentic human fatherhood should be from the Father, one can also determine attributes of divine fatherhood by looking at authentic human fatherhood. Indeed, John Paul suggests that many world religions have expressed the conviction that God is a father based upon their experiences of love and affection from earthly fathers. See John Paul II, *A Catechesis on Salvation History*, vol. 6, *The Trinity's Embrace: God's Saving Plan* (Boston: Pauline Books and Media, 2002), 171.

[18] See John Paul II, Apostolic Exhortation on the Role of the Christian Family in the Modern World *Familiaris consortio* (November 22, 1981), *AAS* 74 (1982), 114–37, §25; Post-Synodal Apostolic Exhortation on the Vocation and the Mission of the Lay Faithful in the Church and in the World *Christifideles laici* (December 30, 1988), *AAS* 81 (1989), 393–521, §61.

[19] John Paul says, "When you are a father . . . 'Go and teach.' When you kneel with your

John Paul notes the tremendous impact that seeing his own father on his knees had on his own spiritual development.[20]

There are also paternal attributes manifested in the Old Testament that are now capable of perfection in Christ. John Paul singles out maintaining family unity, the paternal correction of children, and dependability in times of need.[21] Even the negative example of an unfaithful father can be viewed in contrast to the perfection of paternal fidelity that God the Father embodies. Such failure reveals the human father's obligation to fidelity.[22]

Because both motherhood and fatherhood derive from the fatherhood of God, we find maternal attributes in God's fatherhood. For example, John Paul says that there is a maternal aspect to God's love when it is expressed as compassion and mercy.[23] Yet compassion and mercy is experienced by children differently when it is offered by the father, whose offer is the initiative that can move the child to repentance. In addition to maternal mercy and compassion, the Old Testament also reveals the maternal attributes of tenderness and understanding from God.[24] John Paul believes that it is particularly in tenderness that God's mercy is revealed.[25] But receiving tenderness offered by a father is also a different experience than receiving that readily given by a mother. While compassion, mercy, tenderness, and understanding are maternal attributes, they also should be understood as complementary paternal characteristics. These will be addressed later under the rubric of mercy when we systematize paternal attributes, roles, and tasks.

Let us now draw together the attributes, roles, and tasks of human fatherhood found via analogy to divine fatherhood, while distinguishing each as being unique to human fatherhood, or shared with motherhood,

---

child in prayer: 'Teach!'" John Paul II, *The Way to Christ: Spiritual Exercises*, trans. Leslie Wearne (NY: Harper Collins, 1984), 54.

[20] He remarks that seeing his father each morning and evening silently praying on his knees instilled within him the deep conviction that an authentic life of faith demands interior conversion (see George Weigel, *Witness to Hope* [New York: Harper Collins Publishers, Inc., 1999], 30).

[21] See John Paul II, *The Trinity's Embrace*, 187.

[22] See John Paul II, *The Trinity's Embrace*, 173.

[23] He states: "In light of biblical and Christian revelation, motherhood is seen as a sharing in God's love for men, a love which, according to the Bible, also has a maternal aspect of compassion and mercy (see Is 49:15; Dt 32:11; Ps 86:15; etc.)" (John Paul II, *The Church*, 495).

[24] See John Paul II, *The Trinity's Embrace*, 177.

[25] See John Paul II, *God, Father and Creator*, 147.

but expressed in complementarily distinct manner. John Paul II mentions the paternal task of maintaining family unity which is first apparent from human fatherhood and subsequently came to be seen as an attribute of God in the Old Testament. Considered as a manifestation of masculine initiative, this task is primarily paternal. John Paul further implies this primacy by emphasizing the harmonious character associated with the task of maintaining unity, indicating that the role can never be a cause of division. Nevertheless, one might reasonably expect a role for the mother in helping to ensure family unity, one that incorporates her complementary feminine gifts.

Clearly, the father and mother together explicitly share the task of education. However, again based upon the author's anthropology, the husband and wife would accomplish this common task differently and complementarily. We see this demonstrated in Wojtyła's retreat talk given to men when he was auxiliary bishop of Kraków in 1962. There he discusses the different responsibilities of men and women in teaching the Gospel, based upon their complementary differences.[26] Women's more integrated structure enables them to more easily live the faith in their interior life than is the case for men, and so they are more inclined to teach the faith as experience and commitment.

Men have to work at living and teaching the faith as experience and commitment, but at the same time their masculine characteristics make them more readily suited to engaging the faith in an intellectual manner. In this area, Wojtyła says that men "must take responsibility for the Gospel as *Weltanschauung* and idea . . . the Gospel as idea is primarily a male sphere."[27] While the methods of doing so may differ from man to man, it is the Christian male's responsibility to teach the Gospel as conceptual to others, especially to his children. Moreover, he warns that the fallen masculine tendency to avoid giving of himself will require he achieve adequate self-mastery to live up to this obligation.

Likewise, the task of correcting the children could be inferred to be a common task as well but with the same caveat of complementary roles in carrying out the task. The task of combating concupiscence inasmuch as it inhibits the fulfillment of parenthood also should be a common task but in a complementarily distinct manner. However, John Paul seems to find that this task is more urgent and perhaps often more difficult for men as fathers. Hauke's insight explains this difficulty in view of the man's bias

---

[26] See Wojtyła, *Way to Christ*, 52–55.
[27] Wojtyła, *Way to Christ*, 53–54.

toward individualism, a trait associated with the masculine characteristic of being on the outside and going outside of himself into the world. The man's entire masculine structure, which orients him toward his vocation, also seems to make his struggle against concupiscence more pronounced when trying to live up to his vocation as a father. In general, this particular difficulty also makes the tasks of faithfulness and dependability more acutely in need of attention by men, on average, than by women.

The task of manifesting the Father's merciful love is explicitly required of both fathers and mothers. But John Paul says that mothers manifest this especially through their tenderness. Tenderness receives and embraces the other and integrates the other into self-giving love and compassion. The previous analysis of the parable of the prodigal son indicates there is a paternal complement to maternal tenderness. Integrated into a human father's merciful love, a masculine tenderness which is manifested as a reaching out rather than as receptive acceptance, will be an offer of forgiveness and an implicit call to repentance. Again, according to John Paul II's complementarity as I have described it, these characteristics possess a primary and secondary mode of acting.

The father and mother together would possess the initiating invitation to merciful love as well as the tender reception of the accepted invitation. However, the former mode would be dominant in fathers while the latter would be dominant in mothers. The attribute of initiative is paternal because it is a dominant masculine characteristic. A final attribute is relationality. Fatherhood is a relational vocation, as is motherhood. The father becomes an authentic father only through a nurturing relationship with the mother and child.[28] But obviously fathers play a unique role in the way they relate to their children. And as with a mother, these interrelationships have an irreplaceable effect on his sons as well as on his daughters. Again, fatherhood must have its maternal complement for successful fathering. These tasks, roles, and attributes belong to the man as he answers the vocation to self-fulfillment through a sincere and total gift of self.

JESUS'S EXAMPLE OF FATHERHOOD

Returning to *Radiation of Fatherhood*, Adam recognizes that Jesus, the Father's Son, came into the world to show men how to become adoptive

---

[28] This is true at least, in the general sense of natural fatherhood. However, the role of the mother must be accomplished in some manner even in the case of adoptive or purely spiritual fatherhood.

children of the Father. Adam is awed by the "strain, toil . . . [and] the magnitude of his love."[29] However, Adam is afraid of the suffering required to become a son of the Father. He knows such an undertaking of self-emptying, of the "risk of love," is beyond him. Adam sees limpidly his vocation to transformation into Christ the Bridegroom, but he resists.[30]

The woman fervently calls Adam to the Cross, to join with the Bridegroom's death and be reborn as a son, and to radiate God's father-hood.[31] Wojtyła shows that one can respond to the call to authentic human fatherhood only through the imitation of Christ most exquisitely articu-lated in the great mystery (see Ephesians 5). The Bridegroom is the exemplar and enabler for the Christian husband and father. The husband-father's solicitude for his family must radiate from Christ's concern for them. The man must mediate Christ's love by conforming his love to that of Christ, something possible only through grace. The man must give himself to his wife and family as Christ does.

The task of the husband and father, as head of his wife, is a call to making a gift of himself for the sake of his wife's and family's sanctification. In order to manifest a paternal love of initiative, he must first risk himself and give love in order to receive it back again. But the human father is not the Son, though he attempts to imitate him. So he is not competent to act unilaterally as head. He must subject himself to his wife's primacy in the order of love. John Paul II calls this "mutual submission," in reference to the great mystery.[32] From Wojtyła's play and the preceding discussion, it would appear that the husband's subjection to his wife is subjection in the order of *receptive* love.[33] It is a real subjection.

Subjection to his wife's receptive love is how a man learns the freedom to trust another, to overcome his selfish inclinations and fear of commit-ment, and to be able to radiate God's fatherhood effectively. While John Paul does not provide explicit examples of such submission, I will infer some from his writings. Subjection is practically exercised by a husband when he gives himself to and receives his wife in tenderness and patience in their conjugal intimacy, by dying to his concupiscent inclinations to conquer and possess her. He exercises it as husband when he dies to himself

---

[29] Wojtyła, *Radiation of Fatherhood*, part 1, section 4, "Between Meeting and Fulfillment," 339.

[30] See Wojtyła, *Radiation of Fatherhood*, part 3, section 2, "Radiation and Dying," 362.

[31] See Wojtyła, *Radiation of Fatherhood*, part 3, section 2, "Radiation and Dying," 363.

[32] See John Paul II, Apostolic Letter on the Dignity and Vocation of Women *Mulieris digni-tatem* (August 15, 1988), AAS 80 (1988), 1653–1729, §25, in reference to Ephesians 5:21.

[33] My emphasis.

and supports and collaborates with his wife in the manifold domestic matters important to her, but which do not seem to him to have the same significance.

This subjection is practically exercised as a father when the man submits himself to learning to be a father by watching his wife and following her example because she is more readily equipped in the fallen state to receive and love a new life. The man does so when he defers to his wife when she suggests a gentler approach to disciplining a child, or when he incorporates considerations from her that accommodate the specific characteristics of the individual child, because as our author says: "[In] God's eternal plan, woman is the one in whom the order of love in the created world of persons takes first root."[34] The man must learn to submit to his wife as Adam eventually does to the woman who teaches him that to love like the Son, he must learn to die like Christ and so become a father radiating God's fatherhood.

The husband and father's headship is leadership most authentically exercised through cooperative love with his wife, in mutual submission. The man must lead, not in a one-sided, domineering fashion but rather in the gentle but firm manner of Christ. This review of Christ's example provides a more complete explanation of the findings in the previous section on God's fatherhood. Namely, it articulates the way in which Christ reveals the Father and how a human father must live out Christ's example. These aspects of fatherhood are most explicitly described in St. John Paul II's treatment of St. Joseph as the model of human fatherhood.

St. Joseph: A Model of Fatherhood

St. Joseph is St. John Paul II's model *par excellence* of human fatherhood. Therefore, John Paul's treatment of St. Joseph as father must be our lodestar for applying the divine exemplar to human fatherhood.[35] John Paul begins by indicating that St. Joseph was granted a singular gift analogous to Mary's, which enabled him to reciprocate the Blessed Virgin's perfected

---

[34] *Mulieris dignitatem*, §29.

[35] St. John Paul II indicates that St. Joseph's life and his intercession for them points Christian fathers to God's fatherhood as the model for human fatherhood, which will enable them to provide their children the fathers they need for their healthy maturation and flourishing. See John Paul II, Homily on the Solemnity of St. Joseph, March 19, 1983, Termoli, Italy, available at https://www.vatican.va/content/john-paul-ii/it/homilies/1983/documents/hf_jp-ii_hom_19830319_termoli.html (hereinafter, Homily in Termoli).

love. Together they expressed the exclusive, total self-gift of the marriage covenant as a communion of persons which authentically reflected its Trinitarian archetype.[36]

It is important not to misinterpret their respective, singular gifts of grace as making the Holy Family's love an impossible ideal. Rather, they reveal what marital love should be and the goal for which Christian couples must strive by cooperating with the grace of the Sacrament of Marriage. Every Christian family must look to the Holy Family, the first and exemplar domestic church, as the model of love for God, for one another, and for humanity that they aim to reflect in their family life.[37]

St. Joseph's active, lifelong cooperation with this divine gift, expressed his self-oblation in his self-giving love for Mary, is the essence of marriage. Their marriage was not consummated; nevertheless, it was an authentic marital bond with all of the essential elements required for a Christian sacramental marriage.[38] Moreover, "neither [is Joseph's fatherhood] an 'apparent' or merely 'substitute' fatherhood. Rather, it is one that fully shares in authentic human fatherhood and the mission of a father in the family."[39]

St. Joseph's fatherhood over Jesus was true fatherhood. True fatherhood consists not simply in begetting offspring and, in truth, neither does it necessarily require it.[40] For this reason, St. Joseph is also the exemplar for authentic foster fatherhood.

As with all vocations, the vocation to fatherhood is a gift from God. For his part, Joseph accepts this gift with "the obedience of faith."[41] While Joseph's specific vocation is singular in all of creation, his response with an obedience of faith to the gift of fatherhood can justly be considered the task of all fathers.[42] St. Joseph's response was a total sacrifice of himself,

---

[36] See John Paul II, Apostolic Exhortation on the Person and Mission of Saint Joseph in the Life of Christ and of the Church *Redemptoris custos* (August 15, 1989), AAS 82 (1990), 5–34, §19.

[37] See *Redemptoris custos*, §7.

[38] *Redemptoris custos*, §§7, 20.

[39] *Redemptoris custos*, §21.

[40] See *Redemptoris custos*, §21. Although John Paul II links Joseph's true fatherhood to the mystery of the hypostatic union in which his fatherhood is taken up into the mystery of the Incarnation, this statement does not diminish the gift of authentically lived foster fatherhood as a true fatherhood in all the ways that are essential for the flourishing of children and family. While foster fatherhood and adoptive fatherhood can have different meanings in various civil jurisdictions, we will use them as equivalents meaning permanently accepting a child as one's own.

[41] *Redemptoris custos*, §21.

[42] While St. Joseph's call to marriage with Mary was divinely revealed and so fits technically

the hallmark of authentic fatherhood.[43] John Paul notes that in this way, Joseph's earthly fatherhood over the Incarnate Son reflects divine fatherhood "in a most extraordinary way."[44] Joseph is the preeminent exemplar of a natural father radiating God's fatherhood. St. Joseph was the guardian and protector of his Son and his wife, though he carried those duties out in conjunction with Mary his spouse.[45] This collaborative role corresponds with John Paul's application of the great mystery to paternal headship as the mutual subjection of husband and wife.[46]

Joseph's model of authentic fatherhood can, in the first place, be attributed to his total commitment to his calling, sacrificing his whole being to the service of Jesus. As John Paul II states, Joseph "surrendered his whole existence to the demands of [his vocation]."[47] Joseph gave himself as a gift and "turned his human vocation to domestic love into a superhuman oblation of self, an oblation of his heart and all his abilities into love placed at the service of the Messiah growing up in his house."[48]

This self-gift was not only to his Son, it was also a total gift of himself to his spouse, the Holy Mother of God, giving her a husband's self-gift.[49] Joseph's paternal self-sacrifice was a proleptic participation in the oblation of love his Son would make for his Bride, the Church.[50] His fatherhood was a direct service to Jesus as a person as well as to his mission.[51] One can see from *Radiation of Fatherhood* that all authentic Christian fatherhood is service to the mission of Christ in the context of his family. Authentic fatherhood demands the man's total commitment to his wife and family.

To be sure, Joseph's response was profoundly heroic. John Paul attributes this to an intense interior life, the guidance of the Holy Spirit,[52] and to that singular gift of grace enabling him to love his Son with all the love

---

as a response of obedience of faith, so is the general vocation of marriage, along with its obligations, divinely revealed and, as such, a matter of faith.

[43] See John Paul II, "St. Joseph, Image of God's Fatherly Love," Angelus Message of March 21, 1999, on the tenth anniversary of *Redemptoris custos*, *L'Osservatore Romano*, English (March 1999).

[44] "St. Joseph, Image of God's Fatherly Love," Angelus Message of March 21, 1999.

[45] See *Redemptoris custos*, §5ff.

[46] We will address the consistency between the idea of the man being both husband and leader and the idea of mutual submission in part 4.

[47] *Redemptoris custos*, §26.

[48] *Redemptoris custos*, §8.

[49] See *Redemptoris custos*, §20.

[50] See *Redemptoris custos*, §§7-8.

[51] See *Redemptoris custos*, §8.

[52] See *Redemptoris custos*, §21.

that a father can possibly give.[53] These are attributes of a heroically lived vocation to fatherhood and explain Joseph's unique, exemplary paternal status. However, John Paul also identifies some quotidian attributes and duties St. Joseph demonstrated of authentic fatherhood.

Joseph expressed a distinctly fatherly love.[54] Paternal love is one of initiative that first goes out in order to be returned. This initiating love of husband and father comes with what John Paul calls a "fatherly authority"[55] to carry out his roles and duties as "the guardian, head and defender of the Holy Family."[56] His was an authority to which even "the Word of God was subjected.... [H]e obeyed him and rendered to him that honor and reverence that children owe to their father."[57] Joseph was given the ineffable task of raising Jesus, the Son of God and his own adopted Son. To do so he had the obligation of providing his Son with food, clothing, education in the Law along with its religious duties, and in a trade.[58]

One might ask if these are universal paternal tasks or if they are culturally conditioned. John Paul is not explicit but refers to these tasks as the "duties of a father," which implies their universality even if some of the specific ways he did so were specific to the time and place (e.g., teaching Jesus his own carpenter's trade). Our model of masculinity indicates that these tasks are consonant with the masculine structure. They are fundamentally eccentric, going out into the world to possess and conquer in order to provide the family with food, shelter, and the many material needs of life. For example, those aspects of education which deal with the outside world of work and law are areas to which the man is naturally more attuned by virtue of his masculinity, and so they are properly paternal tasks, as John Paul suggested in a retreat with college-aged men.[59]

John Paul draws closely together St. Joseph's model as a father and as a worker.[60] He says there is a bond between work and family life.[61] Joseph's "work of his own hands," by which he provided for the Holy Family, was

[53] See *Redemptoris custos*, §8.
[54] See *Redemptoris custos*, §27.
[55] See *Redemptoris custos*, §§7-8.
[56] *Redemptoris custos*, §28.
[57] *Redemptoris custos*, §8.
[58] See *Redemptoris custos*, §16.
[59] See William May, "The Mission of Fatherhood," *Josephinum Journal of Theology* 9, no. 1 (2002): 52ff. For retreat comment, see Wojtyła, *Way to Christ*, 53–54.
[60] See *Redemptoris custos*, §§22-23; Homily in Termoli.
[61] See John Paul II, "Unity of the Family and Respect for Life," Homily on the Feast of St. Joseph, Liberati Stadium, Terni, Italy, March 19, 1981, *L'Osservatore Romano*, English (March 1981).

also the work he creatively imbued in Jesus, his Son.[62] Work is a source of man's dignity in that he is made in the image of a Creator God, and so he finds his fulfillment in creative work by which he cooperates with God in his plan for creation and redemption.[63] But man is also called to the Sabbath rest in the covenant with God, ultimately entrusting to God the bringing about of his will and making up for what man cannot do.

Man is called out of the sixth day and into covenant rest, separating him from the other animals. He is made to be God's collaborator through work, but not as a beast of burden. He is first a person called to communion with God. John Paul sees in St. Joseph's silence his teaching us the necessity of a virtuous integration of a life of work with quiet contemplation.[64] This worker-contemplative interiority of Joseph's is necessary for him and for all men and fathers to be God's authentic coworkers. It is the manner in which man humbles himself and makes of himself a total sacrifice to God and is thereby transformed, by which he gives his entire life to being a husband and father. This is necessary if he is to nourish his family authentically.[65] A man radiates God's fatherhood by ordering himself, his work, his conjugal life, and his fatherhood according to God's fatherhood, after the manner of St. Joseph whose litany calls him "Cornerstone of families and Glory of family life."[66] This is achieved through an interior life which permits him to submit himself totally to God.

A Theology of Fatherhood from Writings on Women and Motherhood

We have looked at the dominant attention St. John Paul II devotes to women and motherhood in his writings, in contrast to his explicit treatment of men and fatherhood. Yet, we have also seen that he certainly addresses men directly and indirectly in his writings, even when the topic is women and motherhood. Let us now turn to his writings on women and motherhood to gather those masculine and paternal attributes, tasks, and roles which he explicitly attributes to men and fathers. We will apply our complementarity model to infer further masculine and paternal attributes,

---

[62] See John Paul II, Homily in Termoli.

[63] See John Paul II, Encyclical Letter on Human Work *Laborem exercens* (September 14, 1981), AAS 73 (1981), 577–647, §§4–9, and *Redemptoris custos*, §§22–23.

[64] See *Redemptoris custos*, §§23–25.

[65] See *Redemptoris custos*, §26.

[66] See Litany of St. Joseph, available at https://www.usccb.org/prayers/litany-saint-joseph.

tasks, and roles from feminine and maternal attributes, roles, and tasks he explicitly identifies in these texts.

In what follows, we will follow a certain "chronological" order with respect to a man's maturation in the process of becoming a father. This will start with the origins of fatherhood in marriage, which is the conjugal union, then proceed through childbirth and the raising of children, and will finish with a look at a father's societal roles.

The first texts we will consider start even before the husband and wife make the decision to become parents. At the very beginning of the relationship, the husband and potential father has work to do. Flourishing families can only arise from the foundations of flourishing marriages. The goal of flourishing family life today is challenged by a masculine attitude which predominates in many homes, even in certain societies which extol a so-called "macho" attitude.[67] Here John Paul refers to the problem of an oppressive dominance by the man over his wife and family, which he warns is destructive of self, marriage, and children. As a remedy, he recommends St. Ambrose's wisdom to men entering marriage to avoid such a temptation, warning them that they are taking a wife, not a slave. The man is to love his wife, to be attentive to her, and to learn from her. He tells men to treat their wives like Christ treats his Church.[68] John Paul continually returns to the imitation of Christ as head of the Church as the model for husbands and fathers.

For the man in marriage, this imitation of Christ is the great mystery. This mystery is fundamental vocation for Christian husbands and is necessary for a marriage and family life to flourish. Husbands must love their wives with a total gift of self, reflecting the ineffable bond by which they become one flesh. Loving one's wife in this way fundamentally verifies her value as a person. A woman, a wife, requires this affirmation in order for her to develop fruitfully and to actualize her feminine personality, making this an essential husbandly task. In fact, Christ acts in precisely this way as the Bridegroom toward his Bride, as he desires for her "splendor, without spot or wrinkle (Eph 5:27)." This insight captures "the whole 'style' of Christ in dealing with women."[69]

John Paul encourages husbands to make Christ's style their own in their solicitude toward their wives. Indeed, all men ought to behave in this way toward all women in every circumstance. It is through such behavior

---

[67] See *Familiaris consortio*, §25.
[68] See *Familiaris consortio*, §25.
[69] *Mulieris dignitatem*, §24.

that sincere self-gift will be brought into being.[70] The husband's overall task is to imitate Christ and Christ's treatment of the Church in his relationship with his wife. Through this love, husbands play a fundamental part in the formation of their wives and, therefore, in their wives' success as mothers.

John Paul next addresses men and their responsibilities in the conjugal union. The husband's externality, reflected in the spouses' bodies, is an attribute of his masculine eccentricity. Masculine eccentricity comes with intellectual gifts ordered to analysis and problem-solving. These gifts for the man of concupiscence lead him to experience *eros* toward his wife in a complementarily different manner than she experiences toward him. For this reason, she may even promote his reductive inclinations, believing he experiences it in the more person-centered manner that she does. The fallen experience of *eros* is now deprived of its fullness, which should be his interior movement toward the true, the good, and the beautiful, but it now moves the eccentric masculine person to focus on singular, reductive goods.[71]

In marriage, the husband's concupiscent erotic experience concentrates his attention on her sexual value and its potential for his pleasure. This moves him toward the reduction of his wife to these goods at the expense of acknowledging her inestimable value as a person and acting for her integral good. His consent to such temptations turns him inward and, therefore, away from her. This damages his relationship with his wife, with God, and with others, in proportion to the level of his consent and the gravity of any acts which reduce her.

Pope Benedict XVI proposes that a remedy to a reductive *eros* is attentiveness to completing it in *agape*.[72] *Eros* is still good, but its authentic movement must be recovered. This means continually working on the gift of self that both spouses must persistently endeavor to perfect. The

---

[70] See *Mulieris dignitatem*, §24.

[71] See *Man and Woman*, 318ff.

[72] This is discussed in Benedict XVI, Encyclical Letter on Christian Love *Deus caritas est* (December 25, 2005), §§3–8. This was Benedict XVI's first encyclical and the discussion of *eros* and *agape* is clearly by his hand; nevertheless, it shares unmistakably the same insights which we see in John Paul II's *Man and Woman*, in which he discusses *eros* and *ethos* (see 316ff.). They both begin with Plato's definition of *eros* as an interior movement of the person beyond himself and toward the true, the good, and the beautiful. They describe similarly the effect of the fall and the reduction of *eros* to a reductive sexual desire. John Paul II discusses the need to recover *eros's* fullness through purity of heart by constituting *eros* in the *ethos* of the human person who is always treated as an end. Benedict discusses this same phenomenon, but in terms of the interrelationship between *eros* and *agape*, wherein the former must be completed by the latter.

man's practice of rejecting his inclinations to reduce his wife and to giving himself fully and freely in marital love, and in all things large and small, will prepare him to fulfill his role as husband and father more authentically.[73]

The fruitful consequence of sexual intercourse is a particular matter to which the husband must be attentive. His externality creates a biological distance from the process of procreation in comparison to his wife, which can incline him to place the entire responsibility for the pregnancy on her. This distance makes it easier for him to neglect his responsibility for the life which he cocreates with his wife and without his attentiveness to this, makes it more likely that he will. The husband must realize that he may have to work to embrace taking responsibility for his fatherhood. If this is necessary, then he must because the child, his child, is the fruit of a mutual decision which he already made with his wife. It is unconscionable that a father not acknowledge and accept the results of that mutual decision.[74]

His externality necessarily permeates his entire personal constitution, leaving him not only an indirect role after conception but also feeling throughout his fatherhood that he is on the outside looking in. In a certain manner, he experiences the problem of concupiscence working on original solitude in a more acute manner than does his wife. He need not remain there. He can overcome the resulting temptation to turn inward and away from his responsibilities by understanding the root of the problem. Masculine eccentricity includes the manifold gifts needed to fulfill the *telos* of the masculine mode of human nature. Developing self-mastery will give him the freedom to direct these gifts intentionally for the good of his wife and family. Attentiveness to his wife and supporting her throughout the pregnancy will help him experience his fatherhood from the inside.

Both spouses together must assume responsibility for the child they have begotten. Fathers have the obligation to acknowledge and fully accept their children even before a child is born. John Paul explains how the father should do this. Understanding his anthropology is needed to appropriate his meaning, and hylomorphism again is the key. It tells us that the woman's body, her entire psycho-physiology, has much to tell about her roles and tasks because it reveals how her whole person is integrated into the process of pregnancy. This in turn sheds light on the attributes and

---

[73] For more practical suggestions influenced by John Paul II's anthropology, see David H. Delaney, *The Great Mystery*, 2nd ed. (Helotes, TX: Mother of the Americas Institute Press, 2021), 182–98.

[74] See John Paul II, Letter to Families *Gratissimam sane* (February 2, 1994), AAS 86 (1994), 868–925 (New Hope, KY: Urbi Et Orbi Communications, 1994), §12.

the required tasks and roles of the father based upon his complementarity with his wife.

John Paul declares Christ's reconciliation of man with God makes possible his vocation to building a "civilization of love." This is one in which every person lives up to his calling to sincere self-giving. It ought to begin in family life when the husband recognizes his wife's motherhood as a gift from God. It is a gift to her, to him, and to all mankind. His recognition establishes the only adequate framework for raising his children in accord with this civilization. Opening our eyes to the gift of persons and especially to the gift of motherhood gives civilization itself the best chance not simply of surviving but of flourishing. John Paul says that success in this task will depend upon the man's active involvement as a father from the very beginning stages of the pregnancy.[75]

Though indirect during pregnancy, the husband-father's role is nevertheless vitally important for his wife and his child. He must overcome his selfish inclinations and commit himself to supporting his wife and to being attentive to her from the beginning of the pregnancy all the way to the moment of birth, being present with her at delivery, if at all possible. John Paul affirms the beneficial fruits to his wife, children, and society when the man embraces his fatherhood. There can be no civilization of love without a father's authentic participation in family life. John Paul acknowledges the grim statistics and ominous societal impacts of absent fathers.[76]

There is another important aspect of motherhood that must contribute to the husband's fatherhood. "Motherhood *in its personal-ethical sense* expresses a very important creativity on the part of the woman, upon whom the very humanity of the new human being mainly depends. In this sense too, the woman's motherhood presents a special call and a special challenge to the man and to his fatherhood."[77] The mother is more important than the father for the early development of a child because of the biological and psychological priority of the mother in pregnancy and her role as first teacher of the child. Her motherhood therefore "places an essential 'mark' on the whole personal growth process of new children."[78] The gift of motherhood is unique and irreplaceable; it is something for which the father cannot be a substitute. In the early stages of the child's life, his is a

---

[75] See Letter to Families, §16.

[76] See John Paul II, Homily in Termoli, in which he makes references to the crisis of a fatherless society.

[77] *Mulieris dignitatem*, §19.

[78] *Mulieris dignitatem*, §19.

supporting role. Still, it is a role the father must embrace if his children are to have every chance of proper development.[79]

The husband can better appreciate and honor his wife as a mother if he realizes that together he and his wife reflect the "eternal mystery of generation, which is in God himself, the one and Triune God."[80] However, his wife's motherhood shares in this mystery in a unique, more profound way. This is particularly true during her pregnancy because she "pays" more directly for her participation in the mystery of generation than does the man. Her gift to her child is her entire person; she gives him the very "energies" of her soul and of her body. In virtue of this, the man must understand the special debt he owes to his wife.[81] The husband's recognition of the ineffable role his wife plays in the birth of their children cannot but evoke from him a sense of awe and a response of gratitude and love, which can transform him and his fatherhood.

A husband-father needs to be aware that because of man's fallen state, his masculine makeup can be turned into an impediment of his paternal vocation.[82] While women tend to have a natural maternal inclination, men do not generally exhibit a corresponding paternal inclination.[83] In addition to this, the physical ramifications associated with becoming a father

---

[79] John Paul does not cite any sociological studies to support these assertions. Nor does that seem required. He bases his assertions upon a theological anthropology which describes the person as a whole. The first two parts of this study show that his anthropology correlates well with divine revelation. However, given the depth and breadth of his mastery of the associated sociological data that he shows in his book *Love and Responsibility*, it is not unreasonable to assume that he was familiar with the relevant sociological data.

[80] *Mulieris dignitatem*, §18.

[81] *Mulieris dignitatem*, §18.

[82] See *Mulieris dignitatem*, §10.

[83] John Paul II's statements that men must learn their fatherhood from their wives because he is outside the process of pregnancy (*Mulieris dignitatem*, §18) is completely consistent with his earlier thought. Cardinal Wojtyła says: "A man's physical fatherhood has a lesser place in his life, especially in his organism, than a woman's physical motherhood has in her life and organism. Therefore, fatherhood must be specially molded and educated so that it constitutes in the interior life of a man a position as important as motherhood is in the interior life of a woman: the biological facts themselves in a sense impose this on her. We are now speaking about fatherhood and motherhood above all in the bodily, biological sense. It consists in possessing a child to whom life has been given, existence transmitted (*procreatio*)" (Karol Wojtyła, *Love and Responsibility*, trans. Grzegorz Ignatik [Boston: Pauline Books & Media, 2013], 245). While in neither work does the author explicitly cite sociological data, this observation, which he justifies based on his anthropology, is consistent with the sociological data describing the current crisis in fatherhood presented earlier.

are less compelling in a man's day to day experience. Therefore, men must recognize that they have to make a concerted effort to cultivate and train themselves so that paternal affectivity will become as important to their inner lives as maternity is for their wives. Wojtyła's warning is based upon his anthropological insights but is borne out in the sociological data associated with absent fathers.[84] Men who fail to accede to these admonitions run the risks of failing to fulfill themselves, failing to assist their wives in their self-fulfillment and, finally, they risk damaging their children emotionally, psychologically, and spiritually.[85]

John Paul's theological anthropology states that man cannot fulfill himself except through a sincere gift of himself. He declares that for a father this is, in part, achieved in a natural manner through his manifestation of "love for his wife as mother of their children and love for the children themselves."[86] The dangers mentioned above are heightened when the father lives in a society which encourages men to have an attenuated concern for their families and for their fatherhood.

This includes societies in which fatherhood is widely denigrated, where a preponderance of fathers are voluntarily absent for various reasons, where work outside the home is prized over that of being a dedicated father, or perhaps where time spent with the family is seen as a woman's responsibility. John Paul II refers to experience in order to assess that the absentee father has borne a grim harvest for children and society. The resulting ill fruits for the children include psychological damage, degrading of morals, and significant problems in intra-familial relationships.[87] These problems can arise even when paternal involvement in the child's formation is not missing but only diminished, for example, with respect to his education. However, the contrary extreme can be similarly problematic.

When the husband-father exhibits an oppressive presence, he can impede the maturation of sound family relationships. In the end, the indicated manner for the husband-father to understand and fulfill his vocation is to love his wife as mother of their children and to love the children for their own sakes.[88] This exhausts John Paul II's direct addresses to men found in our survey of his corpus of writings. However, this does not exhaust his writings to men which tell them how to be authentic husbands and fathers. We will now look at John Paul II's writings in which

---

[84] See chapter 9.
[85] See John Paul II, Homily in Termoli.
[86] *Familiaris consortio*, §25.
[87] See *Familiaris consortio*, §25.
[88] See *Familiaris consortio*, §25.

he describes the symbols, attributes, tasks, and roles of women in order to extract their inferences for the corresponding complementary tasks of husbands and fathers.

We have already seen that John Paul II integrates theological symbols into his anthropology in order to explain various aspects of sex difference. This is particularly the case with feminine symbols for the Church and the fact that femininity symbolizes humanity's relation to God and its relationship with him. Mankind's relation to God is receptive with respect to existence, love, and other important attributes. Man's relationship with God is now actualized solely through the Church, his Bride. Let us revisit some of these feminine symbols to ascertain whether one might infer masculine attributes from them.

We will follow, as much as possible, the same progression used for the direct attributions. "The 'feminine' humanly symbolizes . . . welcome and care for the human person and giv[ing] birth to life. All this is rooted, in a transcendent way, in the mystery of the eternal divine 'begetting.'"[89] It must be emphasized that God's fatherhood is completely spiritual. Divine begetting communicates eternal, relational reciprocity in the Trinity. This is reflected in a fundamental manner in the created order, by the relational reciprocity of masculinity and femininity. The Trinity is the source of all human fatherhood as well as motherhood, but each symbolizes different aspects of the divine archetype. Femininity as a created symbol manifests the "dimension of love and fruitfulness."[90] These attributes of femininity reflect the free and active reception of love on the part of the woman. John Paul assumes this in discussing the personification of the Blessed Virgin as a symbol for humanity and for the Church.[91]

While femininity symbolizes active receptivity, ultimately this is rooted in man's relation to God, masculinity symbolizes its complement. Masculinity's primary, innate feature is an initiating love, and it so it naturally represents God in his relation toward humanity, for example, as Father, Creator, Word, Bridegroom, Sanctifier, and so on.[92] These images can easily be misunderstood or misconstrued. This does not mean that God is masculine in his essence.[93] Masculinity and femininity both have

---

[89] John Paul II, *The Trinity's Embrace*, 289–90.

[90] John Paul II, *The Trinity's Embrace*, 443; see also 444.

[91] See John Paul II, *The Church*, 118.

[92] See *Mulieris dignitatem*, §§25–26.

[93] Rightly understood, the concept of the "communication of idioms" might allow for speaking of God's masculinity in Jesus (see Aquinas, *ST* IIa-IIae, q. 16, aa. 5-6). However,

their origin in God, but they are created manifestations of the infinite, divine relations.

A fundamental manner in which God's absolute perfection manifests itself in the created order, is as human masculinity and femininity. Masculinity symbolizes the *relation* God has with humanity; God first loves us. In the order of redemption, this is disclosed through the Bridegroom's relation to his feminine Bride.[94] The complementary relationship between love offered by a husband and love received and returned by his wife is in this way a participation in the Trinitarian mystery and manifested in God's relation with man. Masculine symbols for God in relation to man are archetypical for masculine attributes which are ordered to a husband's love and service to his wife and family.

In addition to feminine symbols, John Paul has written copiously about women's and mother's attributes, tasks, and roles. We can derive masculine attributes, roles, and tasks from these writings. What one finds is that these generally affirm those previously identified. Other of his writings may not necessarily infer complementary attributes or tasks, but they do suggest tasks which arise from their educative nature. All of these together contribute to our author's theology of fatherhood, which can help men to excel in their vocation and so help their marriages and families to flourish.

John Paul describes the general need for society, for women and men, to come to a deeper understanding of what it means to be feminine. Earlier we saw women's leading role in this regard and men's need to support them. To do so effectively men need to understand feminine genius adequately. While John Paul is not entirely negative about the trajectory of contemporary society in its appreciation of femininity, he is extremely concerned. He laments the dichotomy between principles which modern society espouses and practical reality.[95]

Society must not only condemn in principle every practice which assaults human dignity, it must also stop it in practice. We have already discussed the problem of the sex industry, with its destruction of women's lives and its distortion of society's view of authentic femininity.[96] Many cultures and governments, for a variety of reasons, look the other way. It is most often men who are in positions which are best suited for putting policies into place to eliminate such practices. Men are also the primary consumers

---

masculinity cannot be attributed to the divine essence itself, for it exists in the category of relation.

[94] See *Mulieris dignitatem*, §§25–26.

[95] See John Paul II, *The Trinity's Embrace*, 288.

[96] See John Paul II, *The Trinity's Embrace*, 288.

and facilitators of such practices. Therefore, men have a grave obligation to work to stop such damaging practices. They must apply their masculine gifts such as initiative, inclination to protect the weak and defenseless, and problem-solving skills to assist in addressing this scourge, beginning in the home with themselves and the formation of their children.

There are vocations which are proper to women because of their femininity, and to men because of their masculinity. The two primary vocations for women are virginity and motherhood.[97] The entire structure of a woman's feminine personhood—body, soul, physiology, psychology, and so on—are oriented toward effecting her vocation. Regardless of the manner in which she expresses it, whether through natural motherhood, consecrated virginity, or spiritual motherhood in a societal role, it is imperative that she live this out in accord with her feminine identity.[98] This is the only way a woman will ultimately fulfill herself. The same admonition applies to men in two ways. He will flourish as a man to the degree that he actively supports and encourages women in his life to live their femininity authentically. In addition, he will flourish as a man to the degree he dies to his fallen inclinations (whether they are ordered to nature or opposed to it) and submits himself to God and in relationships with others in accord with his masculine identity.

Natural fatherhood and spiritual paternity are masculine complements to feminine vocations. As with women, men will fulfill themselves only in accord with their proper masculine vocations. In this regard, let us look at one important aspect of the feminine genius John Paul highlights. He says that woman's vocation can be summarized as a witness to love through her primacy in the order of love.[99] Every particular vocational manifestation in society and in the Church must take this into consideration. He connects the attribute of trust to this primacy in which the woman receives love

---

[97] See *Mulieris dignitatem*, §17.

[98] Elizabeth Johnson identifies three masculine characteristics from *Mulieris dignitatem* in her reaction to John Paul II's warning against the "masculinization" of women. By John Paul's description of feminine qualities Johnson infers "assertiveness, rational argument and independent action" as masculine characteristics that women do not possess (*Truly Our Sister: A Theology of Mary in the Communion of Saints* [New York: Continuum, 2003], 61). Johnson does not describe her rationale or identify the particular female characteristics from which she arrives at this inference. I do not think that these can be defended as proper masculine attributes in John Paul II's thought, at least not without a more precise description of what Johnson means by them and a better explanation as to how she arrives at them. Therefore, I will not use them.

[99] See *Mulieris dignitatem*, §30.

in order to love in return.[100] Women are more habituated to trust, as it is required in some degree when they choose to accept love from others, especially from men.

In addition to this, women are also models of trust because they recognize the special way in which they have been entrusted with another person in motherhood. This is the source of their great strength. The husband must recognize his wife's primacy in the order of love and learn from her example of trust and love. In marriage, this consideration must complement the way a man discharges his husbandly and paternal authority. The husband and wife, mother and father, together in their mutuality, are more complete reflections of Trinitarian love. Therefore, the man will deficiently use his authority, if not abuse it, if it is not complemented by his wife's primacy in love's order. Only in authentic complementarity will marital love reach its *telos*, ordered by its divine archetype. While the man has the authority of headship within marriage, the great mystery contextualizes his headship as existing only in the marriage covenant.

Masculine headship does not extend to broader societal relationships among men and women.[101] However, women's primacy in the order of love does seem to extend to all aspects of life. The trust which is essential to social functioning has its origin in the order of love. For this reason, women ought to be involved in all aspects of social life, in order to complement masculine approaches, which tend to dominate in the absence of feminine influence. Men are not generally attentive to the experience of trust necessary for receptive love because it is secondary in their experience and so easily ignored. Men must learn the trust required for submitting oneself in love. They can do so by attentiveness to the trust manifested by their mothers, wives, relatives, friends, and even female co-workers. Only through a mature actualization of trust will men be prepared to contribute fruitfully to a civilization of love in their families and society.

Within marriage, the man is the one who "knows" and the woman is the one who is "known."[102] John Paul II describes this reciprocal knowledge as the special gift of self, shared between the spouses. However, an

---

[100] See chapter 6 for an account of the reciprocity of trust in relationships.

[101] This is true even if it is also the case that a man's gifts associated with initiating love can incline him to pursue forms of masculine leadership in public life which is more visibly apparent than feminine, receptive leadership.

[102] See *Man and Woman*, 211. Recall that in this context "to know" in the biblical sense of the term is expressed by the Hebrew *jadac*. It is the sharing of intimate love such that one person shares the deepest mystery of himself with his spouse. The most intimate, visible expression of this "knowledge" is marital intercourse. John Paul's use of the term is not

ever-present danger is the concupiscent temptation on the part of the man "to become the 'master' of his wife ('he shall rule over you') or by the woman remaining closed within her own selfish inclinations ('your desire shall be for your husband': *Gen* 3:16)."[103] Here John Paul does not explicitly admonish men about the implications of biblical knowledge, but the implications seem clear. The husband (as well as the wife) must recognize that they are united authentically to the degree they are a mutual self-gift to one another, especially as this is expressed in biblical knowing. Husband-fathers must be aware of and overcome his concupiscent temptations which diminish the fruits of conjugal unity. This is true not only in sexual congress, but in all aspects of daily life he must see and treat his wife as an equal partner, not a possession.

Another feminine feature John Paul points out is a woman's more acute capacity for paying attention to another person.[104] An unstated implication of this is that the man is not as attentive to the personhood of others. A man must recognize his proclivity to be less aware of the other person, as well as recognize his wife's greater sensitivity in order to learn from her. Rather, he will tend to be focused on some particular feature of interest, for example, a task to be accomplished or an outstanding physical attribute. He must recognize that women will have different manners of perceptions, communication and, many times, different expectations. John Paul advises that the husband's recognition of these types of differences is important especially during pregnancy, in which men remain essentially outside the process. He should observe his wife, be attentive to her needs, and listen to her in order to learn from her and thereby become more authentically a husband and father.

The husband must also recognize that his wife's solicitude toward her unborn child will generally be greater than his own. Observing his wife will help him to cultivate a deeper desire for fatherhood than he might achieve on his own. A woman's psycho-physical structure gives her a special openness to new life and attunes her more readily to her self-gift than does a man's corresponding structure.[105] These feminine attributes serve to educate the man about the complementary gifts of masculinity and femininity, in order that he might learn how to live his fatherhood in

---

simply as a synonym for the biological act of sexual intercourse, but it is the whole of this concept of intimate communion.

[103] *Mulieris dignitatem*, §18.
[104] See *Mulieris dignitatem*, §18.
[105] See *Mulieris dignitatem*, §18.

a more fruitful manner. When he does so, he submits himself to his wife in the order of love.

Both women and men must appreciate the uniqueness of the vocation and gift of motherhood for family life to flourish. It is clear from the examples provided above that John Paul wants women to recognize and embrace their gift, especially as it is increasingly denigrated by contemporary society. However, his admonitions also have a great deal to say to men, first with regard to their role as husbands and fathers but also in their roles in broader society. We have already seen the husbands' need to recognize the special entrustment of human persons to women as mothers.[106] Yet there are many other aspects of motherhood John Paul II identifies that reveal its ineffable dignity.

John Paul realizes that the more men and women appreciate this dignity in its manifold facets, the more we can heal family life and broader society. For example, if Christians in society honored women as cocreators with God, it would contribute to dampening the systematic objectification of women in media and other forms of entertainment. This objectification has the effect of giving men license to view and treat women like objects for their pleasure rather than as persons with unspeakable dignity. Moreover, the diminishing sense of the dignity and importance of motherhood weakens our ability to see their unique strengths and personal dignity.

Society's diminishment of motherhood does not thereby ignore their feminine gifts. Rather, we are seeing the instrumentalization of feminine gifts for their economic benefit (e.g., in advertising, entertainment, etc.) deteriorating into the exploding sexual exploitation industry which teaches girls that their bodies and the pleasure they can provide are the source of their value. This undermines their healthy development and negatively affects both family life and interpersonal relations, and all society suffers for it. Society's denigration of the value of motherhood not only exacerbates men's temptation to objectify women, it also promotes many women's mistaken impression that they must adopt masculine modes of behavior in order to recapture their lost dignity.

The solution to society's devaluation of motherhood includes men in family life and in their roles in society recognizing the heroism of motherhood and supporting women in this vocation. John Paul finds this heroism reflected in the unspoken witness of mothers who courageously and selflessly dedicate themselves to the flourishing of their families. It manifests itself in mothers who quietly accept the suffering associated with the

---

[106] See *Mulieris dignitatem*, §30.

gestation and birth of their children. It is shown in mothers "who are ready to make any effort, to face any sacrifice, in order to pass on to [their families] the best of themselves."[107]

John Paul, however, is concerned that the direction of society is toward the voluntary rejection of motherhood out of the wish of many of its members to gain material advantages or else in the mistaken notion that personal fulfillment can only come in performing some larger societal function. In truth, this is a deformation of the feminine person who is made with a *telos* meant to develop connaturally within the vocation of motherhood.[108] Men actually promote this distorted thinking by participating in the diminishment of motherhood, often through their attitudes and actions. In doing so, they rob society of the framework that makes possible well-formed children, stable families, and harmonious societies.[109]

Men and women must work together to transform societal structures into those which recognize the irreplaceable importance of motherhood and which facilitate women taking their places as active members of society without having to sacrifice their motherhood.[110] This strongly implies that the primary responsibility for providing material resources for the family is the husband's, at least during the time in which the mother should remain in the home during the raising of the children.[111] This conforms with John Paul's theology of masculinity in which his masculine structure is more suited to going out into the world, for its "conquering and possessing."[112]

Men in particular must recognize a woman's inherent orientation toward motherhood and her irreplaceable contribution to the nurturing of young children.[113] Men, indeed societies, need to acknowledge and appreciate that while the value of the work of mothers may not directly produce profits, even from a utilitarian perspective it has long-term economic consequences. Authentic motherhood therefore possesses fundamental significance for healthy family life and societal good.[114] Family flourishing is a prerequisite to social and economic flourishing. Men must support, assist,

---

[107] John Paul II, Encyclical Letter on the Value and Inviolability of Human Life *Evangelium vitae* (March 25, 1995), *AAS* 87 (1995), 401–522, §86.

[108] See John Paul II, *The Church*, 494.

[109] See John Paul II, *The Church*, 493.

[110] John Paul II does not provide any concrete recommendations for these structural adaptations, as this task belongs to the competence of the laity.

[111] See *Laborem exercens*, §19.

[112] See Wojtyła, *Love and Responsibility*, 81–82.

[113] See *Laborem exercens*, §19.

[114] See John Paul II, *The Church*, 466.

and even exalt mothers and their motherhood. Without this recognition and support, increasing numbers of women today will be disinclined to recognize and embrace the gift of motherhood which God has given them. Others will even continue to fear it as a source of oppression.

The gift of motherhood also makes women indispensable to larger societal concerns as well. Men must recognize that women are needed in almost every sector of life, except those, which by their very nature, diminish their femininity.[115] Their experience as mothers, but also their very femininity itself, is a needed complement to masculine gifts. Therefore, their unique feminine vocation must be recognized and society accommodated to embrace the feminine vocation. Women of course must also recognize these truths. Both women and men must work toward these proposed new social structures and refuse to require or allow conditions which are destructive of the feminine genius.[116] Fathers can teach their children these truths by their words, but even more by the way their children see them act toward their mothers.

SPIRITUAL HUMAN FATHERHOOD

It is necessary to emphasize that there is no separation between natural fatherhood and spiritual fatherhood because human nature is a unity of body-spirit. For John Paul II, a man's biological generation of a child is only the beginning of the important vocation of fatherhood. The more important aspect of natural paternity is the spiritual nurturing of a child. Nevertheless, spiritual fatherhood extends beyond natural fatherhood and encompasses a man's spiritual nurturing of another in a paternal manner.[117] Because, in the author's thought, the biological aspects of fathering are so closely tied to the obligation for the spiritual development of the child, I have shown them to be integrated in the previous sections.

This separate section on spiritual fatherhood is appropriate because John Paul most commonly uses the term (along with spiritual motherhood) for those who play a role in the development of souls in the capacity of a spiritual father (or mother) but who are not themselves natural parents, at least not natural parents to those whom they are nurturing as spiritual parents. In approaching spiritual fatherhood, we will look to John Paul II's

---

[115] This is an implication from John Paul II's theology of women; however, I have not found him to specifically identify any valid roles which would be incompatible with femininity.

[116] See *Laborem exercens*, §19.

[117] See Wojtyła, *Love and Responsibility*, 245–46.

writings which speak directly of spiritual fatherhood, including the spiritual aspects of natural fatherhood. This will also consider the spiritual fatherhood of those who are not biological fathers, including the spiritual fatherhood of priests. We must also investigate texts on spiritual motherhood in order to determine whether it is possible to infer attributes and roles of spiritual fatherhood from them.

Unlike natural fatherhood, the number of texts which directly address spiritual fatherhood outnumber those which address spiritual motherhood.[118] Speaking of a general spiritual parenthood, Wojtyła explains it as a sign of the spiritual maturity of the person, the goal to which everyone is called.[119] In a very real sense then, everyone is called to be a spiritual parent in some regard, whether within or outside of the marital covenant, the ministerial priesthood, or religious life. "This vocation is implicated, in a sense, in the evangelical call to perfection, which indicates the 'Father' as its supreme model. Thus, man attains a likeness to God the Creator particularly when this primarily spiritual fatherhood-motherhood, whose archetype is God, is also formed in him."[120]

Within marriage, parenthood is authentic to the degree to which parents nurture their children's souls as well as their bodies.[121] Parents express this authenticity through the complete, integral education of their children and the fruit that comes from it.[122] However, spiritual parenthood transcends marriage as an expression of self-communicative good (*bonum est diffusivum sui*).[123] Spiritual parenthood is nothing less than giving birth spiritually. It arises from one's spiritual maturity and from a kind of fullness that one desires to share. In this way, one is drawn to spiritual parenthood. The spiritually mature want spiritual "children" just as so many desire biological children.

Young people are often open to being spiritually begotten and, when they accept this, they become objects of endearment for the spiritual parent, receiving affection not unlike that of natural parents for their children. One might liken this, in part, to a similar phenomenon in which one sees himself living on in his children. There are many forms that this

---

[118] This is the case anyway when one includes those texts which speak of the spiritual fatherhood of Holy Orders.

[119] See Wojtyła, *Love and Responsibility*, 246–47.

[120] Wojtyła, *Love and Responsibility*, 246. Wojtyła says the human person is diminished without spiritual parenthood (see *Love and Responsibility*, 247).

[121] See *Man and Woman*, 432.

[122] See *Man and Woman*, 432; see also *Mulieris dignitatem*, §19.

[123] See Wojtyła, *Love and Responsibility*, 246.

love can take. Wojtyła gives the examples of a priest's love for the souls of his flock or a teacher's love for his students. In fact, spiritual kinship is often deeper than the relationships arising from biological connections. Spiritual parenthood entails the communication, in some sense, of one's entire self.[124]

Both natural parents and those who have no biological children can be spiritual parents. They are not to wait for opportunities to come to them; rather, they ought to seek out others less spiritually mature than themselves and to try to share with them the good and the wisdom that the spiritual parents have already actualized. In addition to the spiritual parenthood of teachers and priests, spiritual fatherhood is part of the consecrated life for men and spiritual motherhood is the vocation of consecrated women. Spiritual parenthood in the consecrated life is manifested when the more spiritually advanced make themselves gifts to God and so make themselves gifts to others through great generosity, serenity, and wisdom.[125]

One finds the preponderance of references to spiritual fatherhood in the context of writings on Holy Orders. Quoting the Council of Florence (1439), John Paul II describes the various attributes and functions of the Roman Pontiff. Among these, he is the spiritual father of all Christians.[126] The vocation of spiritual fatherhood is not reserved to the Bishop of Rome, however. John Paul quotes to the Vatican II document *Christus dominus* (*CD*) to assert that the bishop's office is one of father and pastor who must "'be true fathers who excel in the spirit of love and solicitude for all and to whose divinely conferred authority all gratefully submit themselves' (*CD* 16)."[127]

Every bishop has been appointed by God "in the Church to exercise spiritual fatherhood."[128] In this text, John Paul II speaks of bishops' spiritual paternity in the same manner as he speaks of natural fatherhood.[129]

---

[124] See Wojtyła, *Love and Responsibility*, 246–47.

[125] See John Paul II, Post-Synodal Apostolic Exhortation on the Consecrated Life and Its Mission in the Church and in the World *Vita consecrata* (March 26, 1996), §70.

[126] See John Paul II, *The Church*, 276.

[127] John Paul II, *The Church*, 238.

[128] John Paul II, "Angelus, Sunday, 18 March 2001," §2, Vatican, https://www.vatican.va/content/john-paul-ii/en/angelus/2001/documents/hf_jp-ii_ang_20010318.html; the original Italian uses *paternità spirituale*.

[129] John Paul says:

> St. Joseph lived at the *service* of his Wife and Divine Son; for believers, he thus became an eloquent example of how "to reign" is "to serve." He can be seen as a helpful lesson in life especially by those who have the task of being "fathers" and

Spiritual fatherhood is one of the significant features that "form the spiritual beauty of a Bishop [which also include] Orthodoxy of doctrine, the science and art of preaching, asceticism and chastity, modesty which prevents all jealousy, disregard for material goods, the pursuit of mercy and gentleness with recourse to firmness when necessary, *spiritual fatherhood*, love for the Holy Mysteries."[130]

One of the most excellent expressions of a bishop's spiritual fatherhood is his work of evangelization, because this has as its goal the guiding of souls toward or the strengthening of faith.[131] John Paul finds this in St. Paul when he says to the Corinthians that he became their father in Christ Jesus (1 Cor 4:15). The bishop is thus involved in the continual

---

"guides" in the family, at school and in the Church. I am particularly thinking of fathers, who are celebrating their feast on the day dedicated to St. Joseph. I am also thinking of those whom God has appointed in the Church to exercise spiritual fatherhood. Allow me to mention, among these, the nine Bishops whom I will have the joy of ordaining tomorrow in St. Peter's Basilica. I ask you to pray for them and for all the Church's Pastors.

("Angelus, Sunday, 18 March 2001," §2). Joseph Atkinson's citation of St. Augustine, in the latter's *Sermon 96* and *Commentary on the Gospel of John*, is relevant to this discussion. In those texts, St. Augustine draws a parallel between fathers in a family and bishops in their churches. Based upon *Lumen gentium* §2, which calls the family a "domestic church," Atkinson argues for a primacy of spiritual leadership in the family on the part of the father, to include the "duties of preaching, teaching and admonishing *for Christ* . . . and [the] spiritual charge concerning the spiritual well-being for those within their family" (Atkinson, "Paternity in Crisis: Biblical and Philosophical Roots of Fatherhood," *Josephinum Journal of Theology* 9, no. 1 [2002]:18). He shows this also to be consonant with the biblical understanding of fatherhood as well. John Paul makes allusion to this in the passage from *Familiaris consortio* §25, which I cited earlier. Specifically, the Pope says that the father is called upon to ensure harmonious and united development and is to introduce his children to the living experience of Christ and the Church. While there is certainly an affinity here, these points of contact seem too tenuous to be able to assign to John Paul II St. Augustine's view of the natural father as a domestic priest. Another concern is that John Paul says in the cited text that the father shares the task of education with his wife, not specifically stating the father's primacy. Therefore, one cannot assign St. Augustine's view of the father as a domestic priest to John Paul II based solely on this text.

[130] John Paul II, Address to the Synod of the Chaldean Bishops, June 12, 2000, §3. Italics mine.

[131] See John Paul II, *Pastores gregis*, §26; The Vatican English translation renders the Latin *paternitas* as "spiritual fatherhood."

SPIRITUAL HUMAN FATHERHOOD

process of "begetting new life in the Spirit."[132] Bishops are also spiritual fathers to the priests in their charge.[133]

Priests also exercise their office, which one can call an office of spiritual fatherhood, by virtue of their character as an alter Christus and collaborators with their bishops. An important part of this spiritual fatherhood is the priest's sacramental ministry. Bishops, and priests as their coworkers, are the mediators through which Jesus Christ is continually present in order to bestow his grace through the administration of the sacraments to all of the faithful. This spiritual paternity is especially visible in the priest giving a new birth to life in the Spirit through the regeneration of Baptism.[134]

Priests themselves also share in their bishops' concern for the growth of the Church. Because of this, they are prohibited from political activity which inevitably involves the taking of sides. Priests must avoid political activity if they are to be spiritual fathers over all of their flock.[135] A priest's spiritual paternity is an authentic one, because of his share in Christ's priesthood. Christ's fatherhood is over all his children who are brothers and sisters in his Church.[136] John Paul tells priests that they best manifest their spiritual fatherhood through their celibate witness. In imitation of Christ, they are visible signs of the Bridegroom and his loving attentiveness for his Bride.[137]

As Christ manifested the Father, therefore, the priest also in his celibacy is "a singular sharing in God's fatherhood and in the fruitfulness of the Church, and as a witness to the world of the eschatological kingdom."[138] While the priest manifests spiritual fatherhood, John Paul says that he also manifests spiritual motherhood, giving new birth spiritually. Nevertheless, priests live this "motherhood" in a manly way, which is nothing other than spiritual fatherhood.[139] This is possible because there is close affinity between spiritual fatherhood and spiritual motherhood.[140] Before concluding this section, let us turn to John Paul's writings on

---

[132] *Pastores gregis*, §26.

[133] See John Paul II, *The Church*, 240–41.

[134] See John Paul II, *The Church*, 211.

[135] See John Paul II, *The Church*, 364.

[136] See John Paul II, Letter to Priests for Holy Thursday 1995, §4, in *Letters to My Brother Priests: 1979–2001*, ed. James Socías (Chicago: Scepter Publishers, 2001), 218.

[137] See John Paul II, *The Church*, 353.

[138] *Pastores dabo vobis*, §29.

[139] See John Paul II, Letter to Priests for Holy Thursday 1988, §4. I will evaluate this assertion about the priest being both a spiritual father and mother in part 4.

[140] See Wojtyła, *Love and Responsibility*, 246–47.

spiritual motherhood in order to determine whether there is any application of these to spiritual fatherhood.

Spiritual motherhood is motherhood according to the spirit. It takes on many forms. In the consecrated life, it is the renouncing of physical motherhood, which allows the consecrated person to express her marriage to her Spouse through a concern for all of God's people and to witness to the eschatological vocation to which all are called. Thus, virginity goes hand in hand with spiritual motherhood.[141] There is in fact a complementarity between physical motherhood and the spiritual motherhood of consecrated women. John Paul says that in comparing the two, one is married through the sacrament and the other is married spiritually to her Bridegroom.[142] Both of these represent a sincere gift of self to the G/groom, but in different manners. The spiritual motherhood of consecrated women is a sign *of God's tender love toward the human race* and [a] . . . special witnesses to the mystery of the Church, Virgin, Bride and Mother."[143] It "in a certain way reproduces the features of universality and spiritual fruitfulness of Mary's motherhood."[144]

Women outside the consecrated life manifest this same spiritual motherhood in any situation in which "we see women working with maternal devotion on behalf of orphaned, sick or abandoned children, on behalf of the poor and unfortunate, and in many works and projects inspired by Christian charity."[145] According to John Paul II, men as natural fathers or in living the evangelical counsel of chastity can, while maintaining their masculinity, also witness to these aspects of spiritual motherhood. They can, after a manner, fulfill some roles of spiritual mothers.[146]

In summarizing the attributes, roles, and tasks of spiritual fatherhood, we should recall that all men have the vocation to spiritual fatherhood whether they are married or not. For those within the marriage covenant, fatherhood can only be considered authentic if the father takes part in the nurturing of his children's souls as well as their bodies: in a word, he must nurture each child's person in its entirety. Since all men have a vocation to spiritual fatherhood, they are to seek out opportunities to help form

---

[141] See *Mulieris dignitatem*, §21.

[142] See *Mulieris dignitatem*, §21.

[143] *Vita consecrata*, §57.

[144] John Paul II, *The Church*, 609.

[145] See John Paul II, *The Church*, 495.

[146] There appears to be a tension between John Paul II's anthropology in which he indicates that sex difference is manifested in the soul and his statements that men can, in some sense, be spiritual mothers. I will address the consistency of these statements in part 4.

others who are less spiritually mature than are they. Bishops and priests have a further vocation to spiritual fatherhood in virtue of their office. The bishop is the spiritual father of his diocese. A bishop's primary task as a spiritual father is guiding lost souls to faith and strengthening the faith of his flock. No less important is the task of bishops and priests to exercise their spiritual paternity through their sacramental ministry. They must, therefore, be icons of Christ the Bridegroom through their witness of fidelity and holiness.

SYNOPSIS OF NATURAL AND SPIRITUAL FATHERHOOD IN JOHN PAUL II'S THOUGHT

Natural fathers (and spiritual fathers) have God's fatherhood as their model which they are called to radiate. Jesus's self-oblation of love is the created archetype of divine fatherhood, and St. Joseph is our model of human fatherhood. Men must make a concerted effort to understand ways in which women's femininity is an indispensable complement to their masculinity. Christian men must endeavor to live out the great mystery for the flourishing of their marriages and children. This means pouring themselves out in love to their wives, corresponding to the ineffable bond by which they become one flesh. In this way they overcome the primordial temptation to reduce the marriage to a master-slave relationship.

Husbands' authentically expressed love will help in the formation of their wives as mothers and in the formation of their children. Fathers must endeavor to nurture acceptance of their children from the moment they learn of the pregnancy, understanding the fallen effects of eccentricity on their fatherhood. They begin with a concerted effort to provide their wives with attention and support throughout the pregnancy, interiorizing the truth of the gift of his wife's motherhood. All these aspects of paternal involvement are necessary for the fruitful formation of their wife and children and building a civilization of love.

The husband-father also cultivates and trains himself as a father by recognizing his wife's primacy in the order of love, manifested in her example of trust toward him and solicitude toward others. He must allow her to complement him in the use of his paternal and husbandly authority, making his headship authentic through mutual submission. The man will deficiently use his authority, if not abuse it, if it is not complemented by his wife's loving cooperation.

The father must be aware of his wife's greater solicitude toward her unborn child. He must learn to observe this in order to cultivate his fatherhood by learning to develop the love and affection which seems to come more naturally for his wife. In broader society, men must use this experience to help overcome the diminishment which motherhood has experienced in modern culture. The ills resulting from this will be surmounted when men do their part by recognizing the heroism of motherhood and supporting women in their vocations. Many of the preceding roles and tasks are directly related to natural fatherhood and apply within the nuclear family. However, many of these roles and tasks also apply to spiritual fatherhood. Those which do can transcend the nuclear family and can apply to the manner in which men also should act in broader society.

All men are called to be spiritual fathers, even if they are not natural fathers. Spiritual fatherhood is about giving birth to another who has not yet actualized some maturity the one has attained. Spiritual fatherhood is essential for one's own fulfillment and also for a flourishing society. It is most effectively accomplished through one's being transformed in Christ.

CHAPTER 12

A Synthesis of John Paul II's Theology of Masculinity and Fatherhood

John Paul II's theology of masculinity and fatherhood must be understood from his account of man, made in the image of God with the task of attaining its intended likeness. The category of being of relation is essential to understanding the coherence of his view of personhood and sex difference, along with how fulfillment is attained from metaphysical and personal perspectives. Human personhood and sex difference are analogies which find their archetype in the Trinity, and specifically in the relation between the Father and the Son.

The fact that personhood changes ontologically toward either fulfillment or annihilation through the choices of the person are a *sine qua non* for seeing the connections among his various statements about men and fatherhood, together with their implications. The ontology of this change again requires relation as a category of being for its coherence. Because sex difference determines the specific identity of the human person and configures the mode of his nature as masculine (or feminine), and because sex difference determines the general manner in which one's personhood is fulfilled (or not), the vocational aspect of masculinity and its fulfillment in fatherhood must apprehended. We will flesh these matters out here. We are using this study of attributes, roles, and tasks to describe more specifically what we mean by "the manner of masculine and paternal fulfillment." This chapter will provide an integral account his theology of masculinity and fatherhood in these terms, using what we have extracted from his works.

Theology of Masculinity

Perhaps the best synopsis of John Paul II's theology of masculinity is to say that one can understand a man (male) only in the face of a woman. Masculinity is inherently relational, complementarily relational. It interpenetrates the entire person, having its ontology in the category of relation. Personhood also has the ontology of relation and so sex difference "modulates" the person-relation as one of two complementary possibilities. As such, sex difference forms a complementary-relational duality of masculine and feminine persons.[1]

We can say, therefore, that masculinity is constitutive of the male person inasmuch as it conditions the entirety of his personhood and modulates his nature, body and soul. Since the body expresses the soul, the body reveals the person. From gross anatomy and throughout his entire psychological, physical, emotional, and spiritual structure, down to the level of his gametes, and to every cell in his body, the radical and complete manner in which sex difference permeates the man as a body-soul unity is manifested. This means that masculinity establishes, fundamentally and irrevocably, a human male's personal identity.

One important consequence of this relationality is that while each man is an individual in himself, he is created for and called to a communion of persons with others. Such fulfillment is not self-referential but other-oriented. A man can achieve his fulfillment only through a sincere and disinterested gift of himself to another person. While this self-gift can take many forms, it is most intimately and visibly expressed as an image of the Trinitarian God through the *communio personarum* of the marital covenant. This particular call to communion demands a complementary other, without whom authentic fulfillment is not possible.

John Paul II's theology of the body, with its hylomorphic implications, indicates that the man's body reveals its spousal makeup, who the male person is, and much about his vocation. The body's spousal meaning shows man that he is meant for another person. He can see in his body that he is the natural complement to this other self and that this complementarity, while not reducible to the capacity for procreation, cannot be separated from it.

It is for these reasons that a man who is called to marriage must be

---

[1] This would seem to correspond fairly well with D. C. Schindler's account of sex difference as a mode of the substantial form (see "Perfect Difference: Gender and the Analogy of Being," *Communio* 43 [Summer 2016]: 205-15ff.), the metaphysical space for which, having been opened up by the transcendence of form in matter, is a mode of *esse* (see 210–26).

274

sincerely open to realizing an authentic vocation to natural fatherhood in matrimony. All of this is known from an integral reading of the body through the implications of the divine archetype of masculinity and fatherhood. It is confirmed by the Church, which teaches that there is an indivisible unity between the flourishing of the spouses in their reciprocal communion and the procreative meaning of marriage and the marital act. From this analysis it becomes apparent that authentic marital love is always other-oriented and that it is motivated by self-diffusiveness of the good for the sake of the other in the vocations to marriage and fatherhood. Marriage and fatherhood have their own specific, given structures which determine the manner of the man's fulfillment.

The natural complementarity between masculinity and femininity also reveals that the deepest meaning of masculinity is to offer love first and to receive love second. Masculinity reflects that within the complementarity of love, the man is to initiate love. His love is a love of initiation. John Paul II's constant references to the Trinity as the origin of marriage, particularly in terms of its procreative fruitfulness, and to the Father as the model for human fatherhood suggest there is more to be drawn from the analogy between God's fatherhood and to human masculinity and its fulfillment in fatherhood.

I propose that we find in the Father, as Origin without origin, the archetype for masculine initiative in its manifold expressions, all rooted in initiating love. In fact, as we showed in discussing Balthasar on this matter, there surely is a correspondence between the first procession and the hierarchical structure of masculine and feminine complementary love.[2] Further, as love is the ultimate *telos* of the will, which is ordered to the fulfillment of the person, we find that initiating love must permeate all aspects of the masculine person, the entire masculine mode of his body-soul unity. This permits us to discern more precisely the attributes, roles, and tasks that belong specifically to men from the divine archetype, at least to determine the manner in which they belong to him as masculine and, therefore, as initiating.

Returning to the centrality of hylomorphism in John Paul II's anthropology, we see more how profoundly initiation interpenetrates the masculine organism. The human body is not simply the result of random biological evolutionary progression: it expresses his invisible soul and so his entire personhood. The body can be "read" because a man's physical, psychological, emotional, and spiritual constitution is an expression

---

[2] See chapter 6.

of his masculine soul, which is the substantial principle of his masculine attributes given to him in order to fulfill his vocation. However, a soul is masculine because it is possessed by a masculine person.

The masculine person now experiences his masculinity in a different manner than God intended. Every man now lives in the historical experience of sin. An important result of this is that his psycho-physical structure turns out to be ambivalent when it comes to a man (male) fulfilling his vocation. Both men and women are equally subject to concupiscence; however, men's initiating structure makes them somewhat differently susceptible to temptations that can impede their masculine vocations than is the case for women and their feminine vocations. The effects of concupiscence characterize many of the masculine tasks required for the fulfillment of a man's fatherhood.

Vocation to Fatherhood

The specifically masculine vocation, revealed in part through a man's body, arises from his sex difference. His sex is the principle of properly masculine gifts and attributes that are necessary for fatherhood. Because fatherhood is a vocation, a calling, one must freely respond to it. He can either accept or reject it. However, if a man is to fulfill himself, he must not simply accept his vocation, he must embrace it. A vocation to natural fatherhood requires that one first accept the vocation to marriage and become one flesh, a *communio personarum* with his spouse.[3] His vocations as a husband and as a father are like his masculinity itself in that neither can be understood except in a relationship of reciprocity with his complementary spouse. A husband's vocational model is the great mystery (Eph 5). More specifically, a husband is called to imitate and make visible Jesus Christ, who is the Bridegroom and model for men and fathers. The husband and

---

[3] John Paul II sometimes uses the terms "one flesh" and *communio personarum* as synonyms, but at other times he seems to make a distinction between them. "One flesh" sometimes is a synonym for marital intercourse (see John Paul II, *Man and Woman He Created Them: A Theology of the Body*, trans. Michael Waldstein [Boston: Pauline Books and Media, 2006], 165, 167ff.); however, John Paul also seems to use it to indicate the complete moral unity of husband and wife (see *Man and Woman*, 207, 480, 484). In the latter case, it seems that he wants to use the most intimate expression of marital unity as a synecdoche. By contrast, he most often uses the term *communio personarum*, or communion of persons, to indicate the fullness of the marital union of husband and wife (see *Man and Woman*, 349). Here I intend to use "one flesh" in the second manner, as a synecdoche for the entire *communio personarum* by means of its most intimate visible expression.

father is called to give his very self as an oblation for the sanctification of his wife and family.

Every man is also called to spiritual fatherhood. For natural fathers, this is first directed toward their own children. However, for all men it is a call to employ their masculine gifts to help in the spiritual maturation of those who are put in their lives. This certainly applies to men of all ages who find themselves in the single state, whether or not it is by their own choice. The fatherhood to which all men are called can be expressed toward anyone in need of paternal solicitude. It is essential for such men not to mourn a natural fatherhood lost or never realized, while neglecting to share their paternal love and wisdom with those in front of them who can benefit from it. Some men are called to spiritual fatherhood as priests or as non-ordained in religious life. For such men, spiritual fatherhood is also modeled on Christ, who reveals the love of the Father, even if it differs somewhat from that of natural fathers. These spiritual fathers are responsible for the spiritual maturity of those put in their charge, using the gifts proper to their state.

THEOLOGY OF FATHERHOOD

Man, as male and female, is made in the image of a Trinitarian God. He is made after the image of a divine *communio personarum* for communion with God and with other persons. He also has the capacity for a particular type of communion with a specific complementary person in a way that serves and promotes communions of love. Masculine personhood is made to reflect divine love in the manner of a love of initiative in a relationship with a female person who is ordered to the active reception of his love. Yet the Trinitarian archetype reveals something more about masculine personhood. Masculinity also reflects the Trinitarian Father, after whom all created fatherhood is named (see Ephesians 3:15).

While motherhood also reflects God's perfection, human fatherhood is a unique participation in divine fatherhood bestowing upon human fathers a multiplicity of proper gifts needed to carry out their vocation to fatherhood. All of this comes from the fatherhood of God as Origin of the godhead. The task to radiate God's fatherhood, who is the model for human fatherhood, perhaps best characterizes John Paul II's theology of human fatherhood. To accomplish this task, John Paul emphasizes the need for fathers to be like Jesus Christ in his solicitude for his own Bride, following St. Paul's emphasis on the love men must have for their wives in the great mystery (see Eph 5). It is also because transformation in Christ is the only remedy to the manner in which concupiscence distorts his masculine gifts and threatens the authenticity of his fatherhood. St. Joseph is the extraordinary example of the self-immolation required of husbands and fathers in order for them to flourish in the fallen world.

Fatherhood complementarily cooperates with motherhood in order to bring about covenant communion, reflected in relationships of selfless love. Flourishing marriages and families have the task of contributing to a civilization of love. This is a task which begins with man as a unity of body and soul. The soul is the principle of man's end of communion, made possible through his intellect and will. The body, however, makes him a solitude. This solitude must be transcended through communion, that is, through fruitful relationships of selfless love, the aggregates of which are called communities.

There is a hierarchy of communities which man requires in order to flourish and to fulfill himself. The hierarchy begins with the foundational communities of marriage and family. Families prepare men for and, in a sense, comprise higher levels of human community: local societies, the Church, broader society, the state, etcetera. Fatherhood is the vocation that serves these communities at all levels, in the way of promoting the common good through a love of initiation. Families are served primarily by natural fatherhood, but all levels of community need to be served by authentic spiritual fatherhood.

Fatherhood describes how every man will find his fulfillment. His masculine personhood gives him the faculties of consciousness and efficacy through which he may fulfill himself. But he is fulfilled only through a free human act (*actus humanus*) of love. Only free human acts ordered to the common good (the concurrent good of self, family, and society) can achieve the character of self-transcendence, which characterizes authentic fulfillment. But again, man lives in a fallen state.

His concupiscence inclines him toward rejection of his call to fatherhood because of fear, selfishness, and an intense tendency to reduce the meaning of sex to the pursuit of pleasure. To the degree a human act falls short of selfless love, it is imperfect or even evil. Such acts distort the essence of the person by turning him inward upon himself, leaving him alone. Concupiscence greatly increases the difficulty of the task of developing his self-mastery, self-possession, and self-transcendence. Succumbing to sin inhibits successfully accomplishing the task. In fact, he can only accomplish this tremendous task of self-transcendence because he now lives in the horizon of redemption.

Jesus Christ is the solution to this problem. He manifests the model for all fatherhood in the horizon of redemption. He reveals the Father who is the archetype for all fatherhood. He also reveals man to himself and so makes it clear that man's calling is to fulfillment through a love of total self-gift; its highest expression is the Cross. Man can only fulfill his call to mediate the Father through his transformation in an authentic, masculine life in Christ. This transformation and radiation of authentic fatherhood require tremendous effort and attentiveness to achieving self-possession.

As he increasingly possesses himself, he will make use of this freedom to progressively transcend himself and his selfish interests through increasingly pure, concrete acts of selfless love. The man of concupiscence cannot accomplish this through his own resources. Such self-transcending love can be achieved only through cooperation with the undeserved gift of grace, which is participation in the divine nature (see 2 Peter 1:4).

This personal actualization is essential to human personhood, and as with all real relations the actualization appears as an accidental form inhering in the soul. These accidental forms provide the metaphysically concrete structure for the essence of relations in hylomorphic persons. The forms also "register" the fruits of sanctifying grace (i.e., the theological virtues) and the maturation of the human virtues, allowing them to perdure and permit the man to build upon his achievements in the way of personal fulfillment. The forms also register and make concrete any deformation of relational personhood when the person chooses vice and sin. This is the metaphysical account which underlies John Paul's understanding of self-transcendence and personal fulfillment in holiness.

Every human person is called to holiness, which is perfection in selfless love. Fatherhood is the pathway by which a male person fulfills himself by giving himself away. It ultimately describes the manner in which a man authentically lives out his masculine vocation, which also structures his very identity. As a person, a man must transcend himself, through self-mastery and self-possession, in order to give himself away as a gift. That is, a man is fulfilled according to the measure to which he selflessly gives of himself in order to nurture another person in the way of a love of initiation. The vocation to fatherhood is perhaps fulfilled for most men in natural fatherhood, but spiritual fatherhood characterizes the path to fulfillment for every man. He must seek out and selflessly give himself to others with respect to those among whom he has greater spiritual maturity. His spiritual paternity aims to bring to fruit the same maturity in the other, who becomes his spiritual daughter or son.

Men also have the obligation to participate in contributing to the common good of society as fathers, and to lead their natural and spiritual families to do the same. Participation reflects the person's social identity, one who is created for his own sake, but to fulfill himself by sharing himself with others. Social participation is essential to personal fulfillment because it is a more Trinitarian manner of cooperating with God in his continuing creation. Here again there is a specific manner in which the father participates in society mirroring the unique way in which he reflects God's creative love.

A man's manner of cocreation is shaped by his initiating love. While a woman receives and takes into herself in order to cocreate, a man's masculine structure makes his role extrinsic. John Paul's view corresponds with this as having its origin in the divine archetype, specifically from the Father as sole origin of divinity. The Father as Origin in relation to the Son is the archetype of initiation in the created order.[4]

Masculine creativity is manifested in many manners, but it always has the character of initiation, remaining on the outside, so to speak, of his work. These are tasks which bring the man out into the world to creatively manipulate it in order to have dominion over it, but at the same time they leave him on the outside of the process. This much can be seen through his dominant presence in roles such as that of a hunter to conquer and possess food, as a farmer to manipulate the land to harvest food, in manufacturing to manipulate the world to meet his needs, and in contemporary science and technology which controls the world in more efficient manners to serve his needs and desires.

This masculine characteristic takes a particular form in his creativity and calling to work as a father. John Paul sees in St. Joseph this close connection between fatherhood and work, coming from Joseph's extraordinary manifestation of God's fatherhood.[5] A father's tasks are to cooperate with God in ongoing creation, but they have the purpose of radiating God's paternal love, so of working to support his wife and family. This is seen in the predominant sense of a man that he should provide for his wife and family. While there are certainly exceptions, this inclination transcends societal norms because it arises from his masculine structure. For this reason, I would submit masculine initiative and its implications

---

[4]   This is the reason the tradition refers to the Father as Creator, though this is done under the rubric of divine appropriations, as all three create.

[5]   See John Paul II, Homily on the Solemnity of St. Joseph, March 19, 1983, Termoli, Italy; and Homily on the Feast of St. Joseph during his pastoral visit to the Archdiocese of Sorrento-Castellammare di Stabia, March 19, 1992, *L'Osservatore Romano*, English ed., March 1992.

should be considered in the couple's manifold decisions with respect to organizing their home life.

Facilitating and promoting social participation for himself and his family is a crucial task for fathers because human dignity requires that man fulfill his personhood by promotion of the common good through becoming cocreators with God. This cocreation is seen at its most fundamental manifestation in procreation and nurturing of children, but it also occurs through acts of spiritual fatherhood (and motherhood) in neighborhoods, in the workplace, in parish life, in the economic and political spheres, in academia, and in all manners of intermediate social structures (i.e., those mediating between and among persons, families, and the state). The masculine inclination to go out into the world comes with the gifts necessary for the man to take the lead in keeping the family from turning in on itself, which would attenuate its flourishing, and to go out into the world and share itself as a gift through social participation, and especially through evangelization.

Attributes of a Father

John Paul II's writings reveal a number of paternal attributes explicitly and implicitly. They are important because they either help us to understand more deeply particular paternal roles or tasks, or they dictate to some extent how the father is to perform them. While our list is not exhaustive, they still provide the basis for a man to flourish as a man, husband, and father. They provide an outline of the essential aspects of family life that are necessary to promote the flourishing of his wife and children. They also reflect the manner in which his masculine gifts are brought to maturity as a father through giving himself in an initiating manner of love.

Articulating these attributes is important for two reasons. First, a man possesses his attributes in a fallen state and this conditions the way he experiences himself and his gifts. Masculine gifts bias him in a manner that can contribute to difficulty in his overcoming concupiscent inclinations. This fallen experience of his masculinity can, in turn, tempt him away from his vocations as a husband and father. Second, even when his gifts don't contribute to sin, they still present themselves as a task to him if he is to employ them authentically. Understanding a man's paternal attributes is needed to address these two issues.

The attribute of masculine initiative is rooted in masculine personhood and complementary love in which he first gives love to his wife whose feminine structure responds by accepting and returning his love. All relationships of love require mutual trust. However, his initiative requires that a man take the risk of being rejected by a woman, leaving in him an acute sense of his need to be trusted for his masculine value to be affirmed. His inexperience with and fear of trusting is perhaps connected to the fact that a relationship begins with his initiating love, and if the woman receives it, he need not be attentive either to the secondary responses of initiation on her part or to active reception on his. Therefore, his experience of relationships does not necessarily require of him either submission or the trust necessary for it. Nevertheless, the husband's need to be trusted continues to be manifested in his relationship with his wife and always affects their interpersonal dynamics.

The father's masculine makeup also provides him with the structure for merciful love, which is the way in which masculine initiating love is experienced, especially when it continues to be offered even after it has been rejected. The realization of the steadfastness of paternal love even while being undeserved can move a child to desire his transformation. It permits the child to reinterpret paternal sternness as medicinal love. This fatherly, merciful love has the ability to draw his children to repentance for their transgressions. Merciful love is a powerful attribute in the nurturing of children, and so a father must tirelessly offer his merciful love to his children in imitation of the Father.

Masculine initiative also gives rise to the attribute of headship in the marriage and in the family. However, this headship must be understood in terms of mutual subjection between himself and his wife. Headship can easily tempt the man to abuse his authority for self-serving motivations. St. John Paul II is emphatic that every husband must endeavor to overcome this fallen tendency. For this to happen, there must be a real submission of the husband to his wife's primacy in the order of love. He cannot authentically exercise his husbandly and paternal authority without her tutorship in love and complementary assistance in the order of receptive love.

In addition, a man's masculine initiating structure is manifested as an eccentric and external orientation throughout the entire masculine organism. The husband's externality is most visibly apparent in the process of pregnancy, in which he remains on the outside of the process. This demands that he actively work to overcome the inclination to accept remaining on the outside and within himself. He has to learn to turn out of himself through experiencing the mutuality of their pregnancy by observing his wife. The self-transcendence he learns in his wife's pregnancy must be applied throughout family life, again by his attentiveness to observing his wife. The husband-father has the ongoing obligation to master himself to overcome the fallen tendencies of masculine eccentricity and its inclination to remain on the outside of family life.

As a masculine person, a husband, and a father, the man is metaphysically relational. He has a complementary relation to his wife which is made visible in the complementarity of their bodies, but its foundation is in the complementarity of their persons, ordered to reciprocal love. This relation gives rise to and forms the basis of their marital relationship and their joint vocation as parents. It touches, in some manner, every aspect of their marriage and family life.

TASKS AND ROLES OF A FATHER

John Paul II teaches that fatherhood is a gift from God as well as a participation in God's own fatherhood. As such, a father's role can be successfully fulfilled only to the degree to which he is able to radiate God's fatherhood to his family. Therefore, his tasks and roles must conform to his masculine initiating love, imbued with the paternal attributes we have just discussed.

As we might intuit, the first of these tasks arises from the foundational attribute of masculine initiative. It is the vocation to imitate Christ in the great mystery. The husband-father is called to mediate Christ the Bridegroom, who makes visible the fatherhood of God. In order to manifest the love with which Christ loves the Church, the husband-father needs to make himself a sacrificial offering after the manner of St. Joseph. He must give himself in such a way that his first concerns in life, after his duties to God, are his wife's and children's integral good, which is first their salvation and then all other aspects of their human welfare. As part of this spousal, self-giving love, he has the task of ongoing fidelity by which he habitually manifests and deepens his trustworthiness and commitment to his covenant promises.

The task of fidelity requires that he recognize his fallen state and how it works against his masculine gifts. In general, this requires he intentionally and proactively cultivate his vocation as a husband, and especially as a father. This means being attentive to how he exercises his familial headship. He is responsible for ensuring that his headship conforms to Christ's tender and saving love. Initiating love uncompleted by secondary receptive love can be perceived by the recipient as stern and harsh and can foster rebellion in his children.

In order to share his masculine love in terms of paternal authority in a more authentic manner, he has the task of recognizing his wife's primacy in the order of receptive love and then subjecting himself to her love out of reverence for Christ. When the husband observes his wife's attentiveness to the whole person and listens to her advice to temper his more aggressive inclinations for addressing matters of discipline, for example, he exercises his authority on behalf of the family in a more authentic manner.

A husband also has the task of recognizing the gift of his wife as a person and the gift of her motherhood. This includes the task of treating his wife as a friend in a relationship of equal dignity and reciprocity. It also implies the respect due by all men to every woman in every aspect of society, since marriage and the family are the fundaments of society. In marriage, the husband-father must direct the general Christian task of increasing in virtue and cooperating with the grace of the sacraments toward his more specific vocation in order to overcome his concupiscent inclinations.

Christian marriage gives the husband the task of cooperating with the privileged means of grace proper to the Sacrament of Marriage which he receives from his wife for the sake of his marriage and children. Moreover, the husband has the task of mediating to his wife that very same grace, which he does through his intentional acts of love for her. In this way, he super-naturalizes his efforts as a husband toward his task of helping to form his wife as a person and especially as a mother.[6]

The husband-father has manifold obligations as head of the family. John Paul accepts that he is responsible for the family's overall leadership and guidance. However, he is adamant that the husband must effect his leadership in an authentic way; he must provide it in the way of service to the family. The husband as initiator of love and its attendant quality of leadership, must engage in decision-making with his wife through mutual reciprocity.[7] This is a demand of mutual submission.

---

[6] John Paul II says that the husband must form his wife through his love but he does not indicate a reciprocal formation of the husband through love on the part of the wife. Rather, it appears that the wife's formation of her husband is as a father through her example of motherhood.

[7] The matter of leadership in the context of reciprocal decision making is implicit in John Paul II's work, particularly in his discussion of Joseph as head and defender of the Holy Family (see John Paul II, Apostolic Exhortation on the Person and Mission of Saint Joseph in the Life of Christ and of the Church *Redemptoris custos* [August 15, 1989], AAS 82 [1990], 5–34, §28). Though I have not found him to address it directly. May agrees with the notion that reciprocity between the husband and wife is required in decision making. However, he points out one important implication of the husband's headship with an occasional family situation, which I believe is in concert with John Paul's theology of fatherhood: "Authority, in short, is not power but decision making. Within marriage and family, both husband and wife . . . have their own responsibility to make

As a father, he has the task of jointly raising his children with his wife, but he has the added task of observing his wife to help him to discover and cultivate his fatherhood. These tasks include observing her openness to new life and the tender solicitude she shows for their child. Thereby, he can develop the deep desire to be a father that he likely will not initially experience. He begins the acquisition of this desire by an immediate, interior acceptance of responsibility for his child the moment that he learns of his existence. He can do this through his increased attentiveness to his wife, his solicitude for the added burdens she experiences due to the pregnancy, and his enthusiastic support for the activities to which she is inclined in preparing for the arrival of the child.

The father also has a variety of tasks associated with raising his children. He is called to provide a Christian example to his children in their formation, so that they learn authentic freedom, the sincere gift of self, solidarity, participation in family and society, and respect for others. John Paul wishes men to be aware of the unique influence a father has on his children in this regard. In his love for his children, a father is called to show the masculine dimension of the Father's merciful love. The children must recognize in their father's love his fidelity to his fatherhood and that the offer of forgiveness is always there to be received the moment they repent of any transgressions they might commit.

A father must learn from his wife how to do this with a receptive tenderness. He has the obligation to correct his children in a way which is of one mind with his wife. Together with his wife, he has the obligation to nurture his children as members of his family, of society, and as members of the Church. However, he has the primary responsibility for the family's harmonious and united development and for the witness to God's fatherhood which will introduce the children into the living experience of Christ and the Church.

The father, together with his wife, is responsible for the children's material needs such as food, clothing, and shelter. However, I have inferred

---

decisions. . . . Naturally, the spouses should communicate as fully as possible regarding decisions affecting the family's common good. They should seek consensus. . . . At times consensus is not reached, but a decision must be made. . . . In such instances, the responsibility (and authority) for making a decision lies with the father" (William May, "The Mission of Fatherhood," *Josephinum Journal of Theology* 9, no. 1 [2002]: 55). However, I would add that I believe John Paul would insist these situations should be rare. I will further address the consistency of this with his Apostolic Letter on the Dignity and Vocation of Women *Mulieris dignitatem* (August 15, 1988), AAS 80 (1988), 1653–1729, §24, in part 4.

from John Paul's anthropology that the father has the primary responsibility for providing, through work, the resources which make this material nurturing possible, at least during the period of child development in which it is important for the mother to be in the home. In addition, the father must ensure that his work outside the home is not a cause of family division. His provision for his children's intellectual formation in secular and religious knowledge is a shared responsibility with his wife, but one that respects their complementary masculine and feminine gifts. In terms of the gospel, the father's masculine gifts give him the task of helping his children to experience it as an idea, as truth to which Christians must conform themselves, and as a means for properly directing their lives.

All men have the vocation to spiritual fatherhood. They have the task to seek out opportunities to help form others with less spiritual maturity than they have. Bishops and priests have a vocation to spiritual fatherhood over their dioceses and parishes respectively. A bishop's task of spiritual fatherhood is in leading souls to the faith and in strengthening the faith of those over whom he has charge. Bishops and priests must also exercise their spiritual paternity through their ministry of the sacraments. They are to be icons of the Bridegroom through their witness of fidelity and holiness. Non-ordained religious have a similar task to help bring about spiritual maturity in their brothers.

Part Four

ASSESSING JOHN PAUL II'S THEOLOGY OF MASCULINITY AND FATHERHOOD

CHAPTER 13

Is It Coherent?

There are four main issues that appear to pose difficulties for the internal coherence of John Paul II's theology of masculinity and fatherhood. We will look at each of the following concerns in turn: mutual submission, sexual differences and the spiritual realm, concupiscence and vocation, and consecrated and priestly celibacy.

MUTUAL SUBMISSION

We touched on the issue of mutual submission in chapter 11.[1] To put the problem into context, recall that in John Paul II's theology of fatherhood we saw that while he may not emphasize it, he does explicitly show the husband and father to have a leadership role in the marriage and in family life, and so headship implies having the authority required to exercise it.[2] In his responsibility of headship, the husband's natural initiative must be expressed in a Christlike, selfless, gentle, and strong love for his wife and children in order to accomplish his unique responsibilities authentically, which includes ensuring the family's "harmonious and united development."[3] The husband's headship is foundational to St. John Paul II's interpretation of the great mystery; nevertheless, John Paul is emphatic

---

[1] "Subjection" is the term used in the English translation of *Mulieris dignitatem*, while "submission" is the term Waldstein selects in his critical translation of *Man and Woman*. I will use them interchangeably here.

[2] See, e.g., John Paul II, Apostolic Exhortation on the Person and Mission of Saint Joseph in the Life of Christ and of the Church *Redemptoris custos* (August 15, 1989), AAS 82 (1990), 5–34, §8, in which he acknowledges St. Joseph's headship and authority over the Holy Family.

[3] John Paul II, Apostolic Exhortation on the Role of the Christian Family in the Modern World *Familiaris consortio* (November 22, 1981), *AAS* 74 (1982), 114–37, §25.

that the great mystery presents a "gospel innovation" in terms of headship, which first century Palestinians did not yet appreciate.[4]

John Paul II draws attention to the Pauline admonition that out of reverence for Christ, there is to be mutual subjection between the husband and the wife (see Eph 5:21). The husband is called to give himself up for his wife's sanctification, even to the point of surrendering his own life.[5] He clearly wants to stress that what is new in the "ethos of redemption" is mutuality in submission between husband and wife.[6] Prior to Christ, the old ethos of Israel understood submission to be one-sided, on the part of the woman to her husband.[7] One must ask if John Paul II is consistent in calling the husband head and giving him the position of authority and leadership in the family with this development of mutual submission.[8]

As we have seen, John Paul II never rejects the traditional interpretation, which places the husband-father in authority over his wife and family and which the magisterium has affirmed.[9] In fact, he obliquely ratifies it in discussing the passage from Ephesians 5, in which John Paul affirms that the inspired author himself accepts as the "mentality and customs of that time."[10] He affirms the husband as "head" in the analogy with Christ as head of the Church.[11] Yet, one must also admit that his exposition of the husband's headship is almost exclusively in terms of Jesus Christ's giving himself for his Church.[12] Moreover, John Paul II consistently emphasizes the reciprocity of the relationship between two equal partners in the marriage covenant. Prima facie there might seem to be no room for a headship which entails the submission of the wife to the husband's authority in mutual submission. If this were so, there would be a rupture with prior Magisterial teachings, but of course this is not the case.

---

[4] See John Paul II, Apostolic Letter on the Dignity and Vocation of Women *Mulieris dignitatem* (August 15, 1988), AAS 80 (1988), 1653–1729, §24.

[5] *Mulieris dignitatem*, §24.

[6] *Mulieris dignitatem*, §24.

[7] *Mulieris dignitatem*, §24.

[8] Indeed, Charles Curran claims John Paul II's "mutual submission" is a liberal interpretation which is in contradiction with the meaning of Scripture; see Charles Curran, *The Moral Theology of John Paul II* (New York: T&T Clark, 2005), 56.

[9] See, e.g., Leo XIII, Encyclical Letter on Christian Marriage *Arcanum divinae sapientiae* (February 10, 1880), AAS 12 (1879/80), 389; and Pius XI, Encyclical Letter on Christian Marriage *Casti connubii* (Dec 31, 1930), AAS 22 (1930), 539ff.

[10] John Paul II, *Man and Woman He Created Them: A Theology of the Body*, trans. Michael Waldstein (Boston: Pauline Books and Media, 2006), 474.

[11] *Mulieris dignitatem*, §24.

[12] *Man and Woman*, 481. This point is significant.

John Paul points out that the Pauline text of the great mystery begins by discussing the prescription to mutual subjection of husband and wife out of reverence for Christ (see Eph 5:21). Mutual subjection is an unexplored point of the great mystery pericope that John Paul wishes now to bring to the fore, because he is convinced that it clarifies and deepens the traditional teaching of the wife's submission to her husband.[13] It indicates that the wife's subjection is not one-sided and that it cannot be read as her subservience to her husband. Rather, the deeper meaning of subjection is a mutual subjection out of reverence for Christ who gave himself for his Bride. For husband and wife, subjection is the manner of living the reciprocal marital relationship. It indicates that the husband and wife should be motivated in their relationship by their (and the Church's) relationship with Christ.

The Bride's relationship with the Bridegroom is not one of one-sided domination, so neither can this be the relationship between husband and wife. Moreover, because Christ is Lord of both spouses, the reverence they both have for him must enliven their mutual subjection of each to the other. In other words, Christian piety should motivate and inform the spouses' mutual subjection as expressions of love for Christ.[14] Christ is the source and model for this subjection. He subjected himself in service to his Bride for the sake of redemptive spousal love. The Christian experience of Christ's relationship with his Church teaches that the submission of the wife to the husband can be nothing like domination.[15] Indeed, her subjec-

---

[13] Prudence Allen calls this emphasis on mutual subjection "a contemporary development in papal teaching" ("Sex and Gender Differentiation in Hildegard of Bingen and Edith Stein," *Communio* 20 [Summer 1993]: 410). Allen says that the Pope shifts the traditional thinking of a one-sided subjection based upon creation to an equality at this level (see "Sex and Gender Differentiation," 411). Grabowski agrees, finding that this is "one of the most important yet neglected developments of doctrine found in the teaching of Pope John Paul II" ("Mutual Submission and Trinitarian Self-Giving," *Angelicum* 74 [1997]: 487).

[14] *Man and Woman*, 473.

[15] John Paul is emphatic in repeating this:

Love excludes every kind of submission by which the wife would become a servant or a slave of the husband, an object of one-sided submission. Love makes the *husband simultaneously subject* to the wife, and *subject* in this *to the Lord himself*, as the wife is to the husband. The community or unity that they should constitute because of marriage is realized through a reciprocal gift, which is also a mutual submission. Christ is the source and at the same time the model of that submission—which, being reciprocal "in the fear of Christ," confers on the conjugal union a deep and mature character. Many factors of a psychological and

tion to his headship is synonymous with the submission that constitutes her active reception (her "yes") to her husband's offer of initiating love.

While John Paul II makes it clear that in Christ subjection is mutual, he merely asserts the wife's submission to her husband's headship.[16] He does not seem to see it prudent to explicate the positive content of the wife's submission to her husband beyond his affirmation of the scriptural admonition of ready obedience, which is almost certainly due to the problem that mutual submission has not yet been appropriated into the life of the Church.[17] Yet, neither does he seem to discuss the man's submission to his wife. The majority of his discussion about the man's responsibilities appears to be in regard to qualifying his exercise of authority. This leaves much room for argument about exactly what constitutes the man's submission to his wife.

Grabowski argues that the authentic development of doctrine that St. John Paul II promotes is a mutual submission of the husband in the same order, that is, both spouses owe obedience to one another in the order of authority.[18] If this were not the case, he states that it would violate the

---

moral nature are so transformed in this source and before this model that they give rise, I would say, to a new and precious "fusion" of the conduct and relations on both sides.

(*Man and Woman*, 473–74).

[16] May, however, rightly points out the implications of John Paul II's statements in *Familiaris consortio* §25. May says: "[The Pope] clearly assigns to [the husband] a leadership role, one emphasizing the husband/father's service to his family. He likewise implies that the exercise of authority by the husband/father within the family is both proper and necessary, for how could he 'reveal' and 'relive' the very Fatherhood of God by ensuring the 'harmonious and united development of all the members of the family' unless there was some authority proper and exclusive to him as husband and father." William May, "The Mission of Fatherhood," *Josephinum Journal of Theology* 9, no. 1 (2002): 43.

[17] John Paul writes:

St. Paul not only wrote: "In Christ Jesus . . . there is no more man or woman," but also wrote: "There is no more slave or freeman." Yet how many generations were needed for such a principle to be realized in the history of humanity through the abolition of slavery! And what is one to say of the many forms of slavery to which individuals and peoples are subjected, which have not yet disappeared from history? But *the challenge presented by the "ethos" of the Redemption* is clear and definitive. All the reasons in favour of the "subjection" of woman to man in marriage must be understood in the sense of a "mutual subjection" of both "out of reverence for Christ."

(*Mulieris dignitatem*, §24).

[18] Grabowski, "Mutual Submission," 499ff.

communio personarum of the Trinitarian archetype.[19] We will address first the issue of what the submission of the husband to his wife entails, and then treat the concern over the violation of the *communio personarum* if mutual submission were to be asymmetrical.

John Paul obliquely adopts and develops Pope Pius XI's application of St. Augustine's "order of love" to the complementary relationship of husband to wife.[20] In fact, Pius appears to take initial steps toward articulating a theology of mutual submission in which he declares women to have a primacy in the home in this order of love as a complement to the husband's headship, by which he has a primacy in "ruling" (*regimen*).[21] We see John Paul explicitly embrace this same Augustinian "order of love," which was introduced magisterially in *Casti connubii,* and women's specific relation to it, when he affirms that "the dignity of women is measured by the order of love."[22] In fact, John Paul says that it is in God's providence that "woman is the one in whom the *order of love* in the created world of persons takes first root."[23]

Primacy in the order of love, which Pius says the wife must claim, is the primacy to which St. John Paul II says the man must subject himself.[24] While women are as much subject to concupiscence and sin as are men, the way they possess their human nature means that they are influenced in different manners. All things being equal, the wife is more suited to the living out the order of love than is the husband in this fallen world. For these reasons, much of what John Paul says in qualifying the husband's headship in terms of giving himself up for his wife in order to enter into Christ's transformation of spousal love into redemptive love, I would say, is a description of the man's submission to his wife.[25]

---

[19] Grabowski, "Mutual Submission," 499–508.

[20] See Pius XI, *Casti connubii*, §26.

[21] Pius XI, *Casti connubii*, §27. Michael Healy provides an important analysis of *Casti connubii* in which he shows how Pius XI qualifies headship and subjection in terms of the equality of husband and wife, identifying nine major points showing that Pius is already preparing the ground for what John Paul will more fully articulate in *Mulieris dignitatem* and his doctrine of mutual subjection. Michael Healy, "Reading *Casti Connubii* (and the Tradition) in Light of the Insights of JPII," *The Personalist Project* (blog), August 31, 2012, http://www.thepersonalistproject.org/home/comments/reading_casti_connubii_and_the_tradition_in_light_of_the_insights_of_jpii.

[22] *Mulieris dignitatem*, §29.

[23] *Mulieris dignitatem*, §29, emphasis mine.

[24] See *Casti connubii*, §27; our term "primacy" in the official English translation uses "chief place"; the Latin uses *principatus*.

[25] See *Man and Woman*, 478.

This can be seen more clearly as we now turn to Grabowski's concern over whether denying that the woman has the same authority as the man possesses ruptures John Paul II's Trinitarian analogy for marriage as an image of the Trinitarian *communio personarum*. In other words, authority of one over the other could seem to obviate the reciprocity of the *communio* relationship. The first thing that could be offered is that with all analogies there is both a similarity and difference between the objects of the analogy. In the Trinity, there is one divine will. In marriage, there coexist two human wills, and so each partner has the vocation to confirm his or her will to God's will. The more both do so, the more the individual will of each can conform to that of the other. Though, even where there is no discord there is still the need for leadership, even in unified decision-making.

In a fallen world, the correspondence of human wills to both the divine will and to one another is a difficult task not easily achieved. In the best of cases a lack of accord between two human wills might be due, for example, to a sincere inability to concur on which decision is most in line with God's will before the decision must be made. It is in such circumstances that the hierarchical familial structure (which is a reflection of the Trinitarian archetype) will assist in resolving such an impasse. In these cases, the wife must be willing to subordinate her will to her husband's leadership.[26] His leadership of course must be authentic authority and not abusive power, to which she need not submit. If the husband does need to exercise his *regimen* before a mutual decision can be achieved, he does so authentically only when he is doing so by dying to himself and guiding his family in the direction that will be most beneficial to the entire family's flourishing.[27]

Yet, Grabowski's point does not seem adequately addressed by simply referring to the obvious differences of the analogy. More must be said, then, about the similarity to the Trinitarian archetype in order to show how it is positively manifested in the spousal relationship, and in order to shed more light on what John Paul II means by "mutual submission." The first step in doing so is to reexamine more precisely the orders of authority and of love to achieve more clarity. While it is helpful to refer to the orders of authority and love as distinct orders, a closer look at St. Augustine's description

---

[26] See *Casti connubii*, §15.

[27] In fact, in some cases his exercise of leadership could also be manifested by his deferring to his wife's opinion when he recognizes her thinking could be more likely to conform with God's will than his.

as Pius XI explains it shows that the order of love subsumes the husband's primacy in authority as well as the wife's primacy in love.[28] This brings us closer to understanding what John Paul II means when he explains the husband's subjection in terms of Christ's headship on the Cross, and when he says that the wife's submission, in the context of Ephesians 5:22–23, "means above all the experiencing of love."[29]

To see what I mean, let us fill in the missing mediating analogy between the Trinitarian *communio* and the spousal relationship, which is the great mystery. This is the analogy after all, upon which John Paul devotes most of his attention in explicating mutual submission.[30] The Trinitarian *communio* is most perfectly manifested by Christ in his relationship with his Church.[31] In this great mystery, the analogy of Trinitarian *communio* is revealed for human spousal love. John Paul characterizes love as the transcending of one's own "I" to form a "we," which in spousal love transforms the "we" into reciprocal, total self-giving of persons.[32]

This "I-thou" which forms a "we" in total self-giving, is a one-flesh union, manifesting the radical unity of total self-giving Trinitarian love. In the Bridegroom-Bride, the one-flesh union—the Head and Body of the Church—is formed, John Paul says, when Christ gives himself up for her and transforms spousal love into redeeming love.[33] This is the archetype for spousal love in which the two totally give themselves, entering into the Cross, as only Christian spouses can do, for the salvation of one another. Inasmuch as both husband and wife have a common human nature, there is a certain equivalence here. Yet, as we have said, they possess their natures differently and so they love one another in a complementarily different way—and this complementarity belongs to the essence of human, spousal love.[34]

Returning to the passage which provided the foundation for understanding John Paul II's view of the complementarity of sex difference as the hierarchy of love, we can see where complementary love provides for the husband's headship, which must simultaneously submit itself to his wife's primacy in love. John Paul observes that in the mutual submission of spouses to one another, which is especially expressed in the union of their

---

[28] See *Casti connubii*, §26.

[29] *Man and Woman*, 485.

[30] See *Man and Woman*, 465–91.

[31] See *Man and Woman*, 477–78.

[32] See Karol Wojtyła, *Love and Responsibility*, trans. Grzegorz Ignatik (Boston: Pauline Books & Media, 2013), 78–83.

[33] *Man and Woman*, 478.

[34] See the discussion on sex and the human person in chapter 6 above.

persons manifested in the body, there is a complementary difference which reflects Christ's union with the Church:

> Although the spouses should be "subject to one another in the fear of Christ" . . . , the husband is above all the one who loves and the wife, by contrast, is the one who is loved. One might even venture the idea that the wife's "submission" to the husband, understood in the context of the whole of Ephesians 5:22–23, means above all "the experiencing of love." This is all the more so, because this "submission" refers to the image of the submission of the Church to Christ, which certainly consists in experiencing his love.[35]

In referring to the man who loves and the woman who is loved, John Paul refers to the complementarity of love in which the man first initiates love and the woman first actively receives it. This initiating love is the essence of headship and its authority. The wife submits to her husband's headship by saying yes to his love and all that comes with it, and so John Paul says she experiences (initiating) love. Yet, this is only the first movement in the hierarchy of complementary love. The woman then secondarily initiates love and the man must secondarily and actively receive it. If the woman experiences love in her submission, so must the man.

John Paul infers that the order of love originates in the Trinitarian processions in which the Holy Spirit is the personal hypostasis of love, and he further says that this is manifested by the Incarnate Son—the Bridegroom, in his relationship with the Bride. John Paul then again affirms the hierarchical structure of love manifested by complementarity in the order of love, saying, "The author of the Letter to the Ephesians calls Christ 'the Bridegroom' and the Church 'the Bride,' [so] he indirectly confirms through this analogy *the truth about woman as bride.* The Bridegroom is the one who loves. The Bride is loved: *it is she who receives love, in order to love in return.*"[36]

Spousal love is in fact the mutual submission of each to the offer of the total self-gift of the other, distinguishing it from all other forms of love. This submission (ὑποτάσσω) of the great mystery, then, is the surrender of

---

[35] *Man and Woman*, 485.

[36] *Mulieris dignitatem*, §29. While John Paul does not draw attention to this point, I might point out that the asymmetry in the husband and wife's submission is highlighted by an oblique reference to the husband's headship in relation to Christ's at the end of the great mystery pericope when we read the wife's reverence (Eph 5:33; φοβέω) is that same fear that both have toward Christ (Eph 5:21).

spousal self-gift (see Ephesians 5:21–25). Total, self-giving love demands the reciprocal surrender of both parties. In such submission, there is authority (i.e. headship) and active receptivity, but there must be no hint of coercion or demand lest the purity of self-giving love be diminished.[37] The husband is head (κεφαλή) because the reciprocal exchange of love begins with his initial offer, which the wife must actively accept (see Ephesians 5:23). Further, we've seen this headship is a reflection of the Father's headship, manifested in the Son as Head of the Church. This spousal Headship is ultimately the initiating love of the Bridegroom for his Bride, by which he transforms spousal love into redemptive love. This is the initiating love to which the Christian husband is called to offer his wife. But this must be followed by the man's reception of his wife's love. For the analog of the great mystery, the Bridegroom's submission leads to his death.

While the husband is not usually subject to this level of risk, his submission is not free from fear, even if he is not fully conscious of it. The ongoing risk of rebuff in initiating love can so focus his attention on his wife's reception that when he sees her "yes" he can assume the exchange of love has been completed. Habitually, then, he can have little experience of submission or the full experience of total, self-giving love due to this neglect. Moreover, the man's experience of his primary gifts, which are ordered to going out into the world to possess it and have dominion over it in order to serve his family and the common good, can be misused; as the man of concupiscence, he can be tempted to possess and conquer the world and those in it for himself.

So the husband's task must be to infuse his gifts of possessing and conquering with "a proper attitude and content that also includes self-giving."[38] It is here that the husband must learn to overcome this concupiscent proclivity, which can also distort his initiating love as he tries to serve his family. Because his is the love of headship, it is a task that arises uniquely for the man in order to do his part in maturing the totality of reciprocal self-giving through his submission. In addition, he must also focus his attention on completing the reciprocal self-gift by submitting himself in total entrustment of himself to his wife and her secondary offer of love. John Paul does not say that the man's gifts must be suppressed, gifts which include the authority of leadership and from which arise the

---

[37] Michael Healy suggests that if such appeal to authority seems necessary, there already has been some sort of failure in the reciprocal exchange of persons (see "Reading *Casti Connubii*").

[38] Wojtyła, *Love and Responsibility*, 81–82.

duties of guiding and harmoniously ordering the family, but that they must be rightly ordered. They become so by learning and practicing mutual submission.

The husband's leadership in the family must be transformed by a mature, initiating love, and this love is learned by his attentiveness to submitting to his wife's secondary, initiating love. The husband submits to his wife when he learns his fatherhood by observing her lovingly exercise her motherhood and then infusing what he sees into his fatherhood. He submits to his wife when he "obeys" her who, in all the richness of her feminine interpersonal communication, "receptively" suggests to him patience and temperance when he is inclined to employ an excess of the resources of concupiscent masculinity when their child strays from his expectations, when someone cuts him off in traffic, or when he is inclined to prize efficacy and efficiency over the greater good of persons in trying to accomplish some task. It is in learning to receive and submit to his wife's secondary initiating love, by learning to die to himself and his initiating excesses, that he then will be prepared to lead the family selflessly and authentically serve its integral flourishing in those few occasions in which time constraints prevent the couple from reaching a decision together that integrates the richness of their primary geniuses.

Grabowski's concern over maintaining the archetype of the Trinitarian *communio* between the spouses is well founded. However, I believe I have shown that their equality is maintained in that both are ordered to submit to one another in the order of total self-giving love, although they do so in a complementarily different manner. The husband's authority is inseparable from his headship which permits him to express initiating love. His leadership is a necessary attribute of this headship. If both spouses are the head, the great mystery analogy is lost. Rather, the woman expresses her primacy in love to which the man submits in her feminine manner of love, in the order of receptive love. The woman's primacy is not univocal with the man's love of headship but is complementary with it. So I believe that John Paul II's doctrine of mutual submission, in my presentation of it, is indeed coherent.

SEX DIFFERENCES AND THE SPIRITUAL REALM

John Paul II could be understood to say that the spiritual dimension is unaffected by sexual differences, which appears to be inconsistent with his overall philosophical anthropology.[39] For example, in chapter 6 we saw that he asserts sex difference to be in part constitutive of the human person, and in fact we showed that sex difference must have some kind of manifestation in the person's soul. Thus, these two positions appear to be in conflict with one another.

In *Love and Responsibility,* Karol Wojtyła writes about spiritual maternity and paternity in the context of giving birth to a spiritual child. He says that "spiritual fatherhood and motherhood is a distinctive characteristic of a mature interior personhood of a man and a woman."[40] There is much more in common between parenthood in the spiritual than in the biological dimensions of the human personhood. In explaining what Wojtyła means, it would be helpful to begin by looking at the very next sentence in which he asserts that "[t]he sphere of the spirit stands beyond the scope of sex."[41] Wojtyła makes an important distinction between spiritual and biological parenthood with this text. While this might seem to present a problem for us, it is important to note that he does not say that there are no differences arising from sex differences that influence the spiritual realm but rather that sex differences do not prevent men (males) from spiritually begetting a "child." The original Polish text supports this reading. In Polish, the sentence reads "Dziedzina ducha stoi poza zasięgiem płci."[42] A more literal translation of this would be "the realm (field, domain, arena, province) of the spirit stays beyond (stays out of, stays above, exceeds) the reach (range, radius, coverage) of sex."[43] The author's meaning conveyed by the English translation's terms "sphere," "stands beyond," and "scope" then support our initial interpretation of his meaning. The Polish also confirms that the subject of the sentence is not sex differences but the realm of the spirit (*ducha*). In other words, Wojtyła is concerned here primarily

---

[39] See Wojtyła, *Love and Responsibility*, 246.

[40] Wojtyła, *Love and Responsibility*, 246.

[41] Wojtyła, *Love and Responsibility,* 246. The entire text states: "Spiritual fatherhood and motherhood is a distinctive characteristic of a mature interior personhood of a man and a woman. This spiritual fatherhood is much more similar to spiritual motherhood than bodily fatherhood is to bodily motherhood. The sphere of the spirit stands beyond the scope of sex. Having in mind his spiritual fatherhood with respect to Galatians, the apostle Paul did not hesitate to write: 'My children, to whom I give birth suffering . . .' (Gal 4:19)."

[42] Available online at https://www.katolicki.net/index.php/czytelnia/czytelnia-publikacje/publikacje-milosc-i-odpowiedzialnosc/publikacje-milosc-i-odpowiedzialnosc-17.html; accessed on October 2, 2021.

[43] Again, my thanks go to Fr. Gamrot for his translation of and insights into the Polish text.

with the question of spiritual begetting in the realm of the spirit and its meaning for men and women.

He is not, then, intending to address the meaning and structure of sex difference in the context of the realm of the spirit. This is certainly in accord with the context of the sentence. Furthermore, his use of the term "sex" (*płci*) does not specifically point to the sex differences themselves. Rather, *płci* refers to that element which constitutes a human being as either male or female. In our account of sex difference, it would point especially to the person-relation which is either male or female. All together, Wojtyła is making the point that *płci* does not circumscribe that which *ducha* and its sphere govern. Of course, this must be the case for angelic persons who do not have sex difference, which is connected with the fact that sex differences are inseparable from the material order. Nevertheless, nothing here suggests that human sex difference can be separated from the spiritual order.

So, Wojtyła asserts that sex difference does not prevent a male person from spiritually begetting and nurturing another person. But again, he does not assert or even suggest that sex difference has no influence on the realm of the spirit. In any case, the Polish text does not lead to the conclusion that this is a generalized assertion that sex differences have no relation to the spiritual aspects of the human person. The next question is: How does someone beget spiritually? This brings us to consider Wojtyła's meaning that spiritual parenthood of the sexes has more in common than that of biological parenthood.

A human being is a unity of body-spiritual soul which were not meant to be separated. Human death only comes into the world through sin (see Rom 5:12). Human nature forms a seamless unity comprised of spiritual and material principles, between which there is a hierarchical priority. Concern for the good of the realm of the spirit includes the integral good of the person, but also recognizes that the highest good is the justification and sanctification of a human person. Fostering the entire process of salvation through initial spiritual begetting (i.e., Baptism) and nurturing is possible for both sexes.[44] Spiritual nurturing can entail a wide variety of situations in which one helps another on the path to spiritual maturity. Discrete steps along this path can be understood as further spiritual begetting. That which comprises sex difference does not limit the ability of any Christian to mediate Jesus Christ to others and to bring about within them new birth in the realm of the spirit.

---

[44] Though, of course, male clergy are the ordinary ministers of Baptism.

The reason for this is that justification and sanctification are rooted in the spiritual faculties of intellect and will, in which faith, hope, and love are born and matured. The fact that Wojtyła clarifies the relationship between sex difference and the spiritual realm in the context of Galatians 4:19, which he cites in this passage, supports my interpretation of his meaning: "My children, to whom I give birth suffering . . ." (Gal 4:19).[45] Here, St. Paul is concerned with the formation of the Galatians after the manner of Christ. In other words, he wants them to become Christlike, or to be sanctified.

In fact, Wojtyła goes on to clarify that "spiritual generation is a symptom of the person's maturity and of some fullness, both of which one wills to give to others (*'bonum est diffusivum sui'*)."[46] This could also be described as the appetite or desire "to give birth to" some spiritual good in another which one finds God has brought about in oneself, but which one observes has not reached the same point of spiritual maturity in the other. Wojtyła's use of the scholastic dictum that the good is self-diffusive indicates that he finds the desire toward spiritual parenthood to be a natural manifestation of this truth. So men and women alike can beget and nurture spiritual children and foster the relationship such that it can possess a certain likeness to natural motherhood.[47] In a sense, they beget themselves in the other when they spiritually parent a child.[48]

Moreover, John Paul draws together the Pauline passage above and the great mystery passage, in which Christ "nourishes and cherishes" his Spouse the Church as his own body (Eph 5:29), as a Eucharistic reference to indicate that Scripture itself likens spiritual solicitude for spiritual children in the order of redemption to maternal-bodily solicitude in the order of natural motherhood.[49] This is because there is a real theological analogy

---

[45] Wojtyła, *Love and Responsibility*, 246.

[46] Wojtyła, *Love and Responsibility*, 246.

[47] See Wojtyła, *Love and Responsibility*, 246.

[48] See Wojtyła, *Love and Responsibility*, 246, where Wojtyła says that "[s]piritual father-hood or motherhood contains some transmission of personhood." This of course evokes Thomas's epistemology in which the substantial form of the known, inhering in the soul of the knower, indicates that in a real manner the knower becomes the known.

[49] See John Paul II, Letter to Priests for Holy Thursday 1988, §4. He also states that con-secrated women carry out their spiritual motherhood in a feminine manner. Specifically, he identifies tasks for which feminine qualities are indispensable, such as "many works of charity and assistance to the poor, the sick, the handicapped, the abandoned, especially children and little girls, once described as waifs. These are all cases where dedication and compassion, the treasures of the feminine heart, are involved" (John Paul II, *The Church*, 609).

between natural generation and regeneration by the power of the Holy Spirit, that is, between being born and being born anew.[50] A person being born is given natural life, coming into being out of nothing. A person being born anew is given supernatural life through a character imprinted in the *potentia* of the soul, which can sound like he is given a new nature—a new birth—by which he becomes a partaker of the divine nature.[51]

While the ultimate *telos* of the human person is justification and sanctification, all of the integral human goods which contribute to this are also the proper sphere by which spiritual motherhood and fatherhood can bring to birth a spiritual child (e.g., helping another advance in intellectual maturity, in virtue, and of course in holiness). Nevertheless, Wojtyła does not draw a strict equivalence between spiritual fatherhood and spiritual motherhood, because while the man can "give birth" like the spiritual mother in the order of redemption, he must do so "in a manly way."[52] In other words, this is not a contradiction in his thought. The final question we should address is how a man might live spiritual motherhood in a manly way.

Wojtyła does not provide an explicit articulation as to how a man might do this, but he does give some hints. If we put these hints in the context of our account of his view of complementarity, we can provide some possible examples. In Wojtyła's vision of complementarity, both men and women have all of what it means to be human, but they possess these characteristics in a reciprocally different manner. Men possess their human nature in the manner of eccentricity, reflecting masculinity's principle of initiating love.

While many of a man's masculine characteristics are physically manifested in his body, they are not solely or even primarily of the material order. Rather, they interpenetrate the entirety of his being. In fact, all of a man's (male) characteristics have their root in his masculine personhood and its manner of initiating love. For these reasons, the male "mode" of being human is fulfilled when he loves others in accord with initiating love.

A man must accord with his masculine mode of being human in relation to others when bringing another to some new point of spiritual maturity. Nevertheless, while achieving spiritual maturity begins with an invitation (ultimately from God), at the same time this maturity is experienced as reception into communion, or into deeper communion, with

---

[50] See John Paul II, Letter to Priests for Holy Thursday 1988, §4; see also John 3:3.

[51] See Aquinas, *ST* III, q. 63, a. 4, co.

[52] John Paul II, Letter to Priests for Holy Thursday 1988, §4.

the maternal Church. For this reason, John Paul explains to his priests the importance for them to be formed by the Church's Marian spirituality, which will enable them to manifest to the faithful the maternal solicitude of the Church.[53] He gave to his priests the example of their role as confessors as a place in which they might exhibit this spiritual maternal solicitude. We might infer from what we have seen up to this point that this would include the need for the priest to exhibit a concerned solicitude for the entire person, ensuring he allows the penitent to experience the Church's listening and supportive ear before he hears from the confessor a "masculine" analysis of his situation and proposed solution for it.

This advice for priests can be extended in general to all Christian men in terms of expressing spiritual motherhood in a manly way. Men can spiritually beget a child through a similar attentiveness to the personhood of the child rather than manifesting the common masculine inclination to treat such an encounter as a task to be accomplished. The man might direct his attention to listening to the spiritual child to understand, to responding in ways that indicate he understands and accepts the spiritual child, and that he affirms God's love for the child, the sincere concern of the Church, and his own personal concern for the spiritual child. Yet, he does not do so as a woman would, who is actively receptive from the outset. Rather, he engages the spiritual child in an initiating manner of love, offering himself and waiting for the other's acceptance. Explicit affirmation of the spiritual child can help especially in the case of a male "child," as masculine initiative can sometimes obscure his acceptance of the spiritual child. At the same time, he must temper any temptation to reduce his encounters with the spiritual child to a problem to be overcome.

The fact that John Paul does not provide more clarity about the differences between masculinity and femininity with respect to the spiritual realm is perhaps the aspect of his theology of masculinity and fatherhood most worthy of criticism. This is not simply a matter of theological precision, it has daily practical import if men are to behave like men but still witness to spiritual motherhood. Thus, I grant that the lack of a more complete account of the relation of sex differences to the spiritual realm, as well as the lack of practical examples as to how men might witness to spiritual motherhood in a masculine manner are valid criticisms; however, there is no contradiction here.

---

[53] See John Paul II, Letter to Priests for Holy Thursday 1988, §4.

Concupiscence and Vocation

John Paul II's theology of masculinity/fatherhood suggests that the fall affects men in such a way that it tends to lead them away from their vocations as natural fathers. For this reason, he tells them they must observe their wives to learn to nurture their fatherhood. Moreover, they must learn to foster the desire to be fathers in a way in which their wives generally will not require with respect to their motherhood.[54] In his theology of motherhood, he does not identify any complementary concern on the part of women. This seems to be inconsistent with the fact that he says that concupiscence equally affects men and women.[55] Upon closer examination, it becomes apparent that this is not an inconsistency. Rather, it appears to be an asymmetry in the way that concupiscence affects the complementary structures of men and women.

Concupiscence is due to a lack of harmony within the human person and this interior disharmony overflows into the relationships between women and men. This disruption of interior and interpersonal harmony is the result of original sin.[56] After the fall, masculine eccentricity is the attribute which is most significantly affected by his interior disharmony.[57] One can see that the author was consistent in the way he treated this attribute throughout his career. Wojtyła's work in *Love and Responsibility* provides some background for his papal thought on differences in the way men and women experience the same situations differently due to the man's eccentricity and the woman's interiority.

In discussing the requirement for a mutual gift of self in betrothed love, Wojtyła says that in marriage, men and women's experiences will differ in that women generally have the psychological experience of surrender, while for men "some correlation of 'self-giving' and 'possessing' takes place."[58] Because of this, Wojtyła says that the man must overcome the concupiscible aspects of this psychological experience which lead to the desire to possess or he will end up treating his wife as an object.[59] Wojtyła suggests that the man's particular proclivity to objectify his wife is due to

---

[54] See *Mulieris dignitatem*, §18.

[55] See *Man and Woman*, 123.

[56] See *Mulieris dignitatem*, §10.

[57] The husband's eccentricity also seems to be the reason for his need to learn his fatherhood from his wife (see *Mulieris dignitatem*, §18).

[58] Wojtyła, *Love and Responsibility*, 81.

[59] See Wojtyła, *Love and Responsibility*, 81. In fact, Wojtyła indicates the man's concupiscence of the sexual appetite inclines him more toward an attitude of conquering or possessing, which he must purify. He does not indicate this is commensurate in women.

his psychological makeup in light of the fall. The structure of male person-hood leads him to a different experience of the type of love John Paul calls sentimental love than the female structure brings about for her.

The male structure is significantly more analytical and reductive in orientation. A man is driven to unveil the woman as an object with the potential to satisfy his desires, especially the pleasurable aspects of love. He will be more likely to objectify his wife in terms of pleasure than vice versa.[60] The woman, on the other hand, is more likely to be inclined to remain concealed and hidden, appreciating the experience as expressions of affection for her as a person.[61] She is more inclined to interpret the expe-rience, and to project the same upon the man, as a mutual expression of affection and bonding. John Paul II's theology of the body catecheses con-tinue this teaching.

In discussing the effects of original sin on the man and woman, John Paul II says that the text of Genesis 3:16 suggests that it is especially the man who is inclined to desire in a reductive way. This is consistent with Matthew 5:27–28, where it is the man who is rebuked for his lust. Even so, the woman and the man are both subject to concupiscence and both are left to the perennial experience of shame. Concupiscence and shame pro-foundly reverberate to the core of both male and female persons, though again, they do so in different ways.[62] John Paul unmistakably indicates that there is asymmetry in the way in which the man and woman expe-rience concupiscence and shame. The same Genesis text implies that it is most often the man who gives in to lust.[63] This is not to say that women

---

[60] In John Paul II's treatment of *eros*, is possible to explain the man's different experience of concupiscence in objectifying the other in connection to his eccentricity. He explains *eros* as the interior movement that inclines man out of himself and toward the true, the good, and the beautiful (see *Man and Woman*, 318). *Eros* is manifested in the sexual sphere with the reciprocal desire of the man and the woman for each other, arising from their awareness of the sexual value of the other manifested through the body. With the fullness of *eros*, the body they see reveals the entire person and his goodness. However, the fall has left the man of concupiscence deprived of the fullness of *eros*, and so erotic desire is readily reduced to the sexual value of the other (see *Man and Woman*, 319ff.). The man, in all of the gifts of his eccentric orientation, experiences this reductive *eros* predominantly in his desire for the woman's sexual value manifested in the flesh. John Paul explains that the solution to this problem is purity of the heart, in which *eros* is con-stituted by *ethos*. That is the *ethos* of the person who must be treated as an end and never a means (see *Man and Woman*, 326ff.). See our earlier discussion in chapter 11 in which purification of the heart is described in *Deus caritas est* as *eros* completed in *agape*.

[61] Wojtyła, *Love and Responsibility*, 111–12.

[62] See *Man and Woman*, 255, and 260–61.

[63] See *Man and Woman*, 260–61.

are not subject to concupiscence, that women do not fall away from their vocations as mothers, or that women do not often cooperate in their own objectification.

Nor does it mean that no woman ever gives into lust. But it does suggest that their sinfulness will often be much more interior, hidden, and aimed at achieving more perceived relationally beneficial ends than that of men. It also suggests that when women rebel against their interiority and attempt to pursue concupiscent excess by attempting to imitate that of masculine fallenness, they do so more vigorously against their natural inclinations, and for different primary motivations with quite devastating results.[64] What all this reveals is that in the fallen state the masculine gifts tend to incline men toward infidelity to their vocations more easily and more often than is the case for women, though of course women do certainly succumb to such temptation as well. The sociological data presented at the beginning of chapter 9 referring to the demise of authentic families due to the absentee father support this assertion.

This asymmetry fits well with men's special challenge in their paternal vocations and is consistent with John Paul II's understanding of the integral complementarity between men and women. In particular, masculine eccentricity is the complement to feminine centrality. These are complementary in the sense that women and men possess both features, but eccentricity is the dominant mode in men and the interiority associated with centrality is likewise dominant in women.

The husband-father will naturally tend to go out of himself and in general handle his roles and tasks in an external manner. However, he also has the capacity, even if not the general tendency, to be more holistic and integrative than he achieves without effort. To actualize his integrative capacity, he often requires his wife's example; he must also carefully appropriate her insights and seriously consider her advice and admonitions. This is not with the intention of appropriating feminine manners of behavior, nor does it demand slavish submission. Rather, it is with the purpose of becoming more attentive to his own masculine way of interiorizing and of actualizing the potency of spousal and family unity through the harmonious use of the gifts of both spouses. Thus, we see that the asymmetry in

---

[64] For an insightful but sobering study of the carnage the contemporary feminist movement has inflicted on women as they assert that women's equality demands women adopt the worst of masculine lust and debauchery, see Carrie Gress, *The Anti-Mary Exposed: Rescuing the Culture from Toxic Femininity* (Charlotte, NC: TAN Books, 2019).

CONSECRATED CELIBACY AND PRIESTLY CELIBACY

the way concupiscence affects the vocation of women and men is not an inconsistency in John Paul II's anthropology.

CONSECRATED CELIBACY AND PRIESTLY CELIBACY

The final item for evaluation is the consistency of celibacy in the consecrated life together with priestly celibacy. Immediately upon looking at the two vocations an initial incongruity seems to appear. While both women and men are called to consecrated celibacy, only men are called to priestly celibacy. Priestly celibacy is a sign of the fatherhood of God in his relation to humanity as revealed by the Son—the Bridegroom. However, consecrated virginal celibacy is a sign of the Church as the Bride which is also Virgin and Mother.

Men do not have a natural resemblance to, and so they cannot symbolize the Bride. Therefore, one might suppose that men would only be called to celibacy within Holy Orders. This, obviously, has never been the case in the history of Christianity. Nevertheless, the feminine value of consecrated celibacy is undoubtedly the reason John Paul says that consecrated celibacy has a special meaning for women.[65] As we have seen, humanity has a feminine relation to God in the form of an active receptivity to his first offer of love. Yet men also are members of the Church and so they can and must live a life in conformity with an active receptivity of God's love of initiative.

While this receptivity is secondary with respect to a man's masculine structure, he still possesses the natural capacity for a receptive relationship with God and thus can (and must) be a member of the Church. However, because man is created with a receptive capacity that is secondary with respect to his human relations, he does not possess the natural visible resemblance of feminine, actively receptive love, preventing him from being a symbol of the Church. So men can and do participate in primarily receptive love in relation to God, but they are not symbols of it. Nevertheless, even though men are not appropriate symbols of the Church, there is still the question of whether, in John Paul's anthropology, there is room for men to participate, in any way, in that which celibacy represents in the world other than as signs of Christ in Holy Orders.

John Paul answers this question when he says that men express spiritual fatherhood in their celibacy by living the spiritual motherhood that

---

[65] See John Paul II, Post-Synodal Apostolic Exhortation on the Consecrated Life and Its Mission in the Church and in the World *Vita consecrata* (March 26, 1996), §34.

celibacy represents, but in a masculine way.[66] Bishops and priests manifest God's fatherhood in their celibacy. In keeping with John Paul's view of complementarity, one can infer that they share in the value of celibacy from the perspective of motherhood only in a secondary way. Consequently, men do not provide the sign value of virginal maternity in the vocation of consecrated celibacy as do women.

When John Paul refers to men as spiritual mothers in consecrated celibacy, the context is Holy Orders.[67] However, there seems to be no reason why this participation in spiritual motherhood as spiritual fathers cannot also apply to all men who take vows of consecrated celibacy. Non-ordained, celibate men are signs of spiritual fatherhood, not signs of the Bride, Virgin, or Mother. Like priests, they also share in celibacy's value of spiritual motherhood, but they cannot function as signs of this motherhood. Still, they are participating in spiritual motherhood but in the masculine manner, which John Paul calls "spiritual fatherhood." Through acts of initiating love, consecrated men help to bring to birth holiness, or perfection in love, in those whom they spiritually parent.

Moreover, if one limits a man's participation in spiritual motherhood to spiritually begetting a child, which is all John Paul explicitly assigns to it, one can readily make sense of his statements in this regard. We can conclude then that his thought is consistent, if not somewhat nuanced, in his view of the sign value of consecrated celibacy and priestly celibacy. Even so, the initial appearance of a contradiction here is exacerbated by the fact that he has not provided an explicitly systematized theological explication for spiritual parenthood. Nor has he provided practical examples of lived spiritual fatherhood in contradistinction to lived spiritual motherhood which could help resolve the apparent inconsistencies.

---

[66] See John Paul II, Letter to Priests for Holy Thursday 1988, §4. The context here is obviously Holy Orders.

[67] See John Paul II, Letter to Priests for Holy Thursday 1988, §4.

CHAPTER 14

Assessing Criticisms

There have been many criticisms of key concepts in John Paul II's theology of masculinity and fatherhood, in one form or another, which have been put forward by various scholars. In this chapter, we will look at some of these critiques. The criticisms we will address are those which, if not adequately resolved, could undermine John Paul II's theology of fatherhood. Criticisms which do not fit this criterion will be left aside.[1] With this rationale in mind, let us consider what I believe to be the seven most significant critiques: a Biblical Critique, Gender Dualism, Gender Stereotyping, Biologism, Role Models as Idealizations, A Problematic View of Paternal Roles, and Can It Account for Less Common Situations.[2]

BIBLICAL CRITIQUE

Some feminists point to Galatians 3:28 to indicate the ultimate insignificance of sex difference for the human person.[3] Sonya Quitslund provides

---

[1] As an example, I have shown that John Paul finds Jesus's masculinity to be significant to his mission as Redeemer. I used this fact as partial justification for inferring analogical characteristics for men and fathers. However, two factors make it unnecessary to address the debate about the significance of Jesus's masculinity. In the first place, most of the characteristics identified using this approach were simply confirmation of characteristics identified through other means. Secondly, John Paul's emphasis on the great mystery provided an explicit source of many of the most significant characteristics derived from Jesus's masculinity. Therefore, the elimination of this item would not seriously damage the integrity of the Holy Father's theology of masculinity or fatherhood.

[2] Here I will partially set aside the rubric introduced in part 2 and employ the potentially obfuscatory term "gender." The reason is that this term is used by most feminist critiques and so it is necessarily employed here. In addition, in this chapter I will liberally quote from the critics' writings to permit them, as much as possible, to speak for themselves.

[3] See Rosemary Radford Ruether, *Sexism and God-Talk: Toward a Feminist Theology*

one representative example. In an oblique reference to this verse, Quitslund refers specifically to the issue of women's ordination, stating: "The key issue . . . [is] 'to discover if tradition is simply repetition or if it has no meaning other than to face the future, a future specifically eschatological where there will be neither male nor female.'"[4] Quitslund interprets this to say that sex difference will be done away with in the eschaton. John Paul's anthropology explicitly rejects such a theory.

Sex difference is partially constitutive of personhood modulating the personal relation itself; therefore, it must perdure if the person is to maintain continuous integrity and thereby avoid annihilation. It might be helpful at this point, to look at the manner in which John Paul understands the verse in question. He quotes it three times in *Mulieris dignitatem*. Galatians 3:28 alludes to the Genesis narrative and to the mutual opposition that arises between man and woman which he exposited in his theology of the body catecheses.

This mutual opposition leads John Paul to focus his attention on the mutual opposition of the contrary pairs St. Paul identifies in this verse—Jew/Greek, slave/free, male/female—and the overcoming of this opposition in Christ. The theme of mutual opposition is consonant with the rest of the chapter in which St. Paul also contrasts "spirit versus flesh" (Gal 3:3), "faith versus works of the law" (Gal 3:5), and asserts that "the law versus the promises of God" is a false opposition (Gal 3:21). Madeleine Boucher agrees that in Galatians 3:28 "Paul is speaking not so much of equality as of unity in the Church."[5] A further consideration is that those whose position is advocating the annihilation of sex difference posit that this annihilation will occur in the eschaton, but the eschaton is not the context of this passage.

The context points to an already existing reality. Accordingly, the

---

(Boston: Beacon, 1983), 138; Pauline Turner and Bernard Cooke, "Women Can Have a Natural Resemblance to Christ," in *Women Priests: A Catholic Commentary on the Vatican Declaration*, ed. Leonard Swidler and Arlene Swidler (New York: Paulist Press, 1977), 258; Brigitte Kahl, "No Longer Male: Masculinity Struggles Behind Galatians 3.28?," trans. Brian McNeil, *Journal for the Study of the New Testament* 79 (September 2000): 38; Mary Rose D'Angelo, "Women and the Earliest Church: Reflecting on the Problématique of Christ and Culture," in *Women Priests*, 197; Sonya A. Quitslund, "In the Image of Christ," in *Women Priests*, 261.

4 Quitslund, "In the Image of Christ," 261.
5 Madeleine I. Boucher, "Women and the Apostolic Community," in *Women Priests: A Catholic Commentary on the Vatican Declaration*, ed. Leonard and Arlene Swidler (New York: Paulist Press, 1977), 154. This assertion is perhaps more significant since Boucher is writing an article in which she attempts to argue for women's ordination.

interpretation of this baptismal passage is to be found in the reconciliation of opposition through Christ rather than in the obliteration of sex difference in the eschaton. The mutual opposition which arose between men and women because of original sin, John Paul says, "is essentially overcome" in the redemption wrought by Christ.[6] However, in the same letter, he finds it has yet another sense, that of unity for the sexes.

Humanity in its relation to God can be symbolized by femininity,[7] as we have previously discussed. The fall brought about the alienation of man from God which is restored by the Bridegroom and his Bride. John Paul explains that man's restored unity with God, won through Christ's redemption, is brought about in the supernatural order through grace mediated by the Holy Spirit.[8] But while this unity is perfected in the eschaton, it is a reality even now. Consequently, there is no rationale for arguing that the reconciliation brought about by Christ eliminates diversity in eternity, especially not the diversity of sex difference.[9]

In *Christifideles laici* John Paul draws the logical conclusion demanded by his anthropology and further suggested by Galatians 3:28. He concludes that the equal dignity of men and women demands that women cannot be prevented from taking their rightful place in the Church and in society.[10] John Paul thus finds there to be multivalent meaning associated

---

[6] John Paul II, Apostolic Letter on the Dignity and Vocation of Women *Mulieris dignitatem* (August 15, 1988), §11; AAS 80 (1988), 1653–1729.

[7] See *Mulieris dignitatem*, §25.

[8] John Paul II's interpretation of this passage in which he emphasizes reconciliation in Christ of the oppositions, which arise in man due to the fall, arises from the tradition. The Fathers have understood this passage first to refer to reconciliation of man with God through Jesus Christ (see St. Ambrose, *Three Books of the Holy Spirit* 2.8.73–74), that there is no distinction in Christ between man and woman, Jew and Greek, slave and free in their ability to be reconciled (see St. Augustine, *Our Lord's Sermon on the Mount* 1.15.40), and this reconciliation is simultaneously with one another in the Church (see St. Augustine, *Tractate on the Gospel of John* 110.2). St. Maximus the Confessor, in his *Difficulty 41*, taught that this reconciliation of oppositions in Christ was cosmic and ontological. Maximus viewed man as a microcosm of creation who was to reconcile the cosmos's divisions of being, but who failed, and so the cosmic reconciliation had to occur in Christ (see Andrew Louth, *Maximus the Confessor* [London: Routledge, 2005, first published 1996], 153–60). John Paul II's exegesis that this the reconciliation of oppositions that arise due to the fall is in continuity with this tradition, though it is somewhat nuanced.

[9] See *Mulieris dignitatem*, §16.

[10] John Paul II, Post-Synodal Apostolic Exhortation on the Vocation and the Mission of the Lay Faithful in the Church and in the World *Christifideles laici* (December 30, 1988), *AAS* 81 (1989), 393–521, §50.

with these words; however, this multivalence does not include the supposition that sex difference is accidental to the human person. The critique of sex difference and personhood will be looked at more closely in the next section. However, we can say that John Paul's anthropology has adequately accounted for this particular criticism.

GENDER DUALISM

John Paul II's contention that sex difference is a constitutive aspect of the human person meets with a host of criticisms. Perhaps one of the most important of these is that giving sex difference any ontological significance at all necessarily splits human nature into two halves—this is the critique of so-called gender dualism. This criticism is particularly keen among some feminists. In general, the aim of these critics seems to be to eliminate the importance of sex differentiation. Indeed, John Grabowski says that many feminists "are concerned to make sexual differences not merely 'accidental' in the traditional sense but 'incidental' to what it means to be human."[11] Their argument is that giving any constitutive status to sex differentiation necessarily leads to dualism.

Dualism, therefore, is the charge leveled against the use of the term "complementarity" when applied to the relation between men and women. As we saw in chapter 5, Elizabeth Johnson accuses John Paul II of this gender dualism. She describes gender dualism as

> the view of the human race [which] starts out from the obvious biological sex differences between women and men. Thinking in binary terms, it elevates sexual difference to an ontological principle that cleaves the human race into two radically different types of persons—men who have a masculine nature and women who have a feminine nature. Each comes equipped with a distinct set of characteristics. . . . Gender dualism then extrapolates from the qualities endemic to each nature to assign men and women to different social roles played out in rigidly preassigned spheres.[12]

---

[11] John Grabowski, "Theological Anthropology and Gender since Vatican II: A Critical Appraisal of Recent Trends in Catholic Theology" (Ph.D. diss., Marquette University, 1991), 85.

[12] Elizabeth Johnson, *Truly Our Sister: A Theology of Mary in the Communion of Saints* (New York: Continuum, 2003), 48.

She subsequently declares that John Paul II is committed to gender dualism.[13]

Johnson even considers that he has established a "new version of gender dualism . . . [which makes] women equal in dignity but separate in social roles."[14] Nevertheless, Johnson is more moderate in her views about sex in regard to personhood than other more radical claims which try to eliminate any significance to sex difference. She admits that sex does make a difference in establishing personal identity. However, she contends that sex is simply one of many factors which establish identity. Among these factors she includes

> bodiliness and hence sex and race; relation to the earth, other persons and social groupings; economic, political, and cultural location, and the like. These constants mutually condition one another, and in their endless combinations are constitutive of the humanity of every person. Significantly change any one of them, and a different person results. It is short sighted to single out sexuality as always and everywhere more fundamental to concrete historical existence than any of the other constants.[15]

Lisa Sowle Cahill also criticizes John Paul II over gender dualism. Cahill's rejection of the complementarity of sex difference arises from her fear that it can be used to justify unequal treatment of women. For example, she says that sex differences are used to justify less than equal time devoted by both parents in child rearing such that mothers are deprived of opportunities in the social sphere than fathers might have, because fathers spend less time rearing their children. Consequently, Cahill's view of equality must result in homogenization of everything beyond biological necessity. However, she still desires to retain something proper to femininity while protecting women from what she views to be unfair treatment:

> The feminist critique of gender, often focused on motherhood as constraint and delusion, envisions the possibility [of male domination due to femininity] all too clearly. But if human physicality is to be fully integrated with reflection, emotions, choice,

---

[13] See Johnson, *Truly Our Sister*, 61.

[14] Johnson, *Truly Our Sister*, 62.

[15] Elizabeth Johnson, *She Who Is: The Mystery of God in Feminist Theological Discourse* (New York: The Crossroad Publishing Company, 1992), 155.

and social relations, then the mutuality and equality of men and women must be carved out partly in relation to those very qualities by which we distinguish those two human constituencies.[16]

In her book on the modern papacy, Christine Gudorf does not explicitly contend that complementarity results in dualism, but she implies it when she says that it leaves each person incomplete outside of marriage. She finds this incompleteness in conflict with the Church's position on consecrated celibacy. While not specifically identifying John Paul II, she states:

> Papal assumptions of gender complementarity are problematic in themselves, even without the added complexity of historical shifts in gender roles. The problem is that traditional assertions of gender complementarity have the effect of positing both men and women as being incomplete outside marriage. More recent treatment of complementarity tends to explain gender complementarity in terms of human sociality. . . . [P]apal teaching . . . assumes that traits and roles are essentially sex based, so that a man will be more different from all women than from any man. Because of this, our most intimate human relationship, the marital relationship, is assumed to be the place where we come face to face with our complement and thus are made whole through the challenge to communicate with and bond to this opposite.[17]

If Gudorf is oblique in associating complementarity with gender dualism, Johnson makes the connection explicit.

Johnson believes that the traditional view of complementarity arises from Mariology. She claims that because the Christian tradition views Mary as the ideal woman, Mary then becomes the role model for all women. Johnson thinks that those who adopt this view also

> invariably exaggerate sexual differences between women and men, elevating sex to an ontological principle that results in virtually two types of human nature. Masculine nature, characterized by intelligence, assertiveness, independence, and the ability to make

---

[16] Lisa Sowle Cahill, *Sex, Gender, and Christian Ethics* (New York: Cambridge University Press, 1996), 89–90.

[17] Christine Gudorf, "Encountering the Other: The Modern Papacy on Women," *Social Compass* 36, no. 3 (1989): 301.

decisions, is destined for leadership in the public realm. On the other hand, feminine nature, marked by relationality, gentleness, nurturing, a non-assertiveness, non-competitive attitude, and the giving of service and reassurance, is fit for the private domain of childbearing, homemaking, and care of the vulnerable. . . . Perhaps the most widely-heard proponent of this view is Pope John Paul II.[18]

Johnson emphatically rejects the idea of a "feminine nature" as the product of patriarchal thinking.[19] As with Gudorf, Johnson's concerns with complementarity boil down to her suspicions that it is a tool used to justify limiting women's access to their rightful roles in society. She says that this notion is intended "to keep women in their so-called proper 'place.'"[20]

Johnson's suspicion presupposes a hidden agenda on the part of John Paul II and is not an issue directly impacting the adequacy of his theology of fatherhood, so we may set it aside. However, a valid concern remains over the charge of dualism. Namely, as Johnson claims, does John Paul II's view of complementarity necessarily divide humanity into two separate human natures? If so, there is a well-founded theological implication which goes beyond simply Cartesian philosophical concerns. In terms of soteriology, Jesus would have only assumed the male "species" of humanity and thus left women unreconciled with God. However, as we demonstrated in chapter 6, John Paul's view of complementarity does not succumb to this shortcoming. Let's look at this issue a little more closely.

Prudence Allen assesses several theories, showing how legitimate criticisms of some philosophies of sex difference do not apply to all concepts. She classifies these philosophies into four types.[21] She associates the first, "sex unity," with Plato, who taught that there were no significant differences between women and men. It is characterized by a marked devaluation of sexual differences between men and women. Its modern proponents usually defend it via the Cartesian mischaracterization of human reason, a common faculty shared by all human beings.

The second philosophy is "sex polarity" which she traces back to Aristotle. In this view, sexual differences are philosophically significant.

---

[18] Elizabeth Johnson, "Mary, Friend of God and Prophet: A Critical Reading of the Marian Tradition," *Theology Digest* 47, no. 4 (Winter 2000): 319.

[19] See Johnson, "Mary, Friend of God and Prophet," 320.

[20] See Johnson, "Mary, Friend of God and Prophet," 320.

[21] See Prudence Allen, "Integral Sex Complementarity and the Theology of Communion," *Communio* 17 (Winter 1990): 523–44.

Aristotle held that men and women were two poles of a common nature, the former being superior and the latter being a misbegotten male. She associates this view with scholasticism. The third view is "reverse sex polarity," an inversion of traditional sex polarity. This view adopts the perspective that there is significance to the differences between the sexes but claims for women the position of natural superiority. Reverse sex polarity was first put forth by Heinrich Cornelius Agrippa in the sixteenth century. As might be expected, it has gained followers in some corners of contemporary feminism. Allen says that this has led a few feminists into goddess worship and to advocate for a superior feminine culture.

The fourth view Allen refers to as "sex complementarity." She traces the seeds of this anthropology to St. Augustine, although she finds that he espoused two of the previously mentioned views as well. However, sex complementarity first received its most complete form in the thought of Hildegard of Bingen in the twelfth century. Allen uses Hildegard's anthropology to identify two subtypes of sex complementarity. Hildegard sometimes fell into what Allen calls "fractional complementarity." Fractional complementarity is distinguished by an exclusive possession of a specific sex characteristic by one sex, whereas the other gender exclusively possesses its complement.

Allen classifies the second subtype as "integral complementarity." This is distinguished from fractional complementarity in that each man and woman is understood to be a whole being. They do not partially possess the characteristics of human nature such that two species of human beings arise from a human genus. In other words, the male does not provide characteristics of one-half of a whole human and the female the other half (and so the "fractional" terminology) in order to make up the entirety of being human. Rather, in integral complementarity, each person is more like an integer than a fraction. Allen classifies John Paul II's anthropology as one of integral sex complementarity.[22] Allen criticizes both sex unity and sex polarity views.[23] The sex unity theory either devalues the body or rejects sex as a factor in establishing human identity. She argues that sex polarity is also problematic. She believes that it places the opposite emphasis

---

[22] See Prudence Allen, "Sex and Gender Differentiation in Hildegard of Bingen and Edith Stein," *Communio* 20 (Summer 1993): 412. See also John F. Crosby, "John Paul II on the Complementarity of Man and Woman," in *The Church, Marriage, and the Family*, ed. Kenneth D. Whitehead (South Bend: St. Augustine Press, 2007), 41–52, who assesses the accusation of fractional sex complementarity against John Paul II and demonstrates why it fails.

[23] See Allen, "Integral Sex Complementarity," 530.

on bodily differentiation. For Allen, sex complementarity, and specifically, integral sex complementarity alone seeks "a third way in which bodily factors, among others, play a role, but not necessarily the only role in determining one's identity and vocation."[24] This position is different from Johnson's in that for Allen, sex differences go much deeper. For Johnson sexuality is equal with environment and culture in establishing identity. Allen also seeks to avoid the "biology is destiny" charge. Nevertheless, for her, sex is an ontological factor in personal identity. Thus, she sees complementarity manifested at the lowest levels of procreation. She explains:

> It is . . . clear that in the activity of procreation itself the male and female both provide twenty-three chromosomes, so they give what could be called an equal contribution. At the same time, however, the pathways of access of the male seed and the female seed are the differentiated sperm and egg. In fact, they must be different in order for fertility and conception to occur. Therefore, from a simple reconsideration of the relation of male and female on the biological level of generation we find the two premises of sex complementarity (i.e., equality and differentiation) affirmed.[25]

Other scholars agree that John Paul II's complementarity is not the fractional complementarity, to use Allen's term, that some feminists claim.

Antonio Ruiz Retegui describes John Paul's view of complementarity between man and woman as an asymmetric duality, which is most visibly manifested in the marital union.[26] It is neither dualistic nor does it give way to one of the many versions of egalitarian symmetry that some feminists, such as Johnson, think is required to avoid this schism in human nature. It is simply asymmetrical. David Schindler finds that Johnson in particular succumbs to some extent to this egalitarian (i.e., equality is sameness) fallacy in her view of sex differences. Because of this, she ironically retains a form of the dualism she believes she finds in John Paul's anthropology. Schindler explains:

---

[24] Allen, "Integral Sex Complementarity," 530.

[25] Allen, "Integral Sex Complementarity," 531.

[26] See Antonio Ruiz Retegui, "El tratamiento diferencial de la sexualidad humana en la Carta Apostólica 'Mulieris Dignitatem,'" *Scripta Theologica* 22 (1990): 894: "La alteridad varón-mujer es fuertemente asimétrica y reclama una resolución que es del todo peculiar: varón y mujer resuelven la alteridad en la peculiar unión humana en virtud de la sexualidad, en el hacerse *una caro* con las características que esa unión tiene en todos los estratos de la existencia humana para ser verdaderamente resolutiva y no dispersadora."

Johnson's "egalitarian" (symmetrical) approach to the question of the relation between women and men . . . paradoxically, retains a significant aspect of the dualism rejected . . . in John Paul II's notion of the "spousal body." That is, on Johnson's reading, the differences between women and men can have no "natural" or "essential" significance. The differences in the bodies of women and men as a matter of principle can never serve in an intrinsic way as carriers, precisely *in* their physiological character, of any "transcendent" meaning. It is difficult to see how such a notion of the body amounts in the end to anything more than the dumb-mechanical body of Descartes, whose dualism in this respect is a paradigm of the non-symbolic understanding that it has been our burden to reject.[27]

Other scholars provide additional insights explaining why complementarity between women and men is required for an anthropology which adequately explains sex differences. Benedict Ashley finds that feminists prefer "mutuality" to complementarity because the latter implies to them the inferiority of women. However, he argues that "mutuality is generic to all truly Christian and humane relationships and in the case of the sexual relationship requires to be made more specific by the addition of the term 'complementarity' or 'complementary equality,' which implies not only that woman is in one sense incomplete without man, but that man is incomplete without woman."[28] This incompleteness is not in human nature but in one's personal fulfillment which is realized only in relation to others. Ashley's distinction is instructive because while it doesn't succumb to Allen's theory of fractional sex complementarity, it can seem to do so for those without conceptual resources for an adequate distinction between person and nature, metaphysically accounted for with the category of relation. Ashley's point that mutual completion is always interpersonal, most perfectly expressed in the marital covenant, describes John Paul II's anthropology.

Stephen Long provides a similar assessment of complementarity.[29] He says that sex differences are normative in differentiating human beings into

---

[27] David L. Schindler, "Creation and Nuptiality: A Reflection on Feminism in Light of Schmemann's Liturgical Theology," *Communio* 28 (Summer 2001): 294.

[28] Benedict M. Ashley, *Justice in the Church: Gender and Participation (The Michael J. McGivney Lectures of the John Paul II Institute for Studies on Marriage and Family, 1992)* (Washington, DC: Catholic University of America Press, 1996), 114.

[29] See Stephen Long, "The Metaphysics of Gender and Sacramental Priesthood," *Louvain Studies* 10 (1984–85): 47.

men and women. He warns that fundamental human qualities cannot be denied of either sex. Rather, sex differences are essentially dissimilar in the spiritual realm. More specifically, sex difference is found in the human substantial form. Sex difference is an essential characteristic of the soul and since the soul conditions everything which is human, sex difference influences all aspects of the person.

Long believes that this can be understood by looking at the ontological significance of sex difference in the Catholic theology of marriage and of Marian veneration. In venerating Mary and in describing the mysterious uniqueness of the marital bond, reduction of sex difference to the status of biological accident would render both meaningless, according to Long.[30] He goes on to argue that those who reject sex difference as an essential human characteristic must explain why hermaphrodites are understood to be biological mutations. Science recognizes that this situation is brought about by a physical imperfection which impedes natural sexual expression of the male or female, which is nonetheless still present.[31]

Barbara Albrecht also argues that there are only two ways of being human, as a male or female. Sex differentiation is not a result of any type of conditioning, be it social or cultural, but is rooted in the order of creation. She shows that macro-level sex differences are manifest even at the microscopic level of the gamete: "'The selection of sperm cells by mobility' (to travel the longer distance) and the egg cell by vitality at the price of immobility . . . determines that the egg-producing organism becomes the receiving one. This, in all likelihood, is the most momentous factor in the genesis of sex differentiation,' the determining clue to all differentiation within that which men and women possess in common."[32]

Albrecht, like Allen, finds sex differentiation manifested throughout all aspects of the organism, to its lowest levels of organization. However, Albrecht adds the observation that even at the level of the gamete, sex-specific properties such as receptivity seem evident. Allen and others thus provide compelling arguments that sexual complementarity is obvious, and that it does not necessarily result in gender dualism.

Gudorf raises a final issue associated with gender dualism, claiming that it deprives the person of wholeness outside of marriage, denigrating the entire tradition of consecrated celibacy. We have shown John Paul

---

[30] See Long, "The Metaphysics of Gender," 47.

[31] See Long, "The Metaphysics of Gender," 47–48.

[32] Barbara Albrecht, "Is There an Objective Type 'Woman'?," in *The Church and Women: A Compendium*, ed. Helmut Moll (San Francisco: Ignatius Press, 1988), 44.

II's account of consecrated celibacy as a means of personal fulfillment for those called to it. But is he inconsistent with this claim in light of his views of the role of complementary love in personal fulfillment? Walter Kasper's description of personal fulfillment in marriage closely reflects that of John Paul II. His focus on the manner in which relationships contribute to personal fulfillment helps to address Gudorf's concern.[33]

A person is fulfilled through the free, unconditional, and definitive gift of oneself to another person. This is most intimately achieved in a uniquely human manner in the marital covenant. At root, this reveals that personal fulfillment is never self-referential, but neither is it ultimately achieved in human relationships alone. Fulfillment comes through what might be called the Trinitarian paradox: man finds his fulfillment in selfless relationships of love with others. But personal fulfillment is only achieved when one first gives himself completely to Christ, man's only ultimate end.

As John Paul II shows, in consecrated celibacy the person fulfills himself through a total, complete, and definitive gift of himself to Christ the Bridegroom, unmediated by a spouse.[34] In the consecrated state, the selfless relationship is a direct one with the divine person of the Son, the ultimate fulfillment of every created person.[35] In marriage, the spouses mutually mediate this fulfillment in Christ to one another.[36] Therefore, objectively speaking, consecrated celibacy is a superior path to self-fulfillment (i.e., holiness), but marriage is subjectively superior for those who are called to it.[37]

Any rejection of John Paul II's anthropology on the grounds that it is dualistic is a baseless critique. Those who make this claim do not appear to engage his anthropology adequately and so they miss its integral complementarity. His Thomist metaphysics and the later developments of personalism provide the necessary framework to maintain the unity of nature while establishing the ontology of sex difference in the person.[38]

---

[33] See Walter Kasper, "The Position of Woman as a Problem of Theological Anthropology," in *The Church and Women*, 62.

[34] See John Paul II, Post-Synodal Apostolic Exhortation on the Consecrated Life and Its Mission in the Church and in the World *Vita consecrata* (March 26, 1996), §34.

[35] See John Paul II, *A Catechesis on the Creed*, vol. 4, *The Church: Mystery, Sacrament, Community* (Boston: Pauline Books and Media, 1998), 566.

[36] See John Paul II, *The Church*, 56.

[37] See *Vita consecrata*, §18.

[38] See our previous discussion of sex difference having the ontology of relation in chapter 6 and later.

GENDER STEREOTYPING

There are critics who make the claim that the characteristics which John Paul II associates with sex differences are nothing more than stereotypes. If one can show this to be the case, John Paul II's theology of fatherhood, at least as I have presented it, collapses. Cathleen Kaveny argues:

> It is one thing to say in general terms that men and women are "complementary"; it is quite another to start parceling out specific character traits. Unfortunately, in their effort to distance themselves from an early feminism that denied all differences between men and women, some papal feminists—those who have embraced the pope's "new feminism"—have come close to the old sexism. Women, according to papal feminist Gloria Conde, are "tender, sensitive, easily influenced," while men are "independent, self sufficient, emotionally controlled." Tell that to Condoleezza Rice or Ruth Bader Ginsburg.[39]

In an earlier article for *Commonweal*, Kaveny says that while she appreciates John Paul II's view of complementarity, she finds it to be unrealistic:

> In the abstract, the notion of gender "complementarity" embraced by John Paul II seems (and is) very attractive. Gender complementarity emphasizes that men and women are different but that they need each other. Frequently (though more frequently in the writings of the new feminists than in papal writings), it goes one step further, attempting to define a set of corresponding and mutually exclusive "masculine" and "feminine" traits.[40]

However, she argues that the problem with this theology, especially as espoused by the new feminists, is that they slavishly serve an ideology which stereotypes women in the name of complementarity. She argues: "Real women do not fit into . . . binary categories. . . . For a woman to force herself to conform to such expectations is self-destructive and dangerous."[41] Similarly, commenting on John Paul II's encyclical *Redemptoris mater* and his remarks on Mary's feminine virtues as models for women, Elizabeth

---

[39] Cathleen Kaveny, "What is the Vatican Saying About Women? Conservative Catholics Might Be Surprised," *The Washington Post*, August 15, 2004, B3.

[40] Cathleen Kaveny, "What Women Want: 'Buffy,' The Pope and The New Feminists," *Commonweal* 130, no. 19 (November 7, 2003): 18–24.

[41] Kaveny, "What Women Want."

Johnson balks: "Note that whatever may be the praiseworthy value of this list of virtues, the fact that they are 'feminine,' applied to women but not men, makes them suspect. They are the habits of the helper, the auxiliary, the handmaid, not that of the resister of oppression—let alone the self-actualizing, creative leader."[42] In an earlier work, Johnson explains why she is concerned over such stereotyping. She argues:

> In the view [that men and women are polar opposites each bearing unique characteristics excluded from the other sex] male and female are related by the notion of complementarity, which rigidly predetermines the qualities each should cultivate and the roles each can play. Apart from naiveté about its own social conditioning, its reliance on stereotypes, and the denial of the wholeness of human experience that it mandates, this position functions as a smokescreen for the subordination of women since by its definition women are always relegated to the private, passive realm.[43]

Susan Okin describes her ideal for family and society with regard to what she would like to see as general attitudes about sex characteristics and roles:

> A just future would be one without gender. In its social structures and practices, one's sex would have no more relevance than one's eye color or the length of one's toes. No assumptions would be made about "male" and "female" roles; childbearing would be so conceptually separated from child rearing and other family responsibilities that it would be a cause for surprise, and no little concern, if men and women were not equally responsible for domestic life or if children were to spend more time with one parent than the other. It would be a future in which men and women participated in more or less equal numbers in every sphere of life.[44]

A common concern given by many feminists over stereotyping is that any assignment of sex-based characteristics is simply a pretext for the

---

[42] Johnson, *Truly Our Sister*, 63.
[43] Johnson, *She Who Is*, 154.
[44] Susan Moller Okin, *Justice, Gender, and the Family* (New York: Harper Collins, 1989), 171, cited in Cahill, *Sex, Gender, and Christian Ethics*, 83.

subordination of women. While addressing the "suspicion" argument associated with gender stereotyping is not relevant for our concerns, if the arguments against the existence of sex-specific traits can be sustained, then this is problematic for the author's theology of fatherhood.

Cahill articulates many common feminist arguments against sex-specific traits. She says that strong sex differences which are grounded in reproductive biology, such as intellectual, emotional, and social capacities, work to women's disadvantage because they are always associated with the domestic and subordinate women to men.[45] She suggests that reproductive physiology should have little to say about social roles.[46] In her criticism of John Paul II for doing exactly this in *Mulieris dignitatem*, she asks if he is not guilty of uncritical romanticism.[47]

Commenting on his assertion that a woman's equal dignity fully justifies her equal access to all aspects of public life in *Familiaris consortio* §25, Cahill finds a contradiction. She counters that "the value of women's 'maternal and family role' is supposed to exceed that of 'all other public roles and all other professions'; women should not renounce their 'femininity' or imitate masculine roles. Apparently the full interpersonal and sexual reciprocity of women and men does not imply equality in all spheres of familial and social life."[48] Cahill appears to suggest that if one asserts that women have greater responsibilities in certain aspects of family life which take her away from societal roles outside the family more than they do the man, then one supports a structure with inherent inequality. The common argument is that admitting sex differences inherently justifies inequalities.

Nevertheless, Cahill does not go so far as to deny all differences. She is willing to allow them a role in establishing personal identity. But like Johnson, Cahill wants to limit sex difference's influences to the plane of incidental attributes such as race.[49] She summarizes the argument against gender stereotyping in her answer to the "problem":

---

[45] See Lisa Sowle Cahill, "Notes on Moral Theology: Feminist Ethics," *Theological Studies* 51 (1990): 54.

[46] See Cahill, *Sex, Gender, and Christian Ethics*, 82.

[47] See Cahill, "Feminist Ethics," 58. "Romanticism" is a complaint by some feminists against an unrealistic ideal imposed upon women by men based upon the latter's "romanticized" image of mothers and motherly love.

[48] Cahill, *Sex, Gender, and Christian Ethics*, 204.

[49] See Cahill, *Sex, Gender, and Christian Ethics*, 87.

The solution from the object-relations perspective is more egal-itarian child-nurturance patterns, along with less exhaustive maternal commitment to the infant. This approach reinforces the thesis that the whole panoply of male and female psycholog-ical characteristics which are associated with traditional gender roles are neither innate and "natural" nor unavoidable. Even if the female reproductive roles of pregnancy, birth, and lactation do originally define women's relation to their offspring differently from that of men, the complex institutions which prolong their relationship and entrench male and female role separations go far beyond what is demanded by reproductive biology.[50]

There is a range of differences among feminists' willingness to permit sex difference to influence the establishment of personal identity, but there is general agreement that it cannot be the basis for influencing family or social roles, at least not beyond what is obviously dictated by procreative biology. The arguments against social and family roles can be boiled down to the claim that current cultural and social roles are the result of various forms of unjust patriarchal influence on society. These manifest as cultural and social biases imposed by oppressive male-controlled societies or by a naïve patriarchal idealization of women and motherhood.

The common point of reference among the various feminist arguments is that all seem to implicitly recognize the universality of family roles based upon sex-based differences, but from their feminist perspective these must be deconstructed to some degree or another if women are to attain a just equality with men. However, these critics seem to presuppose that which they deny. Dominican moral theologian Benedict Ashley argues that the very fact that feminists can argue that women have been subjugated by stronger, abusive men because of their physically weaker stature reveal a natural differentiation that we must recognize in non-abusive ways.[51] Ashley indicates that women's fear is not unfounded, but it is based upon the sinful abuse of the natural differences men and women possess.

Those feminists who wish to deny these innate differences are, perhaps unwittingly, attempting to bury the problem instead of addressing it. In contrast to an approach which is in reality built upon denial of the obvious, John Paul's anthropology appears to be much more realistic. He recognizes the innate differences between men and women and the abuse

---

[50] Cahill, "Feminist Ethics," 59–60.
[51] See Ashley, *Justice in the Church*, 100–101.

women can suffer because of them, but rather than deny the differences, his writings emphatically point to the need for educating men and women about this truth in order for both to be transformed in Christ in order to overcome these sinful pitfalls. His implicit call for this education about men is in what we are calling his "theology of masculinity and fatherhood." This education is required not only in order to correct the abuses but also to guide men in fulfilling their calling as men and fathers.

In chapter 6, we saw John Paul II's metaphysical arguments for the partially constitutive character of sex difference for the human person. Walter Kasper provides a different type of metaphysical argument for the strong association between the two and, carrying with it, the societal implications of this constitutive association. He argues that if the body is a real symbol of the person, then the whole person of a man or woman cannot be indifferent to the body and its sexuality, and so protecting the equal value of men and women cannot be achieved by rejecting their real differences.[52] Kasper says that these differences, therefore, must also have an impact on the way that family and culture are organized. It is not simply that God provides to man his nature. This gift comes with a task, that of applying the gifts of human nature to the matter of personal perfection.

Personhood reveals that man cannot be reduced to biology. He is a being made for "culture" and as such being woman or man is a gift that requires "cultivation." The body has a "culture" that permeates the way one organizes and lives his personal life. Culture is not something completely arbitrary which frees one from the structure of nature, but on the other hand, neither is nature deterministic. Human nature is, by definition, endowed with an intellect permitting man to transcend himself and with a free will to choose the good. There is ample room for personal creativity within the envelope of authentic possibilities marked off by human nature.[53] Kasper suggests that we are not justified in ignoring the way we are

---

[52] See Kasper, "The Position of Woman," 58–59. Kasper's term "real symbol" is likely invoking Karl Rahner's *Real Symbol* which is the latter's formulation of Thomist hylomorphism. Rahner says: "All beings are by their very nature symbolic, because they necessarily 'express' themselves in order to attain their own nature" (Karl Rahner, "Theology of the Symbol," in *Theological Investigations* [London: Darton, Longman & Todd; Baltimore: Helicon Press, 1961], 4:224). Kasper means that the body as a symbol is not an abstraction but an ontological reality. It is the visible self-expression of the whole person. Self-communication is only possible because of the ontological unity of the whole person with his body.

[53] See Kasper, "The Position of Woman," 60.

made in considering the structures we establish in the family and society. Kasper's realism corresponds well with that of John Paul II in this context.

John Paul II agrees with the feminist criticism that women have often suffered unjustly due to sex differences, but he avoids the temptation to conflate women's equality with sameness. His Christian theology of fatherhood recognizes that human beings are not random products of evolution. They are created by God with a purpose and are given the necessary gifts to fulfill their calling. Equality cannot mean lack of differences because men and women are by definition different. Jutta Burggraf argues just that, saying that equality is a separate issue from vocation and function.[54] She explains that a woman's vocation arises from her femininity because God has created her for a certain purpose. Woman and man are to work together, in equal but complementary ways, so that they harmonize with each other.

Laura Garcia similarly shows that the recognition of sex-based roles is not stereotyping at all. She argues that while certain feminists might dispute this, it probably would not be disputed "by anyone who has children of both genders. The differences between girls and boys appear early and seem stubbornly resistant to manipulation by well-meaning . . . parents. . . . Nature has a way of asserting herself in unperturbed disregard for our theories."[55] Garcia's last point is a significant one because it suggests consequences for getting this question wrong. This touches on John Paul's assertion that the masculinization of women can deform them. There is at least anecdotal evidence that this is universally true.

Journalist Wendy McElroy relates the story of a little boy named Bruce Reimer who was an infant in 1966. As an eight-month-old baby he underwent a circumcision that went seriously wrong, and Bruce was left without a penis. Medical psychologist Dr. John Money of John Hopkins University in Baltimore was eventually consulted. Money had previously theorized that gender was determined more by environment than biology. Consequently, he recommended that Bruce be raised as a girl. Money was especially interested in Bruce's case because he was an identical twin, and his brother could serve as a control. Bruce was renamed Brenda, underwent castration and twelve years of hormonal treatment and extensive

---

[54] See Jutta Burggraf, "Woman's Dignity and Function in Church and Society," in *The Church and Women*, 104–105.
[55] Laura L. Garcia, "The Role of Women in Society," paper delivered to an *Instituto de Iniciativas de Orientación Familiar* sponsored conference, October 2000.

social indoctrination. Despite Money's well publicized "success" of this case, the truth was much different. McElroy writes:

> Behind the scenes, Reimer's mother told Money that Brenda ripped off dresses, rejected dolls, insisted on standing up to urinate, and asked to shave like her father. Nevertheless, Money's 1972 book *Man and Woman, Boy and Girl* declared the experiment to be a success. Indeed, Money urged the Reimers to complete the gender experiment on the pubescent Brenda by having a vagina surgically constructed. When Brenda threatened to commit suicide rather than undergo more treatment by Money, the Reimers revealed the truth. Brenda adopted the name David and began to live as a man. Of his childhood, David later stated: "It was like brainwashing . . . I'd give just about anything to go to a hypnotist to black out my whole past. Because it's torture. What they did to you in the body is sometimes not near as bad as what they did to you in the mind with the psychological warfare in your head."[56]

McElroy reports that in 1997 two scientists writing in the Journal *Archives of Pediatric and Adolescent Medicine* exposed Money's fraudulence. Milton Diamond, a biologist, and Keith Sigmundson, a psychiatrist, concluded that Money's experiment was a failure and his reporting fraudulent. Johns Hopkins Children Center subsequently released two studies which found that sex identity was dictated by prenatal exposure to male hormones in normal babies born with XY chromosomes. This finding held even with babies born without a penis.

McElroy concludes: "Although Money's research was widely discredited, the belief that sexual identity is socially constructed still deeply impacts our culture. A good first step toward reversing the damage this belief can inflict is to reclaim a word usage that has been virtually abandoned. We should use the word 'sex' and reject the word 'gender' when discussing sexual identity."[57] The tragic ramifications of the rejection of the true depth of sex difference for personal identity in this case appear to have been fatal. On May 4, 2004, David Reimer, after numerous attempts beginning in his teenage years, finally took his own life at the age of

---

[56] Wendy McElroy, "Death by Theory," *Fox News*, May 26, 2004, available online at https://soc.men.narkive.com/9d6c3UQK/death-by-theory; accessed on November 18, 2021.

[57] McElroy, "Death by Theory."

thirty-eight.[58] This case would seem to be an acutely tragic realization of John Paul's admonition that ignoring the realities of sex difference can have dire consequences.[59]

As McElroy points out, the theory that biology plays an insignificant role in establishing sex identity was a widespread notion in academic circles for many decades. An example of this may be found in the work of feminist Sidney Callahan, writing in the mid-1970s about the prevailing state of research which indicated the insignificance of sex differentiation in biological development:

> Sexuality is an example of a simple polar categorization which is now beside the point. Not only is there obviously a wide diversity of social sex roles possible in varying cultures, but even the psycho-biological development of sexual identity is far more complicated than appears on the surface. There exists a relay stage system of sexual development in which first genetic factors, then hormonal influences, then morphological and socio-cognitive factors alternate and mutually influence each other. . . . It seems to be the case that we are all programmed more to be a species model, and that sexual differentiation can be seen as a fairly minor part of the incredibly complicated growth process, unless a culture chooses to exaggerate differences.[60]

However, as McElroy correctly indicates, one can no longer credibly maintain this claim.

For example, Garcia shows that there is vast empirical evidence for ontological differences between women and men which one cannot attribute to environmental causes. She cites recent brain research that reveals different organizational structures for female and male brains. Resulting from this, each sex possesses more acute faculties relative to the other sex. Women are better at listening and detecting changes in tone of voice than are men. Women are more sensitive with respect to spotting subtle emotions in interpersonal exchanges. This is due to the fact that women's brains are much more integrated, allowing them to employ both hemispheres of their brains in processing emotional content. Garcia notes that

---

[58] See McElroy, "Death by Theory."
[59] See *Mulieris dignitatem*, §10.
[60] Sidney Callahan, "Misunderstanding of Sexuality and Resistance to Woman Priests," in *Women Priests*, 292.

women engage both halves of their brains in problem solving while for men, problem solving is generally limited to the brain's analytical centers.[61]

Long also points to biological evidence showing that sex differences touch almost every aspect of the human person. For example, men are much more physically aggressive than are women. Biologists correlate this masculine characteristic with testosterone levels which are many times greater than in females. This characteristic corresponds to all mammalian species that have analogous endocrine systems to humans. Other sex-based characteristics also correlate with this greater physical aggressiveness. As an example, men have greater muscle mass which arises from greater testosterone levels. Additionally, Long makes reference to recent investigations by biologists into the effects of hormonal conditioning on cognitive abilities that provide men with more acute aptitudes for performing geometrical and formal mental tasks.[62] These contentions made by theological and philosophical anthropologists are supported by researchers in their respective fields of natural science.

Paul Vitz, at the time a professor of psychology at New York University, asserted that the old unisex models presumed by psychologists have recently been challenged. He says that there is a growing body of evidence that there are important psycho-biological differences between males and females. For example, the male nervous system is masculinized before birth, and this continues for a time postnatally.[63] Newer research has obviated the androgynous theories of the 1970s. A comprehensive assessment of scientific data on sex-based differences was recently published which further supports John Paul II's assignment of sex-based characteristics to men and women.

Stephen Rhoads, professor of politics at the University of Virginia, provides an extensive survey of the literature in this area.[64] He finds that many recent studies support specific characteristics to be associated with sex difference. For example, a common trend in the studies he surveyed is the finding that women exhibit behaviors that are clearly more empathetic, tender, and nurturing than is the case with men.[65] These sex-based traits

---

[61] See Garcia, "The Role of Woman in Society."

[62] Long, "The Metaphysics of Gender," 49.

[63] See Paul Vitz, "From Personhood to Fatherhood," *Social Justice Review* 77 (November–December 1986): 206.

[64] See Stephen Rhoads, *Taking Sex Differences Seriously* (San Francisco: Encounter Books, 2004).

[65] Rhoads, *Taking Sex Differences Seriously*, 193. Rhoads cites, for example, Alan Feingold, "Gender Differences in Personality: A Meta-Analysis," *Psychological Bulletin* 116, no. 3

explain the cross-cultural trends which generally find women dominating domestic roles. He finds that one cannot attribute these trends to so-called oppressive patriarchal societies.[66] To support this, Rhoads writes of efforts in Sweden and Israel to introduce "a more androgynous pattern of child-care" in their respective societies.[67]

The Swedish experiment began in the 1970s when family leave policies were changed from maternal to parental leave. This was followed by an offer of one month's leave to the family only if it was taken by the father. A substantial advertising campaign was subsequently launched to encourage fathers toward more equitable participation in child rearing. Rhoads says that mothers in Sweden are still twice as likely to take maternity leave than are fathers and it lasts six times longer on average. Much earlier in the 1900s the Israeli kibbutzim explicitly attempted to "break down historic, stereotypical sex roles."[68] Communal kitchens and laundries were established, and children were placed in homes separate from their parents. All of this was aimed at freeing women from domestic responsibilities which limited their working outside the home.

It was young mothers who were instrumental in overturning the rules separating the children from their families. These women wanted to devote more time to their children and so today the nuclear family is the foundation of kibbutz life. Rhoads points out that the men initially resisted but it was the women's will which prevailed. He finds there is a biological foundation for these differences in nurturing between men and women.

Rhoads discusses experiments, which found that these biological differences appeared "at an astonishingly early age—before any socialization could have occurred."[69] These include greater female empathy among day-old infants in their response to other infants crying and greater female empathy among second-year infants exposed to the distress of others.[70]

(1994): 429–56, and Richard Lippa, "Gender-Related Individual Differences and the Structure of Vocational Interests: The Importance of the People-Things Dimension," *Journal of Personality and Social Psychology* 4 (1998): 996–1009. Rhoads includes findings from other studies that support his assertion that daughters are more likely than sons to take care of a sick parent and that women are more likely to take care of the family pet. UCLA's Higher Education Research Institute reports that consistently about 68 percent of female freshmen say that helping others is an important life objective, to only 50 percent of male freshmen.

[66] See Rhoads, *Taking Sex Differences Seriously*, 25ff.

[67] Rhoads, *Taking Sex Differences Seriously*, 196.

[68] Rhoads, *Taking Sex Differences Seriously*, 196.

[69] Rhoads, *Taking Sex Differences Seriously*, 197.

[70] See Rhoads, *Taking Sex Differences Seriously*, 197.

Researchers have identified the peptide oxytocin as the most significant hormone associated with nurturing behavior. It "promotes bonding and a calm, relaxed emotional state" in both men and women.[71] They have found that men release large quantities in sexual orgasm whereas women, by contrast, release it in large quantities during pregnancy and in breastfeeding. Rhoads identifies another hormone, prolactin, which also surges in pregnancy and breastfeeding. These hormones are thought to play a significant factor in accommodating the mother to routines and monotony.

Mothers "are more prone to please and obey—a trait some researchers think is nature's way of making them more ready 'to "take orders" from their babies.' Even the act of stroking her baby releases oxytocin in the mother, causing her to feel a 'beatific calm' and somewhat sedated."[72] Fathers can also bond with their babies. Many men experience increased cortisol levels in response to their baby's cry, and testosterone levels drop when the baby is born. However, Rhoads concludes, "Bonding and nurturing instincts are not as strong in men as in women. A father does not get a 'neurochemical high' from cuddling a baby in the way a mother does."[73]

Other findings associated with nurturing include the fact that a mother can distinguish her baby's cry within a few hours of giving birth whereas a father is much less likely to have this capacity.[74] Childless females experience an increase in heart rate when exposed to the cries of infants, while childless males' rates decrease.[75] Mothers are much lighter sleepers on average than are fathers and so the latter are much less likely to hear their infants crying.[76] When the father is awakened by his baby's cry, he is much more likely to be annoyed than is the mother.[77] Rhoads provides much more data which indicate that John Paul II's characterization of women and mothers is not unfounded stereotyping. They are firmly grounded in his realistic anthropology and confirmed by empirical data.

In agreement with McElroy, Rhoads shows that the "gender neutral" presuppositions of many feminists were based on biased and faulty studies. He cites psychologist Alice Eagly[78] as one who does not think there is much

---

[71] Rhoads, *Taking Sex Differences Seriously*, 198.
[72] Rhoads, *Taking Sex Differences Seriously*, 198.
[73] Rhoads, *Taking Sex Differences Seriously*, 199.
[74] See Rhoads, *Taking Sex Differences Seriously*, 199.
[75] See Rhoads, *Taking Sex Differences Seriously*, 200.
[76] See Rhoads, *Taking Sex Differences Seriously*, 200.
[77] See Rhoads, *Taking Sex Differences Seriously*, 200.
[78] See Alice H. Eagly, "The Science and Politics of Comparing Women and Men," *American Psychologist* 50, no. 3 (1995): 145–58.

consequence in biological sex distinctions.[79] Nevertheless, Eagly asserts that the still widely quoted psychology texts on the inconclusiveness of sex differences are out of date. They were based upon 1970s feminist research that was biased toward the elimination of sex differentiation, which was seen as a source of exclusion. Eagly says, rather, that men and women really do conform to sexual "stereotypes." For instance, women "tend to manifest behaviors that can be described as socially sensitive, friendly, and concerned with others' welfare, whereas men tend to manifest behaviors that can be described as dominant, controlling and independent." In other words, ordinary people's gender stereotypes are, as Eagly says, "fairly accurate," and most people do recognize that men and women occupy "partially over-lapping groups, possessing different average levels of various attributes." Eagly concludes that scientists currently studying men and women "have begun to realize" that they have shattered "not cultural stereotypes" but the "scientific consensus forged in the feminist movement of the 1970s."[80]

Rhoads also provides data which supports Garcia's assertion about brain organization and how it facilitates different tasks. In analyzing the medical literature on brain research, he says that the data manifest inherent differences between the sexes. One example is the finding that men have fewer connecting neurons in the corpus callosum, which connects the two hemispheres of the brain, than do women. This possibly plays a part in women's superior capacity to discuss their emotions. The way men and women use their brains differently and the effect of the brain's hormones are even more significant than the physical differences between masculine and feminine brain structure. Women's brains use significantly more neurons for just about every activity tested. This has been shown using positron emission tomography (PET) scans.

Women's brains generally seem to be a highly integrated network across the entire brain whereas men's seem to be "wired" in a much more compartmentalized manner. This provides women advantages in stroke recovery as well as in performing verbal tasks. Men experience a general advantage in working on spatial tasks.[81] These empirical findings support John Paul II's theology of fatherhood quite well and help to confirm the eccentric account we have used to describe masculine traits. Far from being stereotypes, the characteristics of men and fathers (as well as women and mothers) which he presents objectively correlate to empirical studies of sex differences.

---

[79] See Rhoads, *Taking Sex Differences Seriously*, 18ff.
[80] Rhoads, *Taking Sex Differences Seriously*, 18ff.
[81] See Rhoads, *Taking Sex Differences Seriously*, 27–28.

Rhoads also does an extensive review of the literature which looks at behavior patterns correlated to testosterone levels. He reports that high-testosterone men "are more likely to be big-boned, muscular, rambunctious and self-confident, always seeking to dominate."[82] Low-testosterone men on average have superior capacities with spatial tasks, tend to do better in academic settings, and maintain jobs that have more social status.[83] Nevertheless, the lower-testosterone man is "almost always masculine"[84] and is usually competitive with his male peers.[85] Girls who were prenatally exposed to very high levels of testosterone experience a "dramatic and persistent effect."[86] "They 'prefer boys' toys which are more mechanical than girls' toys. They like transportation and construction toys, including helicopters, cars, fire engines, blocks, and Lincoln Logs better than dolls, kitchen supplies, toy telephones, and crayons and paper.'"[87]

Those who as adults possess high testosterone "are more assertive, more career-oriented, and more likely to have high-status and traditionally male-dominated careers."[88] Still, Rhoads finds that the studies do not suggest that high-testosterone women look or act like men. Rather, when compared to other women, they simply tend to mix typically masculine behaviors and traits with those that are typically feminine.[89] So it would seem that while hormone levels both before birth and later in life have significant effects on behavior, they are not the sole determinant. This is an important observation which corresponds to John Paul's anthropology which is based upon his metaphysics.[90]

Agreeing with John Paul II, Long cautions that biological conditioning must not be misread as a rigid determination of roles and responsibilities in family and society. He states that attributes such as male aggressiveness,

---

[82] Rhoads, *Taking Sex Differences Seriously*, 32.

[83] See Rhoads, *Taking Sex Differences Seriously*, 32.

[84] Rhoads, *Taking Sex Differences Seriously*, 32–33.

[85] See Rhoads, *Taking Sex Differences Seriously*, 33.

[86] See Rhoads, *Taking Sex Differences Seriously*, 29.

[87] See Rhoads, *Taking Sex Differences Seriously*, 29.

[88] Rhoads, *Taking Sex Differences Seriously*, 31.

[89] Rhoads, *Taking Sex Differences Seriously*, 32.

[90] John Paul II states: "We must consider that . . . man and woman [are] not just a passive object, defined by his or her own body and sex, and in this way determined 'by nature.' On the contrary, because they are a man and a woman, each of them is 'given' to the other as a unique and unrepeatable subject, as 'self,' as a person" (*Man and Woman He Created Them: A Theology of the Body*, trans. Michael Waldstein [Boston: Pauline Books and Media, 2006], 79).

which is a feature arising from a man's soul, does not override his intellect.[91] This attribute may in some ways make it more difficult, but it does not prevent him from assuming an important role in raising his child.[92] Likewise, a woman's metaphysical predisposition toward receptive nurturing does not prevent her from intellectual, moral, or physical aggression if the situation demands it. Long refers back to the same integral sex complementarity which Allen articulated and John Paul II espouses. He states: "For whatever the profundity of the specific differences of man and woman still each possesses the intrinsic spiritual dignity of beings capable of love and understanding. No essentially human quality is denied of men or women and parcelled [sic] out exclusively to one sex, but these essential human qualities are given typically and substantially different form in the spiritual souls of man and woman."[93] John Paul II's theology of fatherhood recognizes that the characteristics associated with one's sex difference help to orient and facilitate a man (or woman) toward his vocation but they do not deny him his free will.

Karl Lehman also cautions against too strict an association of roles and sex difference. He argues that sex difference must not be overvalued, as many are the products of social conditioning.[94] However, he also warns against androgenizing trends which try to erase these differences. Lehman states: "The appeal to biology must not . . . mean the fixation of an inalterable fate. But if one ignores this in its significance, then women themselves must pay the price."[95] He quotes Margaret Mead to summarize what he sees as the proper balance in regard to the differences between sexes, taking into account the motivation to diminish the differences:

---

[91] Long's assertion that male aggressiveness arises from the masculine soul is not in contradiction to the earlier discussion showing that exposure to high or low levels of testosterone in a person's developmental stages provides a bias toward or away from aggressiveness, respectively. Hylomorphism indicates that the soul, to some degree, is responsible for testosterone production because the soul provides the person's vegetative, animal, and intellectual faculties. I say to some degree because environmental factors also come into play. Furthermore, biochemistry does not mean determinism. The rational faculties of the soul are still responsible for developing habits which either succumb to or overcome a person's concupiscent proclivities associated with the vegetative and/or animal faculties.

[92] See Long, "The Metaphysics of Gender," 50.

[93] Long, "The Metaphysics of Gender," 50.

[94] See Karl Lehman, "The Place of Women as a Problem in Theological Anthropology," in *The Church and Women*, 25.

[95] Lehman, "The Place of Women," 28.

> Our tendency at present is to minimize all these differences . . . or
> at most to try to obliterate particular differences that are seen as
> handicaps on one sex. . . . . But every adjustment that minimizes a
> difference, a vulnerability, in one sex, a differential strength in the
> other, diminishes their possibility of complementing each other,
> and corresponds—symbolically—to sealing off the constructive
> receptivity of the female and the vigorous outgoing construc-
> tive activity of the male, muting them both in the end to a duller
> version of human life in which each is denied the fullness of
> humanity that each might have had. Guard each sex in its vulner-
> able moments we must, protect and cherish it through the crises
> that at some times are so much harder for one than for the other.
> But as we guard, we may also keep the differences. . . . Yet both are
> necessary, and the skill of one sex gives only a partial answer. We
> can build a whole society only by using both the gifts special to
> each sex and those shared by both sexes—by using the gifts of the
> whole of humanity.[96]

Clearly, one needs an integral anthropology which appreciates the metaphysical reality of the human person as sexually differentiated. John Paul
II continually eschews those views which would reduce the human person
to his biology or, conversely, would completely cut the person free from his
body-soul composite. Some scholars have correctly identified the origin
of these errors. Grabowski assesses that the latter error arises from the
erroneous use of scientific evidence to support the premise that there is
no ontological grounding for sex difference in personhood. He says that
the fundamental problem here is a presumptive nominalism and Lockean
epistemology.

Feminists claim the empirical sciences as uniquely supporting their
theological methodology, support that, they argue, their version of traditional theological method does not possess. However, as Grabowski points
out, they do not adequately take into consideration that practitioners in
the empirical sciences generally are quite skeptical about the value of philosophical or theological inquiry. Thus, it should not be surprising that
the results of empirical investigations provide no evidence for an ontological fundament for sex difference. Grabowski criticizes such feminists

---

[96] Margaret Mead, *Male and Female: A Study of the Sexes in a Changing World* (New York:
W. Morrow, 1952, originally published 1949), 371–72, 384, quoted in Lehman, "The
Place of Women," 28.

for exceeding the reasonable employment of empirical data in theological reflection by completely embracing a method that is ignorant of its limits and philosophical presuppositions.[97]

Grabowski identifies an important methodological caution in the use of data from the human sciences. One must take into account that the scientific method requires a metaphysical reduction to be able to isolate certain aspects of the human person for investigation. However, many scientists ontologize this methodological reduction in order to make universal claims which the science itself does not—indeed cannot—demonstrate. Rather, the claims result from unarticulated and therefore unexamined philosophies that these scientists presuppose. The fear of oppression seems to lead some feminists to disregard this caution. John Paul II is aware of this understandable fear.[98] His theology of masculinity and fatherhood provides the insights necessary to begin to correct the source of the fear without undermining an authentic vision of the human person.

John Paul II's theology of fatherhood takes seriously the Second Vatican Council's assertion that "Christ reveals man to himself" (GS §22). His anthropology is more consonant with the Incarnation, which indicates the importance of the whole person who possesses a body and soul, than are those theologies which end up diminishing the body's significance for personhood, dismissing it as being simply biological. Along these lines, Joseph Ratzinger provides an assessment of the errors which lead some to claim no correlation between sex difference and family and social roles. He uncovers another side to the problem.[99] Part of the trouble is rooted in original sin which today manifests itself as a desire for radical emancipation from all constraints. It is, in essence, a desire to be like God without him, as did Adam and Eve. This idea, he says, incorporates the desire to separate man from the biological conditioning in which he was created.

Ratzinger explains that this is wrongheaded because sex differentiation is an integral and unavoidable aspect of man's being. It is deeply rooted in his nature as a unity of body and soul. However, he warns that when the corporal aspect of man is dismissed as merely biological, it becomes licit to manipulate the body as a thing external to the spiritual person. Some scholars take as given this perceived liberation from dependency from one's nature which frees the person to use his will with no prior limitations. Ratzinger says that the ramifications of this attitude include a

---

[97] See Grabowski, "Theological Anthropology and Gender," 91.
[98] See *Mulieris dignitatem*, §10.
[99] See Joseph Ratzinger, "On the Position of Mariology and Marian Spirituality Within the Totality of Faith and Theology," in *The Church and Women*, 76–77.

self-wounding at man's deepest level such that he comes to abhor himself, "because, in truth, it is only as a body, only as a man or woman that he is a human being at all."[100] He underscores the implications of the attempt at a false liberation: it rejects the truth of the Incarnation which is uniting the divine with that which is at once spiritual and biological.[101]

These assessments which presuppose an integral anthropology of a like order with John Paul II's are consistent with a more recent, critical view of the data from the natural sciences. It is clear that John Paul II is on solid ground in his anthropology of specific characteristics for men and women which are needed for their roles in their vocations as parents. His anthropology is internally self-consistent and externally corresponds with the recent empirical data arising from the cultural, sociological, psychological, and biological sciences. While it perhaps may not assuage the fears of those feminists who are motivated by suspicion, his anthropology of sex-based characteristics and associated roles adequately answers the specific criticisms of those who would reject it as mere gender stereotyping.

BIOLOGISM

Another criticism closely related to that of gender stereotyping is that of "biologism" or "physicalism." Earlier we saw that these terms originate among moral theologians but that they have implications for a broader anthropology. The concern of those who accuse John Paul II of biologism in his anthropology is essentially one of determinism. It is often stated as "biology is destiny." Phyllis Kaminski is one who accuses John Paul of just such an error. She says: "Patriarchal theology as illustrated in the pope's letter [*Mulieris dignitatem*] assumes that the biology of reproduction is normative and determines certain naturally derivative social relations."[102] Gudorf makes the indictment more directly: "John Paul II represents the 'biology is destiny' school of thought with regard to women and shares with others in that school the failure to understand the male sex in similar biological terms."[103]

Recall also that Grabowski warned of a metaphysicalism which he

---

[100] Ratzinger, "On the Position of Mariology," 76–77.

[101] See Joseph Cardinal Ratzinger, *Daughter Zion: Meditations on the Church's Marian Belief*, trans. John McDermott, S.J. (San Francisco: Ignatius Press, 1983), 52–53.

[102] Phyllis Kaminski, "'Reproducing the World': Mary O'Brien's Theory of Reproductive Consciousness and Implications for Feminist Incarnational Theology," *Horizons* 19, no. 2 (1992): 259.

[103] Gudorf, "The Modern Papacy on Women," 298.

described as the attempt to infer the ontological qualities of the sexes based on the biology of sexual intercourse.[104] Grabowski mentions only Louis Bouyer and Paul Quay as examples of those who are close to this approach. From what I have already presented, it is obvious that John Paul II rejects the "biology is destiny" determinism. Anyone who has carefully read Wojtyła's book *Person and Act*, or John Paul II's Wednesday catecheses where he discussed his theology of the body, is aware of this fact. As noted above, John Paul explicitly rejects any form of determinism, but this is not the same as saying that our nature and sexual personhood have no influence on our fulfillment.

John Paul II recognizes that biology plays a factor in the constitution of the person, but it is not an irresistible factor. Biology does not annihilate free will. Lawrence Porter argues just this, showing that John Paul does not yield to biologism. He finds evidence of this in *Mulieris dignitatem* (§38) where John Paul II states that motherhood corresponds to the psychophysical structure of women but is not limited to it. In this statement, he does not present a simplistic notion that would reduce a woman to her capacity to conceive and bear a child. "On the other hand, no doubt the pope, while rejecting such biologism, nevertheless recognizes that biology conditions freedom, that is, the bio-physiological structure of both the male and the female of the human species creates a specific personal orientation to self and the world to experience."[105]

Here Porter shows that John Paul takes the middle road between the two poles of the false dichotomy posed by some feminists. In other words, biological determinism is not the only alternative to the position taken by many feminists that biology is inconsequential. What accounts for this presupposition that the traditional view leads to determinism? Perhaps a misreading of St. Thomas Aquinas's view of natural law can account for this false charge. Ashley shows that contrary to some critics, St. Thomas did not see natural law as instinctual determinism. Thomas's use of "human nature" in and of itself implies free will, as this is fundamental to what it means to be human. It is true that in some circumstances, nature implies a set way of being. However, with human nature there is only a partially determinist aspect and this corresponds mainly to the animal aspect of man's nature.

---

[104] See John Grabowski, "Mutual Submission and Trinitarian Self-Giving," *Angelicum* 74 (1997): 501–502n30.

[105] Lawrence B. Porter, "Gender in Theology: The Example of John Paul II's *Mulieris dignitatem*," *Gregorianum* 77 (1996): 111.

The animal aspect of man's nature is generic.[106] What specifies man is that to be human is to be a person with an intellect and free will. Ashley concludes that it is not "an error of 'physicalism' or 'biologism' as some theologians today are claiming, to make the physical, animal character of human acts a decisive determinant of morality, although not its sole determinant."[107] John Paul obviously does not limit human beings to instinct. However, the question remains whether or not his anthropological method is guilty of the metaphysicalism Grabowski cautions against.

Earlier I presented a reading of John Paul II's theology of the body whereby he uses sexual intercourse as a means of inferring masculine and feminine characteristics. Assuming Grabowski's caution is valid, the question must be asked whether John Paul II then falls into this metaphysicalism. It appears that Grabowski is concerned primarily with an inference of ontological attributes tied to sex difference but based solely on a reading of the physiology of sexual intercourse. That is, I believe that he is correctly concerned with placing the sole burden of analysis on biology which is disconnected from a more integral view of the person.

That is not the case with John Paul II. His reading of the body is integrated with a Thomist metaphysics which attributes a final cause to every created good. In addition, he recognizes the soul as the substantial form of the body. Therefore, the body visibly manifests the soul, and so the configuration and function of the sexual organs points to a deeper reality about men and women. But it is not simply his metaphysical anthropology that he relies upon. As we saw earlier, John Paul also integrates divine revelation, that is, Scripture and Tradition, into all of his biological-metaphysical extrapolations.

Man as a body-soul unity—the whole person—can be analyzed by a reading of biology as long as that reading is grounded in a valid metaphysical system and in accordance with an authentic interpretation of divine revelation. On these grounds, John Paul II does not succumb either to metaphysicalism or to the charge of biologism, so these criticisms fail to undermine John Paul II's theology of fatherhood. In what seems to be an inconsistency, Kaminski appears to withdraw her charge of biologism and, rather, attributes John Paul II's fault in assigning roles to women based upon a faulty idealism, providing a segue to addressing this criticism.[108]

---

[106] Ashley cites *ST* Ia-IIae, q. 18, a. 5, co.

[107] Ashley, *Justice in the Church*, 41–42.

[108] Kaminski says: "The pope's affirmation of women's specific role is linked not so much with biology as to patriarchal dualistic thought. He takes motherhood as a paradigm associated with an entire system of feminine nurturing characteristics and expresses these in

Role Models as Idealizations

I have not found any critics who make the claim that Christ is an impossible idealization as a model of masculinity for men, which would be the direct concern for us. However, some feminists do reject the Blessed Virgin Mary as a model for women because her traditional depiction presents an impossible and unrealistic ideal for them. Certainly there is not the same motivation for men to reject this characterization because they have not generally experienced the same sex-based oppression as have many women down through history. Nonetheless, regardless of the motivations, one must address this concern. If the criticism is valid as applied to the Blessed Virgin as the model for women, it applies *a fortiori* to Jesus vis-à-vis men. After all, it is one thing to try to imitate the example of a sinless human person; it would seem quite another to attempt to live up to the example of a divine person.

Elizabeth Johnson weighed in on this issue in an article, which then expanded into a book, addressing what she thinks is the problem with Mary as a model for women. Her view begins with what she understands to be traditional Mariology:

> Drawing from the unquestioned assumption that men are by nature active, rational, and capable of exercising authority, while women are naturally receptive, emotional, and oriented to obedience and service, male theologians over the centuries created an image of Mary as the ideal feminine person. They then either contrasted her unique virtue with that of all other women or held her up as the norm whom all other women should seek, impossibly, to emulate.... Picturing Mary as the most perfect of women, the patriarchal marian tradition functions paradoxically to disparage all other women.[109]

She claims this as a fallacy of which "perhaps the most widely-heard proponent ... is Pope John Paul II."[110] As with her other criticisms of John Paul's anthropology, she believes that the depiction of Mary as the feminine ideal cannot but lead to women's subordination in the family and society in ways psychological, political, and spiritual.[111]

---

terms of an anthropology rooted in mystery rather than historical construction.... [T]he pope transcends natural realities by abstracting motherhood and by idealizing women" (Kaminski, "'Reproducing the World,'" 254).

[109] Johnson, *Truly Our Sister*, 22–23.
[110] Johnson, "Mary, Friend of God and Prophet," 319.
[111] See Johnson, "Mary, Friend of God and Prophet," 319–20.

More specifically, she says that John Paul exhorts all women to be like Mary and to be oriented toward giving love without measure after having received it, toward physical or spiritual motherhood, having the strength to bear the greatest of sorrows, having limitless fidelity, tireless devotion to work, and the ability to combine penetrating intuition with encouragement and support.[112] Johnson suggests that by presenting Mary as the feminine model, women are necessarily going to be stunted in their personal growth and prevented from developing the capacity for critical thought, righteous anger, and other characteristics that she considers to be part of a mature personality.[113] Women are thus left vulnerable to abusive situations because of an ingrained passivity and are then consigned to a life of domesticity.[114] Not surprisingly then, she rejects a "traditional" reading of Mary as a model for women.

One could find a parallel problem with Christ as the model for men that some feminists find with Mary as the model for women. With Christ as his model, a husband is called to humility and a quiet solicitude for his wife and family, even if it should require his death.[115] If men were to live this out authentically, they could easily be taken advantage of by their wives. However, this concern presupposes an ill will on the part of the spouse, which is certainly no basis for a Christian marriage. Rather, it would seem that if both spouses were to make every effort to follow their models, this issue and the issues Johnson identifies would be rendered moot. In John Paul's theology of fatherhood and motherhood, skepticism and distrust must give way to an attitude of charity, conditioned of course by a prudence that recognizes we are living east of Eden. However, there remains a more substantial criticism to address.

Cahill quotes Margaret O'Brien's criticism of *Mulieris dignitatem* for

---

[112] Here she cites John Paul II, Encyclical Letter on the Blessed Virgin Mary in the Life of the Pilgrim Church *Redemptoris mater* (March 25, 1987), *AAS* 79 (1987), 361–433, §46.

[113] In *Truly Our Sister*, Johnson makes clear that she is criticizing the "traditional" model of Mary, which in her view does not correspond with the historical reality. Interestingly enough, to arrive at the "historical" Mary, Johnson must avail herself of the general knowledge of Jewish women in first century Palestine because there is admittedly little historical data on the Blessed Virgin. Thus, one could raise the question whether she really does arrive at the concrete, historical Mary? Is she not really replacing the concrete incarnation of the transcendent feminine and ecclesial symbol *par excellence* with a twenty-first-century feminist interpretation of a first-century Jewish feminine symbol? (See *Truly Our Sister*, 95ff.) Perhaps more astutely put: Is not Johnson replicating in Mariology the false Christological dichotomy between the "Jesus of history" and the "Christ of faith"? (I thank John Grabowski for this latter insight.)

[114] Johnson, "Mary, Friend of God," 319–20.

[115] See *Mulieris dignitatem*, §§23–24.

its presentation of the Blessed Virgin as the model of femininity. She says that O'Brien

> casts some common sense on the volatile rhetoric which often voices concern about women's changing roles. Finding the magisterium's "idealized image" of women's "nurturing, maternal qualities" to be "strangely implausible," she observes that it is separated by a chasm from the ordinary experience of an increasing number of women and men. Accountability to experience will not be achieved by brandishing the term "radical feminism" to ward off threats to the episcopacy's foregone conclusions; nor by reviving the word "complementarity" to advance hierarchically ordered links between reproductive characteristics and social roles, thus to "evade real equality in the church."[116]

Cahill relies on her lived experience to tell her that the traditional Mary is "strangely implausible." Kaveny has similar concerns, but she more explicitly articulates what Cahill implies. Namely, that the traditional view of Mary lionizes an abstract ideal to the extent of misrepresenting the concrete reality.

Kaveny criticizes the cardinal prefect of the Congregation for the Doctrine of the Faith in her review of the document "On the Collaboration of Men and Women in the Church and in the World," for failing to abide by the document's contents. She states:

> If Ratzinger is serious about his stated desire for "dialogue with all men and women of good will," he will start by taking his own advice. He notes that women often have a "sense and a respect for what is concrete," as opposed to "abstractions which are so often fatal for the existence of individuals and society." Unfortunately, his invocation of the Blessed Virgin Mary to demonstrate the Church's inclusion of women risks becoming just such a potentially fatal abstraction.[117]

This is a serious concern. Is the Blessed Virgin an abstraction which opposes

---

[116] Cahill, "Feminist Ethics," 49–50, quoting Margaret O'Brien, "The Church and Its Public Life," *America* 160 (1989): 553–54.
[117] Kaveny, "What is the Vatican Saying About Women?"

the concrete experiences of women? In other words, do the concrete experiences of women prove that Mary is an impossible ideal for them?

This argument, if valid, directly applies even more strongly to Christ as the model for husbands and fathers, in the context of the great mystery. However, it appears that the error in the Marian criticism arises because the critics assume that what they call "the idealization of the feminine" is independent of the concrete lived experience of women. Schindler articulates this point:

> Consider the intrinsic link between spiritual and physical womb affirmed archetypically in the link between Mary's Immaculate Conception, *fiat* and being *Theotokos*. These latter have their meaning first of all as concrete historical occurrences. It is precisely in and through her concrete historical reality as a woman that these fundamental acts of Mary become "figures," as it were, of the feminine, and thereby of created being and action as a whole (MD, nn. 4–5). The point is that (spiritual) receptivity (*fiat*) has primacy within the created order, and that this receptivity becomes concrete first of all in a (physical) woman (and thus bears an intrinsic relation to motherhood; see the *Theotokos*).[118]

John Paul II does not point women (or men) to irrelevant, abstract ideals but rather explicates the theological meaning of the lived experience of concrete persons. Grabowski directly addresses this point with respect to Mary as role model. He argues that in John Paul II's Mariology, Mary indeed retains her identity as a real, concrete feminine person. While it is true that she is a privileged and unique woman, John Paul II never permits her to elide into the status of a principle. Rather, amidst her exemplary life for all Christians she also demonstrates special import as a model of femininity.[119]

This is no surprise. An adequate attending to John Paul II's method demonstrates, as we have shown, that he employs phenomenology to illustrate and explore theological truths as they are manifested in the concrete experiences of women and men. The criticism that the Virgin Mary is invoked only as a principle is unwarranted; rather, the debate becomes

---

[118] David L. Schindler, *Heart of the World, Center of the Church: Communio, Ecclesiology, Liberalism, and Liberation* (Grand Rapids, MI: William B. Eerdmans Publishing Company, 1996), 265.

[119] See Grabowski, "Theological Anthropology and Gender," 336.

whether or not she is a historical person as tradition presents her, which is beyond the scope of this chapter.[120] However, the implications of this is that this feminine model was never lived out. The response to this claim is the same as it is to the question about whether she is an impossible ideal.

John Paul's shows that to be adequate, any evaluation of lived experience must consider the effects of original sin, which distort all human experience. Among the feminist critics making the "impossible ideal" claim, when they attempt to develop an account of authentic women's experience, the consequences of original sin are never considered.[121] The mistake which these scholars make in thinking Mary to be an impossible ideal is their implicit denial of fallen humanity. Rather, they endeavor to make fallen women's lived experience normative.[122]

Those espousing the normativity of postlapsarian experience also implicitly deny the ability of sanctifying grace to help the Christian to overcome the limitations of his fallen state. The distance these critics find themselves from John Paul II's anthropology seems to lie precisely in the fact that he emphasizes that Christ has given fallen man the remedy for the historical experience of sin in sanctifying grace. The sanctifying power of habitual grace is not an idiosyncratic view developed by John Paul II. On the contrary, it is central to the gospel and is articulated in Catholic sacramental teaching. The possibility of personal holiness for all Christians by means of God's sanctifying grace was taught by the Second Vatican Council. *Lumen gentium*'s universal call to holiness authoritatively refutes this presupposition associated with the claim of the impossible ideal.[123]

The same must be said of men who also can live up to their vocation only through assiduous cooperation with sacramental grace. The charge of an impossible ideal takes issue with the fundamentals of the Catholic doctrines of creation, the fall, and the sacraments, not simply with John Paul's anthropology. Yet, it is one thing for a human person perfected in grace to

---

[120] Johnson has denied the historical basis of the traditional view of Mary (see *Truly Our Sister*, 96ff.), citing in passing, Raymond Brown's work. However, she does not make this a central part of her work. Kaveny and Cahill similarly seem to presuppose a dissonance between the historical Mary and the magisterium's teachings on the Blessed Virgin.

[121] See, e.g., Johnson, *She Who Is*, 28–33, in her survey of the problem of precisely identifying what constitutes authentic women's experience talks of culture, race, class, and historical circumstances but does not indicate that the debate is aware that the greater context of women's (and men's) experience is within fallen humanity.

[122] See Johnson, *She Who Is*, 28–33; Cahill, "Feminist Ethics," 49–50.

[123] See Second Vatican Council, Dogmatic Constitution on the Church *Lumen gentium* (November 21, 1964), §§39–42.

be an exemplary feminine model. It is quite another for a divine person, albeit an Incarnate one, to be a model for masculinity. Even if Mary is not an impossible ideal for femininity, is Jesus still not an impossible ideal for masculinity?

The Second Vatican Council says otherwise. John Paul II repeatedly cites *Gaudium et spes* which declares that Jesus Christ is the perfect exemplar for man (see GS §22). Joseph Ratzinger emphasizes the same point, emphasizing that Jesus is not simply a curiosity or an exception but the manifestation of the true figure of man.[124] Jesus is at once the exemplar of what it means to be fully human and of what it means to be fully male. If Jesus Christ was not fully one of us, if he was not fully a man that each one of us could and can be, neither man nor men would have been saved.[125]

A PROBLEMATIC VIEW OF PATERNAL ROLES

Some feminists have identified what they consider to be problematic aspects of John Paul II's theology of fatherhood in the area of paternal roles. For example, Gudorf claims that John Paul II's description of mothers as those who uniquely hear, understand, and love each of their children deprives men of intimacy within the family.[126] She says that John Paul reduces a man's roles to that of material support and remaining loyal to his family, while situated outside of the family with respect to intimate love. She suggests that if men view their roles like this, now that women are breadwinners as well, it is no wonder they desert their families.[127]

It appears that Gudorf is saying more here than she intends. Ignoring for the moment her caricature of John Paul II's statements, we have seen that the crisis in fatherhood in the United States is quite real and that it predates John Paul's pontificate by at least two decades. Regardless, one cannot plausibly assert that his articulation of fatherhood, even if understood in this way, could have had such an immediate and widespread impact in a predominantly post-Protestant society like the United States.

A better explanation is offered by Blankenhorn, who finds that

---

[124] See Joseph Ratzinger, *Introduction to Christianity*, trans. J. R. Foster (San Francisco: Ignatius Press, 1990), 176.

[125] See Gregory of Nazianzus, Epistle 101, 32, trans. Charles Gordon Browne and James Edward Swallow, in *Nicene and Post-Nicene Fathers*, Second Series, Vol. 7; ed. Philip Schaff and Henry Wace (Buffalo, NY: Christian Literature Publishing Co., 1894.), revised and edited for New Advent by Kevin Knight, http://www.newadvent.org/fathers/3103a.htm.

[126] See Gudorf, "The Modern Papacy on Women," 299.

[127] See Gudorf, "The Modern Papacy on Women," 299.

divorce and separation account for the larger portion of absent fathers, but the fastest growing proportion of fatherless households is caused by unwed parenthood.[128] If Gudorf is suggesting that the increased divorce rate in the US is due to men's inability to adjust to the evolving "genderless" family and society, she may have a point. David Popenoe, however, finds the father's coming to identify himself primarily in terms of being the sole breadwinner was simply one step in the evolution of fatherhood, viewed from a historical perspective. He shows that this breadwinner step actually served to begin to isolate him from his family.[129]

This change in the man's role had more to do with societal transition from an agrarian to industrial society than with patriarchal oppression.[130] With the later egalitarianism in broader society, the father's authority in the family was widely devalued and masculinity came to be identified in terms of ambition and achievement, a reductive view of his actual role. This has now led to the further separation of the father from his family and to a resulting dearth of his presence in his children's lives. The consequences are a missing role model for boys and opposite-sex nurturing for girls.[131]

This lack of paternal contact in the formative years is directly traceable to the self-perpetuating decline in family life to the point that the nuclear family is now in total free fall.[132] This corresponds with the description

---

[128] See David Blankenhorn, *Fatherless America: Confronting Our Most Urgent Social Problem* (New York: Harper-Collins Publishers, 1995), 132.

[129] See David Popenoe, "The Fatherhood Problem," *Institute for American Values Working Paper*, Publication No. WP 40 (New York: Institute for American Values, 1993), 31–37.

[130] In pre-industrial agrarian societies, the division of labor along biological lines is much more apparent and, if anything, is more advantageous to women than men. A man's structural and muscular advantages clearly make him the more logical of the spouses for the manual tasks required in pre-industrial farming. However, this model is not absolute, in many cases women worked alongside men in many of these manual tasks (see Popenoe, "The Fatherhood Problem").

[131] Blankenhorn shows that the effect of a voluntarily absent father on girls, especially in mid to late adolescence, is a greatly increased risk of early sexual activity, adolescent and out-of-wedlock childbearing, divorce, and lack of personal confidence. He recounts studies which conclude that this is due to the opposite-sex example of fathers who provide daughters with "a stable relationship with a nonexploitative adult male who loves them . . . [who provides] a sense of security and trust. . . . When a girl cannot trust and love the first man in her life, her father, what she is missing cannot be replaced by money, friends, teachers, social workers, or well designed public policies aimed helping her. She simply loses. Moreover, as more and more girls grow up without fathers, society loses" (*Fatherless America*, 47–48).

[132] See Popenoe, "The Fatherhood Problem," 37.

of the fatherhood crisis presented earlier. If androgyny in childrearing seems the answer, Sweden's experience in this regard should serve as a warning. Blankenhorn shows that the Swedish experiment in androgynous child-rearing beginning in the 1970s has actually led to an increase in the divorce rate.[133] He cites studies by Jay Belsky, Mary Lang, and Ted L. Huston, showing that marital satisfaction for those espousing androgynous norms in child rearing drops when children arrive.

This is borne out by recent research in Sweden and Norway, both countries influenced by these androgynous norms, which finds that the increasing reason for divorce in these two countries is given by the wives as sheer boredom with their husbands, including a lack of sexual interest. The resulting analysis concluded that the behaviors that the husbands began to develop in their roles as an androgynous parent caused them to become too much like women. Blankenhorn finds that the mystery in marriage is partly of a complementary other, and this was lost.[134] There would appear to be subliminal recognition by Swedish and Norwegian wives of the necessity of sex differences, not just for biological reproduction but also for interpersonal nurturing between the spouses.

This study appears to undermine the articulated beliefs of some feminists to the contrary. Consequently, if the experiences in Sweden and Norway are indicative, it is not just the loss of husband's identity as a breadwinner that is to blame but a broader loss of his masculine identity. All of these empirical findings are consonant with John Paul II's theology of fatherhood explicated thus far. Nevertheless, the question remains to be answered: does John Paul's theology of fatherhood leave the man as an outside observer with no other role to play than provider?

Returning to Gudorf's criticisms, she further elaborates on her claim of deficiency in John Paul II's views of paternal roles. She argues that while sexual equality for him is clearly an equality of dignity, she does not understand why this does not extend to equality in vocation. Specifically, she opines that if a man's only responsibility is material support of his family, then John Paul denigrates men as much as he does women. She asks:

Can men be regarded as other than deficient humans when they seem to carry few relational responsibilities? How can they be Christians? Where are men's opportunities for personal service, for sensitivity, for love in any intimate sense? If men's roles in the

[133] See Blankenhorn, *Fatherless America*, 281–82n89.
[134] See Blankenhorn, *Fatherless America*.

family do not teach them to be sensitive to the needs of others, to the demands of justice within the home, how can they possibly love well? How will their sons have models for learning to love well as men?[135]

She goes on to characterize her view of John Paul's theology of fatherhood as one in which the man is unconstrained in his animal drives and, therefore, he must be tamed by the woman. The woman does this by entrapping him in the role of husband and father, capitalizing on the man's need for intimacy. She thereby attains his material support for her and her children. She says: "His role within his family, which both gratifies him and traps him, is material support, a role in which he must be able to take pride if his benefits from the arrangement are to outweigh his sacrifice."[136] To say that this is a caricature of John Paul's theology of men and fatherhood is to understate the case.

It is unnecessary to conjecture about the reasons behind this unfortunate misrepresentation of John Paul II's thought. Rather, it is sufficient to recall his assertions of the husband-father's role in forming his children and his wife, providing selfless leadership, actively cultivating his vocation, and revealing Christ's love as examples of roles and tasks that Gudorf has overlooked in her misrepresentation. Clearly her understanding of John Paul II's theology of fatherhood is deficient. However, she does point to a partial truth. John Paul does identify masculine weaknesses which require feminine support in order to be overcome. Does he succumb to an instinctual determinism here?

From the above discussion it is clear that this is not the case, as he demands that the man use his rational faculties, cooperating with grace in order to overcome his concupiscible inclinations. Rather, Gudorf seems to betray her own deterministic presuppositions. That is, she appears to assume that if the biological characteristics exist, they must be irresistible. A careful study of *Person and Act* and the theology of the body catecheses demonstrates that the author asserts that human nature is characterized by free, responsible, decision-making. John Paul II cannot be accused of reducing conjugal relationships to instinct. If anything, he is an emphatic opponent of this view.

Cahill finds a different kind of problem with regard to roles of husband-fathers. This criticism strikes at one of the foundational concepts

---

[135] See Gudorf, "The Modern Papacy on Women," 300.
[136] Gudorf, "The Modern Papacy on Women," 302.

in John Paul II's theological anthropology. Specifically, she argues that the "total gift of self" is unrealistic and reductive. Cahill's claim that a subjective total gift of self is unrealistic everywhere and always seems compelling. If her argument is sustainable, then the author's theology of men and fatherhood—not to mention his entire anthropology—by and large proves to be inadequate for real life.

The context of her argument is an attempt to justify artificial contraception. In her analysis, she believes that she finds reductionism in John Paul II's view of the integrated nature of sexual intercourse. However, she does this by absolutizing pleasure as an end of the sex act in order to justify posing it against the reproductive end. This results in "three bodily dimensions of sex ... developed through three levels (bodily, personal, social)."[137] She argues that the problem with the John Paul's positions is that

> sexual pleasure and its integration with intimacy is largely ignored. In the end the sex act as a "mutual self-gift" seems strangely disembodied, as well as severed from the dimensions of memory, trust, and hope that make human sexuality unique. Deficient moral behavior or inadequate moral analysis can result from the truncation or division of the pleasurable, intimate, and procreative meanings.[138]

Further, she finds that John Paul pays too little attention to social conditions necessary to make authentic reciprocity "in sexuality, marriage, and parenthood a genuine possibility. The 'mutual self-gift' language must be placed against a backdrop of gender roles, especially the pre-eminence of motherhood for women, which clearly color the picture John Paul II paints of sexual fulfillment in marriage."[139] Again, she appeals to real-life experience to claim that true and complete self-gift is rarely, if ever achievable:

> In *Familiaris Consortio* (Apostolic Exhortation *On the Family*, 1981), the pope elaborates sex as a language of totality. Adherence to *Humanae vitae's* use of "each" sex act as final measure of the interpersonal and parental commitment of spouses is still demanded. Every act of sexual intercourse is invested with the full weight of the couple's love and relationship, and that weight is

---

[137] Cahill, *Sex, Gender, and Christian Ethics*, 113.
[138] Cahill, *Sex, Gender, and Christian Ethics*, 112–13.
[139] Cahill, *Sex, Gender, and Christian Ethics*, 205.

pinned, not on the emotional or pleasurable aspects of the act, but on its procreativity, reduced to pristine biological format. . . . The idea that each act is a total self-gift depends upon a very romanticized depiction of sex, and even of marital love. Certainly there will be times when an act of sexual sharing is hampered or disturbed by factors, intrinsically or extrinsically generated, which impinge, either temporarily or permanently on the couple's relationship. . . . But even more than that, in the *most* ideal of circumstances, human beings rarely if ever accomplish "total self-gift."[140]

Thus, Cahill accuses John Paul II of reductionism. In other words, John Paul disregards pleasure as an end of the sex act. This combines with his naiveté in suggesting that each sex act must incorporate a total gift of self, to result in a deficient anthropology and, for our concerns, a deficient theology of fatherhood as well.

While these critiques are aimed primarily at the issue of contraception, if either can be sustained as valid, they would destabilize John Paul's entire theology of fatherhood. This would especially affect the husband-father's tasks laid out by the great mystery: revealing Christ's love to the man's wife and family, participating in and cooperating with the grace of the sacraments, and his self-giving leadership in his family.

There is a common error which underlies both of Cahill's assertions. Once again, she seems to ignore the fact that mankind is in a fallen state, that all are tempted to sin, and that all have the need for grace. Thus, she herself seems to fall prey to reductionism. This will become apparent as I address two criticisms which one may identify in her argument. Let us first turn to her claim of reductionism in John Paul's failure to integrate pleasure into the unitive and procreative aspects of the sex act.

Karol Wojtyła addresses the issue of sexual pleasure in some detail in his book *Love and Responsibility*.[141] Unfortunately, either Cahill is unaware of this or for some other reason chooses not to engage with it. Wojtyła agrees that sexual pleasure is a good and that the good is to be sought. However, he rejects the assertion that sexual pleasure can be made equal in importance to love (i.e., total self-gift), as seems the case for Cahill. Wojtyła says that this inevitably will lead to a calculus by which the

---

[140] Cahill, *Sex, Gender, and Christian Ethics*, 203.
[141] See Karol Wojtyła, *Love and Responsibility*, trans. Grzegorz Ignatik (Boston: Pauline Books & Media, 2013), 12–53, 168–69.

person will try to weigh pleasure against love and devolve into treating the other person as a means to pleasure. It is never permissible to treat another person as a means to an end.

Let me try to summarize Wojtyła's rationale for this assertion. He asserts that "pleasure is essentially incidental, contingent, something which may occur in the course of an action. Naturally then, to organize your actions with pleasure itself as the exclusive or primary aim is in contradiction with the proper structure of human action."[142] When pleasure becomes a primary criterion for taking an action or discerning good from bad, the result is utilitarianism. Besides the impossibility of precalculating the pleasure or pain quotient, this ignores the fact that many necessary good acts will come with some pleasure and/or some pain.

Another problem with treating pleasure as an end is that the attempt to harmonize inevitable differences in sexual pleasure leads away from love and results in each ego using the other as a means of sexual pleasure. In this way, Cahill, ironically, becomes the reductionist. She recognizes the integrated nature of pleasure with the sex act but in raising it to an end rather than an incidental good (that is, a fruit), she unravels the real integration and now places pleasure in competition with love. The result, as Wojtyła demonstrates, is a reduction of the person to a means rather than treating him as an end.

Failing to recognize that we are in a fallen state, she also ignores the additional problem that concupiscence means that human affects are no longer easily subordinated to reason. Because of concupiscence, reason must evaluate whether the good of a particular pleasure is in concert with the demands of the greater good and the avoidance moral evils. Hence, because there is no calculus for a pleasure quotient, and because the magnitude of pleasure does not provide rationale for deciding between good and evil, making pleasure an end leaves no place for reason. This demonstrates why Cahill's reliance on what Wojtyła calls a "libidinistic interpretation" is unworkable.[143]

---

[142] Wojtyła, *Love and Responsibility*, 36.

[143] "Libidinistic interpretation" is a term used by Karol Wojtyła to describe interpretations of the human person in which sexual pleasure is declared to be a legitimate end of sexual intercourse, because when pleasure is made an end, the person is always reduced to a means. This term is not intended either by Wojtyła or by my use here to be rhetorically inflammatory but rather descriptive of the problem of making pleasure an end. Reduction of another to a means cannot be made legitimate even by mutual agreement because this violates the personalistic norm. Use is always opposed to love and the person is made only for love, so libidinistic anthropologies in which sexual pleasure is declared a good

Cahill's second criticism is that a total self-gift is not possible. Here she appears to fall into the logical fallacy of a false dichotomy. Essentially, she appears to be saying that because we often fall short in perfectly giving ourselves as a total self-gift (which in her examples would seem to be a venial sin at most) then there is no justification for opposing purposeful prevention of total self-gift through contraception (a mortal sin).[144] This is a *non sequitur*.

If Cahill is asserting that a perfectly, morally good intention (total self-gift) is impossible, she also implicitly rejects the Christian vocation to holiness which can ultimately be achieved only through nature cooperating with grace to overcome concupiscent inclinations. In the meantime, the objective language of the body in marital intercourse continues to witness to the subjective vocation of a total self-gift.[145] The criticisms addressed here are mischaracterizations of John Paul II's theology of fatherhood and/ or rejections of definitive Catholic teaching. I find that these criticisms leave our extracted theology of masculinity and fatherhood undamaged.

CAN IT ACCOUNT FOR LESS COMMON SITUATIONS?

One could ask whether John Paul II's theology of fatherhood is adequate for less common family situations. However, I must first rule out immoral situations such as couplings of those suffering from same-sex attraction and/or identity disorders or out-of-wedlock childbearing.[146] One cannot expect John Paul's theology of fatherhood to accommodate these situations

---

in itself to be pursued rather than a fruit to be accepted with joy and thanksgiving is never legitimate. Nor is it practical for flourishing relationships (see Wojtyła, *Love and Responsibility*, 46–53).

[144] I must issue a caveat concerning my treatment by saying that it is not clear to me that Cahill is actually thinking of sinful circumstances in her criticism. Her feminist hermeneutic, which privileges subjective experience over all other criteria, could allow one to read her understanding of John Paul II's "total gift of self" primarily in terms of affectivity rather than subjective intention. In this case, she is quite correct that her misinterpreted notion of total self-gift is an impossible ideal. Regardless, she misses the point that the author's "prophetism of the body" (see *Man and Woman*, 357) includes the objective symbolization of total gift of self in the sexual act (*Man and Woman*, 358–59) together with the vocation to subjectively live it in truth through purity (i.e., free of lust), fidelity, and morality (*Man and Woman*, 360). Within the marital covenant, the objective language of the body is always manifest; it only becomes a lie to the degree that one culpably intends to deny its purity, fidelity, or morality. I thank John Grabowski for the insight regarding Cahill's feminist hermeneutic.

[145] See *Man and Woman*, 357–60.

[146] For an application of St. John Paul II's theology of the body to the question of same-sex

because they do not correspond to the created order. However, there are other situations in which the father is absent by other than a free decision of the mother, but where the mother chooses not to remarry. These include death or desertion by the father.

The question is whether John Paul II's theology of fatherhood can accommodate the missing father, given the significant role that he is called to play. The answer to this is both yes and no. In other words, the author's theology of fatherhood explains the roles that a father is called to play in his fatherly vocation. These paternal roles must be filled in some manner, even if suboptimally. It turns out that there is a qualitative difference between volitional and non-volitional fatherless households which affects childrearing.

Blankenhorn shows that volitional fatherlessness has a different impact on children and, therefore, on society.[147] The death of a father is experienced differently by a child than when a father leaves through divorce or desertion. In the former case, a mother often helps to keep the father's love alive for her children. In a sense, she helps him to still father his children from the grave. In divorce or desertion, the child very usually experiences a sense of abandonment, anxiety, and self-blame. This is often exacerbated by the mother's explicit or implicit expression of resentment for her former husband. Blankenhorn argues that this explains the difference in the current crisis in the nuclear family where 27 percent of all children live in fatherless households and the situation in 1900 when 10 percent lived in single parent households but where there was no corresponding crisis.[148] From the perspective of John Paul II's theology of fatherhood, considering the needs of children and the roles and tasks of the father, one would not be surprised by this situation.

It seems that fatherhood can, in some measure, transcend death, but that is not the case with a father's desertion. While children whose fathers die avoid many of the pathologies children suffer when their fathers voluntarily leave them, there are important paternal tasks which will remain unaccomplished or will need to be accomplished by the mother in either case. John Paul does not provide an explicit solution to the problem of fatherlessness. Whether one could develop a theology of surrogate fatherhood through an assessment of the roles and tasks of the father while

---

attraction, see Eduardo J. Echeverria, *"In the Beginning . . . ": A Theology of the Body* (Eugene, OR: Pickwick Publishers, 2011).

[147] See Blankenhorn, *Fatherless America*, 23–24.

[148] See Blankenhorn, *Fatherless America*, 23–24.

staying grounded in John Paul's anthropology is beyond the scope of this chapter to ascertain.

It is sufficient to demonstrate that this theology of fatherhood is adequate by showing that it can account for the current crisis engendered by absent fathers. Nor would the possibility that there might not be an adequate theology of surrogate fatherhood be a valid criticism of this theology of fatherhood. Any theology pertains to the order of creation and can be used to understand the problems arising when this order is not obeyed. The loss of the father was not part of God's original plan for creation and so it is not certain that any theology could overcome all of the difficulties associated with this ill fruit of the fall.

Another case to consider is that of so-called intersex conditions upon which we obliquely touched in chapter 6. This is a term which collectively refers to sex development disorders that can include sex chromosomal disorders, disorders associated with the reproductive endocrine system, and atypical anatomical manifestations.[149] The medical community now most commonly refers to intersex conditions as "disorders of sex development" (DSD), basing classification on genetics to avoid the ever-changing pitfalls of gender theory. However, there is still debate about this move to genetics-based classification in and out of the medical community.

DSDs are a set of disorders distinct from sexual identity disorders.[150] There is a counter-movement to reject classifying these "variations" as disorders.[151] The ideology called gender theory wishes to conflate DSDs with sexual identity disorders as a means of denying that binary sexual complementarity ordered to procreation is the foundation for sexual relationships, family, and social order.[152] The "normalization" of sexual identity disorders appears to have gained the ascendency in the West. Its conflation with DSDs means the question is important: does John Paul II's anthropology account for DSD/intersex conditions?

I would note here that these cases can be devastating to those who

---

[149] See Margaret Schneider et al., *Answers to Your Questions About Individuals with Intersex Conditions* (Washington, DC: American Psychological Association Office of Public Communication, 2006); available at https://www.apa.org/topics/lgbtq/intersex.pdf.

[150] See Julio Tudela et al., "The Vatican Opinion on Gender Theory," *The Linacre Quarterly* 88, no. 1 (2021): 37–41.

[151] See, e.g., David Andrew Griffiths, "Shifting Syndromes: Sex Chromosome Variations and Intersex Classifications," *Social Studies of Science* 48, no. 1 (Feb. 9, 2018): 125–48, and Timothy F. Murphy, "The Vatican on Gender Theory and the Responsibilities of Medicine," *Bioethics* 33 (2019): 981–83.

[152] See Pope Francis, Post-Synodal Apostolic Exhortation *Amoris laetitia* (March 19, 2016), §56.

suffer from them and their obvious desire to be normal can make for difficult pastoral challenges. Yet, pastoral accompaniment, if it has any meaning, implies leadership and guidance toward Truth himself and so such pastoral guidance can only be good for the person if it conforms with his integral good. This integral good includes affective well-being but that is not its end; rather, it is a fruit of healing and holiness. The pastoral implications of this problem are significant but not our purpose to address here. Rather, we must keep to the question of coherence. The claims of those who reject the binary-complementarity essence of sex have a different understanding of human nature in relation to sex difference. Today, the primary argument seems rarely to be based upon explicit philosophical arguments, but rather it seems to come from implicit, philosophical, anthropological assumptions.

Gender ideology theorists commonly assert that human nature must be described as a continuity of experiences on a spectrum that ranges between those whose "gender identity" and "sex-typical bodies" correspond to one another and those for whom their identities and bodies differ in varying degrees.[153] Timothy Murphy summarizes this view in the form of a question which he contrasts between what he calls the view of "contemporary science" and that of the "Vatican" when he asks: "'What are we?' and 'Who are we?' Are we all instantiations of some master blueprint, some more flawed than others in regard to sex and gender? Or are we self-defining beings wresting identity from our bodies, interests, and the possibilities open to us?"[154] The consequences of binary sex and gender, it is argued, is their social stigmatization and dismal treatment leading to manifold negative mental health outcomes.[155]

There seem to be primarily three anthropological assumptions implicit here. First, that human personhood is essentially what Wojtyła defines as a post-Cartesian, stream of consciousness with no metaphysical foundation. Second, that anything called "nature" is purely descriptive with no ontological foundation, and so biological sex is simply the presentation of biological matter holding little to no part in constituting the person, at least in terms of the sociological aspect of sex which they call gender. Third and consequently, one's gender identity must be based upon experience and the freedom of self-determination, or perhaps more accurately, of self-construction. Anything other than a self-determining

---

[153] See Murphy, "Gender Theory," 982.
[154] Murphy, "Gender Theory," 982.
[155] See Murphy, "Gender Theory," 982.

will, certainly any outward "constraint," is considered damaging to the person. It is perhaps not hyperbolic to suggest we are now seeing the success of Nietzsche's *Gay Science* in which we have killed God, and now a vast sea of possibilities, through the will to power, has now opened up before us as never before.[156] This is offered not as social commentary but to emphasize the importance of Wojtyła's anthropology for our time.

In part 1 we studied the manner in which Wojtyła convincingly corrects Ockham's mistake of nature as purely descriptive and the mistaken post-Cartesian reduction of human personhood to a transitory stream of conscious experience, using his phenomenological analysis metaphysically grounded in hylomorphic theory. Indeed, Wojtyła's phenomenological analysis in *Person and Act* demonstrates that systematic attention to human experience validates hylomorphic theory and the necessity of the concreteness of human personhood. In chapter 6, we saw that he is aware of what is now called DSD, even if the medical insights then were not as robust as they are today. Nevertheless, John Paul's affirmation of the sole existence of male and female persons still holds today for the same reasons. While reasoned responses may not carry the day in contemporary public discourse, we can still see the coherence of Wojtyła's vision of complementary sex difference in contrast to these present-day criticisms.

John Paul II understands sex difference to have a foundational, constituting function for human personhood. He implies that sex difference has its origin in the Trinitarian archetype, and while he does not develop a metaphysical explanation for it, we saw that his anthropology can be best explained if human personhood is understood to be in the category of being of relation in analogy with the Trinitarian persons. In this case, the constituting function of sex difference would also be in the same category of being, not as an added relation but as a mode of personhood based upon the hierarchy of love. Moreover, Christology shows us that it must be the person who possesses his nature, which in the case of humans is a composite but seamlessly unified nature.

The result of this with John Paul's hylomorphic presuppositions is that the bodily expression of biological sex has its root in the soul, which is the substantial form of the body, but the deeper foundation is the sex of the person in the category of relation. Relation implies another with which to relate. The most visible bodily expression of this relation is complementarity ordered to procreation, though of course John Paul's anthropology

---

[156] See Friedrich Nietzsche, *The Complete Works of Friedrich Nietzsche,* vol. 10, *Joyful Wisdom,* ed. Oscar Levy (Edinburgh: T. N. Foulis, 1910), 167–69, and 275–75.

is not reductionist. The meaning of sex difference is not reducible to its biological procreative expression, but neither can it be separated from it. Thus, it follows that sex difference interpenetrates the entirety of the person and his nature, establishing each complementary sex as one of two "modes" of being human, as we have seen.

This metaphysical account of sex differences provides a compelling explanation for the normative experience of human persons, notwithstanding the existence of the tragedy of DSD.[157] The philosophical presupposition that one might "feel" trapped by one's body is much more compellingly explained as a mental health disorder than by the supposed cause, that of restrictive and damaging social structures. The assertion that poor mental health outcomes for those who suffer from DSD (and sexual identity disorders) is due to societal non-acceptance has not been demonstrated and is in fact belied by relevant empirical evidence.[158] In the end, John Paul II's vision of sex difference does account for the existence of persons suffering from DSD.

Our assessment of potential issues in part 4 indicates that John Paul II's theology of personhood, masculinity, and fatherhood is essentially self-consistent and it is able to address adequately the criticisms leveled against it.

---

[157] It is estimated that the frequency of DSD cases is 4.5 per 100,000, a number which reflects a disorder, not a variant of normal human sex. See Tudela, "Vatican Opinion," 38.

[158] A Swedish study, a society which has been actively acceptive of non-standard sexual modes of behavior for at least the last fifty years, shows that as late as 2011 suicides for those who had undergone medical transitioning to permit their bodies to visibly conform to their felt sex is nineteen times greater than the rate for the background population. See Paul W. Hruz, "Deficiencies in Scientific Evidence for Medical Management of Gender Dysphoria," *The Linacre Quarterly* 87, no. 1 (2020): 38.

Conclusion

John Paul the Great's writings have provided us with a theology of masculinity and fatherhood, the fruit of his pastoral heart's encounter with his academic career, which he was initially compelled to take up by his bishop.[1] We have seen that it ultimately arises, as does his entire anthropology, from his use of the *analogia entis*. Personhood, masculinity, and fatherhood are so intertwined that they must be treated as a whole. Moreover, all are implied in the treatment of each aspect of the person. Our author's starting point is the human person made in the image of God, so his anthropology begins with Trinitarian theology. Jesus Christ reveals the authentic meaning of the human person, so his anthropology is also christocentric, providing the normative, practical example of what personal self-transcendence looks like. Wojtyła's concern with post-Cartesian philosophers' diminishment of the person to a stream of consciousness

---

[1] Buttiglione says that Wojtyła's bishop, Cardinal Sapieha, was adamant that Fr. Wojtyła would pursue his habilitation dissertation, which would permit him to teach, after Wojtyła made clear his preference for pastoral work (see Rocco Buttiglione, *Karol Wojtyła: The Thought of the Man Who Became John Paul* II, trans. Paolo Guietti and Francesca Murphy [Grand Rapids, MI: William B. Eerdmans Publishing Co., 1997], 36). Swieżawski indicates that Wojtyła was an integral part of ensuring that the philosophy department maintained an orientation in their work for its practical application, which is unsurprising given his primary concern for pastoral accompaniment (see Stefan Swieżawski, "Karol Wojtyła at the Catholic University of Lublin," in *Person and Community: Selected Essays*, vol. 4, trans. Theresa Sandok, O.S.M. [New York: Peter Lang, 1993], xiv). Members of Wojtyła's Środowisko were unanimous in saying that he spent the bulk of his free time with them, indicating he always made time for them when they needed him as he accompanied them through the questions and challenges of life (see George Weigel, *Witness to Hope* [New York: Harper Collins Publishers, Inc., 1999], 98–108). See also especially footnote 29 in chapter 1.

through a "hypostatization of consciousness" is a dominant influence for his philosophical project.

The threat this poses to understanding man and to fulfilling authentically his sublime call had already been realized in the dual horrors Poland experienced in the twentieth century—Nazism and Marxist Communism. While there are post-Cartesians who have valuable contributions to make in the study of the human person, especially phenomenology as a method for studying the dynamics of human experience, an adequate anthropology demands Thomism, and especially Thomist metaphysics, for a concrete philosophical foundation for human personhood and for his fulfillment. Central to understanding John Paul II's anthropology is his use of Thomas's hylomorphism and its manifold implications for human nature. But implicit in his anthropology—and necessary for its coherence—is the reliance on the distinction between person and nature in terms of categories of being, again using the *analogia entis*.

The human person has a concreteness that can be adequately accounted for only in the category of relation. Relation provides the foundation for the person constituting character of masculinity and femininity, which are two ways of reciprocally modulating the person in two complementary modes of human nature. Moreover, the relational person together with hylomorphism provides an account for personal fulfillment by which one's free actions (*actus humanus*) accrue to the person, either making him holier or else diminishing him and making him more evil. The fulfillment of the human person comes by responding to the Christian vocation to holiness through one of two paths: fatherhood or motherhood. Fatherhood, authentically lived, can be succinctly defined as the fulfillment of the masculine person. Whether or not this is lived out in natural fatherhood (either biological or adoptive), fatherhood must be authentically lived out in every relationship in a man's life.

Natural fatherhood is a vocation and state ordered by the primary complementary relation of initiating love, to the feminine complement of actively receptive love. This hierarchical exchange of love is completed by secondary feminine initiating love to the complement of secondary masculine actively receptive love. The husband-father's responsibilities which arise from this complementarity are characterized by his primary initiating love and by his masculine gifts, which are ordered to living out his masculine vocation. However, the man must focus special attention on the problem that concupiscence poses for his fatherhood. Understanding the great mystery and its call to mutual submission in the context of our account of sex difference and relation, are keys to a husband-father's authentically living his vocation.

This present study also serves as an initial step toward unpacking and developing some of the many hidden implications of John Paul II's theology of personhood, masculinity, and fatherhood. In its broadest-reaching implications, I would point to his overall Thomistic-phenomenological personalist project as ripe for development. His initial purpose for integrating phenomenology as a method of investigation into Thomist metaphysics is best understood by the title to his book *Person and Act*. In this project, his purpose was to develop a coherent and compelling account of personhood and personal fulfillment adequate to the task of accounting for the dynamics of human experience. The efficacy of the *actus humanus* for personal fulfillment meant his account emphasizes the second spiritual faculty, the will.

A complementary personalist project has been carried out by Msgr. Robert Sokolowski, but with a focus on the first spiritual faculty, the intellect. His Thomistic-phenomenological account of the human person might be entitled "Person and Knowing."[2] Sokolowski's surprising contention that the act of reasoning is fundamentally interpersonal is ripe for further development.[3] The premise that the act of intellection is itself a public enterprise and always carried out in some fashion with an interlocutor seems to be redolent of the first Trinitarian procession. With this procession comprising the archetype for both created reason and complementary sex difference, it seems that an attempt to integrate the findings of these two thinkers, with particular attention to their implications for sex difference and subsequent praxis, could bear much fruit for Christian anthropology and pastoral ministry.

The insights we have noted from John Paul II's Trinitarian and christological anthropology and his use of the *analogia entis* for understanding personhood and sex difference are pregnant with opportunities for delving deeper into their theological and practical implications. I have made an initial step in this direction in an article on John Paul II's use of the nuptial mystery and *imago Dei* in his writings.[4] It is also full of possibilities for pas-

---

[2] See Robert Sokolowski, *Phenomenology of the Human Person* (New York: Cambridge University Press, 2008).

[3] See Sokolowski, *Phenomenology of the Human Person*, 68–79.

[4] For further considerations of John Paul's Trinitarian and christological anthropology, see David H. Delaney, "The Nuptial Mystery, the Sacrament of Marriage and John Paul II's *Man and Woman He Created Them*," *Antiphon* 18, no. 1 (2014): 69–105.

toral application for the formation of young people for marriage, especially focusing on his use of the great mystery.[5]

There is also much more work to be done developing the theological, practical, and pastoral implications of the human person and sex difference in the category of being of relation. I envision a work investigating active spiration, the non-personal Trinitarian relation, as the archetype of created relations and the subsequent cosmological and anthropological implications. A review of the Trinitarian, metaphysical speculations in the East's use of relation (σχέση; starting with St. Gregory of Nazianzus) and *hypostasis* (beginning with St. Basil the Great) and the West's introduction of relation with St. Augustine as well as the Western appropriation of the East's *hypostasis* under the Latin equivalent *suppositum* (particularly in the work of St. Thomas Aquinas) would be a good starting point.

The role of relation as its own category of being in the created order is still controverted, especially for human personhood.[6] However, further research could help reduce this resistance by clarifying the difference between absolute relations of opposition (i.e., subsisting relations) and created relations as analogies of these, by showing how created relations can resolve christological questions (e.g., a fuller metaphysical articulation of the Incarnation which accounts for the criticism that it is a logical contradiction), by accounting for the essential character of sex difference, by deepening our account of angelology in relation to the material order of creation, and by providing a more complete cosmological account of existence and essence in terms of the categories of relation and substance.

This research might also further develop our understanding of the manner in which sex difference modulates the masculine and feminine personal relation. There is much fruit to be found in applying to this foundational research, the findings of the empirical sciences on the matter of sex difference in general, and of masculinity and femininity more specifically. The pastoral implications of this research are potentially significant. The confusion about the meaning of sex difference to which young people today are subjected at the tenderest of ages means that pastors will be dealing with its negative spiritual consequences for decades to come.

There is a great opportunity to use the findings of our study for a deeper understanding and articulation of how masculinity and femininity

---

[5]   See, for example, David H. Delaney, *The Great Mystery*, 2nd ed. (Helotes, TX: Mother of the Americas Institute Press, 2021), 182–98.

[6]   See, e.g., Giles Emery, O.P., "The Dignity of Being a Substance: Person, Subsistence, and Nature," *Nova et Vetera* 9, no. 4, English ed. (2011): 997ff.

should affect the manner in which each might more authentically carry out various roles and tasks of life. This account might begin with the general vocations of fatherhood and motherhood and then apply the findings to such areas as leadership in various secular realms and to describe manners in which each sex can more authentically engage in roles for which the other sex is the primary role model (e.g., military specialties, nursing, engineering and sciences, elementary school teachers, etc.). An important starting point for this would be a deeper dive into specific manners in which the husband and wife mutually submit to one another.

Finally, we should look at the most urgent task toward which this work can provide some contribution. We live in a time in which the loss of the meaning of the human person that had already reached a crisis point in the twentieth century has further corrupted into an aggressive assault on the authentic meaning and significance of sex difference. An increasingly dominant public message now asserts that one's determination of his personal and sexual identity must be left to the individual. This is accompanied by growing societal and political pressure for all others to endorse actively even the most disordered ideas. Moreover, once a disordered identity has been adopted, there is hostility toward any attempt to revert to an authentic identity.

The attempt to normalize this confusion results in the demand that not only society but increasingly every individual accept the redefinition of the meaning of the person, his sex difference, fatherhood, motherhood, and family. These crises of personhood and sex difference are accelerating the decades-long decline of family life toward widespread collapse. While this downward trajectory is disquieting, there is hope. The early "mustard seed" Church intrepidly ventured out into pagan lands, confident in the gospel message and in the power of the Holy Spirit. They recognized that as bad as things might be in terms of moral decay, the *logoi spermatikoi* still existed among the nations and these provided a starting point for evangelization. We must apply the same lessons to evangelization today, especially with the good news about the human person and marriage redeemed. Though now the challenge retreats from one of evangelization to pre-evangelization.

While some of the challenges of a post-Christian society are different than those faced by the early Church, the seeds of the *Logos* in the human person and society are always present. These must serve as points of contact by which we engage people of good will about the authentic meaning both of the human person and of sex, and about the promise of a more just civilization. This pre-evangelization is essential preparation for reception of the gospel. John Paul II's anthropology and his vision of sex difference and fatherhood are effective means by which to help Christians articulate the truth and enable them to engage in dialogue with others of good will. St. John Paul II's anthropology provides the outlines for a compelling account of the human person, of sex difference, and of fatherhood and motherhood. Admittedly, this account must be fleshed out and reformulated for a popular audience. I hope that this study can provide a step in that direction.

Bibliography

PRIMARY SOURCES

John Paul II. Apostolic Exhortation on Reconciliation and Penance in the Mission of the Church Today *Reconciliatio et paenitentia*. December 2, 1984. *AAS* 77 (1985), 185–275.

_____. Apostolic Letter on the Dignity and Vocation of Women *Mulieris dignitatem*. August 15, 1988. *AAS* 80 (1988), 1653–1729. Boston: Pauline Books and Media, 1997. https://www.vatican.va/content/john-paul-ii/en/apost_exhortations/documents/hf_jp-ii_exh_02121984_reconciliatio-et-paenitentia.html.

_____. Apostolic Exhortation on the Formation of Priests in the Circumstances of the Present Day *Pastores dabo vobis*. March 15, 1992. *AAS* 84 (1992), 657–804. Boston: Pauline Books and Media, 1992.

_____. Apostolic Exhortation on the Role of the Christian Family in the Modern World *Familiaris consortio*. November 22, 1981. *AAS* 74 (1982), 114–37. https://www.vatican.va/content/john-paul-ii/en/apost_exhortations/documents/hf_jp-ii_exh_19811122_familiaris-consortio.html.

_____. Apostolic Exhortation on the Person and Mission of Saint Joseph in the Life of Christ and of the Church *Redemptoris custos*. August 15, 1989. *AAS* 82 (1990), 5–34. https://www.vatican.va/content/john-paul-ii/en/apost_exhortations/documents/hf_jp-ii_exh_15081989_redemptoris-custos.html.

_____. *Audiences of Pope John Paul II* (English). Vatican City: Libreria Editrice Vaticana, 2014.

_____. *A Catechesis on the Creed*. Vol. 1, *God, Father and Creator*. Boston: Pauline Books and Media, 1996.

_____. *A Catechesis on the Creed*. Vol. 2, *Jesus, Son and Savior*. Boston: Pauline Books and Media, 1996.

_____. *A Catechesis on the Creed*. Vol. 3, *The Spirit, Giver of Life and Love*. Boston: Pauline Books and Media, 1996.

_____. *A Catechesis on the Creed*. Vol. 4, *The Church: Mystery, Sacrament, Community*. Boston: Pauline Books and Media, 1998.

_____. *A Catechesis on Salvation History*. Vol. 6, *The Trinity's Embrace: God's Saving Plan*. Boston: Pauline Books and Media, 2002.

_____. *Crossing the Threshold of Hope*. Edited by Vittorio Messori. Translated by Jenny McPhee and Martha McPhee. New York: Alfred A. Knopf, Inc., 1994.

_____. Encyclical Letter at the Beginning of His Papacy *Redemptor hominis*. March 4, 1979. *AAS* 71 (1979), 257–324. https://www.vatican.va/content/john-paul-ii/en/encyclicals/documents/hf_jp-ii_enc_04031979_redemptor-hominis.html.

_____. Encyclical Letter *Dives in misericordia*. November 30, 1980. *AAS* 72 (1980), 1177–1232. https://www.vatican.va/content/john-paul-ii/en/encyclicals/documents/hf_jp-ii_enc_30111980_dives-in-misericordia.html.

_____. Encyclical Letter for the Twentieth Anniversary of *Populorum progressio Sollicitudo rei socialis*. December 30, 1987. *AAS* 80 (1988), 513–86. https://www.vatican.va/content/john-paul-ii/en/encyclicals/documents/hf_jp-ii_enc_30121987_sollicitudo-rei-socialis.html.

_____. Encyclical Letter on the Blessed Virgin Mary in the Life of the Pilgrim Church *Redemptoris mater*. March 25, 1987. https://www.vatican.va/content/john-paul-ii/en/encyclicals/documents/hf_jp-ii_enc_25031987_redemptoris-mater.html.

_____. Encyclical Letter on the Eucharist in Its Relationship to the Church *Ecclesia de Eucharistia*. April 17, 2003. *AAS* 95 (2003), 433–75. https://www.vatican.va/holy_father/special_features/encyclicals/documents/hf_jp-ii_enc_20030417_ecclesia_eucharistia_en.html.

_____. Encyclical Letter on Human Work *Laborem exercens*. September 14, 1981. AAS 73 (1981), 577–647. https://www.vatican.va/content/john-paul-ii/en/encyclicals/documents/hf_jp-ii_enc_14091981_laborem-exercens.html.

_____. Encyclical Letter on the Holy Spirit in the Life of the Church and the World *Dominum et vivificantem*. May 18, 1986. *AAS* 78 (1986), 809–900. https://www.vatican.va/content/john-paul-ii/en/encyclicals/documents/hf_jp-ii_enc_18051986_dominum-et-vivificantem.html.

_____. Encyclical Letter on the Hundredth Anniversary of *Rerum Novarum Centesimus annus*. May 1, 1991. *AAS* 83 (1991), 793–867. https://www.vatican.va/content/john-paul-ii/en/encyclicals/documents/hf_jp-ii_enc_01051991_centesimus-annus.html.

_____. Encyclical Letter on the Permanent Validity of the Church's Missionary Mandate *Redemptoris missio*. December 7, 1990. *AAS* 83 (1991), 249–340. https://www.vatican.va/content/john-paul-ii/en/encyclicals/documents/hf_jp-ii_enc_07121990_redemptoris-missio.html.

_____. Encyclical Letter on the Relationship between Faith and Reason *Fides et ratio*. September 14, 1998. *AAS* 91 (1999), 5–88. Boston: Pauline Books & Media, 1998. https://www.vatican.va/content/john-paul-ii/en/encyclicals/documents/hf_jp-ii_enc_14091998_fides-et-ratio.html.

_____. Encyclical Letter on the Value and Inviolability of Human Life *Evangelium vitae*. March 25, 1995. *AAS* 87 (1995), 401–522. https://www.vatican.va/content/

john-paul-ii/en/encyclicals/documents/hf_jp-ii_enc_25031995_evangelium-vitae.html.

_____. Homily for the Jubilee for Priests and 80th Birthday of the Holy Father. May 18, 2000.

_____. Letter to Families *Gratissimam sane*. February 2, 1994. *AAS* 86 (1994), 868–925. New Hope, KY: Urbi Et Orbi Communications, 1994.

_____. *Letters to My Brother Priests: 1979–2001*. Edited by James Socías. Chicago: Scepter Publishers, 2001.

_____. *Letter to Women*. June 29, 1995. New Hope, KY: Urbi Et Orbi Communications, 1995.

_____. *Man and Woman He Created Them: A Theology of the Body*. Translated by Michael Waldstein. Boston: Pauline Books and Media, 2006.

_____. "Only Christ Can Fulfill Man's Hopes." *Communio* 23 (Spring 1996): 122–28.

_____. Post-Synodal Apostolic Exhortation *Pastores gregis*. October 16, 2003.

_____. Post-Synodal Apostolic Exhortation on the Consecrated Life and Its Mission in the Church and In the World *Vita consecrata*. March 25, 1996. https://www.vatican.va/content/john-paul-ii/en/apost_exhortations/documents/hf_jp-ii_exh_25031996_vita-consecrata.html.

_____. Post-Synodal Apostolic Exhortation on the Vocation and the Mission of the Lay Faithful in the Church and in the World *Christifideles laici*. December 30, 1988. *AAS* 81 (1989), 393–521. https://www.vatican.va/content/john-paul-ii/en/apost_exhortations/documents/hf_jp-ii_exh_30121988_christifideles-laici.html.

Wojtyła, Karol. *The Acting Person*. Translated by Andrezej Potocki. Edited by A. Tymieniecka. Analecta Husserliana: The Yearbook of Phenomenological Research, vol. 10. Dordrecht: Reidel Publishing Co., 1979.

_____. "In Search of the Basis of Perfectionism in Ethics." In *Person and Community: Selected Essays*, vol. 4, edited by Theresa Sandok, O.S.M., 45–56. New York: Peter Lang, 1993. Originally published in Polish as "W poszukiwaniu podstaw perfekcjoryzmu w etyce." *Roczniki Filozoficzne* 5, no. 4 (1955–57): 303–17.

_____. *Love and Responsibility*. Translated by Grzegorz Ignatik. Boston: Pauline Books & Media, 2013.

_____. "On the Dignity of the Human Person." In *Person and Community: Selected Essays*, vol. 4, edited by Theresa Sandok, O.S.M., 177–80. New York: Peter Lang, 1993. Originally published in Polish as "O godnosci osoby ludzkiej." *Notificationes a Curia Principis Metropolitae Cracoviensis* (1964): 287–89.

_____. "Parenthood as a Community of Persons." In *Person and Community: Selected Essays*, vol. 4, edited by Theresa Sandok, O.S.M., 329–42. New York: Peter Lang, 1993. Originally published in Polish as "Rodzicielstwo jako 'communio personarum.'" *Ateneum Kaplanskie* 67 (1975): 17–31.

_____. "Participation or Alienation?" In *Person and Community: Selected Essays*, vol. 4, edited by Theresa Sandok, O.S.M., 197–207. New York: Peter Lang, 1993.

Originally published in Polish as "Uczestnictwo czy alienacja." *Summarium* 7, no. 27 (1978): 7–16.

_____. "Pastoral Reflections on the Family." In *Person and Community: Selected Essays*, vol. 4, edited by Theresa Sandok, O.S.M., 343–61. New York: Peter Lang, 1993. Originally published in Polish as "Rozwazania pastoralne o rodzinie." *Roczniki Nauk Spolecznych* 3 (1975): 59–76.

_____. *Person and Act and Related Essays*. Washington, DC: The Catholic University of America Press, 2021.

_____. *Radiation of Fatherhood*. In *The Collected Plays and Writings on Theater: Karol Wojtyła*. Translated by Bolesław Taborski. Berkeley: University of California Press, 1987.

_____. *Sources of Renewal: The Implementation of the Second Vatican Council.* Translated by P. S. Falla. New York: Harper & Row Publishers, San Francisco, 1979. Originally published in Polish as *U Podstaw Odnowy*. Cracow: Pol Tow. Teol., 1972.

_____. "Subjectivity and the Irreducible in the Human Being." In *Person and Community: Selected Essays*, vol. 4, edited by Theresa Sandok, O.S.M., 209–17. New York: Peter Lang, 1993. Originally published in Polish as "Podmiotowosci i 'to, co nieredukowalne' w czlowieku." *Ethos* 1, nos. 2–3 (1988): 21–28.

_____. "The Family as a Community of Persons." In *Person and Community: Selected Essays*, vol. 4, edited by Theresa Sandok, O.S.M., 315–28. New York: Peter Lang, 1993. Originally published in Polish as "Rodzina jako 'communio personarum.'" *Ateneum Kaplanskie* 66 (1974): 347–61.

_____. "The Human Person and Natural Law." In *Person and Community: Selected Essays*, vol. 4, edited by Theresa Sandok, O.S.M., 181–85. New York: Peter Lang, 1993. Originally published in Polish as "Osoba ludzka a prawo naturalne." *Roczniki Filozoficzne* 18, no. 2 (1970): 53–59.

_____. "The Personal Structure of Self Determination." In *Person and Community: Selected Essays*, vol. 4, edited by Theresa Sandok, O.S.M., 187–95. New York: Peter Lang, 1993. Originally published in Polish as "Osobowa struktura samostanowienia." *Roczniki Filozoficzne* 29, no. 2 (1981): 5–12.

Secondary Sources

Aland, Barbara, Kurt Aland, et al., eds. *The Greek New Testament*. 4th rev. ed. Stuttgart: United Bible Societies, 1994.

Allen, Prudence. "Integral Sex Complementarity and the Theology of Communion." *Communio* 17 (Winter 1990): 523–44.

_____. "Sex and Gender Differentiation in Hildegard of Bingen and Edith Stein." *Communio* 20 (Summer 1993): 389–414.

_____. *The Concept of Woman*. Vol. 1, *The Aristotelian Revolution, 750 BC–AD 1250*. Grand Rapids, MI: William B. Eerdmans, 1997.

_____. *The Concept of Woman*. Vol. 2, *The Early Humanist Reformation, 1250–1500*. Grand Rapids, MI: William B. Eerdmans, 2002.

Albrecht, Barbara. "Is There an Objective Type "Woman?" In *The Church and Women: A Compendium*, edited by Helmut Moll, 35–49. San Francisco: Ignatius Press, 1988.

Aquinas, St. Thomas. *Summa Theologica*. Translated by the Fathers of the English Dominican Province. New York: Benziger Bros., 1948. Reprint, Allen, TX: Christian Classics, 1981.

Ashley, Benedict M. *Justice in the Church: Gender and Participation (The Michael J. McGivney Lectures of the John Paul II Institute for Studies on Marriage and Family, 1992)*. Washington, DC: The Catholic University of America Press, 1996.

_____. *Theologies of the Body: Humanist and Christian*. Braintree, MA: The Pope John Center, 1985. Reprint, 1995.

Atkinson, Joseph. "Paternity in Crisis: Biblical and Philosophical Roots of Fatherhood." *Josephinum Journal of Theology* 9, no. 1 (2002): 3–21.

Balthasar, Hans Urs von. "A Word on Humanae Vitae." In *New Elucidations*, 213–14. San Francisco: Ignatius Press, 1986.

_____. *Theo-Drama: Theological Dramatic Theory*. Vol 5, *The Last Act*, translated by Graham Harrison. San Francisco: Ignatius Press, 1998.

_____. *The Office of Peter and the Structure of the Church*. San Francisco: Ignatius Press, 1986.

Beigel, Gerard Paul. "'The Person Revealed in Action': A Framework for Understanding How Social Justice is an Essential Part of the Gospel in the Teaching of Pope John Paul II." Ph.D. diss., The Catholic University of America, 1994.

Benedict XVI, Encyclical Letter on Christian Love *Deus caritas est*. December 25, 2005.

Biffi, Giacomo. "The Action of the Holy Spirit in the Church and in the World." In *John Paul II: A Panorama of His Teachings*, 38–47. New York: New City Press, 1989.

Blankenhorn, David. *Fatherless America: Confronting Our Most Urgent Social Problem*. New York: Harper-Collins Publishers, 1995.

Bogónez Herreras, Fernando. "La persona humana en su relación con Dios según la Constitución Pastoral *Gaudium et spes*." *Estudio Augustiniano* 35 (2000): 533–73.

Bourgeault, Cynthia. "Why Feminizing the Trinity Will Not Work: A Metaphysical Perspective." *Sewanee Theological Review* 44 (2000–2001): 27–35.

Bransfield, J. Brian. *The Human Person: According to John Paul II*. Boston, MA: Pauline Books & Media, 2010.

Burggraf, Jutta. "Woman's Dignity and Function in Church and Society. In *The Church and Women: A Compendium*, edited by Helmut Moll, 103–14. San Francisco: Ignatius Press, 1988.

Buttiglione, Rocco. *Karol Wojtyła: The Thought of the Man Who Became John Paul II*. Translated by Paolo Guietti and Francesca Murphy. Grand Rapids, MI: William B. Eerdmans Publishing Co., 1997.

Cahill, Lisa Sowle. "Accent on the Masculine." In *Considering* Veritatis splendor, 53–60. Cleveland: Pilgrim Press, 1994.

————. "Current Theology, Notes on Moral Theology: Feminist Ethics." *Theological Studies* 51 (1990): 49–64.

————. "Humanity as Female and Male: The Ethics of Sexuality." In *Called to Love: Towards a Contemporary Christina Ethic*, edited by Francis A. Eigo, 75–95. Villanova, PA: Villanova University Press, 1985.

————. *Sex, Gender, and Christian Ethics*. New York: Cambridge University Press, 1996.

Callahan, Sidney. "Misunderstanding of Sexuality and Resistance to Woman Priests." In *Women Priests: A Catholic Commentary on the Vatican Declaration*, edited by Leonard Swidler and Arlene Swidler, 291–94. New York: Paulist Press, 1977.

Cessario, Romanus. *Introduction to Moral Theology*. Washington, DC: The Catholic University of America Press, 2001.

Clarke, W. Norris. "Person, Being, and St. Thomas." *Communio* 19 (Winter 1992): 601–18.

————. *The One and the Many: A Contemporary Thomistic Metaphysics*. Notre Dame, IN: University of Notre Dame Press, 2001.

Coda, Piero. "Per una rilettura dell' 'antropologia trinitaria' di Giovanni Paolo II." *Aquinas* 41 (1998): 641–46.

Compagnoni, Francesco. "La persona nella comunità umana e nella chiesa. Il magistero di Giovanni Paolo II." *Studia Patavina* 40 (1993): 45–57.

Conley, John J., S.J. "The Philosophical Foundations of the Thought of John Paul II: Response." In *The Thought of Pope John Paul II: A Collection of Essays and Studies*, edited by John M. McDermott, 23–28. Rome: Editrice Pontificia Università Gregoriana, 2000.

Crosby, John F. "John Paul II on the Complementarity of Man and Woman." In *The Church, Marriage, and the Family*, edited by Kenneth D. Whitehead, 41–52. South Bend, IN: St. Augustine Press, 2007.

Cross, Nancy. "Toward a Totally Christian Anthropology." *Priest* 42 (May 1986): 35–38.

Dec, Ignacy. "Person als Subjekt. Zum Personbegriff bei Karol Wojtyła." *Theologie und Glaube* 76 (1986): 294–307.

Delaney, David H. *The Great Mystery*. 2nd ed. Helotes, TX: Mother of the Americas Institute Press, 2021.

————. "The Nuptial Mystery, the Sacrament of Marriage and John Paul II's Man and Woman He Created Them." *Antiphon* 18.1 (2014): 69–105.

Denzinger, Henry. *The Sources of Catholic Dogma*. Translated by Roy Deferrari. Saint Louis: B. Herder Book Co., 1957. Originally published in Latin as *Enchiridion symbolorum*. 30th rev. ed. Freiburg: Herder & Co., 1954.

De Vogel, C. J. "The Concept of Personality in Greek and Christian Thought." *Studies in Philosophy and the History of Philosophy* 2 (1963): 20–60.

Dinan, Stephen. "John Paul II and the Mystery of the Human Person." *America* 190, no. 3 (2004): 10–22.

_____. "The Phenomenological Anthropology of Karol Wojtyla." *New Scholasticism* 55 (1981): 317–30.

Dulles, Avery. "The Prophetic Humanism of John Paul II." *America* 169 (1993): 6–11.

_____. *The Splendor of Faith: The Theological Vision of Pope John Paul II*. New York: Crossroad Publishing Co., 1999.

Echeverria, Eduardo J. *"In the Beginning . . . "*: A Theology of the Body*. Eugene, OR: Pickwick Publishers, 2011.

Evdokimov, Paul. *Woman and the Salvation of the World*. Crestwood, NY: St. Vladimir's Seminary Press, 1994.

Emery, Giles, O.P. "The Dignity of Being a Substance: Person, Subsistence, and Nature." *Nova et Vetera* 9, no. 4, English ed. (2011): 991–1001.

Feingold, Alan. "Gender Differences in Personality: A Meta-Analysis." *Psychological Bulletin* 116, no. 3 (1994): 429–56.

Fernández, Fernando Aguado. "Algunas reflexiones sobre el concepto de persona en Juan Pablo II." *Sapientia* 47 (1992): 295–304.

Franquet Casas, María José. "Persona, acción y libertad en Karol Wojtyła." Ph.D. diss., Universidad de Navarra, 1995.

Gałkowski, Jerzy W. "The Place of Thomism in the Anthropology of K. Wojtyla." *Angelicum* 65 (1998): 181–94.

Garcia, Laura L. "The Role of Woman in Society." Paper delivered to an *Instituto de Iniciativas de Orientación Familiar* sponsored conference, October 2000.

Grabowski, John. "Mutual Submission and Trinitarian Self-Giving." *Angelicum* 74 (1997):489–512.

_____. "Person: Substance and relation." *Communio* 22 (1995): 139–63.

_____. "Theological Anthropology and Gender since Vatican II: A Critical Appraisal of Recent Trends in Catholic Theology." Ph.D. diss., Marquette University, 1991.

_____. "The Status of the Sexual Good as a Direction for Moral Theology." *The Heythrop Journal* 35 (1994): 15–34.

Gress, Carrie. *The Anti-Mary Exposed: Rescuing the Culture from Toxic Femininity*. Charlotte, NC: TAN Books, 2019.

Groër, Hans. "The Church: Sacrament of Salvation." In *John Paul II: A Panorama of His Teachings*, 27–37. New York: New City Press, 1989.

Gudorf, Christine. "Encountering the Other: The Modern Papacy on Women." *Social Compass* 36, no. 3 (1989): 295–310.

_____. "Probing the Politics of Difference: What's Wrong with an All-Male Priesthood?" *Journal of Religious Ethics* 27, no. 3 (Fall 1999): 377–405.

Guillem, Gonzalo Gironés. "Hacia una teología del cuerpo humano." *Anales Valentinos* 26 (2000): 25–43.

Harris, Harriet A. "Should We Say That Personhood Is Relational?" *Scottish Theological Journal* 51 (1998): 214–34.

Harvanek, Robert F., S.J. "The Philosophical Foundations of the Thought of John Paul II." In *The Thought of Pope John Paul II: A Collection of Essays and Studies*, edited by John M. McDermott. Rome: Editrice Pontificia Università Gregoriana, 2000.

Hauke, Manfred. *Women in the Priesthood? A Systematic Analysis in the Light of the Order of Creation and Redemption*. Translated by David Kipp. San Francisco: Ignatius Press, 1988.

Healy, Michael. "Reading *Casti Connubii* (and the Tradition) in Light of the Insights of JPII." *The Personalist Project* (blog). August 31, 2012. http://www.thepersonalistproject.org/home/comments/reading_casti_connubii_and_the_tradition_in_light_of_the_insights_of_jpii.

Henninger, Mark G., S.J. *Relations: Medieval Theories, 1250–1325*. Oxford: Clarendon Press, 1989.

Honoré, J. "Christ the Redeemer, Core of John Paul II's Teaching." In *John Paul II: A Panorama of His Teachings*, 12–26. New York: New City Press, 1989.

Hruz, Paul W. "Deficiencies in Scientific Evidence for Medical Management of Gender Dysphoria." *The Linacre Quarterly* 87, no. 1 (2020): 34-42.

Hume, David. *A Treatise of Human Nature: Being an Attempt to Introduce the Experimental Method of Reasoning into Moral Subjects*. Book III, *Of Morals*. Oxford, UK: Clarendon Press, 1896.

Ibrahim, M. H. *Grammatical Gender: Its Origins and Development*. Paris: Maton, 1973.

Jobert, Philippe. "Complémentarité de l'anthropologie de Saint Thomas d'Aquin et de l'anthropologie de Jean Paul II." In *Antropologia Tomista. Atti del IX Congresso tomistico internazionale*, 432–37. Rome: Libreria Editrice Vaticana, 1990.

Johnson, Elizabeth. "Mary, Friend of God and Prophet: A Critical Reading of the Marian Tradition." *Theology Digest* 47, no. 4 (Winter 2000): 317–25.

_____. *She Who Is: The Mystery of God in Feminist Theological Discourse*. New York: The Crossroad Publishing Company, 1992.

_____. *Truly Our Sister: A Theology of Mary in the Communion of Saints*. New York: Continuum, 2003.

Johnson, Luke Timothy. "A Disembodied 'Theology of the Body': John Paul II on Love, Sex and Pleasure." *Commonweal* 128, no. 2 (January 26, 2001): 11–17.

Kaminski, Phyllis. "Reproducing the World: Mary O'Brien's Theory of Reproductive Consciousness and Implications for Feminist Incarnational Theology." Horizons 19, no. 2 (1992): 240–62.

Kasper, Walter. "The Position of Woman as a Problem of Theological Anthropology." In *The Church and Women: A Compendium*, edited by Helmut Moll, 51–64. San Francisco: Ignatius Press, 1988.

————. "The Theological Anthropology of *Gaudium et Spes*." *Communio* 23 (1996): 129–40.

Kaveny, Cathleen. "What is the Vatican Saying About Women? Conservative Catholics Might Be Surprised." *The Washington Post*. August 15, 2004.

————. "What Women Want: 'Buffy,' The Pope and The New Feminists." *Commonweal* 130, no. 19 (November 7, 2003): 18–24.

Lawler, Ronald. *The Christian Personalism of Pope John Paul II*. Chicago: Franciscan Herald Press, 1982.

Lehman, Karl. "The Place of Women as a Problem in Theological Anthropology." In *The Church and Women: A Compendium*, edited by Helmut Moll, 11–33. San Francisco: Ignatius Press, 1988.

Leo XIII. Encyclical Letter on Christian Marriage *Arcanum divinae sapientiae*. February 10, 1880. AAS 12 (1879/1880).

Lippa, Richard. "Gender-Related Individual Differences and the Structure of Vocational Interests: The Importance of the People-Things Dimension." *Journal of Personality and Social Psychology* 4 (1998): 996–1009.

Long, Stephen. "The Metaphysics of Gender and Sacramental Priesthood." *Louvain Studies* 10 (1984–1985): 41–59.

López Trujillo, Alfonso. "The Truth of the Human Being in Christ." In *John Paul II: A Panorama of His Teachings*, 122–43. New York: New City Press, 1989.

Louth, Andrew. *Maximus the Confessor*. London: Routledge, 2005.

————. "The Body in Western Catholic Christianity." In *Religion and the Body*, edited by Sarah Coakley, 111–30. New York: Cambridge University Press, 1997.

Malone, Richard. "On John Paul II's *Pastores Dabo Vobis*." *Communio* 20 (Fall 1993): 569–79.

Marcel, Gabriel. *The Philosophy of Existentialism*. New York: The Citadel Press, 1956.

Martin, Francis. "Feminist Theology: A Proposal." *Communio* 20 (Summer 1993): 334–76.

————. "Male and Female He Created Them: A Summary of the Teaching of Genesis Chapter One." *Communio* 20 (Summer 1993): 240–65.

————. "Radiation of Fatherhood: Some Biblical Reflections." *Josephinum Journal of Theology* 9, no. 1 (2002): 22–41.

Martin, Robert. "Person." In *The Philosopher's Dictionary*. 2nd ed. Ontario, Canada: Broadview Press, 1994.

May, William. "Marriage and the Complementarity of Male and Female." *Anthropotes: Rivista sulla persona e la famiglia* 8, no. 1 (1992): 41–60.

————. "The Mission of Fatherhood." *Josephinum Journal of Theology* 9, no. 1 (2002): 42–55.

McCool, Gerald A., S.J. "The Theology of John Paul II." In *The Thought of Pope John Paul*

II: A Collection of Essays and Studies, edited by John M. McDermott, 29–53. Rome: Editrice Pontificia Università Gregoriana, 2000.

McDermott, John M. *The Thought of Pope John Paul II: A Collection of Essays and Studies*. Roma: Editrice Pontificia Università Gregoriana, 2000.

McElroy, Wendy. "Death by Theory." *Fox News*. May 26, 2004. https://soc.men.narkive.com/9d6c3UQK/death-by-theory.

McGovern, Thomas. "The Christian Anthropology of John Paul II." *Josephinum Journal of Theology* 8, no. 1 (2001): 132–47.

Meconi, David V. "Deification in the Thought of John Paul II." *Irish Theological Quarterly* 71 (2006): 127–41.

Meyer, John R. "An *Ek-static* View of the Person." *Josephinum Journal of Theology* 8, no. 1 (2002): 22–41.

Miller, John W. *Calling God "Father": Essays on the Bible, Fatherhood, and Culture*. New York: Paulist Press, 1999.

Min, Anselm K. "John Paul II's Anthropology of Concrete Totality." *American Catholic Philosophical Association Proceedings* 58 (1984): 120–29.

Molina Leon, Maria. "*Mulieris dignitatem*. Hacia una teología de la mujer y del varón." Ph.D. diss. Universidad de Navarra, 1995.

Moll, Helmut, ed. *The Church and Women: A Compendium*. San Francisco: Ignatius Press, 1988.

Moreno, Fernando. "La verdad sobre el hombre en el Magisterio de Juan Pablo II." *Scripta Theologica* 20.2–3 (1988): 681–707.

Muller, Earl C., S.J. "'Person' in Christian Thought, East and West." Report on the Seminar on Trinitarian Theology. *Proceedings of the 46th Annual Convention of the Catholic Theological Society of America*. Atlanta, GA. June 12–15, 1991. Silver Spring, MD: CTSA, 1991 (46): 171–73.

Müller, Max, and Alois Halder. "Person." In *Sacramentum Mundi: An Encyclopedia of Theology*, 404–409. New York: Herder and Herder, 1969.

Nachef, Antoine. *The Mystery of the Trinity in the Theological Thought of Pope John Paul II*. New York: Peter Lang Publishing, 1999.

Nietzsche, Friedrich. *The Complete Works of Friedrich Nietzsche*. Vol. 10, *Joyful Wisdom*, edited by Oscar Levy (Edinburgh: T. N. Foulis, 1910).

Nilsen, Tina Dykesteen. "A Critique of Arguments against the Ordination of Women to Priesthood with Special Emphasis on the Argument from Jesus' Maleness." *Milltown Studies* 46 (2000): 33–57.

O'Brien, Margaret. "The Church and Its Public Life." *America* 160 (1989): 553–54.

————. "Theological Anthropology in the Encyclicals of John Paul II." In *Continuity and Plurality in Catholic Theology. Essays in Honor of Gerald A. McCool, S.J.*, edited by Anthony J. Cernera, 107–26. Fairfield, CT: Sacred Heart University Press, 1998.

O'Donnell, John. "Man and Woman as *Imago Dei* in the Theology of Hans Urs von Balthasar." *Clergy Review* 68 (April 1983): 117–28.

Oxford-Carpenter, Rebecca. "Gender and The Trinity." *Theology Today* 41 (1984–1985): 7–25.

Pagé, Jean-Guy. "La pensée de Karol Wojtyła (Jean-Paul II) sur la relation homme-femme." *Laval théologique et philosophique* 40 (Février 1984): 3–29.

Pesarchick, Robert. *The Trinitarian Foundation of Human Sexuality as Revealed by Christ According to Hans Urs von Balthasar*. Rome: Gregorian University Press, 2000.

Petri, Thomas, O.P. *Aquinas and the Theology of the Body: The Thomistic Foundations of John Paul II's Anthropology*. Washington, DC: The Catholic University of America Press, 2016.

Pius XI. Encyclical on Christian Marriage *Casti connubii*. December 31, 1930. AAS 22 (1930).

Porter, Lawrence. "Gender in Theology: The Example of John Paul II's *Mulieris Dignitatem*." *Gregorianum* 77 (1996): 97–131.

Power, Dermot. *A Spiritual Theology of the Priesthood: The Mystery of Christ and the Mission of the Priest*. Washington, DC: The Catholic University of America Press, 1998.

Prokes, Mary Timothy. *Toward a Theology of the Body*. Grand Rapids, MI: William B. Eerdmans, 1996.

Quitslund, Sonya. "In the Image of Christ." In *Women Priests: A Catholic Commentary on the Vatican Declaration*, edited by Leonard Swidler and Arlene Swidler, 260–69. New York: Paulist Press, 1977.

Rahner, Karl. "Theology of the Symbol." In *Theological Investigations*. Vol. 4. Baltimore: Helicon Press, 1961.

Rahner, Karl, and Herbert Vorgrimler. "Person." In *Dictionary of Theology*, 378. New York: Crossroad Publishing Company, 1981.

Ratzinger, Joseph. "Concerning the Notion of Person in Theology." *Communio* 17 (Fall 1990): 439–54.

_____. *Daughter Zion: Meditations on the Church's Marian Belief*. Translated by John McDermott, S.J. San Francisco: Ignatius Press, 1983.

_____. "God in Pope John Paul II's Crossing the Threshold of Hope." *Communio* 22 (1995): 107–38.

_____. *Introduction to Christianity*. Translated by J. R. Foster. San Francisco: Ignatius Press, 1990.

_____. "On the Position of Mariology and Marian Spirituality Within the Totality of Faith and Theology." In *The Church and Women: A Compendium*, edited by Helmut Moll, 67–79. San Francisco: Ignatius Press, 1988.

Rhoads, Stephen. *Taking Sex Differences Seriously*. San Francisco: Encounter Books, 2004.

Rolnick, Philip A. *Person, Grace and God*. Grand Rapids, MI: William B. Eerdmans Publishing Company, 2007.

Roten, Johann G. "Hans Urs von Balthasar's Anthropology in Light of His Marian Thinking." *Communio* 20 (Summer 1993): 306–33.

Ruiz Retegui, Antonio. "El tratamiento diferencial de la sexualidad humana en la Carta Apostólica 'Mulieris Dignitatem.'" *Scripta Theologica* 22 (1990): 881–97.

Rulla, Luigi. *Anthropology of the Christian Vocation*. Vol. 1, *Interdisciplinary Bases*. Rome: Gregorian University Press, 1986.

_____. *Anthropology of the Christian Vocation*. Vol. 2, *Existential Confirmation*. Rome: Gregorian University Press, 1989.

Savage, Deborah. "Masculine Genius." In *Promise Challenge: Catholic Women Reflect on Feminism, Complementarity, and the Church*, edited by Mary Rice Hasson, 129–53. Huntington, IN: Our Sunday Visitor Publishing, 2015.

_____. "The Nature of Woman in Relation to Man: Genesis 1 and 2 Through the Lens of the Metaphysical Anthropology of Aquinas." *Logos* 18, no. 1 (Winter 2015): 71–93.

_____. "Woman and Man: Identity, Genius and Mission." In *The Complementarity of Women and Men*, edited by Paul C. Vitz, 89–131. Washington, DC: Catholic University of America Press, 2021.

Saward, John. *Christ is the Answer: The Christ-Centered Teaching of Pope John Paul II*. New York: Alba House, 1995.

Schmemann, Alexander. *For the Life of the World*. Crestwood, NY: St. Vladimir's Seminary Press, 2000.

Schmitz, Kenneth L. *At the Center of the Human Drama: The Philosophical Anthropology of Karol Wojtyla/Pope John Paul II*. Washington, DC: The Catholic University of America Press, 1993.

_____. "The Geography of the Human Person." *Communio* 13 (1986): 28–48.

_____. "The Passage of Love: Wojtyla's Radiation of Fatherhood." *Communio* 22 (1995): 99–106.

_____. "The Solidarity of Personalism and the Metaphysics of Existential Act." *Fides Quaerens Intellectum* 1 (Summer 2001): 183–99.

_____. "Who Has Seen the Father." *Josephinum Journal of Theology* 9, no. 1 (2002): 42–73.

Scola, Angelo. "The Dignity and Mission of Women: The Anthropological and Theological Foundations." *Communio* 25 (Spring 1998): 42–56.

_____. *The Nuptial Mystery*. Translated by Michelle K. Borras. Grand Rapids, MI: William B. Eerdmans Publishing Company, 2005.

Second Vatican Council, Dogmatic Constitution on the Church *Lumen gentium*. November 21, 1964.

Séguin, Michael. "The Biblical Foundations of the Thought of John Paul II on Human Sexuality." *Communio* 20 (Summer 1993): 266–89.

Seidl, Horst. "The Concept of Person in St. Thomas Aquinas: A Contribution to Recent Discussion." *The Thomist* 51 (1987): 435–60.

Shivanandan, Mary. *Crossing the Threshold of Love: A New Vision of Marriage in the Light of John Paul II's Anthropology*. Washington, DC: The Catholic University of America Press, 1999.

Sicari, Anthony. "The Family: A Place of Fraternity." *Communio* 20 (Summer 1993): 290–305.

Sikorski, John. "Towards a Conjugal Spirituality: Karol Wojtyła's Vision of Marriage Before, During and After Vatican II." *Journal of Moral Theology* 6, no. 2 (2017): 103–29.

Sokolowski, Robert. *Phenomenology of the Human Person*. New York: Cambridge University Press, 2008.

Strukelj, Anton. "Man and Woman under God: The Dignity of the Human Being according to Hans Urs von Balthasar." *Communio* 20 (Summer 1993): 377–88.

Stuhlmueller, Carroll. "Bridegroom: A Biblical Symbol of Union, Not Separation." In *Women Priests: A Catholic Commentary on the Vatican Declaration*, edited by Leonard Swidler and Arlene Swidler, 278–83. New York: Paulist Press, 1977.

Swieżawski, Stefan, "Karol Wojtyła at the Catholic University of Lublin." In *Person and Community: Selected Essays*, vol. 4, trans. Theresa Sandok, O.S.M. New York: Peter Lang, 1993.

Tavard, George. "A Theologian Responds to Margaret Farley." In *Women and Catholic Priesthood: An Expanded Vision*, edited by Anne Marie Gardiner. New York: Paulist Press, 1976.

————. "The Contemporary Role of Women in the Catholic Church." *American Theological Library Association Summary of Proceedings* 43, no. 1 (2001): 95–103.

Trendelenburg, Adolph. "A Contribution to the History of the Word Person." *Monist* 20 (1910): 336–63.

Tudela, Julio et al. "The Vatican Opinion on Gender Theory." *The Linacre Quarterly* 88, no. 1 (2021): 37–41.

Turner, Pauline, and Bernard Cooke. "Women Can Have a Natural Resemblance to Christ." In *Women Priests: A Catholic Commentary on the Vatican Declaration*, edited by Leonard Swidler and Arlene Swidler, 258–59. New York: Paulist Press, 1977.

Vitz, Paul C. "From Personhood to Fatherhood." *Social Justice Review* 77 (1986): 203–209.

————. "The Fatherhood of God: Support from Psychology." *Josephinum Journal of Theology* 9, no. 1 (2002): 74–86.

Williams, George Huntston. *The Mind of John Paul II: Origins of His Thoughts and Action*. New York: The Seabury Press, 1981.

Wolicka, Elzbieta. "Participation in Community: Wojtyla's Social Anthropology." *Communio* 8 (1981): 108–18.

Zizioulas, John. *Being as Communion*. Crestwood, NJ: St. Vladimir's Seminary Press, 1997.

Index